Comparative Characterization in the Sermon on the Mount

Comparative Characterization in the Sermon on the Mount

Characterization of the Ideal Disciple

ARREN BENNET LAWRENCE

WIPF & STOCK · Eugene, Oregon

COMPARATIVE CHARACTERIZATION IN THE SERMON ON THE MOUNT
Characterization of the Ideal Disciple

Copyright © 2017 Arren Bennet Lawrence. All rights reserved. Except for brief quotations in critical publications or reviews, no part of this book may be reproduced in any manner without prior written permission from the publisher. Write: Permissions, Wipf and Stock Publishers, 199 W. 8th Ave., Suite 3, Eugene, OR 97401.

Wipf & Stock
An Imprint of Wipf and Stock Publishers
199 W. 8th Ave., Suite 3
Eugene, OR 97401

www.wipfandstock.com

PAPERBACK ISBN: 978-1-5326-1351-7
HARDCOVER ISBN: 978-1-5326-1353-1
EBOOK ISBN: 978-1-5326-1352-4

Manufactured in the U.S.A. FEBRUARY 14, 2017

To my wife, Joyce, for her many sacrifices

And to my daughter, Netanya

Contents

List of Figures | xii
List of Tables | xii
Preface | xiii
Acknowledgments | xv
Abbreviations | xvii

Chapter 1: Comparative Characterization as a Methodology to Interpret the Comparisons in the Sermon on the Mount | 1

    1.1 The Role of Comparisons in the Sermon on the Mount
    1.2 The Importance of Comparison in the Study of the Sermon on the Mount
    1.3 Comparative Characterization: A Methodology
    1.4 Definition of Terms
        1.4.1 Characterization
        1.4.2 Foil
        1.4.3 Comparative Characterization
        1.4.4 Ideal Disciple
    1.5 The Use of Comparative Characterization
    1.6 The Significance of Comparative Characterization

Chapter 2: Sermon on the Mount in Literature | 14

    2.1 Justin Martyr
    2.2 Irenaeus
    2.3 Tertullian
    2.4 Augustine of Hippo
    2.5 John Chrysostom

2.6 Thomas Aquinas
2.7 Martin Luther
2.8 John Calvin
2.9 Anabaptists
2.10 Robert Barclay
2.11 Leo Tolstoy
2.12 Mahatma Gandhi
2.13 Johannes Weiss
2.14 Albert Schweitzer
2.15 Martin Dibelius
2.16 C. H. Dodd
2.17 W. D. Davies
2.18 Stephen Westerholm
2.19 Conclusion

Chapter 3: Narrative Criticism in New Testament | 64

    3.1 Introduction
    3.2 Literary Criticism
    3.3 Narrative Criticism
        3.3.1 Narrator
        3.3.2 Point of View
        3.3.3 Narrative and Dialogue
        3.3.4 Repetition
        3.3.5 Leitwort
        3.3.6 Allusions
        3.3.7 Characters
            3.3.7.1 Classification of Characters
        3.3.8 Characterization
            3.3.8.1 Showing and Telling Characterization
            3.3.8.2 Characterization and Inner Life
            3.3.8.3 Characterization through Speeches and Actions
            3.3.8.4 Self Characterization
            3.3.8.5 Contrast Characterization
    3.4 Conclusion

Chapter 4: Comparative Characterization as a Methodology to Interpret Matthew 5–7 | 86

    4.1 Introduction
    4.2 Characters
    4.3 Characterization

4.3.1 Use of Foil Characters in Literature
4.3.2 Comparative Characterization in the Hebrew Bible
    4.3.2.1 Samuel and Eli's Sons
    4.3.2.2 David and Saul
4.3.3 Comparisons in Greco-Roman Literature
4.3.4 Comparison in Rhetoric
4.4 Synkrisis
4.5 Conclusion
    4.5.1 Comparative Characterization in Praxis

Chapter 5: Characterization of the Ideal Disciple in Matthew 5:1–16 | 109

5.1. Introduction
5.2 Sermon on the Mount as Characterizing the Ideal Disciple
5.3 Beatitudes as Characterizing the Ideal Disciple
    5.3.1. Blessed are the Poor in Spirit
    5.3.2. Blessed are the Mourners
    5.3.3 Blessed are the Meek
    5.3.4 Blessed are the Hungry and Thirsty for Righteousness
    5.3.5. Blessed are the Merciful
    5.3.6. Blessed are the Pure in Heart
    5.3.7 Blessed are the Peacemakers
    5.3.8 Blessed are the Persecuted
5.4 Salt and Light
    5.4.1 You are the Salt of the Earth
    5.4.2 You are the Light of the World
5.5 Conclusion

Chapter 6: Comparative Characterization in Matthew 5:17–48 | 139

6.1 Introduction
6.2 Characterizations in Matt 5:17–20
    6.2.1 The Interpretation of πληρῶσαι
        6.2.1.1. Richard E. Menninger
        6.2.1.2. John P. Meier
        6.2.1.3 Norvald Yri
        6.2.1.4. Ed Glasscock
        6.2.1.5 Watchman Nee
        6.2.1.6 John Wesley
        6.2.1.7 "To Fulfill:" πληρῶσαι
        6.2.1.8 Matthew's Use of πληρόω in the Infinitive
    6.2.2 Law Abiding Ideal Disciple (5:18–20)

6.2.3 The Law and the Ideal Disciple (5:19-20)
  6.2.3.1 The Ideal Disciple Compared with Paul?
  6.2.3.2 The Ideal Disciple Compared with Pharisees and Scribes
  6.2.3.3 Karma vs. Dharma
 6.3 Jesus, the Law and the Antitheses (5:21-48)
  6.3.1 Are the Antitheses Anti-theses?
  6.3.2 Jesus' Interpretation vs. Pharisaic and Scribal Interpretation
  6.3.3 Murder vs. Anger
  6.3.4 Adultery vs. Lust
  6.3.5 Divorce vs. No Divorce
  6.3.6 Vows and Oaths
  6.3.7 Eye for an Eye vs. Do not Resist
  6.3.8 Love your Neighbors vs. Love your Enemies
 6.4 Jesus vs. Teachers of Judaisms of His Time
  6.4.1 Teacher of Righteousness and the Law
  6.4.2 Rabbi Hillel and the Law
  6.4.3 Building Fence Around the Torah
 6.5 Conclusion

Chapter 7: Comparative Characterization in Matthew 6:1—7:29 | 194

 7.1 Introduction
 7.2 Beware of Practicing Righteousness (6:1-34)
  7.2.1 Not Giving Alms before Men like the Hypocrites (6:1-4)
  7.2.2 Not Praying before People like the Hypocrites (6:5-6)
  7.2.3 Not Praying with Meaningless Words like the Gentiles (6:7-15)
   7.2.3.1 Lord's Prayer
    7.2.3.1.1 First Petition: Hallowed be Thy Name
    7.2.3.1.2 Second and Third Petition: Thy Kingdom Come, Thy Will be Done
    7.2.3.1.3 Fourth Petition: Give us the Daily Bread
    7.2.3.1.4 Fifth Petition: Forgive Us our Debts
    7.2.3.1.5 Sixth Petition: Lead us not into Temptations
    7.2.3.1.6 Forgive others to be Forgiven
  7.2.4 Not Fasting before Men like the Pharisees (6:16-18)
  7.2.5 Not Storing on Earth but in Heaven (6:19-23)
  7.2.6 Not Serving Money like Gentiles but God (6:24-34)
   7.2.6.1 Not Worrying
 7.3 Comparisons and Their Function in Matthew 7 (7:1-29)

7.3.1 Not Judging Others like the Hypocrites (7:1–6)
    7.3.1.1 Swine and Dogs
7.3.2 Asking like a Child to Receive (7:7–12)
    7.3.2.1 Golden Rule: Treating Others Better
7.3.3 Final Comparisons and Entering the Narrow Gates (7:12–27)
    7.3.3.1 Entering the Narrow Gate
    7.3.3.2 Beware of False Prophets (7:15–23)
        7.3.3.2.1 Sheep vs. Wolves
        7.3.3.2.2 Grapes vs. Thorns and Figs vs. Thistles
        7.3.3.2.3 Good Tree vs. Bad Tree and Good Fruit vs. Bad Fruit
        7.3.3.2.4 False Prophets vs. True Disciple
        7.3.3.2.5 House Built on Rock vs. House Built on Sand (7:24–27)
7.4 Conclusion

Chapter 8: Comparative Characterization of the Ideal Disciple in the Sermon on the Mount and Its Implications | 241

8.1 Introduction
8.2 Significance of Comparative Characterization in the Sermon on the Mount
    8.2.1 Comparative Characterization in the Beatitudes (5:1–16)
    8.2.2 Comparative Characterization in the Antitheses (5:17–48)
    8.2.3 Comparative Characterization in Matt 6–7
8.3 Conclusion

Bibliography | 251

List of Figures

Comparisons of Cain and Abel in Gen 4:1–8 | 90
Comparison of Samuel with Eli's Sons in 1 Sam 1 & 2 | 91
Structure of Matthew 5:18 | 158

List of Tables

Wide Gate vs. Narrow Gate (7:13–14) | 231
House Built on Rock vs. House Built on Sand (7:24–27) | 237

Preface

My interest in writing this book began with my interest in literary criticism, narrative criticism, and the topic of the Law in the New Testament. Primarily I was working on Jesus' teaching on the Law in the Sermon on the Mount. Further, I began my research in identifying why the author was writing about the Law. Later, I moved to study on how the author was writing about it. Through this I identified that the author keeps the teaching on the Law (5:17–48) in a broader framework where he characterizes the ideal disciple in Matt 5–7. The idea of chratacterization of the ideal disciple fascinated me. As I was already interested in narrative criticism I began to work on characterization in the Sermon on the Mount. I realized that there are many comparisons in the Sermon on the Mount. Comparisons were not widely used in the study on characterization. Thus, I wanted to do a research on the function of the comparisons in the characterization of the ideal disciple in the Sermon on the Mount.

The Sermon on the Mount contains many comparisons. In this study, the functions of these comparisons are identified by the methodology called comparative characterization. Characterization is nothing but the way a character is characterized in a narrative. Comparative characterization is the characterization of a character using comparisons. In comparative characterization, another character is used as a foil to bring out a characteristic trait of a concerned character. Thus, comparative characterization identifies the functions of the comparisons in the characterization.

Jesus characterized the ideal disciple in the Sermon on the Mount with many descriptions and imperatives. To characterize the ideal disciple Jesus used many comparisons and highlighted the characteristic features that embody the ideal disciple. Jesus described who this ideal disciple is in the beatitudes by descriptions such as the one who is "poor in the spirit," and also as the one who possesses "the kingdom of heaven," etc. (5:3 & 10). Interestingly here, Jesus used comparisons of who this ideal disciple is in the present world and also who this ideal disciple is in the light of the kingdom of heaven. Thus, the present state of the ideal disciple is compared with the blessedness of the ideal disciple in the kingdom perspective. This brings a complex portrayal of the ideal disciple. Therefore, comparative characterization yields in understanding the characterization of the ideal disciple in the Sermon on the Mount.

While the comparisons such as *"You have heard that . . . But I say to you . . . "* in 5:17–48 were considered as antitheses by many a closer look at the comparisons show that Jesus was not giving a new law in 5:17–48 and thus, he was not portraying the ideal disciple as an antinomian. Jesus used the comparisons as foils to highlight how the ideal disciple should obey the Law in 5:21–48. Similarly, in Matt 6, Jesus characterized the ideal disciple as the one who practices the acts of righteousness such as giving alms, praying, and fasting sincerely unlike the hypocrites and gentiles who do them ostentatiously to please men. The comparisons with the hypocrites and gentiles function as foils to characterize the ideal disciple. In addition, through the many comparisons in Matt 7, Jesus shows how the ideal disciple should live using comparisons as the one who does not worry about the essentials of life, such as what to eat, what to drink and what to wear but as the one who lives with trust and dependency in God (as in 6:33).

The many comparisons used in the Sermon on the Mount are identified in this study through comparative characterization. In addition, the teleological purpose of the comparisons which is to play as foil to the characterization of the ideal disciple is identified and highlighted in this study of the comparisons and their functions in the Sermon on the Mount. Thus, this study of comparative characterization in the Sermon on the Mount identifies Jesus' characterization of the ideal disciple and his complex portrayal of the ideal disciple with the many uses of comparisons in the descriptions and imperatives of Jesus in the Sermon on the Mount.

Acknowledgments

THIS BOOK IS AN updated version of my Ph.D dissertation called, "Comparative Characterization as a Methodology to Interpret the Comparisons in the Sermon on the Mount." First of all, I am deeply indebted to thank Dr. Joseph Shao for his immense encouragement to complete my Ph.D. I must thank Biblical Seminary of the Philippines, Asia Graduate School of Theology and Dr. Theresa Lua for their helps rendered during my study. My heartfelt gratitude is also due to Paulien, Anton and Boaz friends for their continual support. I also must thank Dr. Charles and Sherry Quinley. Without their initiative I wouldn't have started my Ph.D program. I must also express my gratitude to Uncle David West who encouraged me to go for higher studies in theology. I must also thank Ptr. Sungwon for his continual support which helped me continue my Ph.D studies. I am grateful to Uncle Bhagi Mirpuri who was a great support while I was doing this research. I am indebted to Dr. Edwin Perona, who constantly encouraged me during my research. In addition, I am also thankful to Dr. Kenneth Fox and Dr. Edgar Ebojo for their valuable suggestions which made this manuscript a better one.

I would like to extend my heartfelt gratitude to Dr. Michael Malessa for his valuable suggestions. I must thank Revathi Bout for reading the whole manuscript and copyediting it which obviously made it better in many ways. In spite of all these I take full responsibilities for any mistakes still found. I must also thank Wipf and Stock for their willgness to publish this book. Especially I am indebted to Matthew Wimer and Brian Palmer for their continual help in making this manuscript ready for print. They patiently answered my many queries and helped me in making this book come to reality.

Special thanks are due to my loving wife, Joyce for the many contributions she made towards the completion of my research; may it be by giving me the time and freedom to work on the manuscript or by typing the many pages of this book. My gratitude is due also to my parents, M. S. Lawrence and Selvamani Lawrence for their constant love and encouragements. In addition, I am thankful to my daughter, Netanya for giving me the space and time to complete my requirements, and for understanding that even the grownup-dad needs to finish his "homework." *Soli Deo Gloria!*

Abbreviations

Old Testament

Gen	Genesis	Song	Song of Songs
Exod	Exodus	Isa	Isaiah
Lev	Leviticus	Jer	Jeremiah
Num	Numbers	Lam	Lamentations
Deut	Deuteronomy	Ezek	Ezekiel
Josh	Joshua	Dan	Daniel
Judg	Judges	Hos	Hosea
Ruth	Ruth	Joel	Joel
1–2 Sam	1–2 Samuel	Amos	Amos
1–2 Kgs	1–2 Kings	Obad	Obadiah
1–2 Chr	1–2 Chronicles	Jonah	Jonah
Ezra	Ezra	Mic	Micah
Neh	Nehemiah	Nah	Nahum
Esth	Esther	Hab	Habakkuk
Job	Job	Zeph	Zephaniah
Ps/Pss	Psalms	Hag	Haggai
Prov	Proverbs	Zech	Zechariah
Eccl	Ecclesiastes	Mal	Malachi

New Testament

Matt	Matthew	Acts	Acts
Mark	Mark	Rom	Romans
Luke	Luke	1–2 Cor	Corinthians
John	John	Gal	Galatians

Eph	Ephesians	Heb	Hebrews
Phil	Philippians	Jas	James
Col	Colossians	1–2 Pet	1–2 Peter
1–2 Thess	1–2 Thessalonians	1–3 John	1–3 John
1–2 Tim	1–2 Timothy	Jude	Jude
Titus	Titus	Revelation	Revelation
Phlm	Philemon		

Other Books

1 *Apol.*	Justin Martyr, *First Apology*	*J.W.*	Josephus, *Jewish Wars*
1*QM*	War Scroll	JSOT	Journal of the Study of the Old Testament
1*QpMic*	Pesher Micah		
1*QpPs*	Pesher Psalms		
1*QpZeph*	Pesher Zephaniah	JSOPTSup	Journal of the Study of the Old Testament Supplement Series
1*QH*	Thanksgiving Hymns		
1*QS*	Rule of the Congregation	LXX	Septuagint
1–2 Macc	1–2 Maccabees	*m. Šabb.*	Mishnah Shabbat
3–4 Macc	3–4 Maccabees	*Marc.*	Tertullian, *Against Marcion*
3*QpIsa*	Pesher Isaiah		
4*QpHos*	Pesher Hosea	*Metam.*	Apuleius, *Metamorphoses*
4*QpNah*	Pesher Nehamiah		
A.J.	Josephus, *Antiquitates Judaicae*	*Mor.*	Plutarch, *Moralia*
		NAU	New American Standard Bible Updated (1996)
CD	The Damascus Document,		
Ep.	Seneca, *Epistulae Morales*	NIV	New International Version
Haer.	Irenaeus, *Against Heresies*	*Part. or.*	Cicero, *Partitiones oratoria*
Hom. Matt.	Chrysostom, *Homiliae Matthaeum*	QpHab	Pesher Habakkuk
		Rhet.	Aristotle, *Rhetoric*
Inst.	Quintilian, *Institutio Oratoria*	*Serm. Dom.*	Augustine, *De Sermone Domini in Monte*
Inv.	Cicero, *de Inventione rhetorica*		
		Sir	Sirach
		Sifre Deut	Sifre Deuteronomy

T. Iss	Testament of Issachar	*Top.*	Aristotle, *Topica*
Tob.	Tobit	*'Avot R. Nat.*	*Avot of Rabbi Nathan*

Chapter 1

Comparative Characterization as a Methodology to Interpret the Comparisons in the Sermon on the Mount

THE SERMON ON THE Mount has been an important document in the history of Christianity. Luke Timothy Johnson says, "In the history of Christian thought—indeed in the history of those observing Christianity—the Sermon on the Mount has been considered an epitome of the teaching of Jesus and therefore, for many, the essence of Christianity."[1] In addition, W. D. Davies highlights the importance of the Sermon on the Mount in these words: some "have seen in it the finest statement of the highest ethic that mankind has known."[2] The Sermon on the Mount gives the essence of Jesus' teaching in three chapters, Matt 5, 6 and 7. However, though it is an important document of Christianity, it was not accepted and understood by all in the same way. Claurence Bauman says, "The Sermon on the Mount is the most important and most controversial biblical text."[3] John Stott adds, "The Sermon on the Mount is probably the best known part of the teaching of Jesus, though arguably it is the least understood, and certainly it is the least obeyed."[4] One of the reasons for the complexities of the Sermon on the Mount is its comparisons.

Many comparisons are found in the Sermon on the Mount. While some are explicit others are subtle. The following are some of the verses where the comparisons come to the fore in Matt 5–7:

---

1. Johnson, "The Sermon on the Mount," 654.
2. Davies, *The Sermon on the Mount* (1983), 1.
3. Bauman, *The Sermon on the Mount*, 3.
4. Stott, *The Sermon on the Mount*, 5.

5:17	Do not think that *I came to abolish the Law* or the Prophets; *I did not come to abolish* but to fulfill.
5:20	For I say to you, that unless your righteousness *surpasses that of the scribes and Pharisees*, you shall not enter the kingdom of heaven
5:21	*You have heard that* the ancients were told, v.22 *But I say to you* . . .
5:27	*You have heard that* the ancients were told, v.28 *But I say to you* . . .
5:31	*And it was said*, v.32 *but I say to you* . . .
5:33	*Again, you have heard* that the ancients were told, v.34 *But I say to you* . . .
5:38	*You have heard that it was said*, v.39 *But I say to you* . . .
5:43	*You have heard that it was said*, v.44 *But I say to you* . . .
5:47	"And *if you greet your brothers only, what do you do more than others? Do not even the Gentiles do the same?*
6:2	When therefore *you give alms*, do not sound a trumpet before you, *as the hypocrites*
6:5	And when *you pray, you are not to be as the hypocrites*
6:7	And *when you are praying*, do not use meaningless repetition, *as the Gentiles*
6:8	Therefore do *not be like them*
6:16	And whenever *you fast*, do not put on a gloomy face *as the hypocrites do*
6:19	Do not *lay up for yourselves treasures upon earth*
6:32	For *all these things the Gentiles eagerly seek*
7:15	Beware *of the false prophets*

Many questions arise with the number of comparisons in the Sermon on the Mount: Why did Matthean Jesus use so many comparisons in this Sermon? Why did Matthean Jesus use the comparisons while he was teaching about the way in which the disciples should live? These questions are highlighted when we see how the interpreters of the Sermon on the Mount interpret this literature.

For John Stott, comparisons are an essential part of the Sermon on the Mount. He says, "To me the key text in the Sermon on the Mount is Matt 6:8: 'Do not be like them.'"[5] Comparisons in the Sermon on the Mount call for difference in the disciples from the others. Comparisons call for repentance and to be different from the others. John Stott shows the importance of comparisons in the Sermon on the Mount in these words: "There is no single paragraph of the Sermon on the Mount where this contrast between Christian and non-Christian standards is not drawn. It is the underlying and uniting theme of the sermon; everything else is a variation of it. Sometimes

---

5. Ibid., 6.

it is the Gentiles or pagan nations with which Jesus contrasts his followers. At other times he contrasts them with Jews."[6] One must take note of these words: comparisons are "the underlying and uniting theme" of the Sermon on the Mount. This is how comparisons are important in the Sermon on the Mount. Therefore, this study is about comparisons and their function in the Sermon on the Mount.

1.1 The Role of Comparisons in the Sermon on the Mount

Comparisons in the Sermon on the Mount could function as a key in understanding Jesus' characterization of the ideal disciple. The research question of this study is this: what is the function of the comparisons in the Sermon on the Mount? Could the comparisons in the Sermon on the Mount function as a key to understand Jesus' characterization of the ideal disciple? Jesus uses many comparisons in the Sermon on the Mount. In addition, Jesus also portrays how a disciple should live. This portrayal is done in several ways. In the first part, in 5:1–16, Jesus describes who his disciple is. Jesus describes the disciple as the one who is blessed. In addition, this blessed disciple is the one who is poor in spirit (v.3), the one who mourns (v.4), who is gentle (v.5), who hungers and thirsts for righteousness (v.6), who is merciful (v.7), who is pure in heart (v.8), and the one who is a peacemaker (v.9). Through these descriptions Jesus describes who this ideal disciple is in 5:1–16.

Moreover, from 5:17–48, Jesus compares his teachings with the Old Testament Law and teaches how the disciple must obey the Law in a better way. The comparisons are obvious in his formula such as, "you have heard the ancients were told,"Ἠκούσατε ὅτι ἐρρέθη τοῖς ἀρχαίοις, but "I tell you . . . ," ἐγὼ δὲ λέγω ὑμῖν (5:21, 22). These comparisons were considered by many to be contrasting comparisons as Jesus is considered giving antithetical teachings to the Old Testament. However, a closer look into the function of these comparisons shows that Jesus' teaching concentrates on how the ideal disciple should obey the Law better than the ones who obey the Law as 'they have heard from the ancients.' Apart from this, Jesus includes several other comparisons which indicates how the disciple should greet (5:47); give alms (6:2); pray (6:5, 7); fast (6:16); and handle money (6:19), etc.

Through these comparisons, Jesus wants to show how the ideal disciple should behave in particular situations. In addition, in these teachings Jesus compares this ideal disciple with how the hypocrites, Pharisees, and

---

6. Ibid., 6.

Gentiles and tax collectors behave. Thus, comparisons in Sermon on the Mount have an important function in the characterization of the ideal disciple..

Comparisons are common in literature and especially in characterization. Foil characters are used to illuminate the characteristic traits of a desired character in a narrative. Saul in the books of Samuels functions as a foil to David, as he brings out the good characteristic traits of David. While Saul frequently tries to kill David, David spares King Saul, though God handed Saul over to David in Engedi (1 Sam 24) and Hachilah (1Sam 26). Saul is then compared with David to bring out the good characteristic traits of David as the merciful king. This method of characterization is called as comparative characterization in this study. As Jesus uses comparisons to elucidate how an ideal disciple should live in the Sermon on the Mount could comparative characterization be used as a method to interpret the Sermon on the Mount? This will be the enquiry of this study.

1.2 The Importance of Comparison in the Study of the Sermon on the Mount

The comparisons in 5:21–48, *"You have heard that the ancients were told,"* *"... But I say to you,"*"Ηκούσατε ὅτι ἐρρέθη τοῖς ἀρχαίοις ... ἐγὼ δὲ λέγω ὑμῖν are called as antitheses. Antithesis is contrast, or an opposition. Matt 5:21–48 are called antitheses because of the assumption that Jesus contrasts his teaching with the teachings of the Pharisees.[7] Daniel Harrington says, "Christians often overemphasize the difference between the Old Testament teachings quoted in the first part of the antithesis and Jesus' instruction in the second part. They talk about the opposition between the Law and the gospel, or refer to the 'new law' promulgated by Jesus."[8] This indeed is true in the many interpretations of the Sermon on the Mount.

The teachings or antitheses in 5:21–48 are identified as Jesus undoing the old law and giving his disciples new laws to follow. To this extent, many scholars have penned. It is good to draw on a few of their conclusions found in Jules Isaac's *Jesus and Israel*.[9] Isaac quotes a few of them, which are important to understand the perspective of this school of thought. Ernest Renan says:

---

7. Harrington, *The Gospel of Matthew*, 90.
8. Ibid., 90.
9. Isaac, *Jesus and Israel*.

... all these old Jewish institutions ... An idea ... that henceforth seemed rooted in his mind was that there was no possible pact with the old Jewish cult. The abolition of the sacrifices that had caused him such disgust, the suppression of an impious and haughty priesthood, and in general the abrogation of the Law appeared to be of absolute necessity to him. From this moment on, *his chosen role was no longer as a Jewish reformer but as a destroyer of Judaism* ... In other words, Jesus was no longer Jewish ... The Law would be abolished, and he would be the one to abolish it.[10] [Emphasis mine]

In addition, Edmond Stapfer says: "Up till now, [Jesus] had been a Jewish reformer; henceforth he would be the destroyer of Judaism ... He was convinced that he would abolish the Law of Moses ... Mosaism was dead, it had only to disappear."[11] Maurice Goguel says: "Jesus' ministry in Jerusalem ended in a break with Judaism ... It was the accomplishment of the Law ... which led Jesus to discover that the role of the Law and the prophets ... had been outlived, and that a new era had opened in the history of religion."[12] Father Albert Vincent says: "There was ... an abrogation of everything that constituted the specificity of Judaism and gave it an essentially transitory character. *This is what Christianity teaches: Jesus Christ abrogated the Law*"[13] [emphasis mine].

Notice the last statement of Vincent: "This is what Christianity teaches: Jesus Christ abrogated the Law." How could he derive such a statement when Jesus himself in 5:17 mentioned that he did not come *"to abolish the Law or the Prophets"*? This shows the complications involved in the interpretation of the Sermon on the Mount. If the comparisons in Matt 5:21–48 are understood as antithetical then one could also assume that Jesus abrogated the Law. However, if the comparisons are not antithetical then Jesus would not have abrogated the law. Thus, the main concern of this study is this, how do comparisons function in the Sermon on the Mount.

Therefore, in this study, comparative characterization is used to identify how these comparisons function in the Sermon on the Mount. If comparisons in 5:21–48 are taken out of the context, without taking 5:1—7:29 in to considerations, or even without 5:17-20, one could come up with the statement that Jesus abrogated the Law. However, when these comparisons in 5:21–48 are studied with the other comparisons in the Sermon on the

10. Renan, *Vie de Jesus*, 215 cited in Isaac, *Jesus and Israel*, 49.

11. Stapfer, *Jesus-Christ pendant son ministere*, 255 cited in Isaac, *Jesus and Israel*, 49.

12. Goguel, *La Vie de Jesus*, 294 cited in Isaac, *Jesus and Israel*, 50.

13. Vincent, *Le Judaisme*, 74 cited in Isaac, *Jesus and Israel*, 50.

Mount in their overall function of the characterization of the ideal disciple, a different canvas appears and the caricatures of the antithetical teachings of Jesus fade out but the imperatives on how an ideal disciple should live unlike the Pharisees and gentiles are stressed. The question then lies in the understanding of the functions of these comparisons. If these comparisons are considered as antitheses then they must be seen as contrasting comparisons. However, if these comparisons are not antithetical then they must have other functions. This is an important query of this study. In literary techniques, comparisons function as foil to highlight the characteristic traits of a concerned character. Thus, the query of this study is this: Do the comparisons function as contrasting comparisons, antithetical or as foils in the Sermon on the Mount, Matt 5:3—7:27?

The purpose of this study is to interpret Matt 5:3 to 7:27 in the light of comparative characterization to elucidate Jesus' characterization of the ideal disciple over and against the characterization of the Pharisees, Scribes and the Gentiles. This study will concentrate only on Matt 5:3—7:27 and will look at the comparisons made by Jesus and identify their functions in the comparative characterization in an endeavor to highlight the portrayal of the ideal disciple. In order to do this, the methodology will be explained first, which is called as comparative characterization. Thus, in explaining the comparative characterization narrative criticism and literary criticism will be explained in chapters 3 & 4. After this, the methodology of comparative characterization will be applied in the text of Matt in 5:3 to 7:27 in chapters 5, 6 & 7. Using comparative characterization, the text in concern will be studied to bring out the functions of the comparisons in the characterization of the ideal disciple.

1.3 Comparative Characterization: A Methodology

This study as a whole is about the usage of the new methodology called comparative characterization to interpret the Sermon on the Mount. Comparative characterization is part of narrative criticism, which in turn is a part of literary criticism. One of the important presuppositions and contributions of the literary criticism is its emphasis on treating the literature as a whole. Literary criticism stressed that the Bible is literature and thus the methodologies used to read other literature must also be applied in the studying of Scripture.[14] This involved studying letters as letters (as Greco-Roman letters), narratives as narratives, historical writings as historical writings, etc. This stress on the treatment of the Bible as literature brought

---

14. Crain, *Reading the Bible as Literature*, 12–13.

forth several other methodologies such as narrative criticism, which treats narratives in the Bible as narratives, and rhetorical criticism, which reads the New Testament writings in light of the Greco-Roman rhetoric, etc. Though narrative criticism was widely used in the interpretation of the Old Testament it gained momentum in the interpretation of the New Testament in recent decades.[15] Narrative portions of the New Testament were read as narratives using narrative elements such as plots, conventions, Lietwort (keyword), motif, dialogues and speeches, repetitions, and characterization, etc.[16] In these elements of narrative criticism this study is more concerned with characterization.

Characterization is nothing but an element in narrative criticism which identifies how a character in a narrative is characterized.[17] To characterize a character sometimes another character or a group was used and compared to bring out certain characteristic traits of the concerned character.[18] This character is called a foil. In most cases, foils are used as antagonist to the protagonist to bring out concerned characteristic traits of the protagonist. This kind of characterization is done by the use of comparisons. This method of characterization is called as comparative characterization in this study. While characterization could be done by the description of the character or through the descriptions of the actions of the character or by the direct speech of the character or through the speech by others, in comparative characterization, characterization is done by the use of comparisons.

One important aspect of comparative characterization is its teleological purpose. Why is a particular character kept as a foil to the concerned character? Why is a particular incident kept as a foil? Why is a particular characteristic trait kept as a foil to the characteristic trait of the concerned character? These questions bring the teleological purpose of the presence of the foil to fore. The mere presence of a longer line adjacent to a shorter line makes the shorter line shorter. Without the presence of the longer line the shorter line would not be considered shorter. Thus, comparisons bring out certain characteristic features of the thing it is compared with. A particular foil is used in a particular setting concerning a particular characteristic trait so that this foil would bring out the particular characteristic trait of the concerned character. For example, Saul is kept as a foil against David, who tried to kill David frequently, to bring out the merciful characteristic traits

---

15. Resseguie, *Narrative Criticism of the New Testament*, 18.

16. Greidanus, *The Modern Preacher and the Ancient Text*, 286.

17. Burnett, "Characterization and Reader Construction of Characters in the Gospels," 3.

18. Turco, *The Book of Literary Terms*, 99.

of David, who in fact withdrew himself from killing Saul in Engedi (1 Sam 24) and in Hachilah (1 Sam 26). Thus, the comparative characterization identifies the teleological purpose of the use of comparisons to identify the characteristic trait(s) that the comparisons bring forth from the characterization of the concerned character. Thus, this comparative characterization is used to interpret the function of the comparisons in the Sermon on the Mount and its teleological purpose(s). In this study, the teleological purpose of the comparisons will be studied with the concentration on their function in characterizing the ideal disciple to highlight several characteristic traits.

1.4 Definition of Terms

Few terms are important to this study and thus must be defined. They are characterization, foil, comparative characterization and ideal disciple. The definitions are as follows:

1.4.1 Characterization

Characterization is nothing but the art of presenting a character in a narrative.[19] It is a process by which a character is revealed by the narrator in a narration. Adele Berlin says, that the reader gets to know a "character from the information provided to him [or her] in the discourse: he [or she] is told by the statements and evaluations of the narrator and other characters, and he [or she] infers from the speech and action of the character himself."[20] The author characterizes a character by giving enough information and thus the character gets life in the story. For example, Jesus is characterized as a compassionate person in Mark 1:41, as he, it was told, was moved with compassion looking at the leper and healed him. He was characterized as a good friend who would cry when he lost his friend, Lazarus in John 11:35. Jesus was characterized as zealous and devout Temple-lover in John 2:14–17. Thus, a character is characterized in a story by the depictions portrayed by the author. In this study, in the direct speech of the Sermon on the Mount: 5:3—7:27, Jesus is the one who characterizes how the ideal disciple is to live. Thus, Jesus characterizes the ideal disciple in the Sermon on the Mount. This would be one of the major concentrations of this study.

---

19. Harrison, *The Language of Theatre*, 51–2.
20. Berlin, *Poetics and Interpretation of Biblical Narrative*, 23.

1.4.2 Foil

Foil is a category of character in a narrative. A foil's main purpose is to stand in contrast to another character or group to bring out certain qualities of that particular character or group. Thus, "A character in a work who, by sharp contrast, serves to stress and highlight the distinctive temperament of the protagonist is termed a foil."[21] Foil is technically a thin sheet of bright metal placed under a jewel to bring out the qualities of the jewel.[22] Howard Suber says, "Foil characters exist to fulfill a particular need of the story, which is usually to reveal something about, not about the foil but about the central character."[23] James L. Resseguie adds, "A foil may also illuminate the deficient qualities of groups of characters."[24] By this he means that a certain character could stand as a foil or contrast to a group to show certain characteristic traits of the group. For example, the poor widow who gave all that she had in a self-less act was a foil against the many, who had more money but did not have that selfless trait (Mk 12:42–44). The women who were present at the cross were kept as foil in contrast to the coward men disciples who were in hiding (Lk 23:27).[25] The definition of the terms, characterization and foil, leads to the next term called comparative characterization.

1.4.3 Comparative Characterization

Comparative Characterization is nothing but the method of characterization which involves using foil character(s) to characterize a character or a group. In many instances, to identify a character as good the author would introduce a bad or worse character to be compared with it, so that the character in concern would be portrayed as being better. Evidences for this can be seen in many literary works. In *Les Misérables*, the goodness of Jean Valjean is seen by his comparison with the strict Inspector Javert.[26] In the Bible, the kindness of Joseph is seen by his comparison with his cruel brothers who sold him to slavery in Egypt (Gen 45). The mercifulness of David is seen by his comparisons with the cruelty of Saul. The godliness of Elisha is shown by his comparisons with the ungodliness of Ahaz and Jezebel (1 Kgs 16–18). Thus, comparison is an effective tool in characterization.

---

21. Abrams and Harpham, *A Glossary of Literary Terms*, 265.
22. Ibid., 265.
23. Suber, *The Power of Film*, 169.
24. Resseguie, *Narrative Criticism of the New Testament*, 124.
25. Ibid., 124.
26. Hugo, *Les Misérables*.

Therefore, comparative characterization is nothing but a characterization that involves comparisons to portray or show certain characteristic traits of the concerned character.

1.4.4 Ideal Disciple

A disciple is the one who follows Christ and obeys his will (Matt 7:20–27). Juan C. Ortiz answers the question "What is a disciple"? He says, "A disciple is one who follows Jesus Christ."[27] An ideal disciple is the one who obeys Christ completely in all the teachings and commands that Christ had given. According to Dietrich Bonhoeffer, "the disciple of Jesus acts simply in obedience to his Lord."[28] For Bonhoeffer, this simple absolute obedience is extraordinary. In addition, for Bonhoeffer, this simple obedience to His will is Christian life.[29]

In the Gospels, Jesus gave many commands on how a disciple should be. Especially, the Sermon on the Mount is full of such teachings on how a faithful disciple should be. In the Sermon on the Mount, Jesus teaches who the disciple is in 5:3–16; and how he or she must obey the Law in 5:17–48; and how he or she must live in the community in 6:1—7:27. Thus, the one who fully follows all these commands of Jesus from the Sermon on the Mount is called by the present writer as an ideal disciple.

It is understandable that no one could successfully evaluate who obeyed Christ completely. Therefore, the phrase "ideal disciple" is used in such a way to express Jesus' depiction of how an ideal disciple should be. Thus, Jesus, in one way, was characterizing the ideal disciple. In his exhortation on how a disciple should be Jesus shows who an ideal disciple is. Thus, in this way, he characterized the ideal disciple. Therefore, from the so-called antitheses (Matt 5:21–48), one could infer that the ideal disciple is the one who does not get angry at his brother, who does not look at a woman lustfully, who does not swear, who does not resist evil, etc. Thus, through the imperatives, Jesus characterized who the ideal disciple is. Hence, in this study, the term ideal disciple is used as Jesus' portrayal of how the disciple should be.

---

27. Ortiz, *Disciple*, 9.
28. Bonhoeffer, *The Cost of Discipleship*, 106.
29. Ibid., 106.

1.5 The Use of Comparative Characterization

The hypothesis of this study is that the use of comparative characterization in the Sermon on the Mount brings out the expected characteristic traits of the ideal disciple who is characterized by the comparisons and imperatives of Jesus in the Sermon on the Mount.

An important limitation to be addressed is that this study concentrates only on the Sermon on the Mount, which is found in the Gospel According to Matthew, from Chapter 5 until 7, especially from 5:3—7:27, leaving out the editorial comment of the author of Matthew in 5:1-2 and 7:28-29. In the methodological framework, one limitation to be stressed at the onset is that this study is not concerned with whether Matthew consciously used the comparative characterization in the Sermon on the Mount. However, it is about identifying how the comparisons function in the interpretation of the Sermon on the Mount. Contributing to this understanding is the presupposition that the Bible is literature and that it must be read as such. Thus, as comparisons are prevalent in this portion of the literature, the Sermon on the Mount and its comparisons are read using comparative characterization to see its function in its literary context.

1.6 The Significance of Comparative Characterization

In this study, the Sermon on the Mount is studied as a whole by identifying the function of comparisons in the Sermon on the Mount in its overall characterization of the ideal disciple. Thus, it avoids making conclusions from just looking at the parts of the passage or its comparisons. It concentrates on elucidating the important functions of the comparisons as being foils in the characterization of the ideal disciple. Thus, it helps to bring a better understanding of the Sermon on the Mount. The significance of the study then is that it helps to study the passage as a whole and also to see the literary function of the comparisons in its literary context.

This study concentrates only on the Sermon on the Mount. The objective in using the Sermon on the Mount to check the hypothesis of comparative characterization is a conscious decision which was made to show how comparative characterization could not only be applicable to a third person narrative but also to first person and second person narratives. In the Sermon on the Mount, Jesus uses first person and second person narrative, such as *"You have heard that the ancients were told, 'you shall not commit murder,' and whoever commits murder shall be liable to the court. But I say to you that everyone who is angry with his brother shall be guilty before the* *court,"*Ἠκούσατε ὅτι ἐρρέθη τοῖς ἀρχαίοις· οὐ φονεύσεις· ὃς δ᾽ ἂν φονεύσῃ, ἔνοχος ἔσται τῇ κρίσει. ἐγὼ δὲ λέγω ὑμῖν ὅτι πᾶς ὁ ὀργιζόμενος τῷ ἀδελφῷ αὐτοῦ ἔνοχος ἔσται τῇ κρίσει (Mat 5:21–22). While he is exhorting his disciples on how they ought to obey the Law he is using comparisons to show the better way to obey. Even here, in the first person and second person narrations Jesus uses comparisons. If comparative characterization could be used in the second person narrative how much more could it be used in third person narratives? Thus, the long range consequences of this research are immense.

This comparative characterization therefore can be used in any narrative and any literature. Comparisons are part of anthropological, and sociological phenomenon which dwell in the history of mankind. Thus, comparisons are part and parcel of our social existence. Therefore, comparative characterization helps understand how the narrator's use comparisons in the Bible. Gospels could be studied to see how the Evangelists use comparisons in relations to their characterization of Jesus, or disciples, or Pharisees, Jews, etc. This would help understand the characterization of the individuals or groups to elucidate the portrait of the characters and groups.

In the book of Mark, the Markan author compares the disciples with Jesus' opponents on many occasions. The Pharisees, Scribes and the Jews have unbelief towards Jesus (2:1–12; 3:1–6; 6:1–6; 11:27–33). This unbelief of theirs is due to the hardening of their hearts (3:5 and 4:12). Likewise, the disciples are also characterized similarly by the author that they did not have faith in Jesus when they were with him on the boat (4:35–41), they did not understand Jesus because of unbelief (8:14–21); they could not perform miracles because of unbelief (9:14–29). Thus, the disciples in Mark are also characterized very similarly to the opponents of Jesus in the following ways: both, the opponents and the disciples have hardness of heart which was the result of their unbelief (3:5 and 6:52, respectively); both of them have eyes but not see, have ears but not hear (4:12 and 8:17). Why would the author depict the disciples very similar to that of the opponents of Jesus? Comparative characterization would help to bring out the characterization of these groups and the literary functions of these comparisons in the narration.

Comparative characterization could be used extensively in the Old Testament narratives. Old Testament narratives are full of comparisons. Noah was compared to the rest of the world, Abraham was compared with Lot, Jacob was compared with Esau, and Laban, Joseph was compared with his brothers, etc. Even in the writings such as Job comparative characterization could be applied. The speech of Job's friends and the speech of Job are kept in comparison that Job's characterization could be well achieved by good analysis of those comparisons.

It is also possible to see how comparisons work in the epistles. Comparative characterization could illuminate the comparisons and their functions in the characterization. For example, to elucidate how important was the contributions of the Philippians, Paul writes to the Philippians *"after I left Macedonia, no church shared with me in the matter of giving and receiving but you alone; for even in Thessalonica you sent a gift more than once for my needs"* (Phi 4:15-16). Paul uses comparisons in his epistles. Thus, Comparative characterization could be used even in the epistles to elucidate the literary functions of the comparisons.

In addition, this comparative characterization can be used in any piece of literature. As long as there are literature and communication, there will always be comparisons. Where comparisons are present comparative characterization could always be used to elucidate their function in the characterizations. Though the idea of foil is used in the narrative analysis of literature, comparative characterization as a methodology could be used to consciously analyze the characterization of the characters in particular literature. Thus, comparative characterization has enormous potential for long term consequences in the field of narrative and literary criticism. With this chapter 1 is concluded. In chapter 2, the literary review of the study of comparisons in the Sermon on the Mount is scanned for the better understanding of the functions of the comparisons in the Sermon on the Mount.

Chapter 2

Sermon on the Mount in Literature

> If anyone piously and soberly considers the Sermon which our Lord Jesus Christ preached on the mount, as we read it in the Gospel according to Matthew, I think that he will find in it, as regards the highest morals, the perfect measure of the Christian life.... All the precepts which have to do with shaping this life are in it.... This sermon is filled with all the precepts by which the Christian life is formed. (Augustin, Serm. Dom.5.1)

THESE WORDS OF ST. Augustine epitomize how several interpreters of the Sermon on the Mount saw this beautiful three chapter composition of Matthew, namely, Matt 5–7. However, on the other side of the spectrum, George Bernard Shaw considered the Sermon on the Mount as an "impractical outburst of anarchism and sentimentality."[1] For Tolstoy, all Christianity is summed up in one phrase of the Sermon on the Mount: "Love your enemies."[2] However, for Johannes Weiss, Jesus' teachings in the Sermon on the Mount are so other-worldly that it is impossible to practice them in this world and that it is unnecessary to practice them in this world.[3] For Mahatma Gandhi, the Sermon on the Mount contained the whole message of Jesus "unadulterated."[4] However Gandhi also said, "But negatively I can tell you that to my mind much of that which passes for Christianity is a negation of the Sermon on the Mount."[5] Thus, the Sermon on the Mount evoked varied responses and criticisms throughout the history of the church. These varying interpretations are to be attributed to the complications these chap-

1. Shaw, "Religion and War," 96.
2. Tolstoy, *What I Believe*, 7–8.
3. Weiss, *Jesus' Proclamation of the Kingdom of God*, 21.
4. Radhakrishnan, *Mahatma Gandhi*, 481.
5. Ibid., 481.

ters bring at the interpretive levels and also at the applicability levels. From the second century onwards, a number of writers wrote on this masterpiece. W. S. Kissinger lists about 150 pages of bibliography in his book, *The Sermon on the Mount*.[6] Thus, to give a comprehensive literary review of the interpretation of the Sermon on the Mount is simply a Herculean task.

In this chapter, then, the literary review is presented with selected scholars from Patristic Period through the Medieval and Reformation period, to Modern and 21st century. Though most scholars' views are kept in somewhat chronological formula, the chronological order is not strictly followed. For example, Mahatma Gandhi's views are presented immediately after Tolstoy's though chronologically he appears much later. This is done, so as to avoid breaking the continuity in content produced from the similar perspective from the Anabaptist, Barclay, and Tolstoy. In addition, it must also be mentioned that several scholars of the 20th century are not mentioned in order to avoid exhaustive presentation of the history of interpretation of the Sermon.

In this literary review, three important aspects are presented: 1. The common interpretive framework of a particular scholar, which would also embody the philosophy behind his or her way of interpretation, 2. Important contributions of the particular author, especially his or her view of the applicability of the Sermon on the Mount. (It must be mentioned here that it is not important for the present writer to show the applicability of the Sermon on the Mount in this literary review. However, most scholars seemed to write extensively on the applicability of the Sermon on the Mount. Therefore, the present writer is, then, obliged to show their view about the applicability as it essentially embodies their point of views in their interpretations of the Sermon on the Mount.) 3. How a particular author sees the function of the comparisons in the Sermon on the Mount. However, it must be said that in certain cases, not all these three areas are essentially present. Therefore, when all three are not present or not prominent these are not presented in entirety. It is only fitting to start the literary review from the Patristic fathers. To this now we turn.

2.1 Justin Martyr

Justin Martyr was one of the important theologians of the second century. His first apology was addressed to Roman Emperor, Antonius Pius, the father of Marcus Aurelius, in which he commented on the Sermon on the Mount in brief (in chapters 15 and 16). Justin Martyr used the Sermon on

6. Kissinger, *The Sermon on the Mount*.

the Mount to show what Jesus taught so that the Emperor and his son would understand the teachings of Jesus and the life of the Christians. He shows that Christians are chaste; they do not murder, they don't even get angry at the brother, and they do not swear, etc. He used the comparisons of Jesus in the Sermon on the Mount to indicate how Christ wanted his disciples to be. However, he did not stress on the comparisons. Nevertheless, it is obvious that the comparisons of the Sermon on the Mount played a vital role in his exhortations as he also mimics comparisons in his own writings in chs. 15 and 16. For example, he says, "For we ought not to strive; neither has He desired us to be imitators of wicked men, but He has exhorted us to lead all men, by patience and gentleness, from shame and the love of evil" (Justin Martyr, 1 *Apol.*16.3).

Justin Martyr, in his *First Apology*, shows that the Sermon on the Mount indicates how an ideal disciple must be. If anyone does not follow the teachings found in the Sermon on the Mount, for him, he/she is not a Christian at all. For he says, "And let those who are not found living as He taught, be understood to be no Christians, even though they profess with the lip the precepts of Christ; for not those who make profession but those who do the works, shall be saved, according to His word . . . " (Justin Martyr, 1 *Apol.* 16.7). In addition, he also condemned all those who do not obey Christ's teachings in the Sermon on the Mount to be punished by the Emperor (Justin Martyr, 1 *Apol.* 16.8). Thus, for Justin Martyr the Sermon on the Mount teaches how a disciple of Christ must live.

2.2 Irenaeus

St. Irenaeus was the Bishop of Lyons, who was associated with Polycarp, the Bishop of Smyrna. His *Against Heresies* is said to be one of the finest writings against the Heresy of Gnosticism. In his accusations against Gnosticism and Marcion, Irenaeus deals with the relationship between the new law and the old, referring to Matt 5:21, and the following verses.

Irenaeus identifies that, Jesus keeps the things said of the men of old and of his own sayings in comparisons in the Sermon on the Mount. For Irenaeus, through the comparisons Jesus was not speaking against the old law, but was only against the watered down traditions of the old law followed by the Pharisees (Irenaeus, *Haer.* IX.12.1). The comparisons Jesus makes in Matt 5 are not about the old law but against the "Pharisaical" interpretation of the Law. Thus, Jesus was not against the old law but against Pharisaical traditions. In his argument against Marcion, Irenaeus points out that Jesus cannot be different from the Father or be another god, as he validated the old law in the Sermon on the Mount and so he also stressed that Jesus came not to abolish the Law but to fulfill it (Irenaeus, *Haer. IV.*12.2). Thus, Christ did not "abrogate the natural precepts of the Law" but he came and "extended them" (Irenaeus, *Haer. IV.*13). Therefore, for Irenaeus, the comparisons in the Sermon on the Mount do not show that Jesus was doing away with the Law but He was just extending it so that his followers would obey and believe in them (Irenaeus, *Haer. IV.*13.3). He says, "Now all these [precepts, . . . not the injunctions] of one doing away with the Law, but of one fulfilling, extending, and widening it among us; just as if one should say, that more extensive operation of liberty implies that a more complete subjection and affection towards our Liberator had been implanted within us" (Irenaeus, *Haer. IV.*13.3). Consequently, Irenaeus sees through the comparisons that Jesus was not showing the contrast between the old law and his teaching, but he was making his teaching extended so that it would create "more complete subjection" from his disciples/followers (Irenaeus, *Haer. IV.*13.3).

2.3 Tertullian

Tertullian is considered as a prolific ecclesiastical writer of the late 2nd century and early 3rd century. He was from Carthage, a Roman province of Africa. He wrote extensively in Latin and was one of the first to do so. Hence, he was called "the father of Latin Christianity." Though Tertullian wrote extensively on various subjects, our concentration is on his five books against Marcion, where he used the Sermon on the Mount quite at length in chapters 14–17 of *Book IV*. He did so, in order to refute the teachings of Marcion by using the teachings of Jesus from the Sermon on the Mount. Through the Sermon on the Mount, Tertullian showed that Jesus was not different from the Father of the Old Testament, as Marcion claimed. Jesus blessed in the beatitudes like the Father blessed all creation in the Old Testament (Tertullian, *Marc. IV.*14.8).

In commenting on the comparisons in 5:21ff, Tertullian identifies that Jesus did not put away the Law but he fulfilled it while Marcion propagated that Jesus put away with the Law. Tertullian accused Marcion's Jesus saying: "what a turncoat is Marcion's Christ! Now the destroyer, now the advocate of the prophets! He destroyed them as their rival, by converting their disciples," (Tertullian, *Marc. IV.*15.20). Thus, Tertullian says, "in His beatitudes just as if it were not competent to the creator, in the preeminence of both His attributes as the good God and judge, that, as He made clemency the preamble of His benediction so He should place severity in the sequel to His curses; thus fully developing His discipline in both directions, both in following out the blessing and in providing against the curse" (Tertullian, *Marc. IV*.15.6–7). Through this, Tertullian stressed that the character of Jesus is not different from the Creator God, who is also the Judge in the Old Testament. In addition, by the same time, he identifies that, in the Sermon on the Mount, Jesus demands discipline from his disciples that they need to follow the precepts given by Christ in the Sermon on the Mount, failing which they will be condemned. Hence, through his apologetic writings against Marcion, Tertullian shows the importance of following the Sermon on the Mount and its precepts in order to be identified as good disciple.

In addition, Marcion seemed to have interpreted Jesus' words "Love your enemies" as a new command of Jesus, which is antithetical to the teachings of the Old Testament God. God of the Old Testament demands Israel to kill all their enemies but Jesus of the New Testament commands his disciple to love their enemies. Thus, Marcion seemed to have said that the Jesus of New Testament is different from the God of the Old Testament. Tertullian commenting on this verse says, "These commands the Creator included in one precept by His prophet Isaiah: 'Say, ye are our brethren, to those who hate you'" (Tertullian, *Marc. XVI*.5). Through his use of Isaiah of the Old Testament, Tertullian shows that the God of the Old Testament is also a loving God, who considered that the ones who hate are to be considered as brethren. Thus, he shows continuity from the Old Testament in the New Testament. The comparisons in the Sermon on the Mount are not seen as antithetical, like Marcion saw them but for Tertullian, they are synonymous and an extension of the old. He presents similar arguments for identifying why Christ changed the law of tooth for tooth to turning the other cheek when slapped on one (Tertullian, *Marc. IV*.17–20). Thus, Tertullian sees continuity in the comparisons rather than a discontinuity or antithesis. "Thus," he says, "whatever (new provision) Christ introduced, he did it not in opposition to the Law, but rather in furtherance of it, without at all impairing the prescription of the Creator" (Tertullian, *Marc. IX* 16.21).

2.4 Augustine of Hippo

St. Augustine was born in 354 CE. He was one of the most influential church fathers in the history of Christianity.[7] Many studies on the writings of Augustine were concerned with his well-known work such as *Confessions*, *The City of God*, and *On the Trinity*. However, his writings on the Gospels and on the Sermon on the Mount display his views in *De Sermone Domini in Monte*. Probably, St. Augustine was the first one to call this document of

---

7. Tillich, *A History of Christian Thought*, 103–4.

Matthew as "The Sermon on the Mount."[8] For St. Augustine, the Sermon on the Mount describes the highest standard of morality and the perfect measure of Christian life demanded by Jesus. In his words he says,

> If anyone will piously and soberly consider the Sermon which our Lord Jesus Christ spoke on the Mount, as we read it in the Gospel according to Matthew, I think that he will find in it, so far as regards the highest morals, a perfect standard of the Christian life: and this we do not rashly venture to promise, but gather it from the very words of the Lord Himself. For the Sermon itself is brought to a close in such a way, that it is clear there are in it all the precepts which go to mold the life. For thus he speaks: 'Therefore, whosoever heareth these words of mine, and doeth them, I will liken him unto a wise man, which built his house upon a rock . . . ' Since, therefore, he has not simply said 'whosoever heareth my words,' but has made an addition, saying 'whosoever heareth these words of mine,' he has sufficiently indicated, as I think, that these sayings which He uttered on the Mount so perfectly guide the life of those who may be willing to live according to them, that they may justly be compared to one building upon a rock. (Augustine, *Serm. Dom.* 1.1)

This shows Augustine's conviction that the Sermon on the Mount is not just a collection of moral code for a selected few but a perfect rule and pattern for every Christian believer. For Augustine, the Sermon on the Mount shows the ethical content by which every follower of Christ should live by because it is "the highest morals and a perfect standard of the Christian life."

St. Augustine used symbolism and numbers to interpret the Sermon on the Mount that for him the eight beatitudes should be considered as seven because the eighth beatitude which also has "for theirs is the Kingdom of God" returns back to the first one because of its similarity to the first beatitude.

St Augustine, in his reply to Faustus, shows his understanding of the relationship between the old law and the new law using the Sermon on the Mount. Faustus was one of the famous Manicheans who wrote against the continuation of the old law in the New Testament. Augustine wrote against him in his *On the Sermon on the Mount*, stressing that Jesus came so that even the iota, "the smallest letter" and a tittle which is a "particle of some sort at the top" would not be lost from the Law (Augustine, *Serm. Dom.* 1.7). He says that by these words, Jesus shows that "in the Law all the smallest particulars even are to be carried into effect" (Augustine, *Serm. Dom.*

---

8. Kissinger, *The Sermon on the Mount*, 13.

1.8). Through these, Augustine shows the continuation of the old law, unlike Faustus who stressed that Jesus came to end the Law and to give a new law. Augustine stressed the continuation of the Law but also showed that there was some kind of addition of Jesus to the old law. In his paraphrased sentences of 5:21, he says: "Unless ye shall fulfill not only those least precepts of the Law which begin the man, but also which are added by me, who am not came to destroy the Law, but to fulfill it, ye shall not enter into the Kingdom of Heaven" (Augustine, *Serm. Dom.* 9). This shows the continuation of the old but also the additions of Jesus which must be obeyed to enter into the Kingdom of Heaven.

The comparisons of 5:21–48 are seen by Augustine as Jesus giving teachings on the internalization of the Law over and against the Pharisaic obedience of the Old law. He says:

> The righteousness of the Pharisees is, that they shall not kill; the righteousness of those who are destined to enter into the kingdom of God, that they be not angry without a cause. The least commandment, therefore, is not to kill; and whosoever shall break that, shall be called least in the kingdom of heaven; but whosoever shall fulfill that commandment not to kill, will not, as necessary consequence, be great and meet for the kingdom of heaven, but yet he ascends a certain step. He will be perfected, however, if he be not angry without a cause; and if he shall do this, he will be much further removed from murder. For this reason he who teaches that we should not be angry, does not break the Law not to kill, but rather fulfills it; so that we preserve our innocence both outwardly when we do not kill and in heart when we are not angry. (Augustine, *Serm. Dom.* 9)

The comparisons are, thus, seen as Jesus teaching the disciples on how to internalize the old law. These comparisons are not to show contrast from the old law to the new teachings of Jesus but these comparisons elucidate the need to internalize the old law so that his disciples will be great in the Kingdom of God.

Therefore, for Augustine, there are two kinds of righteousness: the lesser righteousness which is derived from the obedience of the old law by the Pharisees; however, the greater righteousness is the righteousness derived by obeying Jesus' interpretation of the Law. He repeats this many times in his commentary on the Sermon on the Mount. For example, he says, "the lesser righteousness, therefore, is not to commit adultery by carnal connection, but the greater righteousness of the Kingdom of God is not to commit adultery in the heart" (Augustine, *Serm. Dom.* 12.33). Thus, the internalized qualities of the Law are greater than the literal obedience of the Law, as followed by the Pharisees. This shows Augustine's view on the comparisons and contrasts. However, for Augustine, the internalization is actually to fulfill the old law and is not given as a contrast to the old law. He says, "Now, the man who does not commit adultery in the heart, much more easily guards against committing adultery in actual fact" (Augustine, *Serm. Dom.* 12.33). Thus, "the later precept confirmed the earlier"; Augustine says, "for He came not to destroy the Law, but to fulfill it" (Augustine, *Serm. Dom.* 12.33).

2.5 John Chrysostom

John Chrysostom was born in Antioch and was the Bishop of Constantinople. He was born in 347 CE and was a contemporary of St. Augustine. Chrysostom was so known for his eloquence of speech, that some claim that he was called *Chrysostomos*, meaning "golden-mouthed" on account of his eloquence. Chrysostom was known for his homilies on the parts of the Bible, which are characterized by the literal interpretations of the text, unlike the Alexandrian interpretations which were more spiritual and allegorical in nature. His homilies on the Gospel of St. Matthew have his interpretation of the Sermon on the Mount. As with the other church fathers Chrysostom's interpretations were also filled with apologetical concerns where he encountered Gnostics and Manicheans in his teachings.

Chrysostom identifies comparisons in the Sermon on the Mount. While commenting on the verse *"For I say unto you, except your righteousness shall exceed the righteousness of the Scribes and Pharisees, you shall not enter into the Kingdom of Heaven,"* Chrysostom points out that the comparison of the old law to Jesus' new teaching should not be considered as antithetical but that of "the same tribe and kindred." For he says, "And observe also here, how He commends the old law, by making a comparison between it and the other; which kind of thing implies it to be of the same tribe and kindred. For more or less, is in the same kind" (Chrysostom, *Hom. Matt. XVI.*6). For Chrysostom, Jesus' comparisons should not be considered as contrasting comparatives but a comparison of the same kind. Thus, Jesus did not do away with the Law but he made it stricter. He says, "He cloth not, you see, find fault with the old law, but will have it made stricter. Whereas, had it been evil, He would not have made it more perfect, but would have cast it out" (Chrysostom, *Hom. Matt. XVI.* 6). Further, for Chrysostom, Jesus did not do away with the Law because if it was evil he would not have fulfilled it. Thus, for Chrysostom the comparisons in the Sermon on the Mount do not show antithetical teachings of Jesus to the old law but a teaching of the same kind.

Through these teachings Chrysostom was not only interpreting the Sermon on the Mount but was also attacking his opponents, the heretics. He says, "Now this [Jesus' teaching in the Sermon on the Mount] not only obstructs the obstinacy of the Jew [who misunderstood Jesus and thought that he came to destroy the Law] but stops also the mouths of those heretics, who say that the Old Covenant is of the devil," (Chrysostom, *Hom. Matt. XVI.*3). Thus, Chrysostom stressed that Jesus' disciples must obey all that Jesus taught in the Sermon on the Mount to prove that they are his disciples. For Chrysostom, the Sermon on the Mount was not only demanded of Jesus' immediate disciples, the twelve, but to all the followers of Jesus. He says, "But when you hear that he taught them [in the Mount], do not think of Him as discoursing with His disciples only, but rather with all through them" (Chrysostom, *Hom. Matt. XV.*1). Thus, for Chrysostom all the followers of Jesus must obey the Sermon on the Mount. Therefore, Chrysostom, like the other Patristic writers seen above exhorted Christ's followers to obey the Sermon on the Mount.

This ends the review of literature in the Patristic period's interpretation of the Sermon on the Mount. The middle ages, which were dark ages, were not really dark but provided ways for the Christianity to develop, strengthen and also to have deep roots in several countries. Out of these Middle Ages comes a fine scholar, Thomas Aquinas, a systematic theologian, who nevertheless used the Sermon on the Mount for his exposition.

2.6 Thomas Aquinas

Thomas Aquinas, "The father of Catholic Theology" addressed the interpretation of the Sermon on the Mount in questions 107 and 108 of "Treatise on Law" in *Summa theologica*, part 2.1. For the old law is not distinct from the new law in one sense, while the old is quite distinct to the new law Jesus exposed in the Sermon on the Mount in another sense. He explains it in this way:

> We must therefore say that, according to the first way, the New Law is not distinct from the old law: because they both have the same end, namely, man's subjection to God; and there is but one God of the New and of the Old Testament . . . According to the second way, the New Law is distinct from the Old law; because the old law is like a pedagogue of Children, . . . whereas the New

Law is the Law of perfection, since it is the law of charity. (Aquinas, *Summa theologica* 2.107)

While commenting on the comparisons in the Sermon on the Mount, Aquinas says that "the New Law is compared to the old as the perfect to the imperfect" (Aquinas. *Summa theologica* 2.107). Aquinas points out that the New Law fulfills the old law as it perfects the imperfect, the whole law, in its end, which is "justifying men."

As we closely read Aquinas, he shows the unique stand of the Catholic Church from the middle ages onwards, which shows that not all the demands of the Lord are needed to be obeyed by all. A careful reading of the following shows his classic exposition of this interpretation:

> Now Christ fulfilled the precepts of the old law both in His works and in His doctrine, In His works, because He was willing to be circumcised and to fulfill the other legal observances, which were binding for the time being . . . In His doctrine He fulfilled the precepts of the Law in three ways. First, by explaining the true sense of the Law. This is clear in the case of murder and adultery, the prohibition of which the Scribes and Pharisees thought to refer only to the exterior act: wherefore our Lord fulfilled the precepts Law by showing that the prohibition extended also to the interior acts of sins. Secondly, our Lord fulfilled the precepts of the Law by prescribing the safest way of complying with the *statutes of the Law*. Thus, the old law forbade perjury: and this is more safely avoided, by abstaining altogether from swearing, save in cases of urgency. Thirdly, our Lord fulfilled the precepts of the Law, by adding some *counsels of perfection*: this is clearly seen in Mat. 19:21, where our Lord said to the man who affirmed that he had kept all the precepts of the old law: "one thing is wanting to thee: If thou wilt be perfect, go, sell whatsoever thou hast." (Aquinas, *Summa theologica* 2.107, Emphasis mine)

Aquinas, here, distinguishes two things from each other: "precepts" or "statutes," and "counsels of perfection." This distinction later became the basics for catholic moral theology which was called a "double standard view" in the obedience of the new Law.[9] While the former entity, the "precepts" or "statutes" sometimes were called as "moral precepts," the latter "counsels of perfection" was called "Evangelical counsels."[10] According to Aquinas and the Catholic theologians who followed him, the moral precepts were

9. Ibid., 18.
10. Ibid., 18.

demanded by all the followers of Jesus while the Evangelical Counsels were only required of those who dedicated themselves for perfection. Kissinger, explains it this way: "The Evangelical Counsels have traditionally been associated with the virtues of poverty, chastity and obedience. Obedience to the precepts or commandments is necessary for salvation, but the evangelical counsels are essential for perfection and they obtain more merit and favor with God."[11] Aquinas shows the distinction between them as follows:

> The difference between a counsel and a commandment is that a commandment implies obligation, whereas a counsel is left to the option of the one to whom it is given. Consequently in the New Law, which is the law of liberty, counsels are added to the commandments, and not in the Old law, which is the Law of bondage. We must therefore understand the commandments if the New Law to have been given about matters that are necessary to gain the end of eternal bliss, to which end the New Law brings us forth with: but that the counsels are about matters that render the gaining of this end more assumed and expeditious... Nevertheless, for man to gain the end aforesaid, he does not need to renounce the things of the world altogether: since he can, while using the things of this world, attain to eternal happiness, provided he does not place his ending them: but he will attain more speedily thereto by giving up the goods of this world entirely: wherefore the evangelical counsels are given for this purpose.
>
> Now the goods of this world which come into use in human life, consist in three things: viz, in external wealth pertaining to the concupiscence of the eyes; carnal pleasures pertaining to the concupiscence of the flesh; and honours which pertain to the pride of life... and it is in renouncing these altogether as far as possible, the evangelical counsels consist. Moreover, every form of the religious life that professes the state of perfection is based on these three: since riches are renounced by poverty; carnal pleasures by perpetual chastity; and the pride of life by the bondage of obedience. (Aquinas, *Summa theologica* 2.108)

Thus, for Aquinas, the Sermon on the Mount cannot be applied to all the believers of Christ but to those who aim for perfection. While the moral codes on adultery and murder are required to be obeyed by all, the evangelical counsels are required only of those who look for a higher calling of perfection. Later, this higher calling was equated to the priesthood.

---

11. Ibid., 18.

From Aquinas onwards, Catholic theology was keen to follow this principle of "double standard" in the sense of the applicability of the Sermon on the Mount by Christ's followers. The impracticality of putting into practice of the Sermon on the Mount fuelled this movement that the Catholic scholars who followed Aquinas stressed that the Sermon on the Mount is not required to be obeyed by all but only by the certain few. This view was challenged heavily by the Protestant scholars such as Martin Luther, and John Calvin. To these now we turn.

2.7 Martin Luther

Martin Luther (1483–1546) was a professor of theology in the 16th century. His seminal works were aimed at the reformation within the Catholic Church and later against the Catholic Church. Martin Luther took up the interpretation of the Catholics who followed Thomas Aquinas first and refuted their interpretations vehemently. He says,

> First of all there have fallen upon this chapter [Matt 5] the vulgar hogs and asses, jurists and sophists, the right hand of the pope and his Mannelukes ... They have covered up Christ ... and have exalted and maintained the antichrist, namely the Christ here does not wish everything which he teaches in the fifth chapter to be regarded by his Christians as commanded and to be observed by them; but that much of it was given merely as advice to such as wish to become perfect, and any who wish may observe these parts; despite the fact that Christ there threatens wrathfully:—no one shall enter heaven who sets aside one of the least of these commands,—and he calls them in plain words commands.[12]

This is an interesting statement Luther makes even in the preface of his book on the Sermon on the Mount, which shows how he was against Thomas Aquinas' interpretation of the Sermon on the Mount. As he accused the Catholic interpreters with such harsh words as "hogs," "asses," etc., he nevertheless shows why he was frustrated. He claims that the Catholic interpreters of the Sermon on the Mount have covered up the original Jesus of the Sermon on the Mount and instead gave an "anti-Christ" because while the original Jesus propagated the obedience of the Sermon on the Mount to all the followers of Christ, the Catholic Jesus seemed to have given these as "advise" to those who want to become perfect. He shows that this interpretation

---

12. Luther, *Commentary on the Sermon on the Mount*, vi.

of the Catholics is entirely antithetical to the teachings of Jesus, who gives his teachings in the Sermon on the Mount as "commands." Thus, Luther refuted catholic interpretation of "double standard view" from the beginning of his treatise on the Sermon on the Mount.

Like the Patristic fathers' apologetic interpretations, Martin Luther's interpretation of the Sermon on the Mount was also dominated by his polemic teachings against the Catholics and Anabaptists. Against the Catholics, he says, "they have thus made not only Christian Salvation, yes even perfection also, dependent aside from faith upon works, but they have made these same works voluntary."[13] Luther accused the Catholics saying that they do not commend the practice of the Sermon on the Mount to all people on the basis of practicality and applicability. He says,

> And the teaching of those twelve "evangelical counsels" is very common among them, viz., not to require wrong doing, not to take vengeance, to offer the other cheek, not to resist evil, to give the cloak along with the coat, to go two miles for one, to give to everyone that asks, to lend him who borrows, to pray for persecutors, to love enemies, to do good to them that hate, etc., as Christ here teaches. All this (they disgustingly say) is not commanded, and the monks at Paris honestly assign reasons, saying, this Christian teaching would be much too hard if it were loaded with such commands as these, etc.[14]

Luther's stand is obvious. He was against the Catholics who did not require obedience to the Sermon on the Mount from all believers on the basis that the Sermon on the Mount is "much too hard" to practice. According to Luther, the Sermon on the Mount should be practiced by all the followers. In addition, for Luther, the ones who do not follow the Sermon on the Mount must be considered as following "anti-Christ" as they are against the teachings of Christ.

Apart from the Catholics, Luther also fought against another group of people in this regard. It is better to read his words to know who they were. "In the second place also against the new jurists and sophists, namely, the factious spirits and Anabaptists, who in their crazy fashion are making new trouble out of this fifth chapter."[15] Unlike the Catholics, who did not obey the Sermon on the Mount, the ones who "condemned and obliterated it" the Anabaptists "teach that one should have nothing of his own, should not swear, should not act as ruler or judge, should not protect or defend, should

---

13. Ibid., vi.
14. Ibid., vii.
15. Ibid., vii.

forsake wife and child and much of such miserable stuff."[16] Thus, Luther laments that both these extremes are the works of the devil in misinterpretation of Matt 5.[17]

To counter the teachings of the Anabaptists, Luther brings the concept of two kingdoms: "an earthly and heavenly kingdom."[18] Luther identifies that much of the misunderstandings of the passage comes because of the lack of understanding about the "secular and spiritual matters" and the difference between "the kingdom of Christ and of the [kingdom] of the world."[19] Jesus' use of comparison, about an eye for an eye and tooth for a tooth, to his new teaching, about turning the other cheek, must be understood in light of the two kingdoms. For Luther, the old law belongs to the earthly secular kingdom. However, the new law expounded by Jesus is commanded by Him as spiritual laws to be held by a Christian individual. However, when the same Christian has to respond to a particular situation in the secular realm he must use the old law, because the old law is not discontinued in Jesus Christ (5:17–20).[20] Thus, for Luther, a Christian who is wronged by somebody must report to the court as it relates to the secular realm but must not take grudge against that man/woman because it relates to the heavenly spiritual kingdom. Luther reacts in this manner:

> For they suppose that to offer the other cheek to the smiter means that one must say to him: see thou hast this cheek too, and smite me again; or that we are to throw the cloak to him who wants to take the coat. If that were the meaning, then we would have to give up at last house and home, wife and child . . .
>
> But still the question and dispute here remain, whether one is to suffer all sorts of things from everybody, and in no case make any resistance; also if we are not to contend or complain before the court, or to claim or demand one's own. For if this were absolutely forbidden, there would be a strange state of affairs, so that everybody's caprice and insolence, and no one could be safe from another, or keep anything, and at last there would thus be no government at all.[21]

Luther's views were practical. If Christians should live a life without resisting evil, then there would be turmoil and confusion that the governance of

16. Ibid., vii.
17. Ibid., vii.
18. Ibid., viii.
19. Ibid., 187.
20. Ibid., 187.
21. Ibid., 189.

the populace would not be a possibility. In order to run a country the thieves must be punished. If a few people do not report the thieves and if a Christian judge does not punish a thief then the thief would be emboldened to steal more and it would cause greater damage to the whole community. Luther identifies that Christ's teaching on the Sermon on the Mount is meant only for the Christian individual and how his/her activities and attitudes must be in relationship to the other Christian.[22] However, when it comes to the secular, would people need to resist evil as it comes under the realm of the secular kingdom? God is in control of both the kingdoms. The secular kingdom must also be ruled by God's law. For this, the old law must be used to rule the secular kingdom while, the Sermon on the Mount must be used in relations to the heavenly kingdom. Luther justifies this from the verse "give to Caesar the things which are Caesar's." Luther shows this dual role of the Christian in the following quote:

> For we are transferred to a different, higher sphere, which is a divine, eternal kingdom, where we need none of the things that belong to the world, but everyone is in Christ a Lord for himself, both over devil and world, as has been told elsewhere. Those now who are part of this same secular administration, must necessarily have control of right and punishment, and observe the distinction of rank, of persons, dispose of and divide properly, so that all things are well-ordered, and everyone may know what he is to do and have; and no one should interfere in the office of another, nor impose upon another, or take what belongs to him. For these things we have lawyers, who are to teach this and manage such matters. But the gospel has nothing to do with such things, but teaches how the heart is to stand related to God; and in all such matters it should be so disposed that it remains pure, and does not stumble upon false righteousness.[23]

Thus, for Luther, the Sermon on the Mount teaches about the things of the heart and not about interpersonal relationships in the secular world. In the Sermon on the Mount, Christ teaches the Christians on "how they are to live before God and in the world, and conduct themselves so that their heart may cleave to God, and have no concern about worldly government, authority, power, punishment, anger, revenge, etc."[24] Thus, Luther forbade a Christian from going to the Law.[25] He says, "Here there should be nothing

22. Ibid., 189.
23. Ibid., 192.
24. Ibid., 192.
25. Ibid., 193.

but mutual love and service, even towards those who do not love us, but are hostile to us, and do us harm and injury, etc. Therefore he says to such that they shall not resist evil, and even not seek revenge, but that they should turn the other cheek to him who strikes them, etc."[26] However, this man when he is in a secular office he must perform his secular duty. This man who holds the secular office is also a Christian. Thus, the "two persons or two offices are joined in one man, and he thus be a Christian and a prince, judge, lord, servant, maid, which are merely worldly persons, for they belong to the sphere of the world."[27] The Christian must involve in the worldly offices because "God had ordained and appointed there worldly spheres."[28] Luther encourages his people to remain in this world but only outwardly but their hearts must be transformed by the teachings of the Sermon on the Mount.

Against Anabaptist, Luther stated that it is foolishness to practice the teachings of the Sermon on the Mount literally. For Luther, one cannot live peacefully without resisting evil. He says, "What kind of a foolish mother would she be, who would not defend her child against a wolf or a dog and deliver it, and then say: A Christian must not defend himself"?[29] Through this, Luther strongly points out the necessity of resisting evil to some degree. Thus, for Luther, the ruler of a place must rule according to the law of the nation and not by the Sermon on the Mount because he must protect his subjects from danger.[30]

Luther saw the difference between the old and the new law, as a difference between law for a community and a law for the hearts of the people. Luther merged these both by his view of two kingdoms. The comparisons in Matt 5 were seen by Luther with the concept of two kingdoms. Thus, when a Christian goes to war or when he sits on a judge bench, punishing his neighbor, or when he registers an official complaint, he is not doing this as a Christian, but as a soldier or a judge or a lawyer. At the same time he keeps a Christian heart. He does not intend anyone any harm, and it grieves him that his neighbor must suffer grief. So he lives simultaneously as a Christian to everyone, personally suffering all sorts of things in the world, and as a secular person maintaining, using, and performing all the functions required by the law of his territory or city, by civil law, and by domestic law.[31]

26. Ibid., 193.
27. Ibid., 193.
28. Ibid., 193.
29. Ibid., 194.
30. Ibid., 194.
31. Ibid., 201.

According to Luther, Jesus Christ addressed these teachings of the Sermon on the Mount to the disciples not to the secular leaders. Thus, the disciples of Jesus, the followers of Jesus must obey all that Jesus had commanded in the Sermon on the Mount. However, this does not apply to the secular leaders and the Christians who hold secular offices. Thus, the secular leaders need not apply the Sermon on the Mount teachings in their secular offices but as for the disciples, they should follow Christ's commandments.

2.8 John Calvin

John Calvin, who was born in 1509, was one of the prominent reformers after Martin Luther. As Huldrych Zwingli was protesting in Zurich, Calvin established a Theocracy in Geneva. His well-known works include *The Institutes of the Christian Religion*. However, much of his views on the Sermon on the Mount come from his *Commentary on a Harmony of the Evangelists, Matthew, Mark and Luke*.

Calvin, in *Institutes*, Book II, in chapter 8, shows that Jesus' comparisons of his new teachings are made against the Pharisaic teachings of the old law. Jesus' interpretations were maintained in comparison with the interpretation of the Pharisees. Pharisees interpreted the old law in such a way that the external act of doing anything against the law was wrong.[32] However, Jesus, the King goes beyond the external act to the internal intentions.[33] Calvin says,

> The reason is, that a human law given does not extend his care beyond outward order, and, therefore, his injunctions are not violated without outward acts. But God, whose eye nothing escapes, and who regards not the outward appearances so much as purity of heart, under the prohibition of murder, adultery, and thefts includes wrath, hatred, lust, covetousness, and all other things of a similar nature. Being a spiritual Lawgiver, he speaks to the soul not less than the body. The murder which the soul commits is wrath and hatred; the theft, covetousness and avarice; the adultery, lust . . . the generality of men, even while they are most anxious to conceal their disregard of the law, only from their hands and feet and other parts of their body to some kind of observance, but in the meanwhile keep the heart utterly estranged from everything like obedience. They think it enough to have carefully concealed from man what they are doing in the

---

32. Calvin, *The Institutes of the Christian Religion*, 337.
33. Ibid., 337.

sight of God. Hearing the commandments, "Thou shalt not kill," "Thou shalt not commit adultery," "Thou shalt not steal," they do not unsheathe their sword for slaughter, nor defile their bodies with harlots, nor put forth their hands to other men's goods. So far well; but with their whole soul they breathe out slaughter, boil with lust, cast a greedy eye at their neighbor's property, and in wish devour it.[34]

Thus, Calvin acclaims Jesus gave the new law, against the Pharisees' outward keeping of the Law, which goes internal and not just external. The new law of Jesus is about the soul while the Pharisaic prohibitions were only about the external acts of the organs of the body. Calvin says, "The Pharisees having instilled into the people the erroneous idea that the Law was fulfilled by everyone who did not in external act do anything against the Law, He [Jesus] pronounces this a most dangerous delusion, and declares that an immodest look is adultery, and that hatred of a brother is murder . . . "[35] Thus, Calvin sees the comparisons of Jesus as him comparing his new teaching to that of the Pharisaic interpretations of the old law. He does not see Jesus as the new law-giver who gave new law over and against the old law. The comparisons in Matt 5 should not be interpreted as Jesus giving new law like a new Moses, according Calvin. For he says, "Those who have not perceived this [His interpretation of the comparisons], have pretended that Christ was only a second Moses, the giver of an evangelical, to supply the deficiency of the Mosaic Law."[36] Thus, Calvin argues against the assumption that the new Moses is better than the old Moses.[37] "This idea" Calvin says, "is in many ways most pernicious."[38] For Calvin, then, Christ did not add anything to the Law but "only restored it to its integrity by maintaining and purifying it when obscured by the falsehood, and defiled by the leaven of the Pharisees."[39] Jesus, thus, was against the Pharisaic interpretations of the Law.

This position of Calvin is based on 5:17 of Matthew. Calvin is known for his careful exegesis. Thus, commenting on this passage, he says, "Christ therefore, now declares that his doctrine is so far being at variance with the law, that it agrees perfectly with the law and the prophets, and not only so, but brings the complete fulfillment of them."[40] How did Christ fulfill the

---

34. Ibid., 337.
35. Ibid., 337.
36. Ibid., 337.
37. Ibid., 337.
38. Ibid., 337.
39. Ibid., 337.
40. Calvin, *Commentary on a Harmony of the Evangelists*, 1:275.

Law, asks Calvin? He says, according to the promise of the new covenant which is to "write the Law in their hearts" (Jer 31:33). Christ fulfilled the Law by making the dead letter come to life in his Spirit. He says, "For he actually fulfilled it, by quickening, with his Spirit, the dead letter, and then exhibiting, in reality, what had hitherto appeared only in figures."[41] Thus, Calvin upheld the Law of the Old Testament and commanded his followers to obey the Law as "it is the eternal rule of a devout and holy life."[42] Thus, Calvin stressed, "Let us therefore learn to maintain inviolable this sacred tie between the Law and the Gospel, which many improperly attempt to break. For it contributes not a little to confirm the authority of the Gospel, when we learn, that it is nothing else than a fulfillment of the Law; so that both, with one consent, declare God to be their Author."[43] Thus, for Calvin, the comparisons of 5:17ff does not show that Christ gave a new law antithetical to the old. For Calvin, there is continuity from the old to the new; both are God's word, which "declare God to be their Author," with an absolute continuity.[44]

Though Calvin is firm in advocating the applicability of the Sermon on the Mount and the old law, in view of them being God's word, he finds an issue with the extreme application of the Sermon on the Mount by the Anabaptists and he criticizes them heavily regarding their interpretations and their use of the Sermon on the Mount. About swearing, Calvin identifies that Bible does not prohibit all kinds of swearing. In fact, for Calvin, Bible commands people to swear. The command that Jesus gives in Mat 5:33 about swearing is to re-enforce the saying "do not take the name of God in vain." Thus, for him as long as swearing is done by not taking the name of God in vain, one can swear. Christ, therefore, meant nothing more than this, that all oaths are unlawful, which in anyway abuse and profane the sacred name of God.[45] Thus, for Calvin, Anabaptists were wrong in prohibiting swearing altogether. This interpretation of Calvin shows his conflict in interpreting the Sermon on the Mount in its context. The context of the text prohibits swearing at all, but in his context swearing is a must, in which one cannot survive without swearing. Calvin's world was just coming out of the newly brought in reformation. Reformation was supported by many rulers. If swearing and protecting were to be prohibited by the reformers, the rulers and ruled subjects would be in great trouble. The practicality and

41. Ibid., 1:275.
42. Ibid., 1:277.
43. Ibid., 1:277.
44. Ibid., 1:277.
45. Ibid., 1:295.

the application of these rules in his context allowed Calvin to customize and contextualize the Sermon on the Mount so that his community would not be harmed by the application of the Sermon on the Mount. The same could be said of non-resistance. For Calvin, not everyone could show the other cheek to the offender every time. He says, "I admit that Christ restrains our hands, as well as our minds, from revenge: but when any has it in his power to protect himself and his property from injury, without exercising revenge, the word of Christ does not prevent him from turning aside gently and inoffensively to avoid the threatened attack."[46] For Calvin, then, as long as one does not use revenge he or she could protect themselves and need not allow themselves to be run over by the offender. While here, Calvin shares the idea that "one must turn aside gently" from the offender, he shows a different view in relation to the lawsuits. Here one need not just submit to the one who sues him or her in court but they must defend themselves in court. He says, "Hence we conclude, that Christians are not entirely prohibited from engaging in lawsuits, provided they have a defense to offer."[47] Thus, for Calvin, resist not evil, is not to be applied literally but must be understood in its canonical context.

2.9 Anabaptists

It is obvious from the writings of Luther and Calvin that Anabaptists were an important group who had different interpretations of the Sermon on the Mount. Though the reformers criticized the Anabaptists regarding their views on re-baptizing the believers, and neglecting the infant baptism, their important contentions against the group comes from their interpretation of the Sermon on the Mount. Both Luther and Calvin (including Zwingli), accused the Anabaptists of applying the Sermon on the Mount too literally. Few of their important doctrines include not swearing, not taking oaths and non-resistance.

For Anabaptists, Christ gave the new law in the Sermon on the Mount. The comparisons in the antithesis show that Christ gave a new law for his new kingdom. Thus, all believers, Anabaptists urged, should literally follow what Jesus said in the Sermon on the Mount. Thus, they forbade swearing or oaths, or use of swords or violence, or taking part in lawsuits, etc.

Hans Denck, the famous Anabaptist in his writing, *Concerning True Love* says,

---

46. Ibid., 1:299.
47. Ibid., 1:300.

This is all that needs to be said concerning swearing about future events. As for testimony concerning things past, according to the Lord's teaching we should do it simply, using as few words as possible—yes or no. For we must answer to God for anything we say. One might call on God as a witness that what he says is true, as Paul did. But do not forget never to use God's name frivolously. This is forbidden in the Law and also in the New Testament, where we are forbidden to swear at all.[48]

Thus, for the Anabaptists, as Christ forbade swearing, they were to not swear at all.

The Anabaptists took the comparisons as antithetical to the point that all that Jesus said in the Sermon on the Mount must be obeyed by all. For Denck, the teachings of the Law of Moses "were good teachings and law for the people of Israel at that time (out of whom God would create and bring forth a new Israel)."[49] Thus, the teachings such as "an eye for an eye, to protect the innocent by force, to defeat evil by force, and concerning usury, divorce, oath and swearing and so on" were the laws of the old ways which were good for their time. But as Jesus, the Messiah had come, "the evil of the old teaching" should go away and the teachings of Jesus should be practiced in the new ways.[50] Thus, the Anabaptists were against using force to protect themselves. Denck declares, "No Christian who wants to bring honor to his Lord can use force or be a ruler. For the governance of our king consists only in teaching and in the power of the Spirit. Whoever truly acknowledges Christ as Lord should not act contrary to his commandments."[51] Anabaptists were taught to love their enemies, and not resist evil. A good example comes from the life of Dirk Willems. When the "rebellious" Anabaptists were targeted as heretics, many were captured, imprisoned, and killed. In 1569, in Holland, Dirk Willems, a Mennonite was fleeing from the arrest as the threat was capital punishment. As Willems was fleeing, he ran across a frozen lake and crossed it safe. However, the deputy who was chasing him fell through the ice and was about to drown. Willems, who could have escaped and have run, went back to save the deputy as it was commanded to love his enemy. The deputy upon being saved, arrested Dirk Willems and imprisoned him and he was later burnt at the stake.[52] Thus, the teachings, of

---

48. Denck, "Concerning True Love," 119.
49. Ibid., 114.
50. Ibid., 114.
51. Ibid., 120.
52. Bercot, *Will the Real Heretics Please Stand Up*, 156.

the Sermon on the Mount were literally put to practice by the Anabaptists in the midst of persecution and martyrdom.

2.10 Robert Barclay

Robert Barclay belongs to the group called Quakers. He was born in Scotland in 1648 and wrote extensively in defense of the Quakers and its founder, George Fox. George Fox himself was a staunch believer against the use of violence and swearing. He interpreted the Sermon on the Mount literally and exhorted his believers to refrain from swearing, taking oaths, and from using the sword. Barclay, in the footsteps of Fox used Matt 5:33–37 to reject the use of oaths and swearing. He says, "I say, considering these words, it is admirable how anyone that professeth the name of Christ can produce any oath with a quiet conscience, as far less to persecute other Christians, that dare not swear, because of their Master Christ's authority."[53] He criticized the other Christians who killed and persecuted the believers who did not swear or use violence. Barclay points out that in the teachings of Jesus, in the Sermon on the Mount, there is no exception in obeying swearing. As there is no exception all must refrain from swearing. He says,

> Which words both all and every one of them do make such a full prohibition, and so free of all exception, that it is strange how men that boast the scripture is the rule of their faith and life, can counterfeit any exceptions certainly reason ought to teach everyone; that it is not lawful to make void a general prohibition coming from a God by such opposition, unless the exception to be as clearly and evidently expressed as the prohibition.[54]

For Barclay, there is no exception in forbidding swearing. Jesus forbade divorce but gave an exceptional clause. However, the exhortation on swearing does not have any exceptional clause, and thus all must forbid swearing.[55] Barclay also criticized the Christians who used force and violence, inorder to stress that all Christians must refrain violence. He says,

> Truly the words are so clear in themselves, that, in my judgment, they need no illustration to explain their sense: for it is as easy to reconcile the greatest contradictions, as these laws of our Lord Jesus Christ with the wicked practices of wars; for they are plainly inconsistent. Whoever can reconcile this, Resist no evil,

---

53. Barclay, "An Apology for the True Christian Divinity," 2:543.
54. Ibid., 543.
55. Ibid., 543.

with resist violence by force; again, give also thy other cheek, with strike again; also love thine enemies, with spoil them, make a prey of them, pursue them with fire and sword; or pray for those that persecute you, and those that calumniate you, with persecute them by fines, imprisonments, and death itself; and not only such as do not persecute you, but who heartily seek and desire your eternal and temporal welfare: whoever, I say, can find a means to reconcile these things, may be supposed also to have found a way to reconcile God with the devil, Christ with Antichrist, light with darkness, and good with evil. But if this be impossible, as indeed it is, so will also the other be impossible; and men do but deceive themselves and others, while they boldly profess to establish such absurd and impossible things.[56]

Therefore, for Barclay, the follower of Christ should not use force and should not use violence. For Barclay and Quakers, war is unlawful for the disciples of Christ. They exhorted their people to live peacefully. One of the important contributions of the Quakers is their Ambulance service at the time of world wars.[57]

2.11 Leo Tolstoy

Count Leo Nikolaevitch Tolstoy was born in 1828 at Yasnaya Polyana near Moscow. From a young age he was serious in his faith and was regular at his orthodox church. He was a Count and he was rich. He spent his time in his country estate looking after his holdings and writing. Tolstoy was famous for his long novels. In addition, he was possessed by the idea of the meaning of life. He looked for answers from the evolutionists. However, the spectacle of a public execution in Paris put an end to his trust in evolution as a way to find meaning in life. He wrote in his *My Confession*: "When I saw the head divided from the body and heard the sound with which it fell separately into the box, I understood, not with my reason, but with my whole being, that no theory of the wisdom of all established things, nor of progress, could justify such an act."[58] Thus, he pursued his quest for meaning in other areas such as church. However, church activities also disappointed him. The priests were not open to the exploration of the meaning of life. In addition, the priests' affirmation of the wars shocked him. The priests, then, sanctioned the war by blessing the battleships and praying to God to confound their enemies.

56. Ibid., 560.
57. Abbott, *Historical Dictionary of the Friends*, 137.
58. Tolstoy, "My Confession," 9.

He says, "Russians slew their brethren in the name of Christian love. Not to think of this was impossible. Not to see that murder is an evil. Contrary to the very first principle of every faith, was impossible. In the churches, however, men prayed for the success of our arms, and the teachers of religion accepted these murders as acts which were the consequences of faith."[59] These things disappointed Tolstoy in his quest for the meaning of life and thus he turned to the Sermon on the Mount. Finally, the Sermon on the Mount showed the meaning for which he was searching. He later admitted that "the Sermon on the Mount was the portion which impressed me most. Nowhere else does Christ speak with such solemnity, nowhere else does He give us so many clear and intelligible moral precepts, which commend themselves to everyone."[60] However, when he tried to understand the Sermon on the Mount, the commentaries said that "man, being full of sin, cannot attain this perfection by own unaided strength, and that the salvation of man lies in faith, prayer, and the gifts of the grace of God."[61] This did not satisfy him. He asked:

> Why should Christ have given us such clear and good precepts, applicable to us all, if he knew beforehand that the keeping of them was impossible by man in his own unaided strength? On reading these precepts, it always seemed to me that they applied to myself, and that I was morally bound to obey them. I even felt convinced that I could, immediately and from that very hour, do all that they enjoined. I wished and tried to do so, but as soon as any difficulty arose in the way of my keeping them, I involuntarily remembered the teaching of the church, that 'man is weak, and can do no good thing by himself,' and then I became weak. I have been told that it was necessary to believe and pray, but I felt that my faith was weak and that I could not pray. I had been told that it was necessary to pray for faith—for the faith without which prayer is of no avail. I was told that faith comes through prayer and that prayer comes through faith which to say the least was certainly bewildering. Such statements commended themselves neither to reason nor experience.[62]

To those theologians who say we cannot fulfill the commandments of the Sermon on the Mount on our own strength, Tolstoy replies:

---

59. Ibid., 70.
60. Tolstoy, *What I believe*, 7–8.
61. Ibid., 8.
62. Ibid., 8–10.

> If my master were to say to me, "Go and cut wood," and I were to answer that I could not do it in my own strength, would it not show that either I had no faith in my master's words or that I did not choose to obey him? God has given us a commandment which he requires us to obey, he says that only those who keep his commandments shall enter life eternal . . . He does not say that it is hard to keep this law; he says, on the contrary, 'My yoke is easy and my burden light.'[63]

Tolstoy's obedience to the Sermon on the Mount was not only taken to his private realm, but also to other aspects of his life. His membership in law court which protected his property came under his scrutiny through the words of the Sermon on the Mount. Tolstoy said,

> The human courts were not only contrary to this commandment but in direct opposition to the whole doctrine of Christ and that therefore he must certainly have forbidden them . . . Christ enjoins us to return good for evil. Courts of law return evil for evil. Christ says: 'Make no distinction between the just and the unjust.' Courts of law do nothing else. Christ says: 'forgive all; forgive at once, not seven times, forgive without end.' 'Love your enemies.' 'Do good to them that hate you.' Courts of law do not forgive, but they punish, they do not do good but evil to those whom they call the enemies of society. So that the true sense of the doctrine is that Christ forbids all courts of law.[64]

For Tolstoy, Matt 5:39 which says, "I say unto you that ye resist not evil" became the key verse to interpret the whole Sermon on the Mount. He said the whole force of the Sermon on the Mount lay on the words, "resist not evil" while the whole the Sermon on the Mount itself is the application of this great principle.[65] He knew the complexities this principle brought if he practiced it fully. He knew he would be "forsaken, miserable, persecuted and sorrowing, as Christ tells his followers would be."[66] He continues, "I knew that if I accepted the law of man, I should have the approbation of my fellow-men; I should be at peace and in safety; all possible sophisms would be at hand to quiet my conscience, and I should 'laugh and be merry,' as Christ says."[67] However, he took up the hard path. He followed Christ, though it made him forsaken, miserable, and poor. However, his life and

---

63. Ibid., 14.
64. Ibid., 25.
65. Ibid., 13.
66. Ibid., 22.
67. Ibid., 22.

teachings changed several generations, especially his view on 'Love your enemy' (Matt 5:43–48). He condemned the killing of enemies in the name of war. He says "it is persistently instilled into us that it is our border duty to oppose our enemy."[68] In addition, he says, "We have grown so used to calling 'a Christ-loving army,' the men who devote their lives to murder, who put up prayers to Christ for victory over the enemy, whose pride and glory are in murder . . . that it now appears to us that Christ did not forbid war."[69] Tolstoy, thus, believed that if all people obeyed these words the world would be a peaceful place to live.

Tolstoy, thus, concluded that "Christianity in its true sense puts an end to the state. It was so understood from its very beginning, and for that Christ was crucified."[70] Thus, Tolstoy condemned the atrocities of the Czarist government, and the wars and unjust judicial system and advocated that should be done away with by following the teachings of Jesus in the Sermon on the Mount. Therefore, Tolstoy reasoned that the increase of Christianity should bring the decrease of the state till all governments are replaced by the spontaneity of brotherly love without oaths of allegiance, legal proceeding, or war taxes which were kept to maintain military defenses. The important presupposition of Tolstoy in his teachings is his conviction that good finally will triumph all evil. And thus, those who follow the Sermon on the Mount will succeed in bringing a world of peace. Thus, Tolstoy clearly identified that in the Sermon on the Mount Jesus taught the christian ideals for the disciples to follow.[71]

Tolstoy's words influenced many who changed history. Mahatma Gandhi, when he was a young barrister in South Africa, surrounded by apprehension of the colored Indians, read Tolstoy's writings and was overwhelmed that he actually wrote to him and got permission from him to publish his writings in South Africa and India. Tolstoy wrote *A Letter to A Hindu* as a response to C. R. Das, a revolutionary representative of Indians in Europe.[72] Tolstoy wrote in *The Letter to A Hindu* that freedom to India could only be attained by not resisting evil and by not using violence. He said, "Do not resist the evil-doer and take no part in doing so, either in the violent deeds of the administration, in the law courts, the collection of taxes, or above all in soldiering, and no one in the world will be able to enslave

---

68. Ibid., 99.
69. Ibid., 99.
70. Tolstoy, *The Kingdom of God is Within You*, 152.
71. Ibid., 117.
72. Murthy, *Mahatma Gandhi and Leo Tolstoy Letters*.

you."[73] This letter influenced Gandhi so much that his biographer Reverend Doke writes, "Undoubtedly Tolstoy has profoundly influenced him. The old Russian reformer, in the simplicity of his life, the fearless of his utterances, and the nature of his teachings on war and work, has found a warm-hearted disciple in Mr. Gandhi."[74] Gandhi himself attested that "Three moderns have left a deep impression on my life and captivated me; Ray Chand Bhai—by his living contrast, Tolstoy—by his book *The Kingdom of God is Within You*, and Ruskin—by his book *Unto This Last*."[75] Tolstoy's views were so influential in Gandhi's life that Murthy says, "The core of religion for both Tolstoy and Gandhi was primarily love."[76] Gandhi even opened a monastic ashram near Johannesburg and named it as Tolstoy Farm.[77] He took the ideals of Tolstoy of Bread Labor, non-violence and non-possession and practiced it there. The non-violence of Tolstoy was expressed as Ahimsa in Gandhian Philosophy. Gandhi says, Ahimsa, "in its negative form . . . means not injuring any living being whether by body or mind. I may not, therefore, hurt the person of any wrong-doer or bear any ill-will to him and so cause him mental suffering . . . In its positive form," he says "Ahimsa means the largest love, the greatest charity. If I am a follower of Ahimsa, I must love my enemy or a stranger to me as I would my wrong-doing father or son."[78] Thus, Tolstoy's interpretation of the Sermon on the Mount influenced Gandhi who influenced many to liberate India, Pakistan and Bangladesh. Gandhi in turn influenced Martin Luther King Jr., who influenced the laws on blacks and minority in the United States of America and beyond.

2.12 Mahatma Gandhi

Mohandas Karamchand Gandhi is the national hero of India who fought against British domination of India and was instrumental in the freedom of India. He was born on 2 October 1869 into a Hindu family. He travelled to London in 1888 to become barrister, attorney, at University College London. After completion of his degree, he came back to work in India as an attorney of Law. He then got a job in an Indian company, Dada Abdullah and Co. to work in the colony of Natal, South Africa, which was part of British Empire

---

73. Tolstoy, *A Letter to Hindu*, cited in Murthy, *Mahatma Gandhi*, 55–56.
74. Doke, *M.K. Gandhi*, 88.
75. Gandhi, *An Autobiography*, 90.
76. Murthy, *Mahatma Gandhi*, 14.
77. Ibid., 14.
78. Gandhi, "Letter to Tolstoy," cited in Murthy, *Mahatma Gandhi*, 15.

then.⁷⁹ He left for South Africa in 1893 and returned to India in 1914. In his 21 years in South Africa, Gandhi developed his political views and leadership skills. His infamous encounter at Pietermaritzburg and other incidents in South Africa paved the way for his civil rights activism. Boarded on a train in the first class compartment, Gandhi was asked by white men to vacate his seat from the first class because he was black. His refusal made the events violent and he was thrown out by the whites at the station, Pietermaritzburg. These activities against colored people made Gandhi stand up for racial oppression and it continued even after he came to India.

After his coming back from South Africa in 1915, Gandhi joined the Indian National Congress, the major political party in India then. He slowly grew through the ranks in Congress and by 1920 he was recognized as a key-leader in the party. Then, through his experiences, he began to raise his voice against all British oppression, through non-cooperation, non-violence and peaceful resistance. The non-violence, peaceful resistant movement set him apart from others, who fought against British rule at that time, such as, Netaji Subhash Chandra Bose.

Gandhi upheld the Sermon on the Mount. Gandhi upheld the teachings of Jesus. Though Tolstoy's writings led Gandhi to see deeper light in Jesus' words in the Sermon on the Mount, he grasped the Sermon on the Mount as life-teachings very important to his liberation and for the liberation of the whole Indian Nation. He says, "The message of Jesus is contained in the Sermon on the Mount, unadulterated and takes as a whole."⁸⁰ Murthy says, "Gandhi found the Sermon on the Mount to be the essence of Christ's teaching."⁸¹ The Sermon on the Mount summarized the whole teaching of Jesus Christ. He followed the Sermon on the Mount. Thus, he assumed he followed Jesus Christ. In one sense, Gandhi considered himself as a Christian by his following of the Sermon on the Mount. He says, "If then I had to face only the Sermon on the Mount and my interpretation of it, I should not hesitate to say, 'oh yes, I am a Christian.'"⁸² Stanley Jones, an American missionary wrote: "I am still an evangelist. I bow to Mahatma Gandhi, but I kneel at the feet of Christ and give him my full and final allegiance. And yet a little man, who fought a system in the framework of which I stand, has taught me more of the Spirit of Christ than perhaps any other man in the East or West."⁸³ Though he considered himself a Christian Mahatma Gandhi

79. Murthy, *Mahatma Gandhi*, 14.
80. Gandhi, "The Place of Jesus," 481.
81. Murthy, *Mahatma Gandhi*, 16.
82. Gandhi, "The Place of Jesus," 481.
83. Jones, "Gandhi-Portrayal of a Friend," 492.

strongly criticized the behavior of the Christians which did not fall in accordance to the teachings of Jesus Christ. He says, "It may be presumptuous for me to say so, but I did not agree with their interpretation of Christ's words."[84]

What Gandhi was trying to say is this: when the Sermon on the Mount explicitly shares that the Christian disciple must "resist no evil" how could the Britain, a Christian nation do evil to others, like the Indians. When Christ taught them to show the other cheek when someone slapped one cheek how could His followers, the British, oppress the Indians. Thus, he despised the then popular Christianity. He says, "But negatively I can tell you that to my mind much of that which passes for Christianity is a negation of the Sermon on the Mount. I am placing before you my fundamental difficulties with regard to the appearance of Christianity in the world and the formulation of Christian beliefs."[85] He lamented, "When I began as a prayerful student to study Christian literature in SA in 1893, I asked myself again and again, 'Is this Christianity?' And I could only say, 'No, no. Certainly this that I see is not Christianity.' And the deepest in me tells me that I was right; for it was unworthy to Jesus and untrue to the Sermon on the Mount."[86]

Gandhi, while addressing the British Christian missionaries to India said this, "I miss receptiveness, humility, willingness on your part to identify yourselves with the masses of India."[87] Mahatma Gandhi's attitude against Christianity stems from his observations that Christians do not follow the Sermon on the Mount as mentioned by Jesus himself. He criticized Christianity because the essence of the Sermon on the Mount and the teachings of Jesus were not present in the practice of Christianity. However, he upheld the teachings of Jesus and contextualized it and followed it the rest of his life. He borrowed the idea of non-violence from Tolstoy's interpretation of the Sermon on the Mount. He revitalized the message of the Sermon on the Mount by giving Indian names so that it could be easily understood by the masses. Terrence J. Rynne says, "The second appeal that Gandhi has to the masses was the use he made of common Hindu symbols and ideals and the stories used to convey them."[88] The word 'Ahimsa,' a Sanskrit word, appears in Indian writings from as early as *Chandogya Upanishad*.[89] Ahimsa was

---

84. Gandhi, "The Place of Jesus," 481.
85. Ibid., 481–482.
86. Ibid., 482.
87. Gandhi, "Christianity and Hinduism," 496.
88. Rynne, *Gandhi & Jesus*, 19.
89. Ibid., 19.

also an important concept in Mahabharata.[90] However, Gandhi's concept of *Ahimsa* was derived from Tolstoy's interpretation of the Sermon on the Mount. Thus, Gandhi took the "Resist no evil" concept from the Sermon on the Mount and baptized it to the Indian Philosophy and made it into *Ahimsa*. Gandhi explains this beautifully in this way:

> Literally speaking, *Ahimsa* means "non-killing." But to me, it has a world of meaning, and takes me into realms much higher, infinitely higher. It really means that you may not offend anybody; you may not harbour an uncharitable thought, even in connection with one who may consider himself to be your enemy. To one who follows this doctrine, there is no room for an enemy. But there may be people who consider themselves to be his enemies, so it is held that we may not harbour an evil thought even in connection with such persons. If we return blow for blow we depart from the doctrine of *Ahimsa*. But I go farther. If we reset friend's action or the so—called enemy's action, we still fall short of this doctrine. But I say we should not resent, I do not say that we should acquiesce; by the word 'resenting' I mean wishing that some harm should be done to the enemy; or that he should be put out of the way, not even by any action of ours, but by the action of somebody else, or, say by divine agency. If we harbour even this thought we depart from this doctrine of non-violence. Those who join the Ashram have literally to accept that meaning.[91]

There are three observations here to be made:

1. Gandhi understands that the Indian concept of *Ahimsa* is just 'non killing.'
2. However, for Gandhi its meaning is "much higher," which is "not to offend anyone".
3. Interestingly, this offense should not even be done in the form of an uncharitable thought.

For Gandhi this *Ahimsa* was not just non-violence but love itself. He says, "If you express your love—*Ahimsa*—in such a manner that it impresses itself indelible upon your so-called enemy, he must return the love."[92]

---

90. Ibid.,19.
91. Gandhi, "Christianity and Hinduism," 495.
92. Ibid., 495.

Vincent Sheean, identifies that Gandhi, during his last days, often read the Sermon on the Mount and Bhagavad Gita.[93] He also pointed out that though Gita and the Sermon on the Mount came to him at the same time, while he was twenty years old, "it is hardly surprising that under these circumstances the Sermon on the Mount had an even more powerful influence inspite of the fact that it is canonically Christian and Gandhiji was profoundly Hindu."[94] Sheean also notes that in his last days, Gandhiji used to chant Gita often and that "it seems to have become subtly blended with the Sermon on the Mount in his consciousness."[95] Thus, the Sermon on the Mount and Gita were an essential part of Gandhian Philosophy.

Pattabhi Sitaramayya says, "(Gandhiji) was always strongly attracted to the Christian ideal of self-sacrifice and the Sermon on the Mount, with all its manifold implication, made a deep impression on him."[96] Llewelyn Powys says, "Nietzsche uttered once the piercing paradox, 'There has been only one Christian and he died on the cross.' Perhaps if the frenzied philosopher had lived long enough to observe the manner of life of this other Guru, he would have qualified his celebrated quip."[97] Thus, some attribute that Gandhi imitated Jesus in his life. Gandhi's use of the Sermon on the Mount is praised by Dr. John Haynes Holmes in this way:

> The principle itself, resist not evil and love your enemies, is nothing new. It is at least as ancient as the teachings of Jesus of Nazareth in the Sermon on the Mount. But Gandhi did what had never been done before. Up to this time the practice of these non-resistant principles had been limited to single individuals or to little groups of individuals. Gandhi work out the discipline and the programme for the practicing of this particular kind of principle by unnumbered manner of human beings.[98]

That is how important Gandhi's interpretation of the Sermon on the Mount is. Sadly, this interpreter is not even a Christian. However, his interpretation of the Sermon on the Mount changed history significantly, if not just the history of India.

93. Sheean, "Last Days," 457.
94. Ibid., 457.
95. Ibid., 457.
96. Sitaramayya, "The Wisdom of Gandhiji," 236.
97. Powys, "The Triumph of the Spirit, Radhakrishnan," 236.
98. Holmes, "Homage," 544.

2.13 Johannes Weiss

"Protestant Liberalism" or "Liberal Theology" found its firm growth in the early nineteenth century to the early twentieth century. The significant aspect of Biblical interpretation in this period is the assumption that the Bible is literature and thus all literary analyses could be used to interpret the Bible. This tendency brought forth several aspects into theology such as synoptic problem, historical Jesus, etc. Immanuel Kant's "Critique of the Practical Reason" written in 1788 had a huge impact on nineteenth century theology and bible interpretation. Kant's critique of "pure reason" showed that all knowledge must be based on "practical reason" and not just based on "pure reason." Thus, the talk about God must be based on practical reason.[99] Kantian view hugely impacted the growth and development of Modernization. Thus, Kantian propaganda of practical reason found its emphasis on religious morality, because for Kant, moral aspects are the basis for religion. Albrecht Ritschl took this thought further to emphasize that the Kingdom of God essentially is about establishing morality among the people of God.[100]

Adolf von Harnack, a follower of Ritschl in Ritschlian School speaks about the Kingdom of God in this way,

> The Kingdom of God comes by coming to the individual, by entering into his soul and laying hold of it. True the Kingdom of God is the rule of God; but it is the rule of the holy God in the hearts of individuals; it is God himself in his power. From this point of view everything that is dramatic in the eternal and historical sense has vanquished; and gone, too, are all the external hopes for the future. Take whatever parable you will, the parable of sower, of the pearl of great price, of the treasure buried in the field—the word of God, God himself, is the kingdom. It is not a question of angles and devils, thrones and principalities, but of God and the soul, the soul and its God.[101]

This classic quote shows that, for Harnack, the kingdom of God was not a futuristic element which involves "angles and devils," "thrones and principalities" but it is about the present realization of God in the hearts of men. The moral living of the human being now in this world is the essence of the kingdom of God. For Harnack says, "A large portion of the so-called Sermon on the Mount is occupied with what he says when he goes in detail through the several departments of human relationships and human

---

99. Kant, *The Critique of Practical Reason*, 96.
100. Ritschl, *The Christian Doctrine of Justification & Reconciliation*, 284.
101. Harnack, *What is Christianity?* 56.

failings as to bring the disposition and intention to light in each case, to judge a man's works by them and on them to hang heaven and hell."[102] Thus, for Harnack, the Sermon on the Mount is about Jesus giving moral teaching for the present world to his followers on having the Kingdom of God. For he says, "Jesus defined the sphere of the ethical in a way in which no one before him had ever defined it . . . we must steep ourselves again and again in the Beatitudes of the Sermon on the Mount. They contain his ethics and his religion, united at the root."[103] Thus, for Harnack, the Sermon on the Mount and the Beatitudes shows Jesus' ethic in the present world in which his followers could experience the kingdom of God.

Against this backdrop, Johannes Weiss wrote extensively about his understanding of the Kingdom of God. Even in the preface of his book, *Jesus' Proclamation of the Kingdom of God*, he points out the "completely apocalyptic and eschatological character of Jesus' idea of the kingdom."[104] Weiss was arguing against his teacher and father-in-law, Ritschl and his followers that kingdom of God was not just an ethical, moral expectation present by the teaching and the following of Jesus' followers. For Weiss, the kingdom of God was eschatological. The kingdom of God was not present yet. Jesus anticipated the kingdom of God to come, and to prepare the people towards that kingdom of God he preached the Sermon on the Mount towards repentance which would consequently bring forth the kingdom of God.[105]

For Weiss, the word ἤγγικεν is very important as it is found in Mt. 4:17; Mt. 10:7; Luke 10:9 & 11. Weiss says, "the meaning of this well attested proclamation of Jesus and his disciples seems clear: The kingdom of God has drawn so near that it stands at the door. Therefore, while the βασιλεία is not yet here, it is extremely near."[106] Weiss with his impressive exegetical skills, knowledge of his Greek grammar and persuasive arguments stresses the point that kingdom of God, proclaimed by Jesus, was still in the future. He points out from the passages which seemingly show that the kingdom of God was already present that they too could be read as futuristic. Thus, for Weiss, the kingdom of God was futuristic and eschatological than a present reality. He says, "if in the Kingdom of God the elect are to sit at the table with Abraham, Isaac, and Jacob, then an entirely other worldly bliss without analogies to this world is intended."[107]

102. Ibid., 72.
103. Ibid., 74.
104. Weiss, *Jesus' Proclamation*, 65.
105. Ibid., 65.
106. Ibid., 65–66.
107. Ibid., 95.

Thus, for Weiss, the Sermon on the Mount is not characterizing those who are already in the kingdom of God but it exhorts the disciples to prepare themselves to be eligible to enter into the kingdom of God. The Sermon on the Mount gives the condition by which the disciples could enter into the kingdom of God.[108] Jesus anticipated that the kingdom of God would come soon. He needed to prepare his disciples for it. He preached the Sermon on the Mount so that his disciples would repent and be eligible to enter into the kingdom of God. He says,

> Matthew has arranged several groups of sayings in the Sermon on the Mount in an extremely perceptive order which certainly corresponds to Jesus' meaning. These are the sayings about laying up treasures, about serving two masters and about anxiety, which Matthew grouped around the sayings about the eye (6:19–34). This evidently was to mean that just as man needs a true, single, and unclouded eye in order to see, so likewise he needs ἁπλότης, simplicity, singlemindedness, if he truly wishes to prepare himself for the Kingdom of God. Whoever waits for the kingdom dares not be divided, a man with two souls (James 1:6–8). "No one can serve two masters. You cannot serve God and mammon." . . . Therefore one must not gather up treasures on earth, . . . Christians, though still on earth, already feel themselves to be citizens of heaven (Phil. 3:20), from whence they await the Kingdom of God.[109]

Thus, for Weiss, the Sermon on the Mount was the guidelines for entry requirements into the kingdom of God. He says, "This new morality which he [Jesus] preaches is thought of as condition for entrance into the Kingdom of God."[110]

2.14 Albert Schweitzer

Albert Schweitzer (1875–1965) was a German theologian, physician and a medical missionary to Africa. Schweitzer's idea of the kingdom of God was very similar to Weiss. However, he felt Weiss did not go all the way in his idea of Jesus' kingdom of God. Schweitzer says,

> Toward the end of the nineteenth century, the idea of the eschatological character of the message of Jesus and the thought

---

108. Ibid., 107.
109. Ibid., 107.
110. Ibid., 113.

that Jesus was aware of His role as Messiah gained increasing recognition. This view was especially well articulated by the Heidelberg theologian Johannes Weiss in his book the Sermons of Jesus concerning the Kingdom of God (1892). Nevertheless, historical theology secretly hoped not to have to admit that Weiss had gone any partway. He realized that Jesus thought eschatologically but did not conclude from this that His actions were also determined by eschatology.[111]

Schweitzer's major critic of Weiss is this, "Weiss explained the course of Jesus' activity and His resolution to die using the hypothesis that He was initially successful and later a failure."[112] For Schweitzer, Jesus was not a failure in his later life. He critiqued Weiss that he was only using the psychological framework to evaluate Jesus' actions.[113] Weiss had thought that the reason why Jesus was arrested in his later life must be attributed to his failure to impress his followers. However, Schweitzer disagrees with this assumption and shows that Jesus was fully involved in the eschatological idea that even his actions, his death on the cross, must be based on this conviction, and not on the failure of the lives of his followers.[114] He says, "Because this eschatological solution succeeds in making the thoughts, words, and acts of Jesus consistent and comprehensible, it shows that many passages in the Gospels, which had been considered apocryphal in the past, were indeed intelligible and completely authentic."[115] If Jesus' teachings on eschatology were "completely authentic" then he must be considered as a man fully dominated by the eschatological expectation. However, Schweitzer's point of agreement with Weiss is this: Jesus' view of the kingdom of God was eschatological.

For Schweitzer, Jesus' main contribution to the world is his ethic of love.[116] The Sermon on the Mount shares this ethic of life. He writes, "Jesus introduced into the late Jewish Messianic expectation the powerful idea, expressed in the Beatitudes of the Sermon on the Mount, that we may come to know God and belong to Him through love. Jesus is not concerned with spiritualizing realistic ideas of the Kingdom of God, and of blessedness."[117]

111. Schweitzer, *Out of My Life and Thought*, 50.
112. Ibid., 50.
113. Ibid., 50.
114. Ibid., 50.
115. Ibid., 50.
116. Ibid., 56.
117. Ibid., 56.

In the midst of Protestant Liberalism, Schweitzer proclaimed the validity of Christ's preaching as the spirituality that comes from "the religion of love."[118]

Schweitzer stressed that with this eschatological view, Jesus expected the kingdom of God to come imminently. For Schweitzer, Jesus assumed that the kingdom of God was to come so imminently that he thought the disciples would not even finish their mission according to Matt 10:23: *"for truly, I say to you, you will not have gone through all the towns of Israel, before the Son of Man comes."* For Schweitzer, Jesus did not see himself as the Son of Man because he always addresses the Son of Man in third person.[119] He says, "Just as Jesus announces the Kingdom of God not as something already beginning but as something of the future, he does not think that he is already the Messiah. He is convinced that only at the appearance of the Messianic kingdom, when those predestined enter the supernatural existence intended for them, will he be manifested as the Messiah."[120] Schweitzer added that Jesus thought his disciples were in pre-Messianic times and thus, they "must first endure the pre-Messianic Tribulation and then prove themselves faithful."[121]

With this expectation, Jesus sent the twelve according to Matt 10:23 to go, and preach the good news to all. Schweitzer says, "He does not expect to see them return to Him but assures them that the 'coming of the Son of Man' (which is expected to be simultaneous with the manifestation of the kingdom) will take place even before they have visited all the cities of Israel."[122] However, this expectation of Jesus was "not fulfilled."[123] The disciples returned back to him, that too without any premessianic tribulation. According to Schweitzer, the disciples should have experienced the pre-messianic tribulation as expected by the other Jewish sects.[124] The failure of the arrival of the pre-messianic tribulation was an indication to Jesus that the kingdom of God had not yet come. He says, "Jesus can explain this fact to Himself only by supposing that there is still some event that must take place first."[125]

Then, according to Schweitzer, Jesus saw himself as the Messiah-to-be, must suffer and make atonement for the elect of the kingdom of God so

---

118. Ibid., 56.
119. Ibid., 39.
120. Ibid., 39.
121. Ibid., 39.
122. Ibid., 40.
123. Ibid., 40.
124. Ibid., 39–40.
125. Ibid., 40.

that he would save his disciples from the pre-messianic Tribulation.[126] Schweitzer uses Jesus' prayer from the Sermon on the Mount, "deliver them from evil" to show that Jesus always wanted to spare his disciples from any harm.[127] Thus, his atonement death was the perfect way Jesus thought he could spare his followers from pre-messianic tribulations, and also to bring forth the kingdom of God to the world.[128] Schweitzer says, "The thought, then, with which Jesus meets death is that God is willing to accept His self-chosen death as an atonement made for believers."[129] Jesus, then, did not die on behalf of the sin of the world but on behalf of the pre-messianic tribulation of his followers. Thus, for Schweitzer, Jesus died expecting the kingdom of God to come but the kingdom of God never came.

Though Jesus died with a mistaken expectation, his teachings were important because these teachings show how one must live in his community with love. Jesus, with his, eschatological expectation has given, in the Sermon on the Mount, "interim ethics." He says,

> As repentance unto the Kingdom of God the ethics also of the Sermon on the Mount is interim ethics. In this we perceive that the moral instruction of Jesus remained the same from the first day of his public appearance unto his latest utterances, for the lowliness and serviceable which he recommended to his disciples on the way to Jerusalem correspond exactly to the new moral conduct which he developed in the Sermon on the Mount: they make one meet for the Kingdom of God ... Whosoever at the dawning of the kingdom is in possession of a character morally renovated, he will be found a member of the same. This is the adequate expression for the relation of morality to the coming Kingdom of God.[130]

For Schweitzer, the comparisons in the ch 5:17–48 show that Jesus was not much concerned about the Law of the Old Testament.[131] Jesus did not show whether he was for the Old Testament Law or against it.[132] For Schweitzer, Jesus gave more importance to the new morality, as it was the interim ethics. Unlike the Pharisees, Jesus and John the Baptist concentrated on the inward

---

126. Ibid., 40.
127. Ibid., 40.
128. Ibid., 40.
129. Ibid., 40.
130. Schweitzer, *The Mystery of the Kingdom of God*, 97–99.
131. Schweitzer, *The Mysticism of Paul the Apostle*, 189.
132. Ibid., 189.

ethic than following the Law to its minute details.¹³³ For Schweitzer, Jesus did not concern himself with Old Testament Law because it was going to go away when the kingdom of God was established. While commenting on Matt 5:17–18, *"Think not that I have come to abolish the Law and the Prophets; I have come not to abolish them but to fulfill them. For truly, I say to you, till heaven and earth pass away, not an iota, not a dot, will pass from the Law until all is accomplished,"* he says, "Jesus thus clearly affirms that the Law is only valid until the beginning of the kingdom of God. How indeed, could he have held that it would retain its validity for the men of the resurrection, partakers of the kingdom."¹³⁴ Thus, for Schweitzer, there is no continuity of the Old Testament Law in the teachings of Jesus Christ. Jesus gave a new morality for the interim period until the kingdom of God is established in this world.

2.15 Martin Dibelius

Martin Dibelius (1883–1947), the famous form critic, published a book on the Sermon on the Mount in 1940.¹³⁵ As he himself was a form critic, he used form criticism to interpret the Sermon on the Mount. According to form criticism, not all the words of the evangelists go back to the Historical Jesus. Based on the forms of the Gospel materials one can identify its authenticity. And thus, by taking away the latter additions by the tradition, one could identify the original forms and thus could identify the original words of Jesus Christ. Dibelius says,

> It is important for the understanding of our Lord's message that we should be aware of this method. Form criticism ventures to go back to those small units of which Jesus' teaching consists, to detach them from their framework and to study their original meaning. Such units of tradition are the elements of which the Sermon on the Mount is composed. It is a summary of characteristic sayings whose historical occasion we do not know. They were brought together by the early tradition within communities in order to form a kind of Christian law. Since this was their purpose the evangelists added other sayings of our Lord to the collection which existed in the days of Q thus completing or explaining the older tradition.¹³⁶

133. Ibid., 190.
134. Ibid., 190.
135. Dibelius, *The Sermon on the Mount*.
136. Dibelius, *The Sermon*, 42–43.

Thus, for Dibelius, the Sermon on the Mount was not preached by Jesus as one whole preaching on the Mount. Jesus could have preached it as several smaller units. The church, which saw the need to portray Jesus as a mighty preacher and also had a need to give the local community the laws of the new community, it collected the sayings of Jesus, compiled them and placed them together to form the Sermon on the Mount.[137]

For Dibelius, the Sermon on the Mount has its eschatological qualities. However, he disagrees with Schweitzer that it was an interim ethic. For Dibelius, the Sermon on the Mount was not an interim ethic but commandments given for eternity. For Dibelius, the Sermon on the Mount is the "pure will of God."[138] As it is the pure will of God it has eternal validity. He says, "The Sermon on the Mount, on the whole, is a collection of radical, absolute commands and sayings because the man who uttered them did not consider the circumstances of our life and the conditions of this world. He looks only to the coming world, the Kingdom of Heaven."[139] Thus, for Dibelius, the Sermon on the Mount is purely eschatological and were not meant to be obeyed in this world. He says, "the Sermon on the Mount makes demands too exacting to be fulfilled in life on this earth, even in the life of the Saviour himself, for his life was bound by earthly circumstances too."[140] He further clarifies this statement in this way: "The sayings of the Sermon on the Mount were originally meant in an absolute sense, but as a law for the coming kingdom rather than as a law governing life in this world. Their practicality in the workaday world was therefore originally restricted. The Christians undertook to alter and adapt them in order to make them directly applicable to the circumstances of this life."[141] This is an interesting statement because even in the Sermon on the Mount there are many editorial works which show that the editors tried to make this eschatological ethic intended for the other world, work in this world. Thus, by removing these editorial works one could identify the truly eschatological teachings of Jesus Christ.

Dibelius gives an example from the Sermon on the Mount. He says, "The known of them is the exception which Matthew grants to the prohibition of divorce (5:32). In the case of unchastity divorce is allowed, but, in the original wording of the sentence as preserved in Mark, divorce is absolutely forbidden: 'what God has joined, then, man must not separate'

---

137. Ibid., 44.
138. Ibid., 51.
139. Ibid., 65.
140. Ibid., 87.
141. Ibid., 94–95.

(10:9)."[142] While the original words of Jesus prohibited divorce altogether the practicality of the situations in the early Christian community developed the exceptional clause, so that divorce could be allowed on the basis of unchastity. Thus, he adds, "In their original wording, some of the sayings of Jesus were not rules fitted for the common life . . . They seem too paradoxical to be carried out; they were impracticable. When they were connected with other sayings which were really practicable commands, the more or less paradoxical words were transformed in the direction of a practical and living realism. In this way the paradoxical sayings became practicable, and the whole mass of sayings in the Sermon on the Mount became a Christian Law."[143]

According to Dibelius one must be careful when interpreting. The original eschatological message of Jesus is tampered by the earlier traditions to form rules or laws of the community in this world. He blames the Matthean tradition that "wanted to incite the Christians of his own generation to live according to these rules, and he endeavoured to present a program of Christian ethics for all generations of the church."[144] To this complicated material Dibelius gives a complicated interpretation. He says, we must not interpret the Sermon on the Mount as Matthew did. Our interpretation should acknowledge that the Sermon on the Mount is "the pure will of God." He says,

> Jesus proclaims in an absolute way the pure will of God. This will is not confined to an interim and is thus not valid only for the period till the end of the world; it is God's actual demand upon men at all times and for all time. But it will attain its full validity only in the Kingdom of God. It is the sign of this passing age that the fulfillment of God's will is hampered and embarrassed by the conditions of our worldly existence. In the face of the coming end, Jesus proclaims God's demand without regard to any such considerations. God's will does not depend upon the eschatological hope and expectation: it is eternal, like God. The eschatological expectation, however, gives the occasion for the proclamation of the divine will, without regard to the circumstances of everyday existence . . . Therefore . . . the passage is to be taken in an absolute sense because it is eschatological. [145]

---

142. Ibid., 18–19.
143. Ibid., 19.
144. Ibid., 21.
145. Ibid., 51–52.

Thus, for Dibelius, the Sermon on the Mount is eschatological but it shows the pure will of God. However, due to the present world conditions the followers of Christ will not be able to follow these teachings of Jesus. He says,

> The sayings of the Sermon on the Mount were uttered by Jesus in order to prepare men for the kingdom. It was his purpose in these sayings to proclaim the will of God in all its severity, the absolute divine will, unconditioned by the circumstances of this world order. This will is, of course, the law of the Kingdom of God, but under the conditions provided by our earthly life this will in its paradox is a stumbling block for men.[146]

Thus, Dibelius says, we cannot fulfill the demands of the Sermon on the Mount in this world. He says, "The performance of the pure will of God is in the present world, consequently hindered. The real fulfillment of this great Christian law is possible only in the kingdom of God."[147] The full obedience of the Sermon on the Mount is, thus, "impossible."[148] Thus, he criticizes Tolstoy saying,

> [he] does not see their relation to the Kingdom of God in an eschatological sense. Consequently, he puts the rules of the Sermon on the Mount in a wrong context, that is, in the life of this age. He attempts to change the whole course of this life, at least of his own life, in the direction of a static ideal formulated on accordance with the Sermon on the Mount. He does not see that Jesus himself referred to another world, to the Kingdom of God.[149]

However, according to Dibelius, this does not mean that we must ignore the Sermon on the Mount altogether, simply because it is not practicable in this present world. Dibelius says that we must live like "the new type of man who knows the will of God in its ultimate eschatological aim and who wants to live here and now in accordance with his will. But he accepts the conditions of this world as the inescapable basis for all his actions . . . The conditions of this world are not amenable to the Kingdom of God, . . . [therefore] our task is to perform signs, not the signs described in the Bible, but signs of our time . . . "[150]

---

146. Ibid., 63–64.
147. Ibid., 97.
148. Ibid., 98.
149. Ibid., 119.
150. Ibid., 137–138.

Thus, for Dibelius, we must recognize the pure will of God but also must understand that we cannot and need not fulfill the pure will of God in this world. Therefore, we must do the "signs of our own time," meaning we must live our own life, with swearing, oaths, and also joining in the army, to kill our national enemies. Thus, Dibelius gave a complicated application not undermining the complications of the Sermon on the Mount.

2.16 C. H. Dodd

C. H. Dodd (1884–1973) was an influential New Testament Theologian of the twentieth century. His writing career spanned about fifty years and he wrote extensively about many issues in the New Testament Theology. His major contribution to the New Testament Theology is his "realized eschatology." He disagreed with Weiss and Schweitzer that the kingdom of God is entirely eschatological, end of times. He used passages that showed the imminence of the kingdom of God to show that the kingdom of God was not entirely eschatological but realized in the preaching, teaching and works of Jesus Christ.

Dodd says, "with the work of John the Baptist an old order was wound up, and a new order was inaugurated. It is characterized by 'Good news' about the Kingdom of God."[151] For Dodd, kingdom of God is nothing but "the reign of God" or "the reigning of God." This means "God himself exercising his royal power."[152] Dodd was so convinced that Jesus' saying in Mark 1:15: "The Kingdom of God has come upon you," revealed Jesus' realization of God's kingdom in the first kerygma of Jesus Christ.[153] Thus, in the teaching and preaching of Christ the kingdom of God was realized in the present world of Jesus and his followers. Thus, the kingdom of God is not entirely eschatological. It is realized eschatology, where in the preaching and ministry of Jesus Christ the kingdom of God is realized. He says,

> . . . Because in his words and action it was presented with exceptional clarity and operative with exceptional power. Jesus himself pointed to the effects of his work as signs of the coming of the kingdom. 'If by the finger of nod I chive out the devils, then be sure the Kingdom of God has come upon you.' . . . And this, Jesus said, was a sign that God was coming in his kingdom . . . That was the work of God himself, whose perpetual providence, active in every part of his creation, had brought about

---

151. Dodd, *The Founder of Christianity*, 55.
152. Ibid., 56.
153. Ibid., 56.

this significant moment, and the most significant feature in it was the appearance of Jesus himself. In his words and actions he made men aware of it and challenged them to respond. It was 'good news' in the sense that it meant opportunity for a new start and an unprecedented enrichment of experience.[154]

For Dodd, those who followed Christ took part in the kingdom of God but those who rejected him and his message where destined for punishment.[155]

C.H. Dodd's interpretation of the Sermon on the Mount must be viewed against this backdrop. Dodd viewed the Gospels as containing two elements: *Kerygma* and *Didache*. *Kerygma* is nothing but the message of the early church. It primarily involves the life, death and resurrection of Jesus Christ. In addition, *Didache* is the ethical teachings of the early church embedded in the New Testament.[156] *Didache* involves "the instruction in Christian morals and ecclesiastical practice."[157] Thus, the Sermon on the Mount, for Dodd is *Didache* material as it teaches the morals on how the disciple must live. It is "a highly articulated and systematic presentation of the main features of the Christian ethical system."[158]

Dodd says, "The Gospel of primitive Christianity is a gospel of realized eschatology."[159] For Dodd, the Sermon on the Mount is not an "interim ethic" but it is the ethic the disciples must follow because they are presently in 'realized eschatology'. He says,

> It is the absolute ethic of the Kingdom of God, the moral principles of a new order of life. The implied major premise of all his ethical sayings is the affirmation 'The Kingdom of God has come upon you:' . . . The Kingdom of God has come upon you, therefore love your enemies that you may be sons of your Father in heaven . . . The Kingdom of God has come upon you, therefore take no thought for your life, but seek first his kingdom. The Kingdom of God has come upon you, therefore judge not, for with what judgment ye judge, ye shall be judged, in the judgment which is inseparable from the coming of God in his kingdom. The teaching of Jesus is not an ethic for those who expect

---

154. Ibid., 56–57.
155. Ibid., 57.
156. Dodd, *Apostolic Preaching and Its Developments*, 1–4.
157. Ibid., 49.
158. Dodd, *Gospel and Law*, 6.
159. Dodd, *Apostolic Preaching and Its Developments*, 147.

the speedy end of the world, but for those who have experienced the end of this world and the coming of the Kingdom of God.[160]

Thus, Dodd's view of the kingdom of God was antithetical to Schweitzer's and thus, explained that kingdom of God was not purely other worldly but is realized in this world. Hence, the Sermon on the Mount is the ethics which the followers of Jesus must follow as they are in the realized eschatology.

Regarding the comparisons in the Sermon on the Mount, especially the ones in Matt 5:17-48, Dodd sees that the comparisons indicate that Jesus gave new law over and against the old law of the Old Testament.[161] For Dodd, the Law and the Prophets were only active until John the Baptist "since then, there is good news of the Kingdom of God." [162] He says, "It appears, then, that we shall not be far wrong in taking the Sermon on the Mount as Matthew represented it—namely, as the New Law which supercedes the Law of the Old Testament—the Law of the Kingdom of God. That, I believe, is the sense in which any reasonable reader would understand the Sermon upon an unprejudiced reading of it."[163]

Dodd affirms that though the ethical teachings of the Sermon on the Mount is binding on all individuals who follow Christ it may not be binding on societies such as nations to turn the other cheek in their international relationship with other countries. He says, "The Law of Christ, we conclude, is not a specialized code of regulations for a society with optional membership. It is based upon the revelation of the nature of the eternal God, and it affirms the principles upon which His world is built and which men ignore at their peril."[164] Thus, for Dodd, the Sermon on the Mount is the *didache* of Christ for all those experienced the kingdom of God in the realized eschatology through the *kerygma* of Christ and the early church.

2.17 W. D. Davies

W. D. Davies (1911–2001), one of the famous New Testament scholars of the 20th century penned an elaborate study on the Sermon on the Mount called *The Setting of the Sermon on the Mount*.[165] This interesting work was followed by his *The Sermon on the Mount*, which included the lectures de-

---

160. Dodd, *History & the Gospel*, 125.
161. Dodd, *Gospel and Law*, 62.
162. Dodd, *The Founder of Christianity*, 55.
163. Dodd, *Gospel and Law*, 65.
164. Ibid., 81.
165. Davies, *The Setting of the Sermon on the Mount*.

livered at the Protestant Episcopal Theological Seminary, Alexandria, Va.[166] In the latter book he made his views of the Sermon on the Mount more accessible and widely readable. In both these books, Davies' emphasis was to show that the setting of the Sermon on the Mount was placed in the Jewish perspective.

Davies' important contribution is to show that the Sermon on the Mount was the "law of Jesus," the Messiah and the Lord.[167] Davies shows that Matthean portrayal of the teachings in the Sermon on the Mont does not show that he was arguing against the Gnosticism or Qumran sect. For Davies, the setting of the Sermon on the Mount must be kept as teachings against Pharisaic teachings, against especially the group from Jamnia. Though Davies acknowledges that historical Jesus could have taught against the teachings of the Qumran sect, Matthean author seems to keep the teachings of Jesus against Pharisaic Judaism. He says,

> Thus, the original *Sitz im Leben* of much in the Sermon on the Mount involved the Essenes; the *Sitz im Leben* which he gave to this involved particularly Pharisees. This explains the collocation of sectarian and rabbinic forms in Matthew. Material dealing with the confrontation with Qumran has become embedded in that dealing with Pharisaic Judaism and given different relevance. This emerges clearly in the Sermon on the Mount. The sectarians of the Law had been given a rigid interpretation of the Law by the Teacher of Righteousness which was designed to lead to perfection. There is every reason to believe that Jesus offered an interpretation of the Law which was set over against this, his radicalism standing over against that of Qumran. But when Matthew constructed his 'Sermon' he utilized the tradition of the teaching for his own purposes to set the Christian ethic not over against Qumran but over against Pharisaic Judaism, the ethic of Jew Israel over against that of the old.[168]

Thus, the original *Sitz im Leben* of the Sermon on the Mount were set in comparison with the teachings of the Qumran community. However, Matthew, who encountered oppositions with the post-70 CE Judaism had to write against Pharisaism of Jamnia, so as to safeguard his community from assimilation into the Pharisaic community. He says, "much of the content of the Sermon on the Mount originally emerged in the encounter of the sectarians and Jesus: its present form and purpose are dictated by the

---

166. Davies, *The Sermon on the Mount*.
167. Davies, *The Setting*, 108.
168. Ibid., 255.

Pharisaic-Christian encounter after A.D. 70."[169] The main reason for this assumption of Davies is that he sets Matthean writing in 70–100 CE. It is possible that he addresses the problems of that particular time period which were problems from the Pharisaic community.[170] For Davies, the Pharisaic party was not so powerful before 70 CE. Its prominence arose in the post-war Jewish nation.[171] It was Rabbi Jonathan ben Zakki who "laid foundations for the more concentrated and homogenous rabbinic Judaism of later history" at Jamnia after the 70 CE wars.[172] Through this initial endeavor, according to Davies, the many Jewish scholars formed as a band, after the war, under the banner of Pharisaism.[173] Against this group, Davies says, Matthew composed this massive Sermon on the Mount. He says,

> It is our suggestion that one fruitful way of dealing with the Sermon on the Mont is to regard it as the Christian answer to Jamnia. Using terms very loose, the Sermon on the Mount is a kind of Christian, Mishnaic counterpart to the formulation taking place there. It is not our intention to deny other formative influences on Matthew. But neither Gnostic nor sectarian pressures are sufficient to account for the massive elevation of the teaching of Jesus in the Sermon on the Mount. Apart from the internal demands of the Christian community, it was the necessity to provide a Christian counterpart to 'Jamnia' that best illumines this . . . this juxtaposition, it seems to me, best explains the emergence of Matthew's manifesto. It was the desire and necessity to present a formulation of the way of the New Israel at a time when the rabbis were engaged in a parallel task for the old Israel that provided the outside stimulus for the Evangelist to shape the Sermon on the Mount. [174]

Against the Pharisaic interpretation of the old law, Davies says that Matthew portrayed Jesus as the new lawgiver in the Sermon on the Mount.[175] He says, "the mountain is the mountain of the New Moses, the New Sinai . . . Secondly, the disciples are here sent forth, among other things, to teach whatsoever Christ has commanded. He is, in short, the source of the new commandments under which the church is to live. The phrase 'whatsoever

169. Ibid., 256.
170. Ibid., 356.
171. Ibid., 356.
172. Ibid., 356.
173. Ibid., 356.
174. Ibid., 315.
175. Davies, *The Sermon*, 17.

I have commanded you' points back to Matt v-vii where the words of Jesus are set alongside those of Moses."[176] For Davies, Jesus is portrayed as the "New Moses" in the Sermon on the Mount, "who was destined to bring his law to the nations (Isa xlii.4)."[177] He says,

> The case would seem to be that, while the category of a New Moses and a New Sinai is present in v-vii, as elsewhere in Matthew, the strictly Mosaic traits in the figure of the Matthean Christ, both there and in other parts of the Gospel, have been taken up into a deeper and higher context. He is not Moses come as Messiah, if we may put it, so much as Messiah, Son of Man, Emmanuel, who has absorbed the Mosaic function. The Sermon on the Mount is therefore ambiguous: suggestive of the Law of a New Moses, it is also the authoritative word of the Lord, the Messiah: it is the Messianic Torah.[178]

Thus, it must be understood that Jesus in some way had given a New Law, according to Davies.

The Sermon on the Mount, therefore, is a Messianic Torah, for Davies. He repeatedly used the phrase, "the law of Jesus" or "the law of Christ." However, for Davies, Matthew's Jesus did not annul the Law. He says, "The Law remains in force. It is true that the so-called antithesis in vv. 21–48 seem to annul parts of the Law, but the meaning of these antitheses has to be carefully observed. The fact is that in none of the antithesis is there an intention to annul the provisions of the Law but only to carry them out to their ultimate meaning."[179] Thus, he stressed, "We cannot speak of the Law being annulled in the antithesis, but only of its being intensified in its demand, or reinterpreted in a higher key."[180] Jesus' teachings in the Sermon on the Mount were not antithetical to the Law of Moses but it was critical of the oral tradition of the Pharisees.[181] He says, ". . . though it is critical of the oral tradition: it is the full interpretation of the former [Law of Moses] rather than its annulment."[182] Thus, Davies stressed that the new law of Jesus in the Sermon on the Mount was not against the Law of Moses but a full interpretation of it. Thus, for Davies, though the comparisons in 5:17–48 show Jesus as a new lawgiver as he did not do away with the Law but interpreted it fully.

---

176. Ibid., 17.
177. Ibid., 23.
178. Ibid., 27.
179. Ibid., 29.
180. Ibid., 29.
181. Ibid., 30.
182. Ibid., 30.

2.18 Stephen Westerholm

Westerholm explains that an understanding of Matthew's view of the law should be kept in his framework of his proclamation of the kingdom (4:17; 5:3).[183] He says, in the coming of Christ the inauguration of the kingdom has begun: "something new, the truly decisive stage in the history of God's dealings with his people, has begun"[184] This framework, for Westerholm, is the key to interpret the Law-teachings of Jesus in the Sermon on the Mount. He shares that though the Law—teachings of Jesus in the Sermon on the Mount seemingly differ and seemingly appear as a counter to the Mosaic—'old' Law, its newness is to be interpreted in the coming of the kingdom. He says, "When the old revelation is interpreted in the light of a new and decisive stage in salvation history, whatever tensions between the two may arise must be attributed to the partial nature of part revelation and its transcendence in the new."[185]

For Westerholm Jesus' teaching "transcends" the Law because it gives a "more perfect embodiment of divine will"[186] (Matt 5:19). This he deducts from the six antithesis of the Sermon on the Mount. Against Leo Tolstoy, Westerholm says that the Sermon on the Mount "is not included as a blueprint for reforming the Laws or institutions of earthly society."[187] In addition, Westerholm points out that the mention that "give to Caesar what is due to Caesar" is a good indication that the Sermon on the Mount is not against legal systems of the present world.[188]

Westerholm identifies that the comparison of the disciples with the tax collectors, Gentiles, Scribes and Pharisees are intended to show the definition of "surpassing righteousness of those who would inherit the Kingdom of God."[189] Westerholm sees the coherent use of those comparisons relating to the major theme of "surpassing righteousness" required of the disciples.[190] The inherent quality of the comparison is quite evident and cannot be missed if one were to study the Sermon on the Mount carefully.

Westerholm identifies that the Sermon on the Mount's main theme is to portray the righteousness demanded of the disciples. For he says, "The

---

183. Westerholm, "The Law in the Sermon on the Mount," 44.
184. Ibid., 44.
185. Ibid., 44.
186. Ibid., 48.
187. Ibid., 48.
188. Ibid., 48.
189. Ibid., 48.
190. Ibid., 48.

theme of the Sermon on the Mount is evidentially Jesus' expectations of how his followers are to behave."[191] As Matthew's Jesus demands the righteousness which was revived of this new age, which brought the kingdom of God in the present age, he demands it by using comparisons. These comparisons clarify what the true righteousness is. These comparisons bring to light how to surpass the righteousness of the others. It also brings to notice the better quality of this demanded righteousness which is internal and not external. The old righteousness of the Mosaic Law deals with the end product while Jesus' Law reinstate the old law by making it internal. The comparison with Pharisaic behaviors and tax-collectors' and gentiles' behavior are intended to show how righteousness must be practiced internally and not just by actions. Thus, through all these comparisons Jesus shows how the ideal disciple must possess righteousness that is internal and not something that is external. He says, "The Sermon spells out how their righteousness is to go beyond that of others."[192] For Westerholm, the whole thrust of the Sermon on the Mount is to show how the ideal disciples' righteousness should go beyond the others.

Though Westerholm says "it is clear that Matthew does expect Jesus' followers to live by the teaching of the Sermon on the Mount,"[193] he points out that those who merely call him Lord will not inherit the kingdom of God but only those who actually do the will of the Father will enter the kingdom of God (7:21–23). Thus, the Sermon on the Mount shows the will of the Father and those who want to enter the kingdom of God should then obey the Sermon on the Mount.[194] In addition, Westerholm notes that if anyone does not heed the commandment of Jesus he is foolish like the one who builds his house on the sand and not on the rock (7:24–27).[195] In addition, he brings support for the applicability of the Sermon from 28:19–20, which commands the disciples to the gentiles "to observe all that I have commanded." Through these, he stresses that the Sermon on the Mount should be obeyed by all, not just by the Jews but also by the Gentiles. Let this be summarized by his own words, "obedience to what Jesus commands is, then expected (by both Jesus and Matthew) of Jesus' followers."[196]

As Westerholm goes on, he stresses that the teachings of the Sermon on the Mount show that God is in control of establishing the expected

191. Ibid., 48.
192. Ibid., 48.
193. Ibid., 48.
194. Ibid., 48.
195. Ibid., 48.
196. Ibid., 48.

norms explicated in the Sermon on the Mount. In addition, he stressed the Matthew is aware that the disciples themselves do not have the inherent capacity to bring about the requirements demanded by the Sermon on the Mount. Thus, he says, "Human virtue unaided will never take on the character of divine goodness. The latter can only be produced by "cooperation with God."[197] I am not sure if this view of Westerholm is purely Matthean as I think a lot of Pauline interpolations seem to be present in this view.

2.19 Conclusion

This concludes the literary review of the interpretations of the Sermon on the Mount. As mentioned in the introduction of this chapter, this literary review was not meant to be comprehensive. However, what it offers is an overview of various interpretations of the Sermon on the Mount through history. While patristic period saw the Sermon on the Mount as Jesus' law, a continuity of the old law which needed to be practiced by all Christians, the Middle Ages dissected the requirement of obedience to the Sermon on the Mount and assigned to only a few, who wanted to be perfect, the priests, for example. Though this idea was rejected by the reformers they seemed to have worked against Anabaptists who applied the Sermon on the Mount literally. Anabaptists, Quakers, Leo Tolstoy and Mahatma Gandhi emphasized the literal obedience of the Sermon on the Mount. However, the 19th and 20th century saw liberal theology rejecting the Sermon on the Mount's application for their present world as irrelevant to a certain extent. Through all these, scholars throughout the centuries identified that comparisons are present in the Sermon on the Mount and showed its importance in the interpretation and application of the Sermon on the Mount. However, it must be said that most scholars were more interested in the applicability of the Sermon on the Mount rather than the literary function of the comparisons in the Sermon on the Mount. The literary function of the comparisons in the Sermon on the Mount will be the focus of this book. Before this the method by which the Sermon on the Mount will be studied needs to be explained. This will be the concentration of the next chapter.

197. Ibid., 52.

Chapter 3

Narrative Criticism in New Testament
A Methodological Overview

3.1 Introduction

NARRATIVE CRITICISM IS RELATIVELY new to the New Testament.[1] Narrative criticism is basically a part of literary criticism.[2] In order to understand the methodological presuppositions of narrative criticism one must understand literary criticism. This will make up the first part of this chapter. Next, narrative criticism will be explained by looking at the various narrative techniques which could be used in the narrative analysis of the text.

3.2 Literary Criticism

According to Norman C. Habel, literary criticism originated alongside other criticisms such as form criticism, historical criticism, and tradition criticism.[3] While all ask similar questions, literary criticism views biblical literature as a whole. Habel points out that the earlier literary critics were the ones who developed form criticism.[4] For example, Astruc, a literary critic, was the first to see the different names of God used in the book of Genesis and suggested that it could have been due to the several sources from which the book of Genesis was redacted.[5] Later, the form critics took over this idea and developed it to concentrate on the pre-literary history of

1. Resseguie, *Narrative Criticism*, 18.
2. Ibid., 18.
3. Habel, *Literary Criticism of the Bible*, iii.
4. Ibid., iii–v.
5. Ibid., iii.

the literature. Thus, Habel says, "Literary criticism dealt with units of the Bible, and with the historical settings in which the writing occurred. Form criticism deals with an earlier preliterary phase of the story."[6] While in form criticism, forms such as, blessings, oaths, hymns, legends, commandments, etc., were identified to see the history of the pre-literary state of the literature, literary criticism identifies the forms to see their relationship to the end product, that is, the literature as a whole.

Historical criticism concentrated on the history of the literature by dissecting the document into *pericopae* and giving the historical background to each in order to reconstruct the history of the text. Hence, historical criticism asks questions such as: who?, what?, when?, where?, why?, and how? These questions must be addressed in order to understand the text according to historical criticism. However, by doing this, the unity of the text is undermined as the text is divided into pieces in the process. Thus, David M. Gunn says, "Unlike historical criticism, which in practice has segmented the text, formalist narrative criticism has often been an exercise in holism."[7] In addition, while historical criticism's objective was to find the historical reliability of the narrative, literary criticism encourages reading the text in its entirety.

Historical critics dismissed reading the Bible as literature because the bible, for them, did not confirm to the literary characteristics of its time.[8] However, literary critics assert that though biblical writings do not conform to the ancient canons of literature, "they do share features with literary texts and are, therefore, amenable to literary criticism."[9] Biblical literature demonstrates several techniques being used by literary critics. Thus, literary critics in biblical studies could use these techniques in their interpretations which in turn would help them understand the biblical literature better.

Tradition criticism, however, identifies that oral and written sources continued to play an important role in the formation of the tradition which eventually culminated in the end product as Scripture. Tradition criticism, which is widely called in the New Testament as Redaction criticism, took mainly the editorial comments or additions of the redactors, or the tradition, into consideration while not viewing the text as a whole. The alterations of the tradition of the text, and the theology behind the alterations were the main concern of tradition criticism. Thus, the important contribution of literary criticism is seeing the text as a whole. While historical criticism,

---

6. Ibid., vi.
7. Gunn, "Narrative Criticism," 251.
8. Peterson, *Literary Criticism for New Testament Critics*, 11.
9. Ibid., 11.

including form and redaction criticisms, concentrated on dissecting the text into smaller forms and seeing the history behind those texts, literary criticism stressed the importance of seeing the text as a whole. Richard G. Mouton says, "No principle of literary study is more important than that of grasping clearly a literary work as a single whole."[10] Leland Ryken shows this important presupposition in these words: "Literary critics accept the New Testament text in its final form as the focus of their study. Furthermore, they assume unity in the text . . ."[11]

Habel defines literary criticism as the following: "Literary criticism in the traditional sense can be defined as the task of analyzing the literary features of a given document to determine its literary character, origins, and states of written composition."[12] According to Habel, literary critical analysis is nothing but identifying the literary features of a given work to identify its literary character, origins and how it was composed, and so on. Moreover, David E. Aune defines literary criticism as a methodology, which "deals with the interpretation and evaluation of a literary work through the careful examination and analysis of the work itself on the basis of both internal factors (eg., genre, structure, content, style, source) and external factors (eg., historical setting, social setting, biographical data, psychological information)."[13] According to Aune, literary critical analysis is not just identifying a piece of literature as literature but also using these literary techniques to interpret and evaluate it. Ryken, on the other hand, goes a little further to say, "A literary approach to the New Testament is one that makes a reader sensitive to the sensations and vividness and experiential qualities of a passage."[14] Ryken identifies that literature is an "art form."[15] The art form of the literature is seen in the presence of "beauty, form, craftsmanship, [and] technique."[16] For Ryken, these qualities, present in whole or part, are the evidence to say that a particular piece of literary material has literary properties. Thus, he strongly suggests using literary criticism to interpret the New Testament, as it contains many literary properties.

---

10. Mouton, *The Modern Reader's Bible*, 1719 cited in Ryken, *The New Testament in Literary Criticism*, 7.
11. Ryken, *The New Testament*, 8.
12. Habel, *Literary Criticism*, 6.
13. Aune, *The New Testament in Its Literary Environment*, 19.
14. Ryken, *The New Testament*, 4
15. Ibid., 5.
16. Ibid., 5.

Habel says, "Literary criticism is to provide the literary spadework for a better understanding of the function and import of a document."[17] Habel, thus, gives essential steps of using literary criticism.[18]

1. One must identify the internal arrangement of the given passage. This includes identifying its themes, structure, and literary units, and to see how these units are interrelated. This must involve identifying the presence of any thematic, formal, chronological, or haphazard connection between them. This will further lead the literary critic to discover if there is more than one sequence, or motif, or incidents developed in the same document.[19]

2. The literary critic must "trace these elements through a series of passages in the document concerned."[20] This will lead him/her to ask following questions. "Are there logical or thematic inconsistencies within the documents? Is one unit interrupted by a digression or secondary comment? Is there a sudden change in literary style? Do variant versions of the same account appear in the document? Do specific groupings of words keep reappearing in different contexts? Is a definite viewpoint espoused, lost and then reaffirmed later in the same text?"[21]

3. After the literary critic has collected enough information from the previous steps he/she must "propose a hypothesis concerning the origins and composition of the document under scrutiny."[22]

4. The literary critic must relate his/her literary findings to the historical context of the document. "To do this he [or she] will need to use all the pertinent information at his [or her] disposal about the language, culture, history, thought forms, and religions of the ancient world."[23] This will give the final information needed to interpret the text, that is, what made the author write what was written.

Thus, through the four steps, the interpreter identifies the literary elements in the text and analyzes the presence of the literary markers to find repetitions. After this, he or she must propose a hypothesis which in fact would

---

17. Habel, *Literary Criticism*, 7.
18. Ibid., 6–7.
19. Ibid., 6.
20. Ibid., 6.
21. Ibid., 6–7.
22. Ibid., 7.
23. Ibid., 7.

explain the meaning of the text. The last step would allow the interpreter to situate the interpretation in its historical context.

Though literary criticism has been used widely and differently, Ryken gives one way to test if the literary analysis is in fact literary critical analysis. If a commentator links biblical literature with that of the familiar modern literature then it is conclusive that that commentator is using literary criticism.[24] Most literary critics of the Bible use literature of the biblical times to expose the literary nature of the biblical text. Most literary critical works compare the literary works of the New Testament to the literature of antiquity like Aeschylus and Sophocles, or Agamemnon, or Odyssey or Iliad. The use of literary elements of modern times is not often used in the biblical literary critical studies. Thus, Ryken stresses that a literary study should consider the bible as literature, even similar to that of literature of our age.[25] Though from a literary point of view Ryken's criticism is interesting, I think this view also limits the literary analysis of the Bible. If literary critical analysis is to be applied to the Bible, then the Bible must be considered as literature similar to any literature, from antiquity to our age. In contrast to Ryken, Habel warns the literary critic sternly not to use modern literary techniques in the assessment of an ancient text.[26] Interestingly, one must notice that Habel does not reject the use of the modern literary techniques but he warns the literary critic of using the modern literary techniques without taking into consideration of the historical, literary context of the literature. William A. Beardslee says, "Literary criticism of the New Testament means setting the New Testament in the context of other literature and perceiving it as literature. It means trying to understand the biblical books by methods of approach and standards which can be useful in the study of other writings as well."[27] Beardslee says, through this recognition that the Bible is "just like any other books," many important advances have occured in the literary study of the Bible.[28] This means that the narratives in the Bible must be treated as litereary narratives not only as sources which will shed light on the history of pre-literary era of the narrative. Letters must be treated as letters, not only as as doctrinal statements of the church or tradition.

Through the identification that the Bible is a literature, it is also important to identify the three important literary genres in the New Testament.

---

24. Ryken, *The New Testament*, 10.
25. Ibid., 8–12.
26. Habel, *Literary Criticism*, 7.
27. Beardslee, *Literary Criticism of the New Testament*, 3.
28. Ibid., 3.

They are, story or narrative, letter or epistle, and vision or apocalypse.[29] Ryken says that the presence of these three common literary genres in the New Testament is clear evidence that the New Testament must be considered as literature.[30] Ryken rightly points out,

> Every literary genre has its 'rules' of operation and its underlying principles. Being aware of them tells a reader what to expect and look for. Literary genres are also important to literary taxonomy and as such provide the basic framework for how we organize individual works and literature as a whole. And since every genre has its own set of procedures, placing a work into the right literary family can be a prerequisite to the correct interpretation of a text.[31]

Interestingly, Ryken stresses that for a good (right, according to him) interpretation of the text one must know the literary value of the text.[32] The literary awareness about the text will help a person to get a good interpretation of the text. This shows the need to use literary criticism.

Literary criticism of the Old Testament narratives and the narratives of the Gospels are quite similar in that they exhibit similar literary techniques, as they are universal to most of the third person narrations. The major difference between the Old Testament narratives and the Gospel narratives is that Old Testament narratives are constructed around heroic figures much too closely with an elongated plot and some unifying themes, while Gospel narrations are "collection of stories" about the life, death, and resurrection of Jesus.[33] "What, then, are the essential features of the gospel as a literary kind?" asks Ryken, and answers:

> The gospels are collections of stories, far more packed with action than is customary in narrative. The overriding purpose of the gospel stories is to explain and praise the person and work of Jesus, who is always the moving force behind the writers' presentation. The impulse to get the facts of Jesus' life and meaning before the reader is combined with the impulse to celebrate what is recorded. The person and work of Jesus are presented through several familiar narrative devices—through

---

29. Ryken, *The New Testament*, 6.
30. Ibid., 6.
31. Ibid., 6.
32. Ibid., 6.
33. Ryken, *The Literature of the Bible*, 274.

His actions, through His words, and through the response of other people to Him.³⁴

Thus, as seen above, in order to interpret a narrative better the interpreter must understand the literary characteristics of the narrative. This is the important contribution of narrative criticism. Comparative characterization is the methodology which will be used in this book. It is part of narrative criticism. To this now we turn.

3.3 Narrative Criticism

Narrative criticism is nothing but a methodology that applies literary theory to biblical narratives.³⁵ Narrative criticism "meant interpreting the existing text (in its 'final form') in terms primarily of our story world, seen as replete with meaning, rather than understanding the text by attempting to reconstruct its sources and editorial history, its original setting and audience, and its author's or editor's intention in writing."³⁶ The meaning of the text is found by reading the text closely and identifying formal and conventional structure of the narrative, determining the plots, developing characterization, and by distinguishing point of view, etc. Narrative criticism focuses on the bible in its final form and analyzes the literary methods and the artistry of the biblical authors. Thus, in this book, the text, the Sermon on the Mount will be studied in its final form not concentrating on its traditions, or forms, etc.

Resseguie explains, "Narrative critics are primarily concerned with the literariness of biblical narrative—that is, the qualities that make them literature, form and content are generally regarded as an indissoluble whole. Narrative criticism is a shift away from traditional historical-critical methods to the way a text communicates meaning as a self-contained unit, a literary artifact, an undivided whole."³⁷ The uniqueness of narrative criticism is its approach, which is unlike that of other methods. Resseguie argues that historical-sociological and anthropological approaches to the Bible seek to interpret the text in their context respectively.³⁸ Historical approaches concentrate on the historical background of the text while sociological approaches concentrate on the sociological background of the text. In

---

34. Ibid., 275.
35. Bennema, "A Theory of Character in the Fourth Gospel," 375.
36. Gunn, "Narrative Criticism," 171.
37. Resseguie, *Narrative Criticism*, 19.
38. Ibid., 19.

one way, narrative criticism does not ignore the historical or sociological backgrounds of the text but incorporates them in the reading of the text as literature. Though narrative critism does not place as much emphasis on the historical and sociological backgrounds of the text, as the fore mentioned approaches do, it does utilize the historical, sociological and anthropological readings as warranteed by the literature.[39] Thus, one of the important functions of narrative criticism is to view the text as a whole, rather than to concentrate on the "historical issues or the development of the text in its *Sitz im Leben*, or life situation. This is in order to focus on the text as freestanding work in which form and content are inseparable."[40]

Why should narrative criticism be privileged over and against the other methods of interpretation? Resseguie answers:[41]

1. It views the text as a whole. While historical criticism and others dissect the text and lead to lose the essence of the whole, narrative criticism views the text as a whole and tries to read it that way.

2. It examines the complexities and nuances of a text by reading it closely. It considers the text as literature and thus close reading is achieved by taking its structure, setting, point of view, symbolism, characterization, and imagery, etc. into consideration. These literary markers are then interpreted in the socio-cultural and historical background of the implied author and the implied reader so as to get a holistic understanding of the text.

3. It also emphasizes the effects of a narrative on the reader.

Narrative criticism is, thus, an important methodology to interpret the narratives. It is now time to explain the narrative techniques so as to understand this narrative criticism better, and also to understand its use in the interpretation of Scripture. Comparative characterization is one of elements of narrative techniques. Thus, to see how comparative characterization functions it is important to also consider a few other elements of narrative techniques. The first in this would be the role of the 'narrator'. To this now we turn.

---

39. Ibid., 19.
40. Ibid., 23.
41. Ibid., 23.

3.3.1 Narrator

In many works of literature, the narrator is felt only indirectly through the characters, but in biblical narratives we hear the narrator's voice alongside the characters. In fact we see and hear only through the narrator's eyes. The narrator is, in a very real way, inside the narrative. Unlike drama, where we feel the author only indirectly through the characters, in narrative, the narrator exists alongside the characters and his voice is heard as well as theirs. There are several qualities of the narrator that we need to understand. Shimon Bar-Efrat gives five important characteristic features of a biblical narrator:[42]

a. He may be everywhere and knows everything.

b. He may intrude into the story and add comments and explanations.

c. He may report what is happening from a distance.

d. He may watch things from above.

e. He may be neutral and objective or have a definite attitude about what is being related.

In most narratives, the narrator appears to be omniscient. He seems to constantly transfer from one place to another as he shows us one character after another. We can't move quickly from one place to another and can only see things from our point of view, but the narrator can move, even across time. He can be, in effect, omniscient. One moment, he can be with Joseph in Bethlehem (Matt 1:19–25), and the next with Magi from the East (Matt 2:1). The narrator can enter the inner chambers and see very intimate things, hear private conversations, even of Herod's conversation with the chief priests and scribes (Matt 2:4). Therefore, we know that Herod secretly told the Magi to see the child and let him know about the whereabouts, and that the Magi did not go back to Herod because they knew of his evil plan. We know where Jesus was but Herod did not know. We know how an angel helped Joseph to safeguard Jesus from the onslaught of the babies in Bethlehem while Herod did not know. The narrator is omniscient and he informs us many things which other characters do not know.

The narrator helps us know things we couldn't otherwise know, like emotions, and what a person's will is in a particular situation, etc. Sometimes, through the narrator we even get brief glimpses of what the characters are thinking. The narrator would show this through the use of inner speech. Narrators usually include negative aspects of characters as well as

---

42. Bar-Efrat, *Narrative Art in the Bible*, 14–15.

the positive ones and relate events in a factual and impassionate manner. However, sometimes narrators might use evaluative terms which would reveal for us the viewpoint of the narrator. In Matt 1:19, the narrator says, "*And Joseph her husband, being a righteous man, and not wanting to disgrace her, desired to put her away secretly.*" Joseph here is evaluated by the narrator for us so that we will know that he is a righteous man. This small detail is important to the story because in the story, Mary is already shown to be righteous, which was the reason for her being with child without having any sexual relationship (Matt 1:18). Likewise, the author must show the righteousness of Joseph to portray him as the earthly father of Jesus, the Messiah. Thus, he adds an evaluation for us to show that Joseph is a righteous man.

The narrator has two ways to portray events; i.e by providing a summary of the events or by showing the events themselves. The first gives us a comprehensive panorama, while the second gives us vivid details.[43] When the narrator summarizes, there is bound to be interpretation and assessment. Usually, however, the writer uses a scenic or dramatic presentation which gives us the illusion of looking at the event itself. This is the method usually followed in order to absorb the reader and involve him/her in the events. However, the narrator needs to control the involvement of the reader in the story otherwise he or she would risk losing out on the analysis of the event. For this, the narrator inserts narrator's comments. Sometimes the narrator may hide his evaluation and show it through another character. The narrator shows the reader what is being described as what one of the characters is seeing at the moment, though we are aware that the narrator actually knew this beforehand or knows more than the character discerns at that moment.[44] In spite of all the showing of the events, the narrator is more obvious when there is a summary provided than in direct speech. However, the point is that, even in the showing of the events, the narrator is never absent, but is at work telling the reader who is speaking, and to whom, and defining the nature of the speech, etc.

In this study, Matthew, the narrator of the Sermon on the Mount, uses Jesus giving speech to describe who the disciple is and how he/she should live. Though Matthew, the author, narrates the story of Jesus' teaching in the Sermon on the Mount, Jesus is technically the narrator in the story world as Matt 5-7 is in the direct speech, from 5:3 to 7:27.

---

43. Ibid., 14–15.
44. Ibid., 35.

3.3.2 Point of View

The Biblical writers had the skill of a great cameraman to give us many viewpoints and angles. Sometimes we are being shown the viewpoint of the narrator; at others, we come to know the viewpoint of the main character; at still others we see the story from the viewpoint of one of the characters. For example, in the birth narrative of Jesus, in Matthew, we see Herod as a perplexed man, who tries his best to kill the child, knowing that another king was born in Bethlehem. He tells the Magi that they should inform him about the child's whereabouts. When they did not return we see him trying to kill all the children in Bethlehem. However, from the other point of view, that is, from the viewpoint of the narrator and from the viewpoint of God [assuming God is the ultimate author of the text], the holy child is kept safe by the Magi, as they did not inform the whereabouts of the child to Herod, and also by the appearance of the angel who said that the baby should be carried to Egypt. Herod does not know this and he tries to do everything to kill the child. However, from the viewpoint of the narrator and God the child is kept safe, and the narrator lets the reader know this viewpoint to appreciate the work of God in the birth of the Messiah. The ability to show different points of views makes the story more exciting. One of the clues that the point of view is changing is the use of the word, "behold" (Hebrew: הִנֵּה, and Greek: ἰδού).

Point of view is an integral part of narrative criticism. Usually, the author shows the point of view, in which way the text must be read and also how the reader must, to a certain extent, respond to the passage. Resseguie says, "Narrative point of view—especially ideological point of view—exists to persuade the reader to see the world in a different way, to adopt a new perspective or to abandon an old point of view. By making strange on firmly held assumptions, values, norms, beliefs, and expectations, the text allows the reader to see a new self—indeed, to become someone else."[45]

The point of view changes dramatically by the use of first person narration and third person narration. First person narration is a narration narrated by an author in first person. Example, in the short story, *A Rose for Emily*, First person narrative is used which shows only a limited perspective, that is of the author.[46] The first person narrated story shows a subjective perspective. However, when an author uses third person narrative, the story is presented somewhat far removed from the personal passions of the narrator

---

45. Resseguie, *Narrative Criticism*, 40.
46. Faulkner, *A Rose for Emily*.

which allows the readers to perceive the story a little more objectively or at least less subjectively to a certain extent.

Robert Alter says third-person narration is a bridge between much larger units of direct speech. Normally if speech is included in the bible, it is direct speech.[47] In the Gospels, narrators use extended direct speech materials to show the teachings, words and acts of Jesus and his disciples. However, though direct speech gives us the feeling of being right there in the scene, it makes the situation more ambiguous. If the narrator were to state it, it would give "authorativeness" to the statement because of the reliability of the narrator.[48] This habit makes the narrative dramatically vivid and stylized.

In Matt 5–7, the Sermon on the Mount is presented by the author as direct speech in a sermon form. This allows the reader to read/hear what Jesus was saying first hand. Though, this portion (Matt 5–7) exists as part of a bigger third person narration, which is the whole book, Sermon on the Mount is a first person narration, in one sense, a first person narration of Jesus Christ. This is quite important for our interpretation of the Sermon of the Mount. In literature, a first person narrative might suggest a less subjective presentation of the story. However, when it comes to the authoritative teachings of Jesus, the first person narrative of Jesus is more authoritative than a third person narrative. The Messiah himself is teaching how the disciple must live. It is not the writing of a disciple or an apostle but of Jesus himself. Thus, it is more authoritative than the third person narrative. Therefore, the author's use of first person narration in Matt 5–7 does not diminish the rhetorical force of the story but multiplies it manifold.

3.3.3 Narrative and Dialogue

The Bible uses more "direct speech" than other narratives. Direct speech has the effect of making us feel like being a part of the "action" and helping us identify with the characters better. The narration, by contrast, has the effect of helping us evaluate what we read by the insertions of narrator's comments with explanations, setting the scene, slowing down or speeding up the action of the story, etc. By adding his comments, the narrator helps us to sufficiently separate ourselves from the story, so that we can evaluate what is happening in the story and understand what the narrative is trying to tell us. The narrator rarely makes comments like "this was evil," etc. Usually, the narrator gives us enough information so that we can evaluate the story

47. Alter, *The Art of Biblical Narrative*, 82.
48. Ibid., 84.

ourselves. For example, by comparing the present story with what has been going on in previous stories we can evaluate and determine who is good and who is not. This is one of the important reasons for the frequent use of the direct speech in the Biblical narratives. As it will be noticed, Jesus' teaching in the Sermon on the Mount is one big discourse, where the reader is invited to listen to Jesus *firsthand* and obey him fully.

3.3.4 Repetition

Repetition is one of the key features of biblical narrative. Bible uses repetition to underscore the importance of certain words or phrases.[49] Sometimes a phrase is repeated in reverse order, which is called a *chiasmus* or *chiasm*. Often this is found at the end of a section or "pericope." Sometimes, repetition simply occurs to underscore an important event. In poetry, repetition occurs in parallelism, which may involve "repetition" of an idea. It may be synonymous, antithetic or synthetic. According to Alter, there are five ways repetition is used in narrative, from the smallest to the largest:[50]

a. Leitwort (keyword)

b. Motif

c. Theme

d. Succession of events (i.e. groups of three), and

e. Type scene

Though the typescenes are not so prevalent in the New Testament there are certain allusions which could be seen as a type scene (eg. Jesus' interaction with the Samaritan woman near a well, which is similar to the betrothal scenes in the Old Testament). Another way in which repetition is used is between what a character says and what the narrator says in relation to it.

In Matt 26, we see the three denials of Peter. The first time when a servant girl asks about Peter he says *"I do not know what you are talking about."* And in the gateway when another person asks about him he says with an oath, *"I do not know the man."* In the third instance, he replies with curses and swears, *"I do not know the man!"* (Mat 26:70-74). Each statement repeats basically the same information but in different ways which reveals the intensity in which Peter is denying. In addition, when the same information is repeated in the words of different characters, it will show each

---

49. Resseguie, *Narrative Criticism*, 42.
50. Alter, *The Art*, 120–121.

character's intentions better. As we do a "close reading" of the text we learn that it is the slight differences in the repitions which make the narrative more interesting and intriguing.

3.3.5 Leitwort

In narration, often stories are organized around a key word. Key words connect different stories together. For example, to "go down" to Egypt is consistently used in the Bible as going away from God's will, while to "go up," particularly to Jerusalem, indicates moving towards God. Interestingly, Matthew uses similar 'going' to Egypt but does not connote any nuances as does the Old Testament.[51] In addition, he is even saying that going to Egypt was a good thing because it in one way proves that Jesus is the Messiah, as the travel justifies the fulfillment of the messianic prophecy from Hosea (Matt 2:15). This in fact could be said as Matthew's reversal theme where he breaks Old Testament conventions in order to show the greatness of the Messiah. All the major characters of the Old Testament, when they went to Egypt, had bad things happen to them or to their family (ex. Abraham, Jacob, Moses, etc.). However, when Jesus went there good things happened to him, being delivered from Herod.

3.3.6 Allusions

Alter asserts that it is "allusions" which hold the Bible together.[52] Every part of the text is to be read with other parts of the text in mind. For example, when David is described in 1 Samuel 16:18 as, "a fine-looking man, and the Lord is with him," the reader will immediately think of Joseph and know that their next hero will have difficulties like the previous one, Joseph, though success would lie ahead for him as it was for Joseph. The previous example in Matt 2:15 could very well be used here also. By showing how Jesus went to Egypt and returned from Egypt, the narrator alludes to the great Moses, the deliverer of the Old, in order to symbolize that Jesus the deliverer of the New Testament is greater than the Moses of the Old. Next element discussed in narrative criticism is characters and characterization, which are important for this book.

---

51. Greidanus, *The Modern Preacher*, 239–240.
52. Alter, *World of Biblical Literature*, 110.

3.3.7 Characters

Characters are 'central' to every story.[53] Characters are the "major players" in a narrative.[54] The bible does not describe every detail of a character for us. If a specific item of description is given that information will be very important in the story and in the characterization of characters. Not everything that is said about one character by another is "true," nor does the Bible tell everything about a character. Sometimes, it is not so easy to judge who is telling the truth and who is not. Alter calls this "reticence" and he gives a scale of reticence so as to help us discern which information is more reliable than others in terms of characterization.[55] For example, the narrator is always reliable—he is able to speak for God. The next reliable, after the narrator, is the inner speech of the character himself, followed by the direct speech of the character himself. After these come the comments about the character by another, further down the line are the report of gestures, actions, appearance, posture, and costumes, in the scale of reticence.

1. Narrator
2. Inner speech of the character himself
3. Speech of the character himself
4. Comments about the character by another character
5. Report of gestures, actions, appearance, posture, costumes

The importance of the scale of reticence is to determine who is telling the truth when there are conflicting views in a narrative.

For example, in the story of Saul we see conflicting information given in the two books of Samuel about the death of Saul. In 1 Samuel 31, we see Saul asking his armor bearer to draw his sword and kill him so that he would not die at the hands of the uncircumcised Philistines. However, as the armor bearer refused to kill, Saul himself took his sword and fell on it. Thus, it is reported by the narrator in 1 Samuel 31 that Saul committed suicide in the wake of his defeat in the battle with Philistine. This detail about his death is given by the narrator, who must be reliable as this is a third person narration. There is a clear indication in 1 Sam 31:5 & 6 that Saul and his three sons died, which also was narrated by the narrator. In addition, in 1 Sam 31:5, it is narrated that only after confirming that Saul was dead the armor bearer kills himself.

---

53. Bock and Fanning, *Interpreting the New Testament Text*, 197.
54. Ibid., 197.
55. Alter, *World of Biblical Literature*, 65–67.

However, in 2 Samuel 1, we have another report, which shows that a young man, an Amelakite, claims that he killed Saul because Saul did not die even after he fell on the spear. The problem here is this—how did Saul die? By suicide or euthanasia? This is when we could use the scale of reticence. The account in 1 Sam 31 shows the narrator's claim that Saul died by suicide, which is no. 1 on the reliability scale in the scale of reticence. However, the account in 2 Sam 1 has a character's comment about the killing of Saul, which falls on the 4th in the scale of reticence. Comparing both, it seems 1 Sam 31 account is more reliable because it is given by the narrator while the account in 2 Sam 1 was narrated by a young man, which could be said to be false. There is a greater probability that this young man wanted a greater reward from the new king, David, and so he claimed that he killed Saul. Thus, scale of reticence is useful in evaluating conflicting accounts of characterizations.

3.3.7.1 *Classification of Characters*

Characters are divided as flat characters and round characters.[56] Flat characters are built around a single trait of a character while round characters are more developed to form a much more complex character with multiple traits. The round characters are also called full-fledged characters.[57] Adele Berlin also finds another type of character which is mere functionary and less developed than others and it is called an agent.[58] In the full-fledged or round characters we see development in the character and not only good but sometimes even bad aspects of these characters are narrated by the narrator. Abraham and David would be examples of "full-fledged" characters. Though they are the heroes of faith their mistakes are also narrated in their characterization. The "flat" characters, however, exhibit only few character traits. Abigail would be an example of this kind of character—a noble woman, industrious, determined with no negative aspects mentioned. Resseguie points out, "major characters are generally round and minor characters are generally flat, but not always. Religious leaders in the Gospels for instance, are major characters, but they lack complexity. They are flat, exhibiting various forms of a single root trait of duplicity and distractiveness."[59] Some characters are just "agents or functionaries" in the story. We do not know much about these characters. An example of a functionary would be Abishag. She is useful only to keep David warm. All we know is that she was beautiful and

---

56. Berlin, *Poetics and Interpretation*, 23.
57. Ibid., 23.
58. Ibid., 27.
59. Resseguie, *Narrative Criticism*, 123.

Adonijah wanted her as his wife to give credence to himself as the 'real' king in opposition to Solomon.

Resseguie points out three other characters other than round, flat and agents:[60] (1) A *Stock character* is like "type character" which frequently appears in literature with established conventions like the stepmother or Prince charming in a fairy tale. (2) A *foil character* is a character kept in contrast with another character or a group to bring out certain characteristic traits of the character in concern. Resseguie says, "In literature, the term [foil] is applied to any person who through contrast underscores the distinctive characteristics of another."[61] Examples include the poor widow who gave generously despite her poverty while those who had money didn't give. Her generosity in poverty plays like a foil, "a sheet of shiny metal that is placed under jewels to increase their brilliance."[62] Another example of the foil character is the gentile centurion in Mark 15:39. The Gentile centurion saw Jesus as the Son of God while people of Israel ignored him as a false Messiah. (3) A *walk-on character* is a "faceless nameless character" that functions just for the plot.[63] This could be similar to the agent in Berlin's classification, as Resseguie doesn't have the category as agent in his nomenclature of characters. Though there are several categories here, our concentration falls on the foil character. It is the assumption of the present author that the Pharisees and scribes of Matt 5:1 to 7:29 play the role of a foil to bring out the characterization of the ideal disciple in that passage.

Walter Kaiser shows that often in Hebrew narratives, characters are contrasted to other characters so as to bring out certain characteristic traits of the subject.[64] In a comparison, one character will play the foil to another character through which the narrator intends to show few characteristic traits of the character of concern. "A foil," Ryken says, "is literally something that 'sets off' or heightens what is most important in a story."[65] Foil, is "in literature, a character who is presented as a contrast to a second character so as to point to or show to advantage some aspect of the second character."[66] In many instances the antagonists of a narrative are considered as the foil to the protagonists.[67] Foil characters are frequently used in the bible though

---

60. Ibid., 123.
61. Harmon and Holman, *A Handbook to Literature*, 216.
62. Resseguie, *Narrative Criticism*, 124.
63. Ibid., 125.
64. Kaiser, Jr. "Narrative," 74.
65. Ryken, *How to Read the Bible as Literature*, 54.
66. "Foil." n.p., *Encyclopædia Britannica*.
67. "Antagonist." n.p., *Encyclopædia Britannica*.

very limited study had been done on the foil characters in the New Testament narrative criticism. This will be the focus of this study. It is time to explain the methods of characterization to understand how the narrators characterize the characters in a story.

3.3.8 Characterization

The reader gets to know a "character from the information provided to him [or her] in the discourse: he [or she] is told by the statements and evaluations of the narrator and other characters, and he [or she] infers from the speech and action of the character himself."[68] This is called characterization. Powell explains characterization as "the process through which the implied author provides the implied reader with what is necessary to reconstruct a character from the narrative."[69] Boris Uspensky points out that characterization can be done in different points of views, such as, the spatial—temporal plane, which refers to actions; the phraseological plane, which refers to speech; the psychological plane, which refers to the thoughts; and the ideological plane, which refers to the beliefs and values of a character.[70]

A narrator could describe a character in adjectives, nouns, etc. This I call as *descriptive characterization*. All characterizations are descriptive in nature where the author describes a character with words, attributes, etc. Berlin says that in descriptive characterization "descriptive terms may be based on status (king, widow, wise man, wealthy, old, etc.), profession (prophet, prostitute, shepherd, etc), gentilic features (Hittite, Amalekite, etc.) or distinctive physical features (beautiful, strong, lame, etc)" may be used.[71] However, direct description is very rare in the stories of the bible.[72] Though description is an important part of characterization, Berlin says that bible uses various other techniques which make characterization interesting.[73]

Adele Berlin brings another element in to this description. Characterization is not just about how a character is presented by the author, but also how it helps a reader to reconstruct the character.[74] She says, "The reader constructs a character from the information provided to him in the discourse: he [or she] is told by the statements and evaluation of the nar-

---

68. Berlin, *Poetics and Interpretation*, 34.
69. Powell, *What is Narrative Criticism?* 52.
70. Uspensky, *Poetics of Composition*, 8–100.
71. Berlin, *Poetics and Interpretation*, 35–36.
72. Ryken, *How to Read*, 37.
73. Berlin, *Poetics and Interpretation*, 37.
74. Ibid., 34.

rator and the other characters and he infers from the speech and actions of the character himself [or herself]."[75] This does not mean that the reader constructs the character as if it is purely reader based hermeneutics. The reader identifies the elements of characterization and sees the function of the characterizations and reconstructs the characters in the narration presented by the narrator. In this case, the narrator of direct speech of the Sermon on the Mount is Jesus himself, who characterizes the ideal disciple at length in three chapters, 5:3—7:27.

3.3.8.1 Showing and Telling Characterization

Two generally recognized narrative techniques of characterization are *showing* and *telling*. *Showing* sometimes is also called the "dramatic method or indirect presentation."[76] Here, the author simply presents the characters talking or acting and "leaves the reader to infer the motives and dispositions that lie behind what they say and do."[77] The narrator could show the nature of the character by showing what the character does, or says. For example, the narrator of the books of Samuel wants to show Saul as an evil king who always plots against David inorder to kill him. In this endeavor, however, he does not say outright that Saul is evil. To David, Saul seems to be a good king who would want to reward David by giving him his daughter's hand if David brings him one hundred foreskins of the Philistines. However, Saul's speech to his inner-self shows that this plan is orchestrated by Saul so that "the hand of the Philistines may be against him [David]" (1Sam 18:21). Though Saul wanted David to be with him all the time, he threw a spear at him and tried to kill him (1 Sam 18:10). The reader is left to view the character of Saul and make up how evil he is over and against David, the good king. The narrator does not outrightly say that Saul is an evil king. If he had mentioned that it could be interpreted as a subjective view of the author. However, as he shows how Saul plans to kill David and how David does nothing against King Saul, the reader is enabled to make up his mind that Saul is a bad king, which is the result the narrator wants.

The next way of characterization is *telling*. Telling is called direct presentation. Here, "the narrator intervenes to comment directly on a character—singling out a trait for us to notice or making an evaluation of a character and his or her motives and disposition."[78] The narrator makes a comment

75. Ibid., 34.
76. Resseguie, *Narrative Criticism*, 126–127.
77. Abrams, *Characters and Characterization*, 47.
78. Resseguie, *Narrative Criticism*, 127.

about Jesus when Lazarus died saying, "He was deeply moved in spirit and was troubled" (John 11:33). Resseguie notes, "This narrator—called an omniscient narrator—exercises the freedom to move at will from the external world to the inner world of the characters" and shows them to the readers to judge the characters and reconstruct that character in the way he wants.[79]

The technique of showing is not quite precise as that of telling. However, it makes the characterization interesting. The reader must collect data thoroughly from the text to reconstruct a character. Moreover, the reliability of a character lies on whose point of view the character is depicted from. John the Baptist's view about the Pharisees as "brood of vipers" in Matt 3:7 must be reliable. However, the view of the Pharisees about Jesus, as the one who "casts out demons by the prince of demons" (Matt 9:34) is not true. The Pharisees are the antagonists and their idea of the protagonist, Jesus, must not be taken as valid. Thus, characterization by showing involves other dynamics also.

3.3.8.2 Characterization and Inner Life

Berlin shows how Characters' inner life could also contribute to characterization of a character. For example, Moses' anger in Exod 32:19 shows him as an angry man, and the disciples of Jesus were repeatedly shown as fearful people (Mark 4:41; 9:32; Luke 9:34; and 9:45), and the thoughts of Eli that Hannah was drunk characterizes both Hannah and Eli in many ways (1 Sam 1:13). Berlin rightly points out that the presentation of the inner life of a character is made to shed insights about the "thoughts, emotions, and motivations" of the characters.[80]

3.3.8.3 Characterization through Speeches and Actions

While description and inner life are conveyed directly by the narrator, speech and action characterizes a character indirectly. Speech of a character shows what kind character he/she is in many ways. For example, the reason for Judas' betrayal of Jesus is showed explicitly in his speech in Matt 26:15: "What are you willing to give me to betray Him to you?" His intention was to get money out of Jesus and he was willing to even betray Jesus for the money. Here, the character of Judas is shown as he is classically understood throughout history as a greedy person. The speech of Judas in Matt 26:15 is instrumental for that characterization of him as a greedy person.

79. Ibid., 127.
80. Berlin, *Poetics and Interpretation*, 38.

Interestingly, a speech of a character about another, if the first character is reliable, could be instrumental in the characterization of the second character. In Luke 9:35, a voice out of the cloud says, *"This is My Son, My Chosen One; listen to Him."* Here, obviously, the voice is identified as God's voice and thus more reliable and must be taken into consideration seriously. This statement thus added value to the characterization of Jesus.

3.3.8.4 Self Characterization

Ryken's *Self-characterization* could be considered as a part of characterization by speech.[81] Jesus calling himself Son of Man or Son of God could be termed as self-characterization of Jesus. Other examples include Job's repeated portrayal of himself as an innocent person, and King Saul's admission that David is more righteous than he is.

Sometimes the actions of the character emphasize characterization of that character. "Character is what produces action, on the other hand, characters are known to us through their actions."[82] Let us take Judas's example again. Immediately after his speech with the high priest, where he asked them how much they would be willing to give him to betray Jesus, the narrator shows the actions of the high priest and Judas which characterizes the character of Judas even better. The narrator shows the actions in Matt 26:15–16 as *"And they weighed out thirty pieces of silver to him. From then on he began looking for a good opportunity to betray Jesus."* This man, the disciple of Jesus, a follower of the Messiah, earlier said in his speech that he was willing to betray his master for money. In addition, immediately after this, the author shows his actions that he received money and that *"he began looking for a good opportunity to betray Jesus."* His actions reinforce his speech and his characterization. Here, characterization is achieved with the speech and actions of a character. The next characterization, contrast characterization is important to this study. Thus, it is important to concentrate on that.

3.3.8.5 Contrast Characterization

Berlin says that some characterization of a character "emerges" when it is compared with another character.[83] Berlin points out that sometime the

---

81. Ryken, *How to Read*, 38.
82. Ibid., 37.
83. Berlin, *Poetics and Interpretation*, 24.

biblical author "invites the comparison by juxtaposing their stories" side by side.[84] She says, "even if a characterization is implicit in the words or deeds of a character, it stands out more clearly if his character is contrasted with its opposite, e.g. Nabal and Abigail, Esau and Jacob."[85] Ryken says, "Many of the famous stories in the Bible are built around great character clashes: Cain and Abel, Jacob and Esau, Joseph and his brothers, the Israelites and their oppressors, Jonah and God, Elijah and Jezebel, Jesus and Jewish leaders, Paul and the Jews. The best way of organizing a discussion of such stories is obviously around the development of character conflict."[86] Contrast characterization uses foil characters in order to characterize a character. Usually, a foil character is used to highlight a particular trait of a character being characterized. The present writer calls this kind of characterization as comparative characterization. This kind of characterization is quite frequently used. This will be concentration of the next Chapter.

3.4 Conclusion

At the outset of the chapter it was mentioned that this chapter is a methodological overview intended to show the importance of narrative criticism, and the major presuppositions of narrative criticism and the elements of narrative criticism in order to apply this methodology in the New Testament. The importance of the methodology was shown through its major presuppositions that bible must be treated as literature and also that it must be studied as a whole unlike the historical or tradition criticisms. It was also shown that narrative criticism is a methodology which applies literary techniques to the narratives of the bible in order to interpret the narratives of the Scripture. The methodology of narrative criticism was shown through series of elements of narratives criticism such as understanding the biblical narrator, point of view, narrative and dialogue, repetition, lietword, allusions, characters, and characterization. The beauty of using narrative criticism was shown by the many examples given to explain the literary techniques which are called narrative techniques. In addition, in the next chapter, comparative characterization will be explained in detail which will be used to interpret the Sermon on the Mount in this study.

---

84. Ibid., 24.
85. Ibid., 40.
86. Ryken, *How to Read*, 41.

Chapter 4

Comparative Characterization as a Methodology to Interpret Matthew 5–7

4.1 Introduction

THE PHRASE 'COMPARATIVE CHARACTERIZATION' is a term coined by the present author to explain the characterization done by comparing one or more characters with a specific so as to bring out some characteristic features of that character. In this chapter, I will describe the methodology by citing examples from the Old Testament. In addition, I will also show the prevalence of comparison in the Greco-Roman literature which shows it's employment as a literary component in the Greco-Roman literature. Thus, it is time to describe characters, characterization and comparative characterization.

4.2 Characters

Shlomith Rimmon-Kenan says that character is one of the neglected areas in literary criticism.[1] Seymour Chatman says, it "is remarkable how little has been said about the theory of character in literary history and criticism."[2] Cornelis Bennema laments that literary criticism "has not advanced beyond the well-known categories of 'flat' and 'round' coined by E.M. Forster in 1927 to classify characters."[3] Fred Burnett points out that "recent works on narrative criticism of the Gospels has emphasized plot and story, but very little has been done with characterization. This is due mostly to the disar-

---

1. Rimmon-Kenan, *Narrative Fiction*, 3, 6.
2. Chatman, *Story and Discourse*, 19.
3. Bennema, "A Theory of Character," 375.

ray of the theoretical discussion about characterization in current literary criticism."[4] Bennema, thus, concludes that "character study is thus still in its infancy."[5] This shows the lack of such scholarship in characterization in the biblical narrative criticism.

4.3 Characterization

The methods of characterization are broadly divided into two categories: Direct and Indirect characterization. In direct characterization, the writer directly states what kind of character he or she is: good, evil, innocent, honest, etc.[6] In the indirect characterization, the writer shows what the character says, does, thinks, and reacts so that the reader can get a better understanding of the character.[7] In addition, indirect characterization also includes the writer showing what other characters think or say about that particular character. Though direct characterization gives much clarity about a particular character it is quite rarely used in the bible. "Showing" or indirect characterization is the most commonly used characterization method in the bible. Indirect characterization makes the readers involved in the story as they evaluate a character by the information given by the author through the five methods of indirect characterization, i.e., the speech, actions, inner thoughts, appearances, and others' views about that character.[8] However, Israel P. Loken identifies another important means of characterization. He calls this one as characterization "Reinforced by Analogy".[9]

This method is usually less stressed or less discussed in the literary criticism of the Bible. This involves the use of contrasted characters. In this kind of characterization, a character is characterized by comparing it with another character. The second character is usually a foil.[10] Sydney Gredaneus calls this use of contrasting characters as "the device in which one character serves as a foil for another."[11] Gredaneus also mentions that usually the minor characters serve as foils. While contrasting characters are kept in contrast, Gredaneus points out parallel characters are to be interpreted

---

4. Burnett, "Characterization," 3.
5. Bennema, "A Theory of Character," 376.
6. Buck and Morris, *A Course in Narrative Writing*, 114.
7. Burroway, *Writing Fiction*, 98.
8. Carlsen, *Encounters*, 4:141.
9. Loken, *The Old Testament Historical Books*, xvii.
10. Ibid., xviii.
11. Greidanus, *The Modern Preacher*, 286.

"in conjunction with each other."[12] Examples of these parallel characters are Mary and Elizabeth in Luke 1, and John the Baptist and Jesus in Mark 1:14 and 6:14–16. They are not contrasted but complimented by the characterization of each other and thus, they are called parallel characters.

4.3.1 Use of Foil Characters in Literature

Modern literary critics say that a foil character is often "a sidekick, a companion who sometimes gives the protagonist important information or insights."[13] A foil character's function in the narrative is to highlight certain characteristic traits of the character in concern. Thus, Berlin calls this method of characterization as characterization by contrast.[14] For example, Shakespeare, in Hamlet, places Laertes and Fortinbras as foil to bring out the moral aspects of Hamlet.[15]

Loken says, in this kind of characterization, "Another character is used to emphasize unique, similar, or contrasting behavioral traits."[16] Loken, in his classification of characters has four kinds of characters. They are: protagonist, antagonist, foil, and archetype. He does not have flat or round characters in his classification but includes foil as one of the important classification of characters in characterization.[17] Indeed, bible is full of foil characters. Saul functions as a foil to David, Cain functions as foil to Abel, Lot for Abraham, Potiphar's wife for Joseph, Jonathan for Saul, Eli's sons for Samuel, etc.

Rimmon-Kenan calls the comparative characterization as "Analogy between Characters."[18] For Rimmon-Kenan, "when two characters are presented in similar circumstances, the similarity or contrast between their behavior emphasizes traits, characteristics of both."[19] This means, both characters, in some way or other, characterize each other. Though this is

---

12. Ibid., 287.
13. Turco, *The Book of Literary Terms*, 99.
14. Berlin, *Poetics and Interpretation*, 40.
15. A good example of contrast in characterization of Laertes and Hamlet, is shown in Act IV and Act III of *Hamlet*, where Laertes, replying to King Claudius saying he would even cut the throat of Hamlet to take vengeance in the church (Act IV, *Hamlet*), while Hamlet is shown not killing King Claudius in revenge because he was praying (Act III, *Hamlet*).
16. Loken, *The Old Testament Historical Books*, xviii.
17. Ibid., xviii.
18. Rimmon-Kenan, *Narrative Fiction*, 70.
19. Ibid., 70.

an interesting observation, from the point of view of the author, the foil is used to show some characteristic features of the character in concern. Thus, comparative characterization is used by the author to elucidate and bring out few characteristic traits of the concerned character. This involves the purpose of the author for the presentation of the foil character as a foil to bring out the characteristic feature of the character in concern. I call this kind of characterization as comparative characterization. The reason for the name is because the narrator compares a certain character with another by placing the second character as a foil to bring out certain characteristic traits from the main character in concern. Comparative characterization is widely used in literature, ancient or modern. This methodology is deeply embedded in story telling, speeches and literature.

4.3.2 Comparative Characterization in the Hebrew Bible

The first of the examples of comparative characterization in the Hebrew Bible is found in Gen 4:1–8. The story of Cain and Abel is carefully narrated intertwining the characterization of both characters. In this narration, the author presents a detail of one character and then gives another detail about that character. The next phrase of the narration gives details of the second character in relation to the characterization of the first character. For example, in A1 of the figure below, Abel's birth is narrated. In B, Abel's profession is mentioned that he was a keeper of the flocks. In these two phrases Abel is the only character being narrated. Immediately after this, in B1, Cain's profession is mentioned that he was the tiller of the ground. In C, Cain's activities are narrated that he brought the offering to the Lord, which is of fruit. In C1, Abel's activity is narrated that he brought offerings to the Lord, which is "the firstlings of the flocks." Careful observation shows that one phrase of the first character's characterization is continued by addition of some details and then that character's description is compared in the next phrase with the second character to display the similarity and difference of these two characters. Thus, a beautiful comparison of characterization emerges by the continuation of comparative characterization. Cain is kept as a foil to Abel to highlight the goodness of Abel.[20]

---

20. McKeown, *Genesis*, 206.

> **Gen 4:1-8**
>
> ¹ Now the man had relations with his wife Eve,
> **A** and ***she conceived and gave birth to Cain***, and
> she said, "I have gotten a manchild with the help of the LORD."
> **A1** ² Again, <u>she gave</u> birth to <u>his brother Abel</u>.
> **B** <u>And Abel was a keeper of flocks,</u>
> **B1** but ***Cain was a tiller of the ground.***
> ³ So it came about in the course of time that ***Cain brought an offering***
> **C** ***to the LORD of the fruit of the ground.***
> **C1** ⁴ <u>Abel, on his part also brought of the firstlings of his flock and of their fat portions. And the LORD had regard for Abel and for his offering</u>;
> **D** ⁵ but ***for Cain and for his offering He had no regard.***
> **D1** So ***Cain became very angry and his countenance fell.***
> ⁶ Then the LORD said to Cain, "Why are you angry? And why has your countenance fallen?
> ⁷ "If you do well, will not your countenance be lifted up? And if you do not do well, sin is crouching at the door; and its desire is for you, but you must master it."
> ⁸ ***Cain*** told <u>Abel</u> his brother. And it came about when they were in the field, that ***Cain rose up*** against <u>Abel</u> his brother and killed him.

Through this comparison the author shows how these two characters are similar and different. This is what I call comparative characterization. Next example comes from the story of Samuel in 1 Samuel.

4.3.2.1 *Samuel and Eli's Sons*

This example for comparative characterization is taken from 1 Samuel 1 & 2. In this story, Paul Borgman identifies that, Hannah is presented as a foil to Eli.[21] He says, "The mother relinquishes a son to God's service proving a foil for what we will see of Eli."[22] Eli should have guided his sons to God's service in a better way. However, he just scolds them (1 Sam 2:22–25). Eventually, God's punishment comes on Eli's sons and they lose the right to be in God's service. However, Hannah's son, who is heard of God (שְׁמוּאֵל, *Shmuel*) hears God's voice and obeys him perfectly throughout his career. Thus, Borgman could be right in pointing out Hannah as a foil to the character, Eli.

While the narrator of 1 Samuel narrates the story of Samuel he also keeps him in contrast with the sons of Eli. Technically, Hophni and Phinehas, the sons of Eli should become the judges after Eli. However, though they were priests of God's Tabernacle, they did evil against the Lord. Hence, God raised Samuel in their place. This story is presented by the narrator

---

21. Borgman, *David, Saul, and God*, 122.
22. Ibid., 122.

in 1 Samuel 1 & 2 in a comparative fashion, which shows the ascension of Samuel to his post as a judge.

The story begins by showing the characters such as Elkanah and Hannah, the parents of Samuel and their habit of visiting Shiloh to worship the Lord. In 1 Sam 1:1–3a, the background for the story of Samuel is mentioned by giving elaborate details of the background of his family. However, this story line is broken by the detail given by the narrator about the sons of Eli in 1 Sam 1:3b. Out of nowhere, the narrator explains who the priests in Shiloh are in 1 Sam 1:3b. This seemingly unconnected mention of the names of Eli's son will play a much bigger role in the course of the narration. After 3b, from v. 4 onwards until 2:11, the birth of Samuel is presented in quite detail. After 2:11, the narrator breaks the story of Samuel again and gives detailed illustrations on how Eli's sons behave badly in the altar of the Lord. From 2:12–17, the narrator shows how evil Eli's sons are and what they do at the altar. They demand raw meat from those who came to sacrifice at the altar rather than just accepting the boiling meat. Their extortion is narrated by author quoting their own words which say, *"but you shall give it to me now; and if not, I will take it by force"* (1 Sam 2:16).

Comparison of Samuel with Eli's Sons in 1 Sam 1 & 2

1 Sam 1:1-3a: Story of Samuel's Parents

1 Sam 1:3b: Introduction to Eli's Sons

1 Sam 1:4-2:11: The Birth of Samuel and the Dedication of Samuel

1 Sam 2:12-17: The Evilness of Eli's Sons

1 Sam 2:18-21: Samuel's Ministry and His Family's Visit

1 Sam 2:22-25: Another Mention of Evilness of Eli's Sons and Eli's Rebuke

1 Sam 2:26: Samuel's Faithfulness

1 Sam 2:27-34: Prophecy against Eli's Sons

1 Sam 2:35: Prophecy for Samuel

1 Sam 2:36: Prophecy about Samuel and Eli's Sons Combined

After the narration of the story of Eli's sons in 2:12–17, the narrator proceeds to narrate the story of Samuel from vv. 18–21. 2:18–25 shows how Samuel began to minister to the Lord in Shiloh. In addition, two verses in this passage are quite important: v. 17 and v. 21. 1 Sam 2:17 gives the summary of portion 2:12–17 and v. 21 gives summary of the portion 2:18–21.

¹² Now the sons of Eli were worthless men; they did not know the Lord ¹³ and the custom of the priests with the people. When any man was offering a sacrifice, the priest's servant would come while the meat was boiling, with a three-pronged fork in his hand.

¹⁴ Then he would thrust it into the pan, or kettle, or caldron, or pot; all that the fork brought up the priest would take for himself. Thus, they did in Shiloh to all the Israelites who came there.

¹⁵ Also, before they burned the fat, the priest's servant would come and say to the man who was sacrificing, 'Give the priest meat for roasting, as he will not take boiled meat from you, only raw.'

¹⁶ And if the man said to him, 'They must surely burn the fat first, and then take as much as you desire,' then he would say, 'No, but you shall give *it to me* now; and if not, I will take it by force.'

¹⁷ *Thus the sin of the young men was very great before the Lord, for the men despised the offering of the Lord.*

¹⁸ Now Samuel was ministering before the Lord, *as* a boy wearing a linen ephod.

¹⁹ And his mother would make him a little robe and bring it to him from year to year when she would come up with her husband to offer the yearly sacrifice.

²⁰ Then Eli would bless Elkanah and his wife and say, 'May the Lord give you children from this woman in place of the one she dedicated to the Lord.' And they went to their own home.

²¹ *And the Lord visited Hannah; and she conceived and gave birth to three sons and two daughters. And the boy Samuel grew before the Lord.*

(1Sam 2:12-21)

While v. 17 gives the summary of the life of Eli's sons, v. 21 gives the summary of the life of Samuel. While v. 17 gives a negative report of Eli's sons v. 21 gives a positive report of Samuel. In v. 17 the narrator says, *"Thus the sin of the young men was very great before the Lord, for the men despised the offering of the Lord."* In contrast to this, in v. 21, the narrator says, *"And the boy Samuel grew before the Lord."* The interesting thing here is that when Eli's sons are identified as doing evil before the Lord, Samuel is mentioned as growing before the Lord favorably. The comparison of these three people gets heightened in the next few verses.

After the mention of Samuel's growth in 2:18-21, the narrator goes on to explain more about the sons of Eli in 2:22-25. In vv. 22-25, the narrator shows how Eli's sons "lay with the women who served at the doorway of the tent of meeting" and how Eli rebukes them (1 Sam 2:22). However, the narrator does not mention the reply of the sons of Eli which indicates the un-repentance of the sons. After that the narrator further shows the evilness done by the sons of Eli in 2:22–25. After that, the narrator goes back to tell a little bit of the story of Samuel in v. 26. In 2:26, the character of Samuel as a boy is described as *"growing in stature and in favor both with the Lord and with men"* (1 Sam 2:26). Interestingly, the narrator need not have provided this detail in this particular place. He could have placed it immediately after v. 21. Why did he purposely keep this detail in this place sandwiched between the details of the story of the sons of Eli in 1 Sam 2:22–25 and 27–34?

In 1 Sam 2:27–34, the author shows how the man of God prophesied against the sons of Eli. Here, both God and the man of God are not in favor of Eli's sons, but, the previous verse, v. 26 tells the readers that God and the men were in favor of Samuel. While Eli's sons lose the favor of God and men, Samuel is shown rising to his post of the judge. The narrator carefully intertwines these two stories to show the decline of the power of Eli's sons, and the ascension of Samuel to the power in the tent of meeting at Shiloh. After the man of God prophesied about Eli's sons in 1 Sam 2:27–34, he also prophesied about Samuel, which brings the comparative characterization to a climax, in 1 Sam 2:36. Here, both these characterizations are tied-up together in a prophecy saying the sons of Eli and their sons will come to Samuel for priestly offices and a piece of bread. Thus, the stories of Samuel and the sons of Eli are kept intertwined to bring out the characterization of Samuel. Samuel's goodness and faithfulness are kept in contrast with the faithlessness and sinfulness of Eli's sons. The extortion and abuse of power of Eli's sons are displayed in contrast to the submission and obedience of Samuel to Eli in ch. 3. The sons of Eli play as foil to Samuel, who is the hero of the book, Samuel(s). In order to bring out the good qualities of Samuel the narrator tells the stories of Eli's sons in such a way that when they are compared, the goodness and greatness of Samuel comes to the fore. This is a beautiful example for comparative characterization in the story of Samuel.

4.3.2.2 David and Saul

The next example comes from the story of Saul and David. Robert D. Bergen points out that the narrator of 1st and 2nd Samuel uses the literary technique of characterization "with unmatched skill" to characterize Samuel, Saul, and David.[23] Even before introducing the character of David, the author already subtly compares him with Saul. "The story of David," Robert Alter says, "cannot be separated from the story of the man he displaces."[24] When Sam-

---

23. Bergen, *First, Second Samuel*, 34.
24. Alter, *The David Story*, xix.

uel went to see Jesse, Jesse made his seven sons pass before Samuel. The first of them was Eliab. When Eliab passed before Samuel, Samuel said, *"surely the Lord's anointed is before him"* (1 Sam 16:6). In reply, God says to Samuel, *"Do not look on his appearance or on the height of his stature, because I have rejected him"* (1 Sam 16:7). Two words in this verse are crucial: "height" and "rejected." Both of these words are associated with Saul. Saul was described as the one who was *"taller than any of the people"* of Israel in 1 Sam 9:2. The idea of height is associated with Saul.[25] In addition, in 1 Sam 15:23 Samuel told Saul, *"you have rejected the word of the Lord, He has also rejected you from being king."* Here, clearly the word 'rejected' is associated with Saul. It is repeated twice in this verse and also twice in v. 26 of the same chapter. Thus, the mere repetition of these words associated with Saul is kept purposefully with Eliab so that the author can introduce David in a grand manner in the same chapter.

In 1 Sam 16:11, David is shown as the faithful shepherd. Even when all his brothers went to the sacrifice done by Samuel he faithfully tended his sheep. However, Saul would go after the lost donkeys (1 Sam 9:3–21). In addition, Saul would sacrifice even before Samuel, the Seer arrived. Saul was rejected but David was the man after his own heart (1 Sam 13:14). Bergen says,

> [The plot] revolving around the character of Saul also supports and enhances the story of David. His primary function is that of a foil, providing a vivid contrast between his own life and that of David. Saul is first portrayed as a bad shepherd; David a faithful shepherd; Saul is a king such as the nations have; David is a king after Yahweh's heart; Saul disobeys the Lord repeatedly throughout his career; David only once; When confronted Saul confesses his sin only begrudgingly; David without hesitation.[26]

Borgman says, "As a foil to David, Saul serves implicitly as a significant introduction to David."[27]

When Goliath came in front of Saul and all Israel, and called out to them for one-on-one battle, the author mentions that *"they were dismayed and greatly afraid"* (1 Sam 17:11). The author says, Saul was "greatly afraid" when he heard Goliath's voice. However, when David heard this, he was

---

25. Bergen, in *First, Second Samuel*, points out an interesting point. He says, the characterization of being tall in the Old Testament is usually used to describe non-covenant people. And Saul was depicted as a tall man, like that of the non-covenant people (Bergen, *First, Second Samuel*, 35).

26. Ibid., 34.

27. Borgman, *David, Saul, and God*, 5.

furious and was ready to kill Goliath saying, *"For who is this uncircumcised Philistine, that he should taunt the armies of the living God?"* (1 Sam 17:26). When Saul hid himself from Goliath, David is depicted as the one who courageously went forward and killed him. David is shown by the author as the valiant warrior who single-handedly killed Goliath while Saul hid in his tents. When he returned from killing the Philistine, the narrator puts these words in the mouth of the women who sang, which again shows his comparative characterization, *"Saul has slain his thousands, And David his ten thousands."* (1 Sam 18:7). This is one of the clear comparative characterizations of Saul and David. Saul is compared by the narrator and so by the women of Israel that David is better at killing than Saul. However, this statement only makes things worse for David. Saul gets jealous of David, even to the point of trying to kill him.

Furthermore, the comparative characterization of David with Saul heightens by the narrator's characterization of Saul and David further in the story. Saul was possessed by an evil Spirit while David was instrumental in releasing him from the evil spirit by playing his harp. When possessed by the evil spirit, Saul tried to kill David by trying to pin him to the wall twice (1 Sam 18:11) while David tried to heal Saul from the evil spirit. In this story, in I Sam 18:10, the author shows that *"David was playing the harp with his hand [to heal Saul], as usual; and a spear was in Saul's hand."* David had the harp in his hands while Saul had a spear in his hand. בְּיָד (in the hand of) plays an important role in the characterization of Saul and David. What David held in his hand is used to heal Saul but what Saul held in his hand was intended to kill David. A clear comparative characterization comes to the fore by the use of בְּיָד in 1 Sam 18:10. In the very next verse the narrator uses another comparative characterization saying, *"for the Lord was with him [David] but had departed from Saul"* (1 Sam 18:12). This comparison is a put down for Saul while it uplifts David, the same way the narrator did with story of Samuel in comparing him with Eli's sons. In 1 Sam 19:9–10, a similar story is told where David was playing the harp while Saul tried to pin him with the spear in his hands.

In 1 Sam 24:1–10, we see Saul pursuing David to kill him in Engedi, near the Rocks of the Wild Goats. While Saul was in pursuit of David in the woods he went into a cave to relieve himself. In 24:4, the narrator shows the words of the men of David saying, *"Behold, this is the day of which the Lord said to you, 'Behold; I am about to give your enemy into your hand, and you shall do to him as it seems good to you'"* (1 Sam 24:4). Immediately after this the readers are shown that David goes out to get Saul. However, he does not kill Saul. While Saul was trying hard to kill David, David only cuts the end of Saul's robe and so spares the life of his opponent. When Saul was shown as the who tries hard to kill David, the narrator shows David as a gracious man who lets Saul live. This comparative characterization puts David on a morally higher ground than Saul. This comparison is even heightened in 1 Sam 24:6 where David says to Saul, *"Far be it from me because of the Lord that I should do this thing to my lord, the Lord's anointed, to stretch out my hand against him, since he is the Lord's anointed."* When Saul was desperately trying to kill David, the Lord's next anointed king, David says he should not have even cut the robes of Saul because he was the Lord's anointed. When Saul's conscience does not trouble him for trying to kill David, the narrator shows in 23:5 that *"David's conscience bothered him because he had cut off the edge of Saul's robe."* In 23:7, the narrator shows that not only did David not kill Saul but he insisted that his men not lay a hand on him. Even when Saul kills all the priests who helped David and all the families with them, David commands his men not to harm Saul. A beautiful comparison of characters is presented here by the narrator of 1 Samuel. To Michal, Saul addressed David as "my enemy" (1 Sam 19:17) but David called Saul "my father" (1 Sam 24:11). This comparative characterization comes to the climax when Saul himself acknowledges to David that *"You are more righteous than I; for you have dealt well with me, while I have dealt wickedly with you"* (1 Sam 24:17). The narrator presents this so beautifully in the words of Saul himself acknowledging that David is a better king than him. This is comparative characterization to the fullest.

In 1 Sam 26, again the narrator shows another event of Saul pursuing David to kill him in the hills of Hachila. David, in the middle of the night, with Abishai goes down to Saul's camp. While Saul and his men are in deep sleep Abishai says to David that he would pin Saul with his spear in one stroke (1 Sam 26:8). However, David is shown by the author as the one saying, *"Do not destroy him, for who can stretch out his hand against the Lord's anointed and be without guilt?"* (1 Sam 26:9). This is Saul whom David was talking about. This Saul came back to kill David even after promising that he would never try to kill him again, in chapter 24. The same Saul is now after David. Nonetheless, David says that he would not kill him because he (Saul) was Lord's anointed. Repeatedly David is shown as a man fearing God and God's anointed while Saul is repeatedly characterized as the one who has no regard for God and God's anointed. David took the spear and the jug of water from beside Saul's head (1 Sam 26:12) but spared Saul's life. Here again, David is characterized as the one who fears God and his anointed, while Saul was trying hard to kill David. The narrator purposefully put these two characters in comparison to show the goodness of David. Thus, the character of Saul plays a foil to show the goodness of David repeatedly.[28]

The courageousness of David is highlighted by Saul's inability to kill Goliath even though he was king. David, though a small boy, small enough that he was not even able to wear the armor, killed Goliath, while Saul was hiding in his tents. The faithfulness of David to his master is repeatedly shown by his acts of not killing Saul, though the latter was handed over to him by the Lord several times. David's faithfulness and kindness is shown by him being compared with Saul who was ruthlessly pursuing David to kill him. Saul pursuing David inorder to kill him and even killing all those who help him is shown, so that David's letting Saul live will be highlighted and that David will emerge as a kind and faithful leader of Israel. Thus, the author purposefully downplays the role of Saul to show the goodness and greatness of David.

Borgman says, "Both Saul and David are afraid in the seemingly unending chase. Both use or refrain from using sword and spear, with differences that tell much about the narrator's characterization of each. The increasing narrative delineation of differences between Saul and David add us to an increased clarity about David through his foil, Saul."[29] Two times David could have killed Saul but he refrained from it. However, Saul tried to kill David sixteen times.[30] This shows Saul's function in the story as a foil to David. This shows the comparative characterization of these characters. Borgman says that "the writer [of Samuels] brings together differing and perhaps contradicting sources to produce a story of Saul that is coherent and compelling, even as it serves as a foil to David's story."[31] Borgman identifies that the selection of the narrator to show Saul in a particular way is dominated by the fact that he must be placed as the foil to David. This comparison in characterization is vital to understand the two main characters of Samuels, Saul and David. Saul is not just a bad king, but he is bad in relation to David. Borgman says, "Saul's story cannot be separated from David's story. God's first choice, Saul proves a complex foil for God's second try, David. Understanding the narrative contrast between Saul and David provides a window on the initiating and responding nature of this story's God. By noting what is missing from Saul's character, we are better prepared for what God might be looking for in King Saul's replacement."[32]

28. Ibid., 51.
29. Ibid., 76.
30. Bergen, *First, Second Samuel*, 35.
31. Borgman, *David, Saul, and God*, 71.
32. Ibid., 18.

Bergen further says, "To create a foil to David, the writer carefully chose details from the life of Saul that emphasized his identity as a king 'such as all the other nations have'—that is, a king unfit to lead the Israelites. From the opening image through the depiction of his death, Saul is shown to be one who was alien to the practices and values of proper Israelite culture."[33] Thus, comparative characterization enables the readers to see the goodness and greatness of David which could only be highlighted to this optimum level by comparing him with Saul. Therefore, comparative characterization is frequently used in the Old Testament, as the writer of Samuels brings out the best of this method.

Therefore, the stories of Cain and Abel, Samuel and Eli's sons, Saul and David illustrate the importance of comparative characterization. In this subtitle we saw how comparative characterization is used in the Old Testament. Now we turn to how comparisons are used in Greco-Roman literature.

4.3.3 Comparisons in Greco-Roman Literature

Comparison is widely used in Greek and Latin literature. Christopher Forbes says that the Greek or Latin students in antiquity, when asked to prepare a piece for presentation, usually would prepare a speech including comparisons. Forbes says, "alongside retelling a well-known fable or historical narrative, confirming or retelling the truth of a fable or a story, arguing the truth or falsehood of a moral generalization, and writing an encomium of a famous person, the student might well be asked to prepare a σύγκρισις (synkrisis), a speech of comparison."[34] As they moved on to higher education they would study other preliminary exercises such as προγυμνάσματα (progymnasmata), which is a "formalized elementary curricula for rhetorical education."[35] The use of προγυμνάσματα in school education is mentioned in *Rhetoric to Alexander* (1436a25), from the fourth century B.C. In addition, Forbes argues that it remained the same way throughout antiquity.[36] It means, most of the writers of the New Testament would have gotten acquainted with this method of the use of comparison, σύγκρισις.

Speeches in Greco-Roman world involved "amplification" (αὔξησις). In the *Rhetoric to Alexander*, the amplification in encomium, the praise speech, is explained as follows:

33. Bergen, *First, Second Samuel*, 35.
34. Forbes, "Paul and Rhetorical Comparison," 134.
35. Ibid., 134.
36. Ibid., 134.

> The eulogistic species of oratory consists, to put it briefly, in the amplification of creditable purposes and actions and speeches and the attribution of qualities that do not exist, while the vituperative species is the opposite, the minimization of creditable qualities and the amplification of discreditable ones. Praiseworthy things are those that are just, lawful, expedient noble, pleasant and easy to accomplish . . .
>
> First, you must show, as I lately explained, that the actions of the person in question have produced many bad, or good results. This is one method of amplification. A second method is to produce judgment—a favourable one if you are praising, an unfavourable one if you are blaming—and then set your own statement beside it and compare them [παραβάλλειν] with one another, enlarging on the strongest points of your own case appear a strong one. A third way is to set in comparison [ἀντιπαραβάλλειν] with the thing you are saying the smallest things that fall into the same class, for thus your case will appear magnified, just as men of medium height appear taller when standing by the side of men shorter than themselves . . . One must also argue one's case by employing comparison [συμβιβάζειν], and amplify it by building it up one point on another, as follows: It is probable that anyone who looks after his friends, also honours his parents; and anyone who honours his parents will also wish to befit his own country. (*Rhetoric to Alexander*, 1425b3–7)[37]

In this long quote, it is mentioned that there are two ways of amplification. The first one just gives details of a person whose actions have given good results or bad results. However, in the second method, a comparison is required to highlight what a person wants to highlight in a praise speech. In giving different methods of amplification (αὔξησις), Airstotle says:"You must compare him (the one who is your subject, συνκρίνειν) with illustrious personages, for this affords grounds for amplification, and is noble, if he can be proved better than men of worth . . . if you cannot compare him with illustrious personages, you must compare him [παραβάλλειν] with ordinary persons, since superiority is thought to indicate virtue" (Aristotle, *Rhet.* 1.9.38, 1368a).[38] Forbes identifies that Quintilian gives *comparatio* a central role in amplification.[39] For Quintilian says, "I consider . . . that there are four

---

37. Following the Translation of Forbes. Forbes, "Paul and Rhetorical Comparison," 134–171.

38. Following the Translation of Forbes. Forbes, "Paul and Rhetorical Comparison," 134–171.

39. Forbes, "Paul and Rhetorical Comparison," 144.

principal methods of amplification: augmentation, comparison, reasoning and accumulation" (Quintilian, *Inst.* 8.4.3). The placement of comparison in the amplification shows the important place of comparison in a speech. Thus, comparison plays a vital role in amplification. Amplification is central to rhetoric. Comparison is an important part of amplification. Thus, comparison is a vital part of rhetoric.

Cicero, then, describes how to compare in much detail in *Topica* 18.68–71 and 84–85. Here he gives detailed instructions on how to compare as follows:

> Comparison is made between things which are greater, or less or equal. And in this connection the following things are considered: quantity, quality, value, and also a particular relation to certain things.
>
> Things will be compared in respect to quantity as follows: more "good" are preferred to fewer, fewer evils to more, goods which last for a long time to those of shorter duration, those which are distributed far and wide to those which are confined to narrow limits, those from which more goods are generated, and those which more people imitate and produce.
>
> In comparing things in respect to their quality we prefer those which are to be sought for their own sake to those which are desired because they make something else possible; also we prefer innate and natural qualities to acquired and adventitious ones, what is pure to what is defiled, the pleasant to the less pleasant, what is honourable to what is profitable itself, the easy task to the difficult, the necessary to the unnecessary, our own good to that of others, things that are rare to those that are common, desirable things to those which you can easily do without, the perfect to the incomplete, the whole to its parts, reasonable actions to those devoid of reason, voluntary to necessary acts, animate things to inanimate objects, the natural to the unnatural, that which is artistic to that which is not.
>
> In regard to value, distinctions are drawn in comparisons as follows: An efficient cause if weightier than one that is not; things which are sufficient in themselves are better than those that require help from others; we prefer what is in our own power to what is in the power of others; the stable to uncertain; what cannot be taken from us to that which can.
>
> Relation to other things is of this nature: the interests of leading citizens are of more importance than those of the rest; a similar value attaches to things that are pleasanter, that are approved by the majority, or are praised by all virtuous men. And

> just as these are the things which in a comparison are regarded
> as better, so the opposites of these are regarded as worse.
>
> When equals are compared there is no superiority or inferiority; everything is on the same plane. But here are many things which are compared because of their very equality. The argument runs something like this: If helping one's fellow-citizens with advice and giving them active assistance are to be regarded as equally praiseworthy, then those who give advice and those who defend ought to receive equal glory. But the first statement is true, therefore the conclusion is also . . .
>
> When the question is about the nature of anything, it is put either simply or by comparison; simply as in the question: Should one seek glory?—by comparison as: Is glory to be preferred to riches? . . . One might ask whether eloquence or jurisprudence is more valuable. (Cicero, *Topica* 18.68–71 and 84–85)[40]

Cicero, thus, gives detailed description on how to compare and what to compare with and for what one should compare. These details of comparisons are to be followed by the students so that they are able to accomplish their rhetorical task better.

Aelius Theon, in his *progrymnasmata*, the rhetorical teaching material from the late first century CE, gives a detailed discussion on how to do comparison:

> Comparison is a form of speech which contrasts the better and the worse. Comparisons are drawn between people and between things: between people, for example Ajax and Odysseus; between things, for example, wisdom and courage. When one distinguishes between people, one takes into consideration their acts, but if there is anything else of merit about them, then the one method would suffice for both.
>
> First, it should be noted that comparisons are not drawn between things which are vastly different from each other. It would be ridiculous to debate whether Achilles is more courageous than Thersites. Like things should be considered, things over which there can be disagreement as to whether a position should be taken up, because of the impossibility of distinguishing any pre-eminence of the one over the other.
>
> In the comparison of people, one firstly juxtaposes their status, education, offspring, positions held, prestige, and physique;

---

40. Following the Translation of Forbes. Forbes, "Paul and Rhetorical Comparison," 134–171.

if there is any other physical matter, or external merit, it should be stated beforehand in the material for the encomia.

Next one compares actions, preferring the finer ones and those responsible for more numerous and greater benefits; those which are more stable and durable; those which were especially opportune; those for which the failure to perform them would have resulted in the occurrence of great injury; those performed out of choice rather than of necessity or chance; and those performed by the few rather than the many. Commonplace and hackneyed things should not be singled out for praise. One should refer to those things done with effort rather than ease, and things done after the appropriate age and opportunity rather than those performed when the possibility was there.[41]

Though this *progymnasmata* is written at the end of the first century, the information it gives about the comparison is quite important for the understanding of the use of comparison in Greco-Roman literature. Quintilian explains how to use comparison in early stages of a student's educational development: "From this [narratives, and their confirmation and refutation] our pupil will begin to proceed to more important themes, such as the praise of famous men and the denunciation of the wicked . . . It is but a step from this to practice in the comparison of the respective merits of two characters" (Quintilian, *Inst.* 2.4.20). This shows that comparison is kept at a higher level of education than the study of narratives or praise speech. Forbes identifies that these kinds of comparison are not just school exercises.[42] Students are asked to practice comparison because "various kinds of comparisons had to be written" in their real lives.[43] Comparison was present everywhere. Comparison was indeed used so widely that students were required to study and apply it in their schooling.

4.3.4 Comparison in Rhetoric

There are three species of rhetoric through which all discourses may be classified. Aristotle points out that "there are three divisions of oratory: (1) political, (2) forensic, and (3) the ceremonial oratory of display" (Aristotle, *Rhet.*, I.3.7). For Aristotle, the *deliberative* or *political* is about a future event,

---

41. R. J. Mortley, *Rhetores Graeci* (trans. L. Spengel; 3 vols.; Frankfurt: Minerva, 1966) 2:112–115.

42. Forbes, "Paul and Rhetorical Comparison," 138.

43. Ibid., 138.

while *forensic* or *judicial* is about a past event, while the *ceremonial* or *epideictic* is about a present event. He explains this in this manner:

> Political speaking urges us either to do or not to do something: one of these two courses is always taken by private counselors, as well as by men who address public assemblies. Forensic speaking either attacks or defends somebody: one or other of these two things must always be done by the parties in a case. The ceremonial oratory of display either praises or censures somebody. These three kinds of rhetoric refer to three different kinds of time. The political orator is concerned with the future: it is about things to be done hereafter that he advises, for or against. The party in a case at law is concerned with the past; one man accuses the other, and the other defends himself, with reference to things already done. The ceremonial orator is, properly speaking, concerned with the present, since all men praise or blame in view of the state of things existing at the time, though they often find it useful also to recall the past and to make guesses at the future. (Aristotle, *Rhet.*, I.3.8–20)[44]

Interestingly, comparison is found to be used in all these three kinds of rhetoric. Though epideictic rhetoric commands most of the comparisons present due to the nature of praise speeches, which require comparisons, other kinds of rhetoric also have been found to have used comparison.

In many occasions, the synkrisis (comparison) is recommended to be used in encomium, praise speech like that of epideictic or ceremonial rhetoric. However, it is also recommended to be used in "deliberative" rhetoric and also "judicial" rhetoric. The epideictic rhetoric usually uses synkrisis in extant. Menander Rhetor who writes from the third Century CE., gives an elaborate description on how to use comparison [synkrisis] in epideictic rhetoric as follows: "Add also a comparison [συνκρίσις] to each of the main heads, comparing nature with nature, upbringing with upbringing, education with education, etc, looking out also examples of Roman Emperors or generals or the most famous of the Greeks" (Menander Rhetor, *II*. 372.20ff). After describing how the student must compare the virtues of the one compared in his *Tyche* he says,

> You should then proceed to the most complete comparison [συνκρίσις], examining his reign in comparison to preceding reigns, not disparaging them (that is bad craftsmanship) but admiring them while granting perfection to the present. You

---

44. Following the Translation of Forbes. Forbes, "Paul and Rhetorical Comparison," 134–171.

must not forget our previous proposition, namely that comparisons [συνκρίσεις] should be made under each head; these comparisons, however, will be partial . . . whereas the complete one will concern the whole subject, as when we compare the reign as a whole and in sum with another reign, e.g., the reign of Alexander with the present one. After the comparison comes the epilogue. (Menander Rhetor, *II*. 376.31–II.377.9)[45]

Cicero, who writes from first century BCE., shows the use of comparison in the "deliberative" rhetoric: "A complex case is made up of several questions, in which several inquiries are made, such as: "Should Carthage be destroyed, or handed back to Carthaginians, or should a colony be established there?" The case involves comparison [*comparatio*] when various actions are contrasted and the question is which one is more desirable to perform . . . " (Cicero, *Inv.* 1.17)[46] This is a clear example for the use of comparison in deliberative rhetoric. In order to choose what the right course of action is one must compare with other courses of actions. Quintilian, who writes in first century CE, gives another example of comparison in deliberative speech in *Inst.* III.8.33–4:

> Nor is expediency compared [*comparantur*] merely with inexpediency. At times we have to choose between two advantages courses after comparison of their respective advantages. The problem may be still more complicated, as for instance when Pompey deliberated whether to Parthia, Africa or Egypt . . . as a rule all deliberative speeches are based simply on comparison [*comparatio*], and we must consider what we shall gain and by what means, that it may be possible to form an estimate whether there is more advantage in the aims we pursue or greater disadvantage in the means we employ to that end. (Quintilian, *Inst.* III.8.33–4)[47]

Cicero is forceful in admitting that deliberative speech should also include comparisons. In his *De Partitione Oratoria*, he says, in deliberative speeches, "the question asked is not only the simple inquiry, what is honorable, what is useful, what is equitable, but it also involves comparison—what is more honorable or useful or equitable, and also what is most honorable"

---

45. Following the Translation of Forbes. Forbes, "Paul and Rhetorical Comparison," 134–171.

46. Following the Translation of Forbes. Forbes, "Paul and Rhetorical Comparison," 134–171.

47. Following the Translation of Forbes. Forbes, "Paul and Rhetorical Comparison," 134–171.

(Cicero, *Part. Or.* 66). Forbes says, "Comparison of alternatives was an important aspect of deliberative speeches, as the comparative benefits of differing policies had to be evaluated."[48]

Forbes identifies that "comparison in judicial [forensic] speeches" are used "for the prosecution or for the defense."[49] An attorney would argue that his client is better than others so as to prove the innocence of his client while he would also argue that his opponent's client is much worse than his client. Comparison is a well-known method in the forensic speeches. Thus, comparison is found in all forms of rhetoric.

4.4 Synkrisis

Synkrisis is a rhetorical methodology commonly used from the 5th century BCE onwards. In this method, a writer would present two lives, biographies of two people, kept parallel with each other. The structure of synkrisis involves a prologue, and then the comparison of two lives, and then an evaluation of one or both characters. This was called synkrisis, a comparison. This kind of comparative analysis of the characters was used to bring out the moral aspects of one character as it was compared with another. George W. M. Harrison who analysed the synkrisis of Plutarch says, "each synkrisis, as the summation of each pair of Lives, illustrates and weighs, among other things, one preeminent virtue, which might loosely be termed its 'moral focus.' If for the Pericles-Fabius Maximus book that virtue is πραότης (even tempered) (5), for Demetrius-Antony it is ἐγκράτεια (self-control) (6) and for Agesilaus-Pompey it is πιθανότης (political acumen)."[50] Synkrisis could be understood as comparison of two biographies while antithesis is a comparison of rhetorical contrast of ideas.

Synkrisis could be a comparison between characters such as Theseus and Heracles, which Menander Rhetor wrote (II.386.19), or it could be a comparison between peas-porridge and lentil soup of Meleager of Gadara, writing in the turn of first century BCE to find out which one was the worse.[51] In literature, synkrisis (comparison) was present inadvertently. Plutarch constructed the whole document called *Lives* comparing the lives of one Greek with one Roman. "The lives in question had been carefully written to prepare for the main themes of the comparison."[52] In his other

48. Forbes, "Paul and Rhetorical Comparison," 150.
49. Ibid., 150.
50. Harrison, "The Semiotics of Plutarch's Συγκρίσεις," 91–104.
51. Forbes, "Paul and Rhetorical Comparison," 135.
52. Ibid., 139.

work, "On the Fortune of Alexander" (*Mor.* 326D–345B), he deals with the question whether luck or brilliance was the reason for the greatness of Alexander. He also wrote whether land animals or aquatic animals are more brilliant in *Mor.* 959A–985C. Plutarch, "On the Virtue of Women," explains comparison as follows:

> It is impossible to learn the similarity and the difference better between the virtues of men and women from any other sources than by putting lives beside lives and actions beside actions, like great works of art, and considering whether the magnificence of Semiramis has the same character as that of Sesostris, or the intelligence of Tanaquil the same as that of Servius the King. (Plutarch, "On the Virtue of Women," *Mor.* 243)

Thus, synkrisis was a common element in the Greco-Roman literature.

Forbes says, "The verbs παραβάλλειν (*paraballein*) and συνκρίνειν (*synkrinein*) were used virtually synonymously for the process of rhetorical comparison as a means of amplification."[53] If this were true the concept of comparison was present deep in the culture and literature of the Greco-Roman people. The "literary comparison, at various levels, spoken or written, was a living feature of Greco-Roman culture, and a feature of which anyone of any formal education would have been thoroughly aware."[54] Thus, Forbes stresses that "comparison was universally accepted as a feature of ancient rhetoric."[55]

4.5 Conclusion

The above mentioned examples of comparison in Greco-Roman literature produce evidence to the prevalent practices of using comparisons in Greco-Roman literature. Comparisons, then, are also done to show one thing as better than another. Aristotle himself gives an example for this:

> Comparisons [τάς ... συγκρίσεις], then, of things with one another should be made in the manner described. The same commonplaces are useful for showing that something is simply worthy of choice or avoidance ... For sometimes, when we are actually comparing two things [σύγκρισιν], we immediately assert that each or one of them is worthy of choice, for example,

---

53. Ibid., 139.
54. Ibid., 140.
55. Ibid., 140.

when we say that one thing is naturally good and another not naturally good . . . (Aristotle, *Top.* 3.4.119a1–11).[56]

Forbes says, "Comparison, in various forms, was a topic dealt with in detail across the spectrum of rhetorical writing. It was both discussed in theory, and widely practiced. As far as the theoreticians were concerned, it was a crucial preliminary exercise, and as the student progressed it could be used to amplify material in encomium and invective."[57]

Forbes, thus, concludes that "the broad convention of rhetorical comparison was so well-known and widespread in both the rhetorical tradition and in the wider literary culture."[58] This comment of Forbes is very important. The presence of comparison is not only prevalent in rhetoric but also in other forms of literature, including narratives. If so, it is not surprising to see comparisons being used in the direct speech of Jesus in the narrative of Matt 5–7.

In the New Testament, there are several instances where comparisons are used. The comparisons usually involve a foil as mentioned above. I call this kind of characterization as comparative characterization. Recently, there are few works which identify the use of foils in the New Testament. Joel Williams identifies that minor characters in the book of Mark function as foils to the disciples.[59] Williams shows that in the passion narratives of Mark, "certain members stand in contrasts to the disciples."[60] While the disciples were hiding and denying knowing Jesus, certain people in the crowd came forward to help Jesus in the passion narratives. These characters, for Williams, play as foils to the disciples. Alan Culpepper identifies that in the book of John, the use of minor characters by the author is to bring out the various aspects of the character of Jesus so that the readers could belive in Jesus Christ.[61]

The prevalence of comparisons in Old Testament literature and in Greco-Roman literature shows the influence the comparisons would have had in the construction of the Sermon on the Mount. In addition, the presence of many comparisons in the Sermon on the Mount validates this point further. Therefore, in this study, it is assumed that, in Matt 5–7, the narrator of Matthew is using the direct speech of Jesus to characterize the ideal

---

56. Following the Translation of Forbes, "Paul and Rhetorical Comparison," 134–171.

57. Forbes, "Paul and Rhetorical Comparison," 150.

58. Ibid., 150.

59. Williams, *Other Followers of Jesus*, 33.

60. Ibid., 33.

61. Culpepper, *Anatomy of the Fourth Gospel*, 147.

disciple by showing how the disciples ought to be. These comparisons in the Sermon on the Mount show comparative characterization by which the ideal disciples is exhorted not to be like Pharisees, Scribes, hypocrites, and gentiles. Thus, I propose that comparative characterization is an instrumental methodology to interpret Matt 5–7.

4.5.1 Comparative Characterization in Praxis

In this section, we will briefly address how comparative characterization must be applied in a text. First of all, to analyze comparative characterization one must identify the comparisons in the piece of literature. The next step in this analysis of comparative characterization is to identify the foil from the protagonist. Usually the foil plays the role to bring out the concerned characteristic traits of the protagonist. Thus, by identifying the foil one must also identify the protagonist.

Comparisons usually have teleological purpose. A certain character is kept as a foil to a protagonist in order to bring out certain characteristic traits of the protagonist. Thus, by mere comparison of the foil with the protagonist there is an outcome which is to highlight certain characteristic traits of the protagonist. If so, then, comparisons are teleological and goal oriented. It means, the comparison itself functions to bring out the characteristic traits of the protagonist. Further, the third identification is to identify the characteristic traits brought forth from the protagonist through this comparison. Thus, these three identifications are important in the process of applying the analysis of comparative characterization. To reiterate, the three steps of the analysis of the comparative characterizations are: 1. Identify the comparisons; 2. Identify the foil and the protagonist; and 3. Identify the characteristic trait(s) brought forth by this comparison. All these identifications work together to identify the function of comparisons in comparative characterization. Thus, in this book all these three parts of comparative characterizations will be used to identify the comparative characterization of the ideal disciple in the Sermon on the Mount.

Chapter 5

Characterization of the Ideal Disciple in Matthew 5:1–16

5.1. Introduction

DANIEL M. DORIANI SAYS, "The Sermon on the Mount is perhaps the most beloved, the best known, the least understood and the hardest to obey."[1] This statement is not an overstatement. The complications in understanding the passage are partly due to the many comparisons the Sermon on the Mount contains. However, Doriani points out one important characteristic feature of the Sermon on the Mount. That is, its characterization of the disciple of Christ. He says, "It (the Sermon on the Mount) describes disciples in stirring terms: 'you are the salt of the earth . . . ' 'You are the light of the world . . . '"[2] The Sermon contains the direct speech of Jesus, the Messiah in 5:3—7:27. Jesus is shown here as the New Moses by Matthew by his teachings such as *"You shall . . . "* and *"You shall not. . . . "*[3] In the Sermon on the Mount, "with about fifty imperatives in roughly one hundred sentences, we certainly hear Jesus' commands. Since the king has arrived and begun to reign, Jesus' commands explain how disciples ought to live under his authority."[4]

In addition, one must notice that, the Sermon on the Mount characterizes the disciple. It describes who the disciple is (the characteristic features of a disciple), and what the disciple would do, how a disciple would behave, etc. Though these characterizations in many instances are kept in imperatives, in command forms, it evidently characterizes the disciples. Doriani says, "Even in passages that are filled with imperatives, Jesus does not simply

1. Dorinani, *The Sermon on the Mount*, 1.
2. Ibid., 1.
3. Chamblin, *Matthew*, 1:301.
4. Dorinani, *The Sermon on the Mount*, 8.

tell us what to do; he invites us to see the world as he does."⁵ Jesus then casts the vision of how the disciple must be. This, then, means Jesus characterizes the disciple. Doriani says, " . . . then, the Sermon on the Mount is law, but much more than law. It tells us what we should do, but it also describes who we are and should be. It probes our character and invites us to see the world in a new way, as Jesus sees it."⁶ Leon Morris calls this depiction of the disciple in the Sermon on the Mount as the characterization of the "servant of Christ."⁷ Donald Senior says, "Matthew's distinctive portrayal of the disciples remains most significant for understanding how the evangelist viewed the demands of Christian life."⁸ Senior further says, "Literary criticism agrees that the reader is expected to identify with the Gospel's portrayal of the disciple . . . "⁹ Thus, scholars do see the Sermon on the Mount as characterizing the ideal disciple.

The Sermon on the Mount gives shape to the ideal disciple on how he/she must live. In the beatitudes, Jesus characterizes the ideal disciples through eight beatitudes. In addition, he also describes the ideal disciple as salt and light in 5:13–16. These will be the concentrations of this chapter. Therefore, in this chapter, Matt 5:1–16 will be studied to see the characterization of the ideal disciple with special concentration on identifying the comparisons and their functions in the characterization of the ideal disciple.

5.2 Sermon on the Mount as Characterizing the Ideal Disciple

Narratives characterize characters. Likewise, New Testament characterizes disciples. Each gospel characterizes the disciple in unique ways. The characterization of the disciple takes new heights in some places where the description of the disciple is also the expected characteristic feature of the readers of the writing. For example, in the Upanishads, when a disciple is characterized as a person who obeys the master (ex. Shvetakethu in *Chhandhogya Upanishad* VI.1–14), the expected expectation of the reader of the Upanishad is that he/she, who is also the disciple of Hinduism must be like that disciple and must obey his/her master. Likewise, when the disciples are characterized in the New Testament there is a heightened expectation that the reader should also confirm to the expectations of the narrative. Thus, the

5. Ibid., 9.
6. Ibid., 9.
7. Morris, *The Gospel According to Matthew*, 56.
8. Senior, *The Gospel of Matthew*, 63.
9. Ibid., 64.

expectation in the Sermon on the Mount is that the disciple should confirm to the expectations of the narrative. Thus, when Jesus teaches his disciples to "Let your word be 'Yes, Yes' or 'No, No'" (Mat 5:37) then, it means that the reader of Matthew and the follower of Christ should also follow these expected norms of Jesus. Therefore, these expected characteristic traits of the disciple create a depiction of the ideal disciple like whom the reader of the Sermon on the Mount should also behave. Thus, the reader of the text should confirm to the expected characteristic traits of the narrated ideal disciple. The ideal disciple is the one who is characterized by Christ as the one who follows all the teachings of Jesus expounded in the Sermon on the Mount. Similar concepts are found in other literature, like in Ben Sira.

Ben Sira describes the scribe in great detail in 38:24—39:11. These details go something like this: the scribe should have leisure time (Sir 38:24); He studies the Law of the Most High (38:34); he seeks wisdom and is concerned with prophecies (Sir 39:1); he preserves sayings (v. 2); he penetrates the subtleties of parables (v. 3); he serves the great, and the rulers, and he travels to foreign lands (v. 4); he prays (v. 5); he receives the spirit of understanding from God (v. 6); Lord directs God's counsel to him (v. 7); he will glory in the Law of the Lord (v. 8); Many praise him (v. 9); Nations will speak of his wisdom (v. 10); and finally, his name will live longer (v. 11). Emmanuel Tov says, "That scribe, one might say, the *ideal scribe*, is portrayed as an expert in all areas of knowledge and administration."[10] Tov identifies that the character, the scribe, characterized by Ben Sira in Sir 38:24—39:11 is the ideal scribe. Most scholars agree that this passage, Sir 38:24—39:11 should be identified as a characterization of the ideal scribe.[11] If Ben Sira's characterization of the scribe could be called as ideal scribe then the exhorted portrayal of the disciple in the Sermon on the Mount should be considered as the characterization of the ideal disciple. Thus, the Sermon on the Mount characterizes the ideal disciple.

In its endeavor to characterize the ideal disciple the Sermon on the Mount uses comparisons. Ben Sira also used comparisons in his characterization of the ideal scribe. When the author of Ben Sira explains the ideal scribe as the one who has leisure time in Sir 38:24, he shows that this scribe is not like the others. The ideal scribe is not like the farmer (38:25–26); nor like the artisan (38:28); nor like the smith (38:28); nor like the potter (38:29–30), as all of whom spend time in their respective trade (38:31–34a),

---

10. Tov, "The Scribes of the Texts Found in the Judean Desert," 183.

11. Newson, "The Self as Symbolic Space: Constructing Identity and Community at Qumran." Arbel, *Beholders of Divine Seccrets*. Wenzel, *Ben Sira's God: Proceedings of the International Ben Sira Conference*. Wright III, "Jubilees, Sirach, and Sapiential Tradition."

and thus do not have the privileged characteristic feature as being leisure to study the Law of the Most High (38:34). To show the privileged status of being a scribe the author of Ben Sira uses comparison. This is comparative characterization. Likewise, Jesus in the Sermon on the Mount used comparisons in his characterization of the ideal disciple. Pierre Kieth identifies that Pharisees and scribes are used in comparison in the Sermon on the mount. He says, "5:20 et en 7:29 *(deux fois dans le cadre du sermon sur la Montagne, comme un élément de comparaison et associés aux scribes)*."[12] Thus, comparisons are present in the Sermon on the Mount.

Jesus begins this comparative characterization even from the beatitudes. Brigitta Stoll, when writing about comparisons in the antitheses (Matt 5:17-48) says that:

> "... *der zum Vergleich beider Gesetze bedacht wird, betrifft deren unterschiedliche Adressaten und, damit zusammenhängend, die unterschiedlichen Einstellungen der Menschen zu den Weisungen der Schrift. Häufig werden die Juden als Adressaten des Alten Gesetzes unterschieden. Die Antithesen stehen dann im Unterschied zur Praxis der Pharisäer und Schriftgelehrten.* ... *Dieser Gedankengang kann weitergeführt werden bis zu der aus der Auslegung der Seligpreisungen geläufigen Kombination der Antithesen...*"[13]

The translation is:

> "... the comparison of the two laws, concerns with their different addressees and, in that context, the different settings of the people are the directives of the Scripture. The Jews are often distinguished as addressees of the old law. Then the opposites are [to be practiced] unlike the practices of the Pharisees and the scribes.... This line of thought can be continued up to the interpretation of the Beatitudes with familiar combination of opposites... [are present]."

Thus, for Stoll, the comparisons found in the antithesis and the comparison in 5:20, ὅτι ἐὰν μὴ περισσεύσῃ ὑμῶν ἡ δικαιοσύνη πλεῖον τῶν γραμματέων καὶ Φαρισαίων, are to be traced back to the beatitudes. Thus, even the beatitudes teach how the ideal disciple should be. They should not be like the Pharisees and scribes. For Stoll says, "Dieser Gedankengang kann weitergeführt werden bis zu der aus der Auslegung der Seligpreisungen geläufigen Kombination der Antithesen..."[14] As the comparisons are found even in

---

12. Keith, "Les Citation d'Osée 6:6 dans les Oracles Sybillius," 62.
13. Stoll, *De Virtute in Virtutem*, 283.
14. Ibid., 283.

the beatitudes comparative characterization could be used even to interpret the beatitudes. Thus, comparative characterization is used in this chapter to interpret Matt 5:1–16.

In addition, Doriani says, "If we simply count verbs, the Sermon describes more than it commands."[15] Doriani adds, "The Beatitudes describe the character of a disciple and the rewards that God promises them (5:3–12)."[16] This should be considered as the main contribution of the Sermon on the Mount. It describes who the ideal disciple is. This description is characterization. The Sermon on the Mount, thus, characterizes who the ideal disciple is. This characterization is done by using beatitudes, which shows that the ideal disciple is a blessed person (Μακάριοι).

5.3 Beatitudes as Characterizing the Ideal Disciple

Beatitudes are beautiful constructions placed in the beginning of Matt 5.[17] The first clauses of the beatitudes are independent clauses, ex. Μακάριοι οἱ πτωχοὶ τῷ πνεύματι.[18] In addition, Daniel Wallace identifies that these independent clauses of the beatitudes are Asyndeton Independent Clauses (a construction "not bound together").[19] Wallace explains it this way: "Occasionally, an independent clause is *not* introduced by a conjunctive word or phrase. . . . In such cases the function of the independent clause is implied from the literary context. Asyndeton is a vivid stylistic feature that occurs often for emphasis, solemnity, or rhetorical value (staccato effect), or when there is an abrupt change in topic."[20] Here, the use of asyndeton is for the rhetorical value so that the beatitudes are structured with the clauses saying "blessed are the . . . " This beauty of the beatitudes is brought together by the "not bound together" Asyndeton Independent Clauses.

Through these clauses, Charles H. Talbert says, "Matthew 5:1–16, the first thought unit, offers a portrait of disciples together with promises and expectations."[21] Talbert identifies that in Matt 5:3–16, Jesus gives a portrait of the ideal disciple, which is characterization, "with promises and expectations" given to the ideal disciple. Thus, the Sermon on the Mount characterizes who the ideal disciple is, and who the ideal disciple is promised to be and

---

15. Dorinani, *The Sermon on the Mount*, 8.
16. Ibid., 8.
17. Croft, *Pilgrim*, 9.
18. Wallace, *Greek Grammar Beyond the Basics*, 657.
19. Ibid., 657.
20. Ibid., 657.
21. Talbert, *Matthew*, 75.

expected to be. For Talbert, in each of the beatitudes, the first clause shows the present "portrait" of the ideal disciple while the second clause shows the "promise" given to the ideal disciple.[22] Thus, for example, in the first beatitude, the first clause, Μακάριοι οἱ πτωχοὶ τῷ πνεύματι, *"Blessed are the poor in spirit"* is the "portrait" of the ideal disciple, while the second clause, ἐδίδασκεν αὐτοὺς λέγων, his *"is the kingdom of heaven"* is identified as the "promise" intended for the ideal disciple.[23] Either way, both clauses characterize the ideal disciple as the one who he/she is at present state and who he/she is promised to be according to the kingdom perspectives.[24] Douglas R. A. Hare ascertains that the kingdom of heaven in Matthew is more eschatological.[25] However, he points out that, "while God's rule in heaven was eternal, that rule was not yet fully actualizes on earth, and consequently the coming of God's kingdom on earth must be the burden of continual prayer ('Thy kingdom come,' Matt 6:10)."[26] Matthew in 24:29, 38–41, identifies that the kingdom will only be fully realized after the dissolution of life as we know it.[27] Thus, the kingdom realities are realized in this world now but the ideal disciple still has to pray for the coming of the kingdom of heaven in its fullness.[28] Thus, Hare says, "the 'poor in spirit' are 'blessed' not only because of their future participation in God's kingdom but because of their present assurance of that blessedness."[29]

F. Hauck identifies that the blessedness of the ideal disciple is characterized by Jesus' use of μακάριοι. He says, "thus the NT beatitudes often contain sacred paradoxes. This is particularly true of the striking beatitudes which obviously formed the introduction to the Sermon on the Mount in the very earliest tradition. In the impressive form of beatitudes basic statements are here made about those who may regard themselves as citizens of the kingdom of God. The power of the statements lies in their status reversal

---

22. Ibid., 75.

23. It must be noticed that the beatitudes use plural verbs and nouns to indicate the disciples. However, as a portrayal of the disciples these verbs and nouns project an image of how the ideal disciples should be. Thus, the ideal disciples are projected and portrayed by the commands and descriptions. Therefore, for practical purposes, here in this study the ideal disciple is mentioned in singular though the narratives describes the disciples in plural.

24. Hendriksen, *Exposition of the Gospel According to Matthew*, 265–266.

25. Hare, *Matthew*, 36.

26. Ibid., 37.

27. Ibid., 37.

28. Blomberg, *Matthew*, 100.

29. Hare, *Matthew*, 37.

of human value."³⁰ Thus, the use of promises shows paradoxes or comparison and contrasts from God's and kingdom values to the human value.

Therefore, the Sermon on the Mount shows comparisons in the form of contrasts in the beatitudes portraying the ideal disciple as the one who is "poor in the spirit" but also as the one who possesses "the kingdom of heaven;" as the "one who mourns" but also as the one who is "comforted"; "the meek" but also as the one who "inherits the earth"; "the hungry and thirsty for righteousness" but also as the one who is "satisfied"; "the merciful" and also the one who "receives mercy"; "the pure in heart" but also the one who "sees God"; "peace makers" but also the ones who are "sons of God"; "persecuted for the sake of righteousness" but also as the one who possesses the "kingdom of heaven" (5:3–10). One must notice here that in these comparisons Jesus is not bringing another foil to highlight the characteristic features of the disciple. In the beatitudes, Jesus uses the present state of the disciple as the foil to identify the awaiting and imbedded blessed characteristic features of the ideal disciple. Therefore, the foil is not the Pharisees, or the hypocrites or the gentiles or tax collectors as mentioned in the rest of the Sermon on the Mount. The foil, then, is the present the state of the ideal disciple. Thus, these beatitudes define the ideal disciple in both who they are at present and who they will be in the coming kingdom of heaven. These comparisons bring the characterization of the ideal disciple to another level. How the world sees the disciples is contrasted with how Jesus sees them. Who they are in this present world is compared and contrasted with who they are and who they will be in the kingdom of heaven. This use of comparisons in the characterization of the disciple is thus identified as comparative characterization.

Comparisons are used to characterize a person to highlight the characteristic traits of a character. Thus, through these comparisons, the Sermon on the Mount characterizes the ideal disciples as the one "who possesses the kingdom of heaven," who is "comforted," who shall "inherit the earth," "who shall be satisfied," "who shall receive mercy," "who shall see God," "who shall be called sons of God," etc. Doriani says, "We must see the beatitudes as a multifaceted description of a whole person. They are not seven or eight random statements about virtue. Rather, they are holistic portrait of a kingdom citizen."³¹ This is the characterization of the ideal disciple. The following subtitles will deal with this characterization in detail.

Knox Chamblin has some interesting observations regarding the beatitudes. He says,

30. Hauck, "μακάριος, μακαρίζω, μακαρισμός," *TDNT*, 5:368.
31. Doriani, *The Sermon on the Mount*, 15.

Each of the first eight beatitudes (Matt 5:2-10) consists of one sentence, in which a main clause is followed by a subordinate clause. Each main clause begins with the predicate adjective μακάριοι ('blessed'), followed by the subject, each of which includes the definite article ('the poor in spirit,' οἱ πτωχοί; 'the mourners,' πενθοῦντες, etc.). Each subordinate clause begins with the conjunction ὅτι ('for,' 'because'), followed by a pronoun in the third person ('theirs,' 'they'). The first and the eighth subordinate clauses are identical ('because theirs is the kingdom of heaven'); four of the remaining six conclude with a future passive indicative verb ('they shall be comforted,' 'they shall be satisfied,' 'they shall be treated mercifully,' 'they shall be called').[32]

He further points out that through these beatitudes Jesus portrays who the blessed ones are in the subjects of the clauses in the beatitudes.[33] Obviously the disciples are described as μακάριοι, the blessed ones in all the beatitudes. Donald A. Hagner says, μακάριοι shows "the nearly incomprehensible happiness of those who participate in the kingdom announced by Jesus."[34] If the ideal disciple is described as the blessed one with μακάριοι, more descriptions are given on who this disciple is by the use of the many adjectives and nouns as the subject of the main clauses in the beatitudes. To this now we turn.

5.3.1. Blessed are the Poor in Spirit

Matt 5:3 reads, "*Blessed are the poor in spirit, for theirs is the kingdom of heaven,*" Μακάριοι οἱ πτωχοὶ τῷ πνεύματι, ὅτι αὐτῶν ἐστιν ἡ βασιλεία τῶν οὐρανῶν. In the first beatitude, Jesus describes the ideal disciple as the 'blessed one.' In the eight beatitudes, all of them start with the plural adjective in the nominative case, μακάριοι, joined with an articular subject in nominative case. While the adjective is μακάριοι, the subjects are, οἱ πτωχοί, οἱ πενθοῦντες, οἱ πραεῖς, οἱ πεινῶντες, οἱ ἐλεήμονες, οἱ καθαροί, οἱ εἰρηνοποιοί, and οἱ δεδιωγμένοι. As μακάριοι is anarthrous it should function as the predicate while the articular nouns function as the subjects in the beatitudes. Thus, the first beatitude, Μακάριοι οἱ πτωχοὶ τῷ πνεύματι, must be translated as "The poor ones in the Spirit are blessed" (6:3). However, most translations translate the beatitude keeping the adjectives first and the subjects later such as, "Blessed are the poor in the spirit." This does not

32. Chamblin, *Matthew,* 311.
33. Ibid., 313.
34. Hagner, *Matthew 1-13,* 91.

mean that μακάριοι becomes the subject. μακάριοι functions as the predicate however, for stylistic reasons (a style followed by Matthew, where he keeps μακάριοι in the front of the phrase) and for emphasis on the blessedness of the disciple. Wallace calls this as the first predicate position of the adjectival use in relation with the noun in attributive position. He says, "The first predicate position is adjective-article-noun (e.g., ἀγαθὸς ὁ βασιλεύς = the king is good). Here, the adjective seems to be slightly more emphatic than the noun. Thus, to bring out the *force* of such a construction, one might translate ἀγαθὸς ὁ βασιλεύς as 'good is the king.' This usage is relatively common."[35] Thus, here too μακάριοι shows emphasis of the blessedness of the disciple. Thus, the ideal disciple is stressed as the blessed person in spite of the present condition he/she is in, like being "poor in spirit," "mourning," etc. The present condition of the disciple functions as the foil to highlight who this ideal disciple is in kingdom perspective.

In addition, keeping μακάριοι in the front indicates style, emphasis, and rhyme present in the Greek text. The rhyme in the beatitudes adds to the beauty with the presence of the personal pronouns in the second clauses of the beatitudes. The personal pronouns of the second clauses are αὐτῶν, αὐτοί, αὐτοί, αὐτοί, αὐτοί, and αὐτοί. Thus, the translation of the second clause of the first beatitude is "theirs is the kingdom of heaven."

The first beatitude describes the ideal disciple as the one who is 'poor in spirit.' Keener points out that "Because the oppressed poor became wholly dependent on God (Jas 2:5), some Jewish people used the title as positive religious as well as economic designation."[36] Thus, the phrase οἱ πτωχοὶ τῷ πνεύματι, could mean both economically poor and also spiritually poor. Further, Jesus describes that this "poor in spirit" as the blessed one. Further, he describes how this spiritually poor disciple is blessed by identifying that 'theirs is the kingdom of heaven,' ὅτι αὐτῶν ἐστιν ἡ βασιλεία τῶν οὐρανῶν. In the clause ὅτι αὐτῶν ἐστιν ἡ βασιλεία τῶν οὐρανῶν, ὅτι functions as causative. Consequently, the blessedness of the poor in the spirit is caused by the disciple having to possess the kingdom of heaven.[37] Thus, the stress here is that the ideal disciple is blessed because (ὅτι) he/she possesses the kingdom of heaven. David Hill says, "the poor saints will obtain what throughout life they desire, the establishment of God's reign."[38] This is the blessedness endowed on the disciple.

---

35. Wallace, *Greek Grammar*, 307–308.
36. Keener, *A Commentary on the Gospel of Matthew*, 168–169.
37. Wallace, *Greek Grammar*, 453.
38. Hill, *The Gospel of Matthew*, 111.

Interesting fact is that except for the first and the eighth beatitudes all the other beatitudes have future tense verbs. If these future tenses indicate time, then, these characterizations are future blessings awaiting the ideal disciple. For Dale C. Allison, even the other two verbs, of the first and the eighth beatitude, though in present tense are "expressions of certainty: the surety of the saints' possession of the Kingdom is underlined by use of a proleptic present."[39] Either the present tenses function as futuristic or the future tenses function as present realities one thing is clear: all these are realities for the ideal disciple. Thus, the ideal disciple will obtain all these or he has all these characteristics already. These are essential characteristic features given by God and that is how this ideal disciple is blessed. If a question may be asked 'how the ideal disciple in the Sermon on the Mount is blessed.' The answer should be through verbs like these: he will 'possess the kingdom,' 'obtain comfort,' 'inherit the earth,' 'obtain satisfaction,' 'obtain mercy,' 'see God,' 'be son (child) of God,' 'possess kingdom,' and 'have reward.' Thus, the blessedness is further characterized by these words. This is the characterization of the ideal disciple in the beatitudes.

In the first beatitude, then, though the ideal disciple is "poor in Spirit" οἱ πτωχοὶ τῷ πνεύματι (5:3a) he/she is blessed because his/her is the "kingdom of heaven," ὅτι αὐτῶν ἐστιν ἡ βασιλεία τῶν οὐρανῶν (5:3b). The disciple is the one who is "poor in spirit." τῷ πνεύματι is a dative of sphere.[40] Thus, the poor whom Jesus is talking about is the poor in the sphere of spiritual aspects. They are not economically poor as we see in Lucan portrayal (Lk 6:20) but the poor in spirit. Ernst Bammel, in *TDNT*, identifies that in οἱ πτωχοὶ τῷ πνεύματι "the emphasis is shifted from the material sphere to the spiritual and hence the religious sphere."[41]

One must notice the comparison and contrast here. The disciple is spiritually bankrupt.[42] However, he/she is the one who is identified as blessed by Jesus, Μακάριοι. Jesus shows contrast through this comparison. This contrast could be said as the contrast in reality—poor in spirit, to the future state of this ideal disciple—his is the kingdom of heaven. Otherwise, this contrast could be of different points of view of the same chronological frame, may even be of the present time.[43] That is, though the disciple seems

---

39. Allison, *The Sermon on the Mount*, 42. Wallace calls the proleptic present as futuristic present: A verb in present indicating a futuristic action. Though the verbal action is futuristic in the aspect of time, its imminence is so expected that it is portrayed in the present action. Wallace, *Greek Grammar*, 536.

40. Wallace, *Greek Grammar*, 154.

41. Ernst Bammel, "πτωχός, πτωχεία, πτωχεύω," *TDNT*, 6:904.

42. Carson, *The Sermon on the Mount*, 18.

43. Glasscock, *Matthew*, 102.

poor in spirit in the sight of others, the reality is that his is the kingdom of heaven. Both interpretations sound appealing. Jesus sets different points of view to look at the disciple. Who is this disciple then? He is the one who is poor in spirit at present, but his will be the kingdom of heaven. The reality seen by everyone is that he is poor in spirit, but in the heavenly realities, i.e., in the kingdom realities, his is the kingdom of heaven. Thus, the depiction of the disciple as the poor in spirit is kept as foil to the depiction of the disciple as the blessed person who possesses the kingdom of heaven.

According to Jesus, the spiritually bankrupt is the one who actually owns the much desired kingdom of heaven not the spiritually rich. It is not the religiously pious people (who are spiritually rich), who own the kingdom of heaven. The spiritually poor, the sinner, is the one who owns this desired kingdom of heaven. αὐτῶν indicates genitive of possession and thus it designates that the disciple possesses the kingdom of heaven, (theirs is the kingdom of heaven, αὐτῶν ἐστιν ἡ βασιλεία τῶν οὐρανῶν). Is this a subtle comparison to the religious people of Jesus' time? Was Jesus comparing the ideal disciple with the religious pious people of his time? Pharisees could be considered as some of the most pious and religious people in the time of Jesus. Could there be a subtle comparison here to the Pharisees where the ideal disciples are characterized as the ones who possess the kingdom of heaven though they are the spiritually poor? Jesus, in Matthew, in other places such as 5:20; 6:1; 6:5; and 6:16 identified that the spirituality of the Pharisees, the hypocrites, are worthless compared to the spirituality of the ideal disciple. Therefore, there is a possibility that, even here, Jesus subtly compares the Pharisees with the spiritually poor to identify that the ideal disciple, who is spiritually poor will inherit the kingdom of heaven, unlike the Pharisees.

This comparison brings irony, as the spiritually poor possessing heavenly kingdom is kept at contrast to the others, may even be against the Pharisees and scribes. This is the beauty of Jesus' communication in the Sermon on the Mount. This is the beauty Jesus creates by his choice of contrasting ideas to characterize the disciple. In this beatitude, then, Jesus describes who the ideal disciple is: he is in fact "poor in spirit" but "he is the one who possesses the kingdom of heaven," οἱ πτωχοὶ τῷ πνεύματι, ὅτι αὐτῶν ἐστιν ἡ βασιλεία τῶν οὐρανῶν (5:3). The comparisons, contrasts and irony follow through in the Sermon on the Mount.

5.3.2. Blessed are the Mourners

The second characteristic feature of the ideal disciple is that he/she is a mourner. Matt 5:4 reads, *"Blessed are those who mourn, for they will be comforted,"* μακάριοι οἱ πενθοῦντες, ὅτι αὐτοὶ παρακληθήσονται. The ideal disciple is in mourning, οἱ πενθοῦντες. Fredrick Dale Brunner advises not to add an object to the mourning too quickly as it would restrict the interpretation of the mourning to a narrowed view.[44] Robert Gundry thinks that this mourning is the disciple's lament under persecution.[45] H. Strack and P. Billerbeck suggest that this mourning is caused by God's commandments, specifically mourning over one's own sinful nature.[46] This could go well with the context of Matt 5, where Jesus deals with the commandments in quite detail. Hill suggests that "those who mourn are the oppressed and the afflicted . . . "[47] However, this mourning Jesus talks about seems to be much more complex, as this mourning of the disciple is compared and contrasted with the promise that the disciple will be "comforted," παρακληθήσονται (5:4b). Thus, the state of mourning, οἱ πενθοῦντες is kept as a foil for being comforted, παρακληθήσονται.

How will this disciple be comforted? The clause, ὅτι αὐτοὶ παρακληθήσονται is kept in passive. Who will comfort this disciple? Who is the agent of this comfort? Wallace says, "The passive is also used when *God is the obvious agent.* Many grammars call this a *divine passive* (or *theological passive*), assuming that its use was due to the Jewish aversion to using the divine name. . . . in the Beatitudes, the passive is used: 'they shall be comforted' (παρακληθήσονται [Matt 5:4]), 'they shall be filled' (χορτασθήσονται [v 6]), 'they shall receive mercy' (ἐλεηθήσονται [v 7])" (Emphasis his).[48] Thus, it is God who comforts this disciple. It is the promise mentioned here in this beatitude, God will comfort the disciple. This is the assurance of the blessedness promised to the disciple when compared with the present state of mourning.

If the promise assured for the mourners is comfort it means that the mourners are in deep need for this comfort. This, in other hand, describes what kind of mourning Jesus talks about. This is, then, a desperate mourning, which comes out of bitter situation, which is beyond the reach of the comfort in the present world or present situation. This mourning is not just the outcome of the persecutions of the present world rather, something

---

44. Brunner, *The Christbook*, 1:163.
45. Gundry, *Matthew*, 68–69.
46. Strack and Billerbeck, *Kommentar zum NT aus Talmud und Midrash*, 195.
47. Hill, *The Gospel of Matthew*, 111.
48. Wallace, *Greek Grammar*, 437.

deeper and much intense and holistic. Brunner explains it this way: "the simple fact of being heartbroken, grief-stricken, in mourning is blessed [according to Jesus Christ]. The participial form of the verb heightens the state of the experience: it is not those who once mourned and no longer do, but it is those who now mourn and, even more specifically (participially), those who are now mourning, who are now heart-broken . . . "[49] Thus, Jesus describes the ideal disciple as the one who is in mourning. It is an all inclusive, may it be for social reasons or spiritual reasons or even economical. Moreover, the ideal disciple is described as the one who mourns at present, οἱ πενθοῦντες, in the sight of the world. On the contrary, the promise laid in front of him is the indescribable satisfaction coming with comfort, ὅτι αὐτοὶ παρακληθήσονται.[50]

The comparison in Matt 5:4 could again be seen in two ways: one chronologically and the other with a different point of view. If the comparison is taken as comparison of time then we must assume that Jesus says that the ideal disciple is the one who mourns at present while he will be comforted in the near future, in the coming kingdom of heaven.[51] Another way to see is that as though both aspects of the comparison are happening at the same time but they are seen from differing point of views. It is as though the disciple may look mourning or in fact is mourning from one perspective but he is the one who is truly comforted, from the perspective of the kingdom of the heaven. The ideal disciple already has a share in the kingdom of heaven, ὅτι αὐτῶν ἐστιν ἡ βασιλεία τῶν οὐρανῶν (5:3b). While the world seems happier at present, in reality, they are the ones who must be mourning. They are not part of the kingdom of heaven and thus, they must be mourning. The mourning disciple, however, is the one who is comforted because he possesses the kingdom of heaven, ὅτι αὐτῶν ἐστιν ἡ βασιλεία τῶν οὐρανῶν. A beautiful comparison emerges by this portrayal. The comparative ideas such as mourning, οἱ πενθοῦντες and being comforted, παρακληθήσονται, lay a beautiful picture in the portrayal of the ideal disciple. He/she is mourning at present but he/she will be comforted. He/she seems mourning in front of the others in the world but he/she is the one who is truly comforted as he/she possesses the kingdom of heaven (6:3). The comparative characterization characterizes the ideal disciple as the one who mourns but he/she is the one who is truly comforted, παρακληθήσονται. The depiction of the ideal disciple offers hope and comfort for the disciple who is at present in distress and mourning, οἱ πενθοῦντες. This is the beauty of the function of a comparison.

49. Brunner, *The Christbook*, 164.
50. Ibid., 164.
51. Allison, *The Sermon on the Mount*, 46.

5.3.3 Blessed are the Meek

In the third beatitude, Jesus says *"Blessed are the meek, for they will inherit the earth,"* μακάριοι οἱ πραεῖς, ὅτι αὐτοὶ κληρονομήσουσιν τὴν γῆν (Mat 5:5). Once again Jesus uses contrasting ideas in his third beatitudes: μακάριοι οἱ πραεῖς, ὅτι αὐτοὶ κληρονομήσουσιν τὴν γῆν. His comparison is now in the present state and the future blessing which awaits this ideal disciple. κληρονομήσουσιν is a future active indicative verb. οἱ πραεῖς indicates the present condition of the disciple. In the present time the ideal disciple looks meek and gentle. However, this disciple is the one who will inherit the earth. In reality, οἱ πραεῖς, the meek people don't inherit the earth. Dominant people inherit much. To rule the earth dominating characters are essential. It is not just about the attitude but it could also be said as the existing state of affairs. The present state of the disciple of Christ might not be a dominating position. He/she may be persecuted or he/she may even be a second class citizen in the Roman Empire. He/she might not be as dominant as a Roman centurion, or a ruler, or even as a Roman citizen. However, in the world to come this disciple will be the one who inherits the whole earth. The disciple possesses the kingdom of heaven, αὐτῶν ἐστιν ἡ βασιλεία τῶν οὐρανῶν and thus, he/she will also inherit the earth, αὐτοὶ κληρονομήσουσιν τὴν γῆν.[52] Hagner suggest that inheriting the earth, κληρονομήσουσιν τὴν γῆν, should mean inheriting the land of Israel.[53] It need not be so. It could well be inheriting the whole earth in the kingdom to come.

Jesus was meek (πραΰς), when he entered Jerusalem on a donkey (21:5) but he was exalted as the king, ὁ βασιλεύς. Likewise, the disciple though meek at present will inherit the earth, in the coming kingdom of heaven. This comparison of who he/she is now and who he/she is in the light of the kingdom of heaven changes the portrayal of the ideal disciple. The ideal disciple is not just characterized by the existing realities around him. Rather, he/she is characterized by who he/she really is in the coming kingdom of heaven.[54] Brunner suggests, "In the Kingdom there will be a complete turnaround: those now on top will be on the bottom, and those now on the low will be lifted very high. All nine promises in the Beatitudes speak of the Great Reversal at the Last judgment."[55] Thus, this comparison brings forth a clearer depiction of who this ideal disciple is and who he will be in the coming kingdom of heaven. These comparisons identify the status

---

52. Ibid., 47.
53. Hill, *The Gospel of Matthew*, 111. So also Hagner, *Matthew 1–13*, 92.
54. Boring, *Matthew and Mark*, 179.
55. Brunner, *The Christbook*, 162.

CHARACTERIZATION OF THE IDEAL DISCIPLE IN MATTHEW 5:1-16   123

reversal of the ideal disciple, from a mourner to the comforted, and from a meek to the one who inherits the earth. This comparison in Matt 5:5, then, highlights that though the ideal disciple is meek, οἱ πραεῖς at present but he/she will inherit the earth, αὐτοὶ κληρονομήσουσιν τὴν γῆν.

5.3.4 Blessed are the Hungry and Thirsty for Righteousness

Matt 5:6 describes the ideal disciple as "blessed" who "hungers and thirsts for righteousness," μακάριοι οἱ πεινῶντες καὶ διψῶντες τὴν δικαιοσύνην, ὅτι αὐτοὶ χορτασθήσονται. While the first three beatitudes identify that the blessedness of the disciple depends on their second clauses, in this beatitude, the blessedness depends much on the first clause itself. In the first three beatitudes, though the disciple is characterized as "poor in spirit," οἱ πτωχοὶ τῷ πνεύματι (5:3a), "mourner," οἱ πενθοῦντες (5:4a), and "meek," οἱ πραεῖς (5:5a), he/she is also blessed because of the second clauses of their respective beatitudes which characterizes him/her as the one who possesses "the kingdom of heaven," αὐτῶν ἐστιν ἡ βασιλεία τῶν οὐρανῶν (5:3b), the one who is "comforted," αὐτοὶ παρακληθήσονται (5:4b), and that he/she will "inherit the earth," αὐτοὶ κληρονομήσουσιν τὴν γῆν (5:5b). However, in the fourth beatitude, the blessedness of the ideal disciple does not just depend on its second clause, "they shall be satisfied," ὅτι αὐτοὶ χορτασθήσονται, but on the first clause itself. Because, the characterization of the present state of the disciple as the one who is hungry and thirsty for righteousness itself demands the blessedness which awaits him/her. Wallace calls the participles, οἱ πεινῶντες καὶ διψῶντες as conditional sentences with substantival participle. He says, "There is no syntactical category of "conditional substantival participle," but the notion of condition can still be implied with substantival participles. This often follows the formula ὁ ` + participle (+ participle) + future indicative."[56] The participles οἱ πεινῶντες καὶ διψῶντες function as condition for the second clause, ὅτι αὐτοὶ χορτασθήσονται. Only when the disciple is hungry and thirsty he/she will be satisfied. This is the beauty of the comparison with conditional sentences with substantival participle.

Hill points out that δικαιοσύνη here should be considered as "life in conformity to God's will."[57] Hagner suggests that δικαιοσύνη here "means 'justice' than 'personal righteousness' . . . from the context."[58] He says, "The poor, the grieving, and the downtrodden are by definition those who long for God to act. They are the righteous who will inherit the kingdom. Yet

---

56. Wallace, *Greek Grammar,* 688.
57. Hill, *The Gospel of Matthew,* 199-200.
58. Hagner, *Matthew 1-13,* 93.

this interpretation altogether does not exclude the sense of δικαιοσύνη as personal righteousness."[59] This hunger and thirst for righteousness of the ideal disciple is promised to have fruition because he/she "will be satisfied," χορτασθήσονται. The one who is truly hungry and thirsty for righteousness will be satisfied. It means that the ideal disciple who is hungry and thirsty for righteousness will be satisfied. It means that the ideal disciple will have the righteousness he/she is thirsting after. If he/she attains this righteousness then, in the characterization, Jesus characterizes the ideal disciple as the one who truly possesses the righteousness. This could be compared with the righteousness of the hypocrites in ch.6.

In Matt 6, the hypocrites, possibly Pharisees, are identified as the ones who practice righteousness before men, by broadcasting their giving to the poor, broadcasting their piety though prayer and fasting. However, Jesus ascertains that practicing righteousness "before men," ἔμπροσθεν τῶν ἀνθρώπων (6:1) "to be honored by men," ὅπως δοξασθῶσιν ὑπὸ τῶν ἀνθρώπων (6:2), and to be "seen by men," ὅπως φανῶσιν τοῖς ἀνθρώποις (6:5), and be "noticed by men," πρὸς τὸ θεαθῆναι αὐτοῖς (6:1) would not produce righteousness. By their practicing of "righteousness before men," τὴν δικαιοσύνην ὑμῶν μὴ ποιεῖν ἔμπροσθεν τῶν ἀνθρώπων, the hypocrites receive the rewards in full by the attention they get from people, [as Jesus says, "they have received their reward in full," ἀπέχουσιν τὸν μισθὸν αὐτῶν (6:2, 5, and 16)], but not righteousness. Righteousness, practiced before men, does not produce righteousness but only attracts attention from people. Rather, true hunger and thirst for righteousness of the ideal disciple will produce true righteousness. Thus, a subtle comparison is alluded here in this beatitude by the use of the word "righteousness," δικαιοσύνη. Matt 6 debunks the practice of the righteousness of the hypocrites, the Pharisees. However, Matt 5:6 promises righteousness for the ideal disciple as he/she is sincerely hungry and thirsty for righteousness.[60] Thus, in this beatitude, the ideal disciple is compared subtly with the hypocrites. Moreover, he/she is characterized as the one who is sincerely hungry and thirsty for righteousness and thus depicted as the one who is satisfied with real righteousness. Consequently, the characterization of the ideal disciple is that he/she is the one who hungers and thirsts for righteousness in the present state and he/she is also the one who receives the true righteousness, unlike the Pharisees (6:1–17), in the kingdom perspectives.

In the first four beatitudes Jesus identified the ideal disciple as needy. Brunner calls these four beatitudes as "the Poor Beatitudes of Grace and

---

59. Ibid., 93.
60. Carson, *The Sermon on the Mount*, 23.

Faith."[61] He says, "All four inaugural Beatitudes present the blessed as persons in need: lacking in spirit, happiness, power and now righteousness. It is to these—the dispirited, the unhappy, the powerless and now the insufficiently righteous—that Jesus gives his first promises."[62] Thus, according to Brunner, in the first four beatitudes, the ideal disciple is in one way characterized as "dispirited, the unhappy, the powerless, and insufficiently righteous."[63] However, the same beatitudes describe the ideal disciple as the one who is blessed because he/she "possesses the kingdom of heaven" in spite of his/her "dispirited-ness," he/she is comforted in spite of his/her state of "mourning," he/she inherits the earth in spite of his/her "powerlessness," he/she is righteous-ed in spite of his/her "insufficiency of righteousness." Thus, these characterizations of the ideal disciple involve comparisons. Hence, these comparative characterizations bring out these complex characteristic traits of the ideal disciple.

5.3.5. Blessed are the Merciful

In Matt 5:7, Jesus gives his fifth beatitude. He says, *"Blessed are the merciful* (οἱ ἐλεήμονες), *for they shall receive mercy* (ἐλεηθήσονται)." In this beatitude, the ideal disciple is characterized as the one who should be merciful to the others. James Montgomery Boice says that the call to be merciful "describe(s) the inner character of a Christian."[64] M. Eugene Boring suggests that merciful suggests, "to concrete acts of mercy rather than merely a merciful attitude."[65] Boice describes mercy in the classical way. He says, "It is like grace in that it comes to those who don't deserve it. But mercy has the additional quality of grace being poured out on those who apart from it are miserable and pitied."[66] Jesus was portrayed as merciful in several passages in Matthew such as Matt 9:27–29; 15:22–28; 17:15–21 and 20:30–34.[67] In addition, Jesus shows that the characteristic trait of being merciful is neglected by many. In Matt 23:23 Jesus says, *"Woe to you, teachers of the law and Pharisees, you hypocrites! You give a tenth of your spices—mint, dill and cummin. But you have neglected the more important matters of the law— justice, mercy and faithfulness. You should have practiced the latter, without*

61. Brunner, *The Christbook*, 167.
62. Ibid., 167.
63. Ibid., 167.
64. Boice, *The Gospel of Matthew*, 1:76.
65. Boring, *Matthew and Mark*, 179.
66. Boice, *The Gospel of Matthew*, 76.
67. Ibid., 76.

neglecting the former." In light of this verse, in Matt 5:7, Jesus subtly identifies that the Pharisees, the hypocrites do not show mercy (ἀφήκατε... τὸ ἔλεος καὶ τὴν πίστιν) to others. Therefore, here Jesus exhorts the ideal disciple to be merciful. Garland says, "It is one of the besetting sins of the scribes and Pharisees in Matthew's story that they fail to grasp the significance of the mandate to be merciful (9:13; 12:7; 23:23)."[68] Thus, it is legitimate to assume that, in some sense, there is a comparison here. Jesus, while exhorting the ideal disciple to be merciful, in 5:7, alludes the comparison to the Pharisees who are repeatedly blamed as merciless. In Matt 9:13 and 12:7, Jesus repeatedly says to the Pharisees, "*Go and learn what this means, 'I desire mercy, not sacrifice,*'" πορευθέντες δὲ μάθετε τί ἐστιν,"Ἔλεος θέλω καὶ οὐ θυσίαν. The Pharisees and scribes did not understand the importance of being merciful. Though the hypocrites gave alms to the poor they did so ostentatiously to receive honor from people and not with sincere merciful acts (Matt 6:1–5). The word for almsgiving ἐλεημοσύνη (Mat 6:2) is showing mercy. The Sermon on the Mount characterizes the Pharisees as the ones who do not show mercy. Thus, there is a possibility that the Pharisees are kept as subtle foil here in 5:7. Therefore, the ideal disciple must then know the importance of being merciful. By being merciful, he will be shown mercy (οἱ ἐλεήμονες, ὅτι αὐτοὶ ἐλεηθήσονται 5:7b). The Pharisees and the scribes do not receive mercy as they are not merciful but they only receive rewards from people (6:1–5). Theirs is not the kingdom of heaven. However, the ideal disciple is shown mercy as his/her is the kingdom of heaven (αὐτῶν ἐστιν ἡ βασιλεία τῶν οὐρανῶν, 5:3 & 10). Thus, through this subtle comparison the fifth beatitude identifies the ideal disciple as the "one who shows mercy" (οἱ ἐλεήμονες, 5:7), and also as the one who "receives mercy" (ὅτι αὐτοὶ ἐλεηθήσονται, 5:7).

5.3.6. Blessed are the Pure in Heart

In Matt 5:8, in the sixth beatitude, Jesus describes the ideal disciple in this way: *"Blessed are the pure in heart, for they shall see God,"* μακάριοι οἱ καθαροὶ τῇ καρδίᾳ, ὅτι αὐτοὶ τὸν θεὸν ὄψονται. What does Jesus mean by οἱ καθαροὶ τῇ καρδίᾳ. The dative could be considered as dative of sphere or dative of reference.[69] If it is dative of sphere then it would mean pure in the sphere of heart. If it is dative of reference then it would mean poor with reference to heart. Who are these pure at heart (οἱ καθαροὶ τῇ καρδίᾳ)? How can one be pure in heart? Glasscock points out that, in Acts 15:9, Peter

---

68. Garland, *Reading Matthew*, 57.
69. Wallace, *Greek Grammar*, 154.

preached that God has cleansed the hearts of those who have faith in Christ. Thus, Glasscock suggests that to be pure in heart "is to be clean inwardly by faith in Christ, which was in contrast to the ceremonial, external cleansing being promoted by Israel's religionists."[70] Though this suggestion sounds very Christian it is a Lukan view mentioned in Acts. Hagner suggests that "Pure in heart refers to the condition of the inner core of a person that is, to thoughts and motivation, and hence anticipates the internalizing of the commandments by Jesus in the material that follows in the sermon."[71]

The heart, καρδία, was considered as "the center of a person's innermost being."[72] Carson says, "In biblical imagery, the heart is the center of the entire personality."[73] In addition, Matthew in 15:19 says, ἐκ γὰρ τῆς καρδίας ἐξέρχονται διαλογισμοὶ πονηροί, φόνοι, μοιχεῖαι, πορνεῖαι, κλοπαί, ψευδομαρτυρίαι, βλασφημίαι, "For out of the heart come evil thoughts, murder, adultery, sexual immorality, theft, false testimony, slander." Thus, to keep the heart pure one must keep the heart cleansed from these evil thoughts (διαλογισμοὶ πονηροί), murder (φόνοι), adultery (μοιχεῖαι), sexual immorality (πορνεῖαι), theft (κλοπαί), etc. This interpretation goes well with the context of the Sermon on the Mount, where Jesus speaks against φονεύω, murder (5:21–26), and against ἐπιθυμέω, lust (5:27–30), etc. Thus, Jesus characterizes the ideal disciple in this beatitude as the one who is pure in heart. Jesus characterizes the ideal disciple as the one who is cleansed from evil thoughts, murder, adultery, sexual immorality, theft and others. As the disciple is pure in heart, οἱ καθαροὶ τῇ καρδίᾳ, the reward for him/her in the kingdom of heaven is to see God, ὅτι αὐτοὶ τὸν θεὸν ὄψονται. Others who are not pure at heart will not see God. ὅτι in ὅτι αὐτοὶ τὸν θεὸν ὄψονται should be considered as causal or adverbial ὅτι because it shows that being pure in heart, οἱ καθαροὶ τῇ καρδίᾳ, causes the ideal disciple to see God, ὅτι αὐτοὶ τὸν θεὸν ὄψονται.[74]

Garland suggests that there is a possible comparison with the Pharisees and scribes here.[75] He says "the pure in heart contrasts with those who fix their attention only on such things as the purification of cups while ignoring the greed and filth within themselves (23:25–26)."[76] In Matt 23:25–28, Jesus

---

70. Glasscock, *Matthew*, 108.
71. Hagner, *Matthew 1–13*, 92.
72. Garland, *Reading Matthew*, 57.
73. Carson, *The Sermon on the Mount*, 26.
74. Wallace, *Greek Grammar*, 461.
75. Garland, *Reading Matthew*, 57.
76. Ibid., 57.

condemned the Pharisees and scribes as those who were only concerned with cleansing the outside of the cups. In Matt 23:25–28 Jesus says:

> [25] Woe to you, teachers of the law and Pharisees, you hypocrites! You clean the outside of the cup and dish, but inside they are full of greed and self-indulgence.
>
> [26] Blind Pharisee! First clean the inside (καθάρισον πρῶτον τὸ ἐντὸς) of the cup and dish, and then the outside also will be clean.
>
> [27] Woe to you, teachers of the law and Pharisees, you hypocrites! You are like whitewashed tombs, which look beautiful on the outside but on the inside are full of dead men's bones and everything unclean.
>
> [28] In the same way, on the outside you appear to people as righteous but on the inside you are full of hypocrisy and wickedness. (NIV)

In the context where the comparisons with the Pharisees and scribes overwhelm (Matt 5–7), the possibility of the presence of comparison is high. Jesus compares the ideal disciple with the Pharisees and scribes frequently in the Sermon on the Mount (5:20; 6:1, 2, 5, and 16). In addition, against these Pharisees, he mentioned that they do not purify their hearts (23:25). In 5:8, he exhorts the ideal disciple to be "pure in heart," οἱ καθαροὶ τῇ καρδίᾳ. Thus, the comparison is quite apparent and well deserved to be noticed. Thus, here, Jesus characterizes the ideal disciple to be "pure in heart," οἱ καθαροὶ τῇ καρδίᾳ, who cleanses his/her heart from murder, sexual immorality and others so that he/she will see God, a privilege not given to the others. Comparative characterization allows us to see the subtle comparisons present in the text.

5.3.7 Blessed are the Peacemakers

In Matt 5:9, Jesus gives his seventh beatitude: *"Blessed are the peacemakers, for they shall be called sons of God,"* μακάριοι οἱ εἰρηνοποιοί, ὅτι αὐτοὶ υἱοὶ θεοῦ κληθήσονται. In this beatitude, Jesus characterizes the disciple as the one who makes peace. It is quite ambiguous what this noun, εἰρηνοποιός (peacemaker) really means as here is the only time this noun is used in the New Testament. However, the idea of exalting the one who makes peace is quite common in Jewish literature. Ps 34:14b says "seek peace, and purse it." Mishnah text, *m. Pe'ah* 1.1 says, "There are the things whose fruits a man enjoys in this world while the capital is laid up for him in the world to come: . . . making peace between a man and his fellow." Rabbi Hillel said, "Be of the disciple of Aaron loving peace and pursuing it" (*m. 'Abot* 1:12). Thus, making peace is considered as an important virtue in Jewish literature.

Brunner identifies that this concept of peace is much more meaningful than the English meaning, peace, which could mean being without conflict. Rather, he suggests, the word εἰρηνη should mean shalom.[77] Blomberg says, "Those who work for shalom (wholeness and harmony rather than strife and discord in all aspects of life) and who reconcile others to God and each others will be called sons of God."[78] Hare points out that "the creators of shalom will deserve to be called the sons and daughters of God, because they have chosen to imitate his magnanimity."[79] Garland identifies that "Examples of peacemakers are those who would leave the altar to seek reconciliation with the one who has been offended (5:23–24; see 17:24–27; 18:15–18), those who love their enemies and pray for them (5:43–44), and those who go to those who hate them with a message of God's love because they are followers of the prince of peace."[80] Thus, the ideal disciple is characterized as the one who makes peace. He/she is called as the child <son> of God because he/she makes peace. He/she must make peace to be called as the child of God. It goes either way. Thus, this beatitude identifies the ideal disciple as the one who makes peace.

The same idea is brought forth in the rest of the chapter. The disciple should make peace before he goes to the altar for sacrifice (5:23–24). He/she should "make friends quickly" (5:25). He should love his neighbor to the point that he does not lust his wife and break the peace with him (5:28). His/her words should be 'yes' and 'yes,' and 'no' and 'no' so that he/she will not offend the peace with his neighbor (5:37). He/she should not resist an evil person to the point that he/she should show the other cheek when someone slaps on the right (5:29) so as to keep the peace with him/her. If anyone sues him/her he/she should let go of his/her coat also so that the peace could be kept (5:40). He/she should go an extra mile when someone forces him to go one mile (5:41). Above all, the ideal disciple should love even his/her enemies so that he/she would keep the peace (5:44). This is a fuller depiction of the ideal disciple that emerges taking the context of Matt 5 into consideration.[81] Brunner says, "'Peacemaking' could almost be called as theme of the fifth chapter of Matthew."[82] Thus, the ideal disciple is the one "who works out peace instead of aggression."[83]

77. Brunner, *The Christbook*, 177.
78. Blomberg, *Matthew*, 100.
79. Hare, *Matthew*, 37.
80. Garland, *Reading Matthew*, 57–58.
81. Brunner, *The Christbook*, 177.
82. Ibid., 177.
83. Glasscock, *Matthew*, 108.

5.3.8 Blessed are the Persecuted

The eighth and final beatitude is presented in two-fold. A brief account is given in Matt 5:10 and its elaboration is given in Matt 5:11-12. In Matt 5:10, Jesus mentions that the *"Blessed are those who have been persecuted for the sake of righteousness, for theirs is the kingdom of heaven,"* μακάριοι οἱ δεδιωγμένοι ἕνεκεν δικαιοσύνης, ὅτι αὐτῶν ἐστιν ἡ βασιλεία τῶν οὐρανῶν. It is an irony that the persecuted disciple, οἱ δεδιωγμένοι,[84] is the one who is identified as the blessed person. How could an afflicted person, not just any afflicted person, but a person who is afflicted for doing what is right be identified as a blessed person? It is unfair. However, this theme of identifying the persecuted 'for the sake of righteousness' as blessed is common in the Judaism of late antiquity.

Josephus narrates the story of two learned men who encouraged their disciples to tear down the golden eagle that Herod had erected in the temple. Those two died in the persecution and are identified as martyrs saying, "It was a noble deed to die for the laws of one's country; for the souls of those who came to an end attained immortality and an eternally abiding sense of felicity" (Josephus, *J. W.* 1.23.2-4 § 648-55). Rabbi Nathan who used Exodus 20:6 said this way when he reflected on the persecution in the time of Emperor Hadrian:

> "Why are you being led out to be decapitated"? "Because I circumcised my son to be an Israelite." "Why are you being led out to be burned"? "Because I read the Torah." "Why are you being led out to be crucified"? "Because I ate the unleavened bread." "Why are you getting the one hundred lashes"? "Because I performed the ceremony of the Lulab." And it says: "Those with which I was wounded in the house of my friends" (Zech 13:6). These wounds caused me to be beloved of My Father in heaven. (*Mekilta Baḥodesh* 6 to Exodus 20:6)

Thus, casting blessings on the persecuted were common in the Judaism of late antiquity. Not only these, similar to the beatitudes, Peter also mentions blessings on the disciples who are persecuted in 1 Peter 3:14 and 1 Peter 4:14:

> *But even if you should suffer for what is right, you are blessed. "Do not fear what they fear; do not be frightened."* (1 Peter 3:14)

> *If you are insulted because of the name of Christ, you are blessed, for the Spirit of glory and of God rests on you.* (1 Peter 4:14)

---

84. οἱ δεδιωγμένοι is a substantival participle. Wallace, *Greek Grammar*, 620.

Thus, casting blessings on the persecuted for the sake of righteousness is not uncommon. This exactly is what Jesus does in 5:10. He characterizes the ideal disciple as the blessed even when he goes through persecution.

Hagner suggests that "the *paradoxes* of the beatitudes reach a climax in the eighth and ninth beatitudes, in which not simply the poor and oppressed are declared to be happy, but also those who experience active persecution precisely for their righteousness."[85] Thus, characterization, here, heightens in 5:11–12 by the use of second person pronoun than just a depiction of the disciple in the third person pronouns. Jesus, who said *"Blessed are those who have been persecuted for the sake of righteousness"* in 5:10, now says *"Blessed are you when people . . . persecute you . . . because of me"* μακάριοί ἐστε ὅταν . . . διώξωσιν . . . ὑμῶν . . . ἕνεκεν ἐμοῦ. Two things must be noticed here: 1. the change in personal pronoun, ὑμῶν; 2. the cause of persecution: "for the sake of me," ἕνεκεν ἐμοῦ. Earlier, according to 5:10, the disciples were persecuted for the sake of righteousness but in 5:11 the ideal disciple is persecuted because of Jesus himself. Is Jesus referring that to follow him is to do righteousness? It could be. In anyways, Jesus characterizes the ideal disciple as the one who will be persecuted for the sake of righteousness and also for the sake of following Jesus. There is persecution. Persecution, including insults, false accusations with all kinds of evil charges laid up against the disciple, should be expected (5:11). However, in the midst of this persecution, Jesus brings another irony and contrast: χαίρετε, "Rejoice!" The disciple is exhorted to rejoice in the persecution. How could the disciple rejoice in the midst of the persecution? This is the beauty of the use of contrast and comparisons. The present state of the disciple, being persecuted is compared with his expected state, χαίρετε, "rejoicing." The disciple must rejoice because of two reasons: 1. they will have great rewards in heaven, and 2. they are equal to that of the prophets who also went through similar persecutions (5:12).

The ideal disciple is, thus, characterized as the one who will get great rewards in heaven while the Pharisees get their rewards only in earth (6:2, 5, & 16). In addition, the ideal disciple is identified as the one who is similar to the prophets of the old who also were persecuted for the sake of righteousness. Through these descriptions the ideal disciple is characterized as the one who possesses the kingdom of heaven (5:10) just like the poor in the spirit (5:3). Thus, the final beatitude characterizes the ideal disciple as the one who undergoes persecution with joy and also as the one who possesses the kingdom of heaven, according to kingdom perspective.

---

85. Hagner, *Matthew 1–13*, 92.

5.4 Salt and Light

In Matt 5:13 and 14–16, Jesus brings another set of concepts to describe the ideal disciple: he/she is salt and light. In 5:13 and 14, Jesus addresses the disciples as *"You are the salt of the earth . . . You are the light of the world,"* ὑμεῖς ἐστε τὸ ἅλας τῆς γῆς . . . ὑμεῖς ἐστε τὸ φῶς τοῦ κόσμου . . . Here, Jesus is describing the ideal disciple with the predicates such as salt and light. The characterization of the ideal disciple as salt and light are significant. Chamblin says, "nature and function are inseparable in both salt and light, the text also contains exhortations implicit (5:13b, 15) and explicit (5:16). What the disciples do discloses what they are: 'Salt salts because it is salt, and light illumines because it is light.' As salt and light are eminently useful, so can the disciples be."[86]

It is not just that salt and light are merely useful, they are essential for the existence of human being. In many ways, one cannot live without salt or light. Thus, the existence of salt and light are much needed for the society. However, more than this imagery Jesus' characterization involves another major component which Chamblin points out: that is the essence of the objects mentioned identifies who they are. That is, salt is salt because it is salty. If the salt is not salty it is of no use. Light is light because of the light it illuminates. If it does not illuminate light it will not be called as light. Thus, through this characterization Jesus wants to points out to his disciples that the ideal disciple is the one who acts as the one who he really is. If the disciple does not behave like a disciple of Jesus Christ he/she consequently and essentially is not a disciple of Christ at all. By definition, a disciple is a disciple when he/she behaves like a disciple. This idea runs through the whole Sermon on the Mount (7:14–25).

Though, until verse 12, Jesus described the ideal disciple with adjectives, from now on he is going to describe the disciple with what the disciple must do and how he must behave. Thus, how to be a disciple is going to be described by the master from verse 17 onwards. However, before this, the master must stress that the disciple is a disciple only when he behaves like a disciple, which is by obeying the commands and following the characterization of the disciple characterized in the rest of the Sermon on the Mount. Thus, the salt and light imageries stress the point that Jesus wanted his disciple to behave like the disciples, the way he characterizes them. It is time to look at functions of the salt of the earth concept first.

---

86. Chamblin, *Matthew*, 331.

5.4.1 You are the Salt of the Earth

In 5:13, Jesus says, *"You are the salt of the earth,"* ὑμεῖς ἐστε τὸ ἅλας τῆς γῆς. Until now, the characterizations of the disciple were done by the third person characterizations such as *"Blessed are the poor in spirit,"* Μακάριοι οἱ πτωχοὶ τῷ πνεύματι. However here, second person personal pronoun is used to direct the attention directly to the disciple. Brunner suggests that this use of second person narration could be an indication of the stress that now the disciples are the New Jerusalem.[87] He says, "From now on it is no longer the Torah, the temple, Jerusalem and Israel that are the salt and light of the world but it is the followers of Jesus."[88] In addition, Brunner points out that the definite article used before salt and light "mean that it is the disciples uniquely who are the world's salt and light."[89] This highlights the characterization of the ideal disciple. The ideal disciple is the salt and light of the world. In the context of Sermon on the Mount, not the Pharisees nor the scribes nor the authoritative religious leaders of Judaism of disciples' time were the salt and light of the world.

The depiction of the disciple as the salt has its function. Salt is an essential element for the survival of the human beings. Leon Morris says, salt is to be considered as an agent functions "as a preservative, as the enemy of decay, and as giving taste to food."[90] Salt has many practical purposes in the Biblical world. Chamblin gives few important uses of salt: "1. Added to Israel's sacrifices, or to a polluted spring, salt was a sign or agent of purification. 2. Salt was a desirable seasoning for food. By synecdoche 'to eat salt' meant to take a meal. 3. Salt was an effective preservative for meats, Similarly, it helped to protect a newborn child from disease. 4. Salt was used in small amounts as a fertilizer. 5. Salt could signal the covenantal bond between God and his people."[91] Glasscock identifies two essential usage of salt: seasoning and preservation.[92] He says, understanding both common uses for salt, one can understand the Lord telling "his disciples that they were to be seasoning in an otherwise tasteless word and a preservative in a decaying world."[93] This is how important the presence of salt in this earth. That is how the disciple ought to be, "the seasoning in a tasteless world"

---

87. Brunner, *The Christbook*, 189.
88. Ibid., 189.
89. Ibid., 189.
90. Morris, *The Gospel According to Matthew*, 104.
91. Chamblin, *Matthew*, 332.
92. Glasscock, *Matthew*, 111–112.
93. Ibid., 112.

and "preservative in a decaying world." Thus, the main characterization of the ideal disciple in 5:13 is that the disciple must remain a disciple so that he/she may be able to "arrest corruption and present moral decay in their world."[94] Thus, being salt of the earth means the disciples' role in the earth is essential for the survival of the earth.[95]

Brunner explains, "as salt exists for food, so disciples exist for the world."[96] He further comments, "Disciples who bring the Messiah into the world are the ones who must preserve, purify, flavor, and convict societies in history. Salt does not exist for itself. Christians should not exist for themselves. Salt's main mission is penetrating food; Christian's main mission is penetrating the earth. Salt a centimeter away from food is useless; Christians not living for people outside themselves are worthless."[97] Thus, the disciple should live for others. This idea is stressed in 5:13 in two ways. First, being the salt is described as "You are the salt *of the earth*," ὑμεῖς ἐστε τὸ ἅλας τῆς γῆς. The disciple is not just the salt but the salt of the earth. Thus, being the salt is for the earth. As salt is important for the food the disciple is important for the world he/she lives in. Second, it is mentioned that when the salt loses its saltiness *"it is no longer good for anything, except to be thrown out and trampled under foot by men,"* ἐν τίνι ἁλισθήσεται; εἰς οὐδὲν ἰσχύει ἔτι εἰ μὴ βληθὲν ἔξω καταπατεῖσθαι ὑπὸ τῶν ἀνθρώπων (5:13c & d). Therefore, the existence of the salt is in relation with its usability for the world. When the salt is deemed useless then it will be thrown out and be trampled under the foot. Thus, the main teaching in 5:13 is that the disciple must be like salt to the earth, an essential ingredient for the taste of the whole world.

While the salt analogy is used to stress it's usability to the whole world there is also one other concept that is stressed by this analogy. Salt is known for its quality, which is salty. When salt is not salty it is not salt anymore and it is not useful. As it is stressed before, the usability of the salt and the ministry of the disciple are dependent on the salt being salty, i.e., the disciple being a disciple of Jesus Christ.[98] When the disciple loses his/her core ingredient which is being a disciple then he/she is not of any use for the world anymore and thus, he/she will be thrown out and trampled.[99] Brunner calls this as "God's rejection at the final judgment."[100] Hence, "if the salt

---

94. Blomberg, *Matthew*, 102.
95. Hagner, *Matthew 1–13*, 99.
96. Brunner, *The Christbook*, 189.
97. Ibid., 189.
98. Hill, *The Gospel of Matthew*, 115.
99. Keener, *A Commentary on the Gospel of Matthew*, 172.
100. Bruner, *The Christbook*, 190.

has become tasteless, how can it be made salty again?" If a disciple stops being a disciple how can he/she be a disciple again? These questions caution the disciple to be watchful of not being a disciple.[101] The disciple should guard himself/herself so that he/she may not stop being a disciple. The only way he/she could continue to be a disciple is by following the teachings of Christ in the Sermon on the Mount. The characterization of the ideal disciple in this analogy is that the ideal disciple should confirm himself/herself continually to be the ideal disciple characterized by Jesus in the Sermon on the Mount. Keener says, "The images of salt and light evoke consideration less of what one does than of what one is."[102] Thus, the disciple should obey the words of Jesus and the will of God to remain who he/she is, a disciple. This is a challenge and a warning.[103] Because, when he/she fails it he/she will be thrown and trampled in the final judgment. The comparison here is the useless salt verses the useful salt. Saltless salt is kept as the foil to the salt. The disciple who does not confirm to the characterization of the ideal disciple is kept as foil to the true disciple. Thus, there is comparison here. Therefore, comparative characterization plays an important role here.

5.4.2 You are the Light of the World

In 5:14–16, Jesus describes the ideal disciple as light saying, *"You are the light of the World,"* ὑμεῖς ἐστε τὸ φῶς τοῦ κόσμου. This teaching on light is also characterized in two fronts: 1. the essence of light; and 2. the utility of light. It is obvious that the whole world would not function without light. That is how important this metaphor is and thus, that is how important the presence of the ideal disciple is in this world.

In addition, Jesus continues to say, *"A city set on a hill cannot be hidden; nor does anyone light a lamp and put it under a basket, but on the lampstand, and it gives light to all who are in the house,"* οὐ δύναται πόλις κρυβῆναι ἐπάνω ὄρους κειμένη· οὐδὲ καίουσιν λύχνον καὶ τιθέασιν αὐτὸν ὑπὸ τὸν μόδιον ἀλλ' ἐπὶ τὴν λυχνίαν, καὶ λάμπει πᾶσιν τοῖς ἐν τῇ οἰκίᾳ (5:14b–15). Through this analogy, Jesus identifies that light should be treated as light.[104] It should not be lit and placed under a basket. Because, the light placed under a basket will die (be put off) and will not be useful either (5:15a). Rather, the light should be placed up, on the lampstand, so that it can burn, and be light, and give light. As salt needs to be salty light also needs to be light.

101. Hill, *The Gospel of Matthew*, 115.
102. Keener, *A Commentary on the Gospel of Matthew*, 172.
103. Brunner, *The Christbook*, 190.
104. Hagner, *Matthew 1–13*, 99.

This analogy invokes an active participation from the disciple to be light. This is shown by the active verbs used in the analogy which show that the light should not be "put" under the basket, τιθέασιν αὐτὸν ὑπὸ τὸν μόδιον (5:15), but should be "put" on the lampstand ἀλλ᾽ τιθέασιν ἐπὶ τὴν λυχνίαν (5:15), so that "it *gives* light to all who are in the house." By the active participation, light remains being light by the same time it is also useful to others in the house.[105] Thus, the ideal disciple should be actively pursuing on being a disciple.

How could this disciple be of use to the others? Should he do some good works? Not by the good works. The ideal disciple is of use to the others by him being an example of the disciple. This concept is unique only to Matt 5:13–16. In other passages in the bible, the disciple is exhorted to be helpful to the others by doing good works or by spreading the Gospel. However, in 5:13–16, he is exhorted to be an example of the disciple, to be an example of the follower of Christ. Jesus says, "*. . . light shine(s) before men in such a way that they may see your good works, and glorify your Father who is in heaven,*" λαμψάτω τὸ φῶς ὑμῶν ἔμπροσθεν τῶν ἀνθρώπων, ὅπως ἴδωσιν ὑμῶν τὰ καλὰ ἔργα καὶ δοξάσωσιν τὸν πατέρα ὑμῶν τὸν ἐν τοῖς οὐρανοῖς (5:16). As the light shines before men, the disciple must be a disciple by showcasing the characteristic features of the disciples, (ὑμῶν τὰ καλὰ ἔργα, your good works, 5:16), so that the others will glorify the Father in heaven. Keener says, "But disciple cannot be content to remain the world's light in a merely theoretical sense; they must 'be what they are,' letting their light shine for their Father's honor."[106]

It is synonymous then to 5:14b which says, "*A City set on a hill cannot be hidden,*" οὐ δύναται πόλις κρυβῆναι ἐπάνω ὄρους κειμένη. Likewise, the ideal disciple cannot be hidden but will provoke others to worship the Father in heaven (5:15). Through this analogy of light, Jesus characterizes the disciple as the one who must continuously work to be the disciple, like actively placing the light on the lampstand and not under the basket. In addition, the ideal disciple is also characterized as the one who must be an example of the disciple of Christ to the others so that the others would see the qualities of the ideal disciple and in return would worship the Father in heaven. Thus, the ideal disciple is the one who constantly behaves as the disciple and also lives as an example to the others, which in itself is an evangelistic tool, as the others would see and glorify God. This is the characterization of the ideal disciple in 5:13–16: salt and light.

---

105. Hill, *The Gospel of Matthew*, 116.
106. Keener, *A Commentary on the Gospel of Matthew*, 175.

Through the use of salt and light concepts, Senior says, "Matthew views the sermon as first of all formative of the community itself and then, through the community's example and teaching, given to the world."[107] Thus, Senior identifies that the Sermon on the Mount characterizes the disciple (formative of the community) and further it teaches the world through the example of the disciple described in the Sermon on the Mount. Thus, Senior ascertains that the Sermon on the Mount characterizes the ideal disciple. The comparison here is that light kept under a basket, useless light, and the light kept on the lampstand, useful light. Disciple who is useful by his/her good works is highlighted by the comparison with the light under a basket, which is the disciple not performing good works (5:16). Thus, comparative characterization brings out the need for the disciple to be the disciple to glorify God.

5.5 Conclusion

Glasscock says, "What contrast [is the depiction of the ideal disciple in the Beatitudes] to the dead and empty religion of self-righteousness and selfish humanity that characterized the religious environment of Israel at this time."[108] Talbert says, "In the beatitudes, Jesus has provided his auditors with a portrait of disciples in both their relation to God and their relations with other humans, on the one hand, and a promise of blessings on such people, on the other hand."[109] What Talbert says is this: The beatitudes in the Sermon on the Mount characterize the disciple by giving a portrait of the disciple in his/her relation to God and other humans and the promises of blessings laid on them. Talbert also says that the beatitudes in 5:3–12, "assume that Jesus' disciples . . . resemble the portrait of 5:3–12."[110] Thus, the ideal disciple is beautifully characterized in the beatitudes, even with the use of comparisons, including contrasts and irony.

In the Sermon on the Mount, Jesus characterized the ideal disciple in comparison with who he/she is in the present world and who he/she is in the kingdom of heaven. Thus, through these comparisons in the beatitudes he portrayed the ideal disciple as the one who is "poor in the spirit" but also as the one who possesses "the kingdom of heaven"; as the "one who mourns" but also as the one who is "comforted"; "the meek" but also as the one who "inherits the earth"; the one "hungry and thirsty for righteousness"

---

107. Senior, *The Gospel of Matthew*, 104.
108. Glasscock, *Matthew*, 102.
109. Talbert, *Matthew*, 78.
110. Ibid., 78.

but as the one who is "satisfied"; "the merciful" and also the one who "receives mercy"; "the pure in heart" but also the one who "sees God"; "peace maker" but also the one who are "sons of God"; "persecuted for the sake of righteousness" but also as the one who possesses the "kingdom of heaven" (5:3–10). In addition, in 5:13–16, Jesus portrayed the ideal disciple as salt and light, the one who should continue to be a disciple by his/her obedience to the teachings of Christ. In the salt and light imagery, the comparisons are made with saltless salt with true salt, and light under a basket compared with light on the lampstand. The disciple who does good works, the will of God, is kept in comparisons with these analogies to the disciple who does not do the will of God, who is deemed useless and is only good to be thrown out. A subtle comparison to the Pharisees is in order as the Pharisees are repeatedly called as the hypocrites who do not act according to their calling. Thus, the ideal disciple should not be like the hypocrites but must be like the salt and light which stay true to their essence and in addition, be useful to the others, unlike the Pharisees who do not help the others but only themselves. Therefore, through the comparisons in salt and light imageries the ideal disciple is characterized as the one who obeys the teachings of the master mentioned in the Sermon on the Mount. Thus, in Matt 5:1–16, a round characterization of the ideal disciple is achieved. In the remaining chapters, the Sermon on the Mount's characterization of the ideal disciple using comparative characterization will be studied from the rest of the Sermon on the Mount, 5:17—7:29.

Chapter 6

Comparative Characterization in Matthew 5:17–48

6.1 Introduction

From Matt 5:1 to 5:16, Jesus described who the ideal disciple is. From 5:17 onwards Jesus describes what the ideal disciple would be like in terms of his/her actions and behavior. From 5:17 onwards, he describes the characteristic features that embody the ideal disciple. The Sermon on the Mount is placed in the beginning of the ministry of the Messiah. It shows the demands made by the Messiah, of those who follow Him. In Qumran community, there was *Rules of the Community*, which was nothing but rules and regulations of the community and rules of correct behavior required of the members of the community. That document was integral to the community's life. Likewise, Jesus, the Messiah, gives rules of the Christian community in this passage, 5:17–48.

John P. Meier rightly points out that "the composition of this whole section by Matthew out of various sources is most carefully done."[1] He continues, "Whatever be the results of the effort, Matthew is obviously attempting to make a major statement about Christ, the Law, and Christian morality."[2] Most scholars acknowledge that 5:17–20 is perhaps the most difficult passage to interpret in the Gospel.[3] Glasscock puts it this way, "to properly relate this periscope to the rest of Scripture is not simple and requires dedicated theological discipline not to err."[4]

1. Meier, *The Vision of Matthew*, 223.
2. Ibid., 223.
3. Also Hare, *Matthew*, 46.
4. Glasscock, *Matthew*, 115.

All Jewish groups used the Torah as the base to form their own doctrines. Pharisees used the whole Old Testament, Torah and Prophets. Sadducees only accepted the Torah (Pentateuch) as the authoritative Scripture, however, interpreted it for their doctrinal statements. Later rabbinic sages used the whole Old Testament along with their own oral traditions. Likewise, the Qumran community had the Teacher of Righteousness, who expounded the Torah and the Prophets. Thus, all sects of Judaism in the time of Jesus used the Old Testament scriptures for the regulations of their sects. Thus, it explains why Jesus had to give his exposition of the Torah (5:21–48), which would be the important teachings for the new community. Therefore, Matt 5:17–48 shows Jesus' allegiance to the Torah (5:17–20) and also gives Jesus' interpretation of the Torah (5:21–48) and his characterization of the ideal disciple as the one who follows the Law.

Interestingly, these expositions of the Old Testament Scriptures are kept in comparisons which are famously called antitheses. Dealing with these comparisons is quite important to identify the characterization of the ideal disciple. If these comparisons, the so-called antitheses, are considered as antithetical comparisons one must come to the conclusion that Jesus was teaching a new law and exhorting his ideal disciple to follow a new law. For example, in his saying in 5:21, *"You have heard that it is said . . . Do not murder . . . But I say to you who is angry with his brother will be subject to judgment,"* Ἠκούσατε ὅτι ἐρρέθη τοῖς ἀρχαίοις· οὐ φονεύσεις· ὃς δ' ἂν φονεύσῃ, ἔνοχος ἔσται τῇ κρίσει. The Old Testament teaching, "Do not murder," οὐ φονεύσεις is kept in comparison with Jesus' teaching 'Do not get angry.' If this is an antithetical comparison then one must assume that Jesus gave antithesis to the ideal disciple, a new law to the ideal disciple. Then his characterization of the ideal disciple would be depicting him/her as the one who obeys the new law of Jesus Christ and as the one who is an antinomian, who does not and need not obey the Old Testament Law. If these comparisons are not antithetical comparisons, then, one must assume that Jesus was characterizing the ideal disciple as the one who obeys the Old Testament Law faithfully. Thus, it is of inordinate importance in identifying the functions of the comparison to identify the characterization of the ideal disciple in the Sermon on the Mount. The following subtitles will study the functions of these comparisons in the characterization of the ideal disciple.

6.2 Characterizations in Matt 5:17–20

Before Jesus shows his portrayal of the disciple, Jesus characterizes himself in 5:17–18. Jesus starts the passage by saying *"Do not think that I came to abolish the Law or the Prophets . . .* " Μὴ νομίσητε ὅτι ἦλθον καταλῦσαι τὸν νόμον ἢ τοὺς προφήτας. ὅτι is a declarative ὅτι in the clause which introduces an indirect speech unlike the ὅτι *recitativum*, which would introduce the direct speech.[5] Through this declarative ὅτι Jesus wants to show that the others should not assume that he had come to destroy the Law and the Prophets. Jesus himself starts giving his relationship with the 'Law and the Prophets.'[6] Jesus starts the section by using μὴ νομίσητε. Wallace calls this as prohibitive subjunctive because it is used to "forbid the occurrence of an action."[7] The audience of Jesus and the readers of the Gospel should not think even in the remote subjunctive reality that Jesus came to abolish the Law. There is a comparison here. Jesus says, *"Do not think that I came to abolish the Law or the Prophets; I did not come to abolish but to fulfill,"* Μὴ νομίσητε ὅτι ἦλθον καταλῦσαι τὸν νόμον ἢ τοὺς προφήτας· οὐκ ἦλθον καταλῦσαι ἀλλὰ πληρῶσαι (Mat 5:17). Jesus compares what the readers possibly think about him with who he really is. People might think that he came to abolish the Law but the truth is that he came to fulfill the Law (ἀλλὰ πληρῶσαι).

Jesus could have simply said that 'I have come to fulfill the Law' avoiding the comparison. However, the polemic aspect of this statement is reinforced by his inclusion of the comparison. It is possible that Jesus was negating an assumption that 'Jesus abrogated the Law' as he was fighting with 'the teachers of the Law,' the Pharisees and scribes, about certain regulations in observing the Law (Matt 15:1–10, etc.). It is probably a polemic way of addressing an error which was circulating about Jesus that he was against the Law.[8] As Jesus was negating certain aspects of the (oral or added) Law (15:1–20) Jewish critics might have blamed Jesus as anti-nomian. Matthew, then, must show that his Messiah is not an anti-nomian but the one who fulfills the Law. As Matthew was writing to a predominantly Jewish congregation he has to show that their Jewish Messiah, Jesus, was not an anti-nomian but a pro-nomian. For this, the comparison plays a vital role. The comparison invites attention to the statement. It draws close attention to identify this statement of Jesus as polemic against a possible prevalent

---

5. Wallace, *Greek Grammar*, 456.

6. Usually, in the New Testament, the phrase Law and the Prophets means the whole Old Testament (Matt 5:17; 7:12; 11:13; 22:40; Luke 16:16; 24:44; John 1:45; Acts 13:15; 24:14; 28:23; Rom 3:21). However, the word writings was also mentioned in the rabbinic mention of the Old Testament though it is not mentioned that way in the New Testament but nevertheless included.

7. Wallace, *Greek Grammar*, 469.

8. Menninger, *Israel and the Church in the Gospel of Matthew*, 105.

antinomian assumption about Jesus. This is the major function of this comparison in 5:17.

The comparison is also intended to show one more thing: Jesus' view of the Law. To understand the use of the comparison in 5:17 we must also know Jesus' view of the Law. It is essential because only by knowing Jesus' view of the Law may we understand how he depicts the ideal disciple, as a Law adhering disciple or as an antinomian. To answer the question about Jesus' perspective on the Law in Matthew, Loader asks a few more interesting questions, "Did Matthew's Jesus replace the Law entirely, written and oral? Replace only parts? Replace only oral tradition? Did he differentiate within Torah? On what basis? Ethical against cultic and ritual? Decalogue against the rest? Intention against behavioral prescription"?[9] Among these questions one vital question needs to be answered and that is "Was Jesus against the Law"? Sanders asks the question, was Jesus against the Law? He further questions, whether it was because of his negative view of the Law that he was murdered?[10] While it is hard to answer the second question it is apparent from 5:17-20 that Jesus was not an antinomian. However, he certainly was against some forms of obedience to the Law which stand out at the forefront of the conflicts between Jesus and the Pharisees (Matt 15:1-10—Law+tradition; 9:10-13—Table fellowship; 12:21-29—Sabbath; 19:3-9—divorce; 22:34-40—Greatest commandment; 23:23-24—tithe; 23:25-28—ritual cleanliness, etc.). Nevertheless, this does not mean that Jesus was against the Law. Jesus was against some aspects of the interpretation of the Law.

While most scholars agree with the idea that Jesus came to fulfill the Law (v.17), and thus, he was not against the Law, they somehow explain that the Law was active only until the time of Jesus. Thus, for them, the ideal disciple need not obey the Law. Somehow, they say, Jesus fulfilled the Law, i.e., ended the Law's requirements such that they are not applicable to the disciples after Christ. Menninger shows an important aspect of this perspective about Jesus' view of the Law. He says, "The Evangelist—at least on the surface—presents a somewhat confusing (even contradictory) attitude toward the Law. Some passages reflect a staunch defense of the Law (5:17-20; 7:12; 11:13; 22:34-40) while others imply a softening of the Law (15:1-20) or even a setting aside of certain commandments of the Law (5:31-42; 12:1-14; 15:11)."[11] The important thing to ask is whether Jesus was contradicting himself? Did Jesus soften the Law? In 15:1-20 Jesus was

---

9. Loader, *Jesus' Attitude Towards the Law*, 151.
10. Sanders, *Jesus and Judaism*, 245.
11. Menninger, *Israel and the Church*, 103.

essentially negating the customs of the Pharisees of washing of the hands but not softening of the Law. In 5:31-42, Jesus does not set aside the Law but makes it *stricter* by teaching not to divorce while the Law allowed divorce (5:31-32); he made the Law stricter in saying no to swearing oaths and vows (5:33-37); he made it stricter in saying no to retribution (38-42). It is hard then to explain how Menninger would consider these things as softening or setting aside of the Law while Jesus himself says in 5:17-20 that he did not come to set aside but to fulfill.

One must remember the predominantly Jewishness of Matthew's Gospel: 1. Matthew starts his Gospel with the genealogy which starts with Abraham, the father of the Jewish nation. 2. He uses the Old Testament scriptures quite often to prove that Jesus is the promised Messiah (1:22; 2:15, 17, 23; 4:14; 8:17; 12:17; 13:14, 35; 21:4; 26:54, 56; 27:9). 3. He mentions of David in 1:1, and mentions of Jesus as the King of the Jews (2:2; 21:5; 27:11; cf. Mark 15:2; Matt 27:29; cf. Mark 15:18; Matt 27:37; cf. Mark 15:26; Matt 27:42; cf. Mark15:32). In this light we see Matthew using much material including the comparisons to portray Jesus as the Messiah of the Jews. Thus, it is understandable that he must show Jesus as the Law-abiding Jewish teacher so that the primary audience would accept Jesus as the Messiah which is one of the primary purpose of Matthew's writing. Thus, Jesus explains his relationship to the Law saying, *"I did not come to abolish, but to fulfill,"* οὐκ ἦλθον καταλῦσαι ἀλλὰ πληρῶσαι (Matt 5:17). The comparison brings the polemic aspect of this communication. The comparison sets the communication over and against Jesus' opponents' worldview—of how they saw Christ. The comparison corrects a wrong assumption of the opponents of Matthew. The comparisons clarifies that Jesus was not against the Law but the one who came to fulfill the Law.

As we try to understand the functions of the comparison in 5:17, one important aspect to consider is the word, πληρῶσαι "to fulfill." Some interpretations of this word take a unique route that it blurs the functions of the comparison. Thus, at this point brief overview of how this word is interpreted is required. Then, an interpretation of the word 'to fulfill,' relevant to the comparison will be considered.

6.2.1 The Interpretation of πληρῶσαι

Hare says that the 'central issue' in the interpretation of 5:17 is the meaning of πληρῶσαι 'to fulfill.'[12] The word πληρῶσαι has several possible interpretations. The following are a selected few:

12. Hare, *Matthew*, 46.

6.2.1.1. Richard E. Menninger

For Menninger, the verb πληρῶσαι should be understood as Christ "both completes and brings it to an end, he is both the goal and the replacement of the Law."[13] Thus, πληρῶσαι means, Christ fulfilled the Law so that the followers of Christ need not obey the Law anymore. Menninger says, "The 'Fulfiller' of the Law displaces the Law in the sense that his interpretation of God's will—not the Law itself—becomes the center and basis of ethical living in Matthew's church."[14]

Menninger says, "While the Law was adequate for the period *before* Jesus, it is inadequate for the time *of* Jesus and afterwards"[15] [Italics his]. Thus, Law somehow has been replaced. He says, "The Law was no longer the basis for God's revelation nor the central authority for community life. The teachings of the Messiah were now the 'Law.'"[16] He continues, "To replace the Law is not to destroy but instead to transcend it,"[17] because the Law contained only the partial will of God.[18] Menninger explains that the Law was not replaced by the teachings of Christ as bad with the good but as "the good with the better."[19] For Menninger, the Torah and the teachings of Jesus are quite different from each other. Menninger points out that the church looks for 'Law of God' provided by Jesus, the Messiah, while the Jewish teachers looked to the Torah for 'the Law.' He says, "While Matthew pictures Jesus' coming as fulfilling OT Law (an important point for Matthew's church), he does so in a way that includes the picture of Jesus setting aside the Law. The new age brings new understanding (9:14–17) and thus Jesus' teaching transcends the letter of the Law while penetrating its inner spirit. The teachings of Jesus (the Messianic King), especially as related to the love commandment (22:34–40), reveal the true will of God."[20] Menninger further makes an ironic statement without much support for this position. He says, "The OT, especially the Law, anticipated the day when the Messiah's teaching would set aside the Law."[21] Where in the Old Testament such a statement be found which says the Law will be replaced by the Messiah?

---

13. Menninger, *Israel and the Church*, 107.
14. Ibid., 108.
15. Ibid., 108.
16. Ibid., 114.
17. Ibid., 116.
18. Ibid., 116.
19. Ibid., 104.
20. Ibid., 104.
21. Ibid., 107.

How could Menninger repeatedly say that Jesus replaced the Law by his teachings while Jesus himself says in 5:17 that he did not come to abrogate the Law? Menninger tries to reason in this fashion: "We must avoid the position that Jesus destroys the Law because this is ruled out by 5:17; at the same time to imply that Jesus' teaching is continuous with the Law is to de-emphasize unnecessarily the radical nature of the new age."[22] Menninger comments that "the locus of God's will is now changed from the Law to the 'teachings of Christ' (i.e., the 'Law' of Christ)."[23] It provokes the question, is the Law of Christ different from the Law of the Old Testament? Does not the Torah and the Prophets give the will of God? If so, could that be set aside? Was Jesus aware of this setting aside of this 'old' will of God by his 'new' will of God?

Obviously, all these questions must be answered with 'No,' at least according to Matt 5–7. Because, Jesus' tone in Matt 5:17–48 does not show a Jesus who would set aside the Law but the one who fulfills, adheres, and abides. He interpreted the 'old' Law in 5:21–48, in light of the Messianic authority, so that it could be adhered properly. If Jesus was giving a 'new' Law why should the so called 'antitheses' be kept in a context which stresses that Jesus did not come to abolish but to fulfill? The comparison in 5:17 just stressed the obvious that Jesus did not come to abolish the Law. Only when this comparison is not taken seriously one could interpret the verb 'to fulfill' as setting aside of the old law. This shows the importance of the comparison in 5:17. Thus, is it not obvious to see that Jesus does not portray himself as an 'anti-nomian' but a 'pro-nomian,' which is quite evident from the tone of 5:17–20. If Jesus' concern was to show himself as pro-nomian is it not proper to view Jesus as one not setting aside the Law but the one who speaks for the continuity of the Law? Hill says, "we must understand this section—the so-called 'antitheses' passage—as setting forth the radical intensification of the demands of the Law. This is not an antithesis to the Mosaic Law set forth by a New Moses: it is 'a messianic intensification,' producing the true righteousness which belongs to the Kingdom."[24]

However, Menninger points out that the Law takes "second place" before Jesus' teachings. The reason he gives for it "is that much of Jesus' instruction is of independent authority and is not related directly to the Old Testament (e.g. 5:11–16; 7:28–29; 10:5ff; 13:3ff; 16:5–11, 17–20, 24–28; 18:3ff; 20:1–16, 23–28; 22:33–43; 23:1–32; 24:1–32; 24–25; 26:26–29;

---

22. Ibid., 118.
23. Ibid., 118.
24. Hill, *The Gospel of Matthew*, 199–200.

28:18ff)."[25] Yes, one must acknowledge that Jesus had a special authority which was lacking in many of the rabbinic elders of his time. The rabbis of the Tannaitic writings usually used the authority of their masters for their interpretations. However, Jesus did not use his masters' or his teachers' or the Scriptures' (in several places) as authoritative but gave his own teachings. This should be understood in light of his Messianic authority. Nevertheless, he himself assured that he was not against the Law in the comparisons in 5:17–20. If he was not against the Law how could he set aside the Law? If he had come to fulfill the Law how could he push the Law to 'the second place' and take its place.

In some ways, Jesus should be thought of as the correct interpreter of the Law rather than the one who gives a new law. It is not clear if Jesus thought of himself as a new law giver. Rather, he worked with the Law and interpreted it with his Messianic authority. These kinds of interpretations were quite natural with the Jewish teachers of his time. A few examples include Hillel and Teacher of Righteousness of the Qumran sect which will be seen in quite detail later in this chapter.

6.2.1.2. John P. Meier

John P. Meier understands the verb πληρῶσαι like the other usages of this verb in Matthew. The verb πληρῶσαι occurs sixteen times in Matthew. Meier observes that out of the sixteen times, twelve times (1:22; 2:15, 17, 23; 4:14; 8:17; 12:17; 13:35; 21:4; 26:54, 56; 27:9) it implies that the Old Testament prophesies have been fulfilled in Christ and in his ministries. He says, "Most of the other occurrences of 'to fulfill' (5:17; 13:48; 23:22) have at least some vague connection with prophets, eschatological fullness, or the final consummation."[26] Thus, for Meier, the passage (5:17–48) also contains apocalyptic tone i.e., it is written as an end-time morality (Eschatological morality).[27]

Meier shows that the verb πληρῶσαι should be understood as prophetic fulfillment of Jesus Christ. As Matthew shows Jesus fulfilling Old Testament prophesies to show that he is the Messiah, πληρῶσαι should here also be considered as the prophetic fulfillment of the Law of the Old Testament. This has been a common interpretation for years. In this view, Jesus fulfilled the Law in a 'predictive' fashion, which means it was predicted by

---

25. Menninger, *Israel and the Church*, 118.
26. Meier, *The Vision of Matthew*, 225.
27. Ibid., 229.

the Torah and Jesus fulfilled it like the other uses of the verb πληρῶσαι in the Gospel.[28]

It is interesting to see that Jesus' fulfillment is called eschatological fulfillment, according to Meier. If this is eschatological fulfillment, the fulfillment of the end times, which began in the ministry of Jesus Christ, the Law was totally completed and thus it need not be obeyed by the ideal disciple anymore because it has been eschatologically completed by Jesus. In this view, to fulfill means Jesus did not come to abolish the Law but to complete it so that no one needs to obey it anymore. As Jesus fulfills the promises of the Old Testament as a completion Jesus completes and accomplishes the Law's requirements so that his followers need not follow it anymore. This is a sound Pauline reading of the passage, I suppose. However, does this interpretation go well with the comparison in 5:17: *"Do not think that I came to abolish the Law or the Prophets; I did not come to abolish but to fulfill,"* Μὴ νομίσητε ὅτι ἦλθον καταλῦσαι τὸν νόμον ἢ τοὺς προφήτας· οὐκ ἦλθον καταλῦσαι ἀλλὰ πληρῶσαι.

Meier says, "In Matthew's mind, the Law, in both its ethical and prophetic utterances, pointed forward to the Messianic events and teachings of Jesus. But, . . . once the Fulfiller came, the prophetic pointer could no longer be the center of attention or the decisive norm."[29] Here, it is evident that Meier is forcing a Pauline idea into Matthew (Rom 3:21; 8:3–4; 10:4; 2 Cor 1:10; Gal 3:12–14; 3:24–25). For Meier, the Law is just a 'prophetic pointer,' which led the human beings to the Messiah. With the arrival of the Messiah, the Law has no importance because it has served its purpose as a pointer. This is a Pauline interpolation. However, for Matthew, the Law is not just a 'prophetic pointer,' though it has some function as such. In Matthew, the Law basically affirms the Messiah and the Messiah should in response affirm the Law. I think that is what Jesus was doing in Matt 5:17–48. He affirms that the Law had been pointing to him and at the same time he is there to affirm the Law and not to destroy it.

6.2.1.3 *Norvald Yri*

Norvald Yri states that, "Through his ministry, suffering, death and resurrection, Jesus completed everything required to fulfill all righteousness."[30] For him, "Jesus is the servant who obeys God: he fulfills all righteousness

---

28. The word 'predictive' was suggested by Carson in Carson, *The Sermon on the Mount*, 36.

29. Meier, *The Vision of Matthew*, 227.

30. Yri, "Seek God's Righteousness," 102.

since ultimately he suffers and dies to *accomplish* redemption in obedience to the will of God"[31] [Italics mine]. He continues to say:

> Jesus did not come in order to abolish the Law and the Prophets (5:17); he came to *fulfill* them. Jesus fulfills the Law and the Prophets in as much as they point to him. They demand righteousness; he himself is the righteous one. To this point the law of God had only been broken, but now one has come who always does what God requires. Thus the eschatological fulfillment of the Law and the Prophets is itself realized in the *obedience of Jesus*, the obedience that leads him to the cross. Thus he not only teaches the righteousness of the requirements of the Law; he himself is willing to satisfy all of God's demands on him in the most absolute sense.[32] [Italics his]

My only problem here is that if Jesus came to fulfill the Law why does he have to teach it to his disciples? Yri identifies that Jesus taught the Law [line six]. With that, he also identifies that Jesus fulfilled, 'satisfied it' so that the disciple need not obey it anymore. Does not teaching others mean he required others to obey what he taught? The six antitheses with the comparisons show that Jesus taught the disciples on how to obey the Law. In addition, the comparison in 5:17 identifies that Jesus did not come to abolish the Law. However, Yri identifies that Jesus fulfilled the Law and thus, Jesus' disciples need not obey the Law. This interpretation goes against the comparison mentioned in 5:17.

6.2.1.4. Ed Glasscock

Ed Glasscock sees this passage in a similar perspective. For him, the Law, in some sense, was completed by Christ.[33] Glasscock points out that the first Adam sent the whole human race to death as he disobeyed the one command of God. Likewise Jesus, the second Adam, by his obedience "accomplished all that the Law demanded."[34] Thus, for Glasscock the word πληρῶσαι means obedience. However, this obedience is the final obedience of Jesus to the Law which culminates the continuity of the Law after Jesus Christ. Because, he says, "those who are in Christ then have through Him

---

31. Ibid., 101.
32. Ibid., 102.
33. Glasscock, *Matthew*, 117.
34. Ibid., 117–118.

met all the requirements of the Law."³⁵ Thus, according to Glasscock the disciple need not obey the Law because Christ already had obeyed it once and for all.

6.2.1.5 *Watchman Nee*

Watchman Nee has a different interpretation of the verb πληρῶσαι. He says, "From the Lord's standpoint, the Law and the Prophets are incomplete. He therefore comes to raise the standard and make it complete: "fulfill" is to fill full, to make something complete."³⁶ Thus, for Nee the Law was 'incomplete' and Jesus 'filled' it to the 'full' and thus, only the teachings of Jesus (vv. 21–48) should be obeyed because the teachings of the Lord is more complete and thus binding on all believers. In addition, in interpreting the word pass away, Watchman Nee points out that "What the Lord, means here is that the Law must be fulfilled before it passes away. This passage does not say that the Law will not pass away, for it will pass away eventually, but not till all things are accomplished. This problem of the Law shall be completely resolved."³⁷ For Nee, Jesus comes to 'fulfill' the Law by his teachings and he 'filled' it to the 'full.' According to Nee, the Law was ready to pass away and thus, the Law is not binding on the believers but the Lord's teachings are.

6.2.1.6 *John Wesley*

John Wesley, the famous Evangelist of England says, "Jesus blotted out, took away and nailed to His cross, the requirement of the written law."³⁸ However, he does not think that Jesus blotted out all the requirements of the Law. He differentiates the Torah into two: Ceremonial and Moral. He says, "The ritual of ceremonial Law was delivered to Israel by Moses. It contained all of the injunctions and ordinances which related to the old sacrifices and service of the Temple. Jesus did indeed come to destroy, to dissolve, and utterly abolish all these laws."³⁹ However, Wesley further goes on to say that, "Jesus did not take away the moral law. The Ten Commandments remained enforced by himself, as well as by the prophets. It was not the intent of His coming to revoke any part of this. This is a law which can never be broken. It

---

35. Ibid., 118.
36. Nee, *Interpreting Matthew*, 81.
37. Ibid., 81.
38. Ibid., 124–125.
39. Wesley and Weakley Jr, *Happiness Unlimited*, 124.

stands fast as the faithful witness in heaven. The moral law stands on an entirely different foundation than the ceremonial law. The latter was designed only for a temporary restraint upon a disobedient and stiff-necked people. Contrary to that, the moral law was from the beginning of the world."[40] He stressed, "No one commandment contained in the moral law, nor the least part of any one, however inconsiderable it might seem, should ever be changed."[41] Thus, he suggests that Jesus did not come just to fulfill the entire law by 'his obedience' but also by his teachings.[42] Thus, the (moral) Law and the teachings of Jesus are still binding to the Christian believers.

To answer the question if the disciple should obey the Law Wesley suggests,

> . . . there is the closest connection that can be conceived between the Law and the gospel. On the one hand, the Law continually makes way for, and points us to, the Gospel. On the other hand, the Gospel continually leads us to a more exact fulfilling of the Law. The Law, for instance, requires us to love God and our neighbor. It requires us to be meek, humble, and holy. We feel that we are not adequate to do these things. With men this is impossible. But we see a promise of God, to give us that love and to make us humble, meek and holy. We grab hold of this gospel, of these glad tidings. This is accomplished in us according to our faith. The righteousness of the law is fulfilled in us through faith which is in Jesus.[43]

Wesley continues,

> We must loudly declare to every penitent sinner, 'Believe in the Lord Jesus Christ and you shall be saved.' At the same time, we must take care to define this faith. We believe in no faith but that which works by love. We have not experienced saving faith until we are also delivered from the power, as well as the guilt, of sin. We have a deep meaning when we say, 'Believe and you shall be saved.' We do not mean, 'Believe and you shall step from sin to heaven without any holiness coming between.' Neither do we believe that faith supplies a substitute for holiness. We believe, 'Believe, and you shall become holy. Believe in Jesus and you shall have peace and power put together.'[44]

40. Ibid., 125.
41. Ibid., 126.
42. Ibid., 125.
43. Ibid., 127–128.
44. Ibid., 133.

For Wesley, the believer should obey the Law but only the moral law. He says, "The righteousness of a real Christian is universal. He does not observe one, or only parts of the law of God, and neglect the rest. He keeps all of God's commandments. He loves them all. He values them above gold or precious stones."[45] However, the believer need not obey the ceremonial law. Thus, Wesley sees Jesus as the one who re-wrote the Law in 5:17–48 to re-emphasize the moral aspect of the Law and as the one who did away with the ceremonial aspects of the Law.

6.2.1.7 "To Fulfill:" πληρῶσαι

In the above summary one could see the diversity of the interpretation of the verb, πληρῶσαι. It is hard to accept the interpretations that Jesus completed the Law by fulfilling it because it goes against the comparison in 5:17, where Jesus himself said that he did not come to abolish the Law. In addition, it is hard to accept the idea that Jesus abolished the ceremonial aspect of the Law but he did not destroy the moral aspect the Law. A few scholars dissected the Law into three major groups: such as: 1. Religious, Ceremonial, Ritual or Cultic; 2. Civil, Social, Political, or Judicial; 3. Moral, Ethical, Personal, or Individual. However, it is hard to dissect the Law as such. The reason is that, if one covets the wife of his neighbor, which could be said as a violation of the judicial law, but it is also a violation against his God, which could mean that he violated religious law. Thus, it is a violation of the moral law also.

D. A. Carson finds two problems in these categorizations: "The first problem with that view is that the expression 'not the smallest letter, not the least stroke of a pen' (5:18) sounds much more all-embracing would be allowed by an exclusive reference to moral law. Moreover, neither the Old nor the New Testaments utilize this three-fold distinction."[46] Carson then points out how these categories are undividable: "The problem with this three-fold division is that it's not clear what 'moral' then means. If it has to do with what is fundamentally right or wrong, I would want to argue that what God approves is fundamentally right and what he forbids is fundamentally wrong; and in that case, when God approved certain ceremonial sacrifices as in the Old Testament, people were morally bound to practice them."[47] If so, the sacrifices and other ceremonial aspects of the Law could not be separated from the moral aspects of the Law because obedience to the ceremonial aspects of the Law is moral. Social aspects of the Law also

---

45. Ibid., 141.
46. Carson, *The Sermon on the Mount*, 35.
47. Ibid., 35.

contain the same dilemma. It is imperative for a citizen of Israel, people of God, to act rightly before God and his neighbor. When he violates a social aspect of the Law he is not only neglecting the social aspect of the Law but committing sin against his God which is the moral aspect of the Law. Thus, ceremonial, social and moral aspects of the Law are inseparable. It is absurd to think of such a distinction in the Jewish biblical world. It is hard to draw a line between ceremonial, social, and civil aspects of the Law. Glasscock rightly stresses, "Nothing in the context [of 5:17–20] implies such a distinction."[48]

How then should the verb, πληρῶσαι be interpreted? It is better to understand the verb πληρῶσαι to mean Jesus' obedience to the Law. The meaning of this verb is clear when we analyze this verb in the light of Matt 3:15. πληρῶσαι could be considered as קום which in pi'el form means 'confirming,' or 'affirming' the Law.[49] "The orientation of the statement is clear: it is in the opposite direction of abrogation; it is confirming and upholding the validity of the Law and the Prophets."[50] Menninger negates this interpretation as appropriate because he says קום was never translated as πληρῶσαι in LXX to mean confirming or affirming.[51] I think it is a narrow approach to restrict Matthew's vocabulary to LXX lexicon. Though Matthew renders several words or usages of the words from LXX it does not mean his vocabulary is limited only to LXX usages.

The verb πληρόω is used in LXX 109 times except its infinitive usages. In all these usages in different moods and participles it usually means to complete a particular time period or to mean "fill," for example "Be fruitful and fill the earth" (Gen 1:8). However, it was never used to mean the fulfilling of God's word. This idea is somehow meant in three verses: 1 Kgs 8:24; 2 Chr 6:4, 15; Jer 44:25, which says, "*You have spoken with Your mouth and have fulfilled it with Your hand as it is this day.*" καὶ ἐλάλησας ἐν τῷ στόματί σου καὶ ἐν χερσίν σου ἐπλήρωσας ὡς ἡ ἡμέρα αὕτη (1Kgs 8:24, LXX). However, here the protagonist of the story talks directly to God and says "your mouth said and your hands fulfilled it" but it does not says that the Word of the Lord says and it has been fulfilled. This idea is used only in infinitive usage of this verb. 1 Kings 2:27 says: "So Solomon expelled Abiathar from being priest to the Lord, thus *fulfilling the word* of the Lord which he had spoken concerning the house of Eli in Shiloh." And 2 Chr 36:21, 22 says:

---

48. Glasscock, *Matthew*, 117.
49. Menninger, *Israel and the Church*, 106.
50. Loader, *Jesus' Attitude towards the Law*, 166.
51. Menninger, *Israel and the Church*, 106.

²⁰ He took into exile in Babylon those who had escaped from the sword, and they became servants to him and to his sons until the establishment of the kingdom of Persia, ²¹ *to fulfill the word* of the Lord by the mouth of Jeremiah, until the land had enjoyed its Sabbaths. All the days that it lay desolate it kept Sabbath, to fulfill seventy years.

²² Now in the first year of Cyrus king of Persia, that the word of the Lord by the mouth of Jeremiah might be accomplished, the Lord stirred up the spirit of Cyrus king of Persia so that he made a proclamation throughout all his kingdom and also put it in writing

Interestingly in both these places the fulfillment of the Word of God spoken by the prophets were stressed by the usage of πληρόω in the infinitive and this way of usage is not found in other moods or participles of the verb, except in infinitive. Interestingly, Matthew does not use this in the same way.

Matthew uses this verb 17 times. In addition, two times he uses πληρόω in the infinitive. While in 15 other instances, 13 times it basically means the fulfillment of the Scripture: (1:22; 2:15, 17, 23; 4:14; 8:17; 12:17; 13:14, 35; 21:4 26:54, 56 Scriptures be fulfilled; 27:9). The important thing to notice is that Matthew's usage of this verb is quite different from LXX. While LXX used πληρόω in the infinitive to mean the fulfillment of the Word, Matthew uses it in other moods also. Thus, Matthew's usage of the πληρόω in the infinitive is quite different. Thus, it is not appropriate to quote LXX usages to interpret Matthew's use of the verb.

6.2.1.8 Matthew's Use of πληρόω in the Infinitive

Matthew uses πληρόω in the infinitive (πληρῶσαι) at two places: 3:15 and 5:17. Interestingly, in 3:15 'fulfilling' has some connotation of doing some requirements demanded of the Jews: *"But Jesus answering said to him [John the Baptist], 'Permit it at this time; for in this way it is fitting for us to fulfill all righteousness.' Then he permitted Him,"* ἀποκριθεὶς δὲ ὁ Ἰησοῦς εἶπεν πρὸς αὐτόν· ἄφες ἄρτι, οὕτως γὰρ πρέπον ἐστὶν ἡμῖν πληρῶσαι πᾶσαν δικαιοσύνην. τότε ἀφίησιν αὐτόν. When John the Baptist resented having to baptize Jesus, Jesus told him to baptize him so that all the requirements of the righteousness would be fulfilled. One must notice that baptism was not required by the Law but it must have been a common practice.[52] In addition, somehow it was considered as fulfilling righteousness. What is

---

52. The archeological evidence of Qumran shows purification tanks were used for baptism.

righteousness for Matthew then? Yri Points out that "there is little consensus as to the meaning of righteousness in this book."[53]

Matthew uses the word δικαιοσύνη seven times in his book: 3:15, 5:6, 5:10, 5:20, 6:1, 6:33, and 21:32.[54] In three places it is clear what Matthew meant by righteousness, which is quite different from Paul. For Paul, righteousness primarily comes by faith in Jesus Christ: *"This righteousness from God comes through faith in Jesus Christ to all who believe,"* δικαιοσύνη δὲ θεοῦ διὰ πίστεως Ἰησοῦ Χριστοῦ εἰς πάντας τοὺς πιστεύοντας (Rom 3:22). However, for Matthew, righteousness is the working out of the faith. Righteousness is the obedience of the Law (Matt 5:20). Jesus himself obeyed to baptism by John the Baptist because *"it is proper for us to do this to fulfill all righteousness,"* οὕτως γὰρ πρέπον ἐστὶν ἡμῖν πληρῶσαι πᾶσαν δικαιοσύνην (Matt 3:15). Here, the word righteousness takes the meaning of obedience to and abiding by the religious norms of the community. In 6:1, Jesus clearly shows what he means by righteousness, in the context of 5:17–48 through the so called antitheses. They are the requirements of the members of the community. They are the rules: the Law expounded by the Messiah. In 6:1—7:29, Matthew shows how the members of the community should properly handle these rules over and against the Pharisees, the rival community to Matthean Christian Jewish community. Thus, in 6:1 he says, *"Be careful not to do your 'acts of righteousness' before men, to be seen by them,"* Προσέχετε δὲ τὴν δικαιοσύνην ὑμῶν μὴ ποιεῖν ἔμπροσθεν τῶν ἀνθρώπων πρὸς τὸ θεαθῆναι αὐτοῖς. Here again δικαιοσύνη is rendered as an action oriented word than having just faith based meaning, as Paul's. Thus, for Matthew, righteousness is obedience to the Torah.

It is not that Matthew is teaching a works-righteousness kind of doctrine. For Matthew, obedience to the Law is the way one remains righteous. In addition, this obedience to the Law is the "acts of righteousness," τὴν δικαιοσύνην, which should be performed carefully, and in private (6:1). These acts of righteousness, for Matthew, are not only obedience of the Law which was expounded by the Messiah in 5:17–48, it also includes, giving alms to the poor (6:2–4), Praying (6:5–13), forgiving (15–16), fasting (16–18), giving (19–24), not worrying (25–34), not judging (7:1–6), etc.

Thus, 'to fulfill,' πληρῶσαι in 3:15 means 'to do' the Law. It is not as same as that of some prophesies being fulfilled in Jesus Christ. Meier suggests, "'To fulfill the Law and the prophets' must not be reduced in meaning to a banal 'doing' or 'observing.' 'To fulfill' is not the usual verb employed in Greek for the idea of putting a law into practice. It is never used that way

---

53. Yri, "Seek God's Righteousness," 96.

54. The δικαι root has been used 26 times in Matthew.

in the Greek Septuagint, which however does speak of the prophetic word of the Lord being fulfilled. Matthew himself supplies no clear example of 'fulfill' in the simple sense of doing or obeying a law."[55] As discussed above it is not appropriate to limit Matthew's meaning of his words to LXX as Matthew obviously uses πληρῶσαι differently from LXX uses.

For Menninger, πληρῶσαι cannot mean 'to do' because Jesus is not 'doing' or obeying the Law in the context of 5:17–48 but teaching. There is no problem in seeing πληρῶσαι to mean "to do" in the context of teaching because, in 5:17–20, Jesus polemically emphasizes that he obeys the Law, while in 5:21–48, he shows his disciples on how to obey the Law. This does not in anyway, distort the meaning of πληρῶσαι in Matthew. If so, if 'to fulfill' is understood to mean 'to do' or 'to obey' the verse should mean: "He [Jesus] announces that he has come to *uphold* the Law and the Prophets and to ensure they are fulfilled (5:17)"[56] [Emphasis mine].

In addition, one other reason why the verb could mean "to do" is that in 5:17 Jesus says he had come to fulfill—'to do' the Law and he teaches his disciples to do the Law effectively in 5:21–48, while in 5:19 he exalts the one who would 'do' the Law and 'teaches' others to do the same: *"but he who does them and teaches them shall be called great in the kingdom of heaven,"* ὃς δ' ἂν ποιήσῃ καὶ διδάξῃ, οὗτος μέγας κληθήσεται ἐν τῇ βασιλείᾳ τῶν οὐρανῶν (5:19). The word ποίεω is used to mean to do and it is kept synonymous to Jesus' fulfilling of the Law which helps us to interpret πληρῶσαι as doing the Law. However, I agree with Hare that "We cannot exclude the possibility that Matthew wished the verb to be understood in more than one sense."[57]

Gundry notices that as Matthew placed the Law before the Prophets in 5:18, Jesus is shown as obeying the Law rather than fulfilling the Law's prophecy as the word 'fulfill' is used in other places in Matthew.[58] He shows this by pointing out that in 11:13, Matthew uses Prophets first over the Law to show the emphasis on the prophetic element but in 5:18 he has the Law in front thus showing Jesus *obeying* the Law than *fulfilling* the prophetic nature of the Law. Thus, Gundry understands the verb fulfill as "teaching in support of the Law, in contrast with abolishing the Law by teaching against it."[59] It is better to incorporate teaching with obeying also because Jesus would not teach the Law if he does not obey the Law. Thus, the verb πληρῶσαι

---

55. Meier, *The Vision of Matthew*, 224.
56. Loader, *Jesus' Attitude towards the Law*, 260.
57. Hare, *Matthew*, 47.
58. Gundry, *Matthew*, 80.
59. Ibid., 80.

should be understood as to mean 'to do' and 'to affirm' or 'confirm' the Law because he did not come to destroy, καταλῦσαι the Law.

Καταλῦσαι seems "too strong for disobedience."[60] Second Maccabees 2:22 praised the Maccabeans who "restored the laws which were about to be abolished." Here καταλῦσαι is used, meaning, the Law was about to be destroyed by the enemies of the Jews. Thus, it must mean abolishing to the point that it does not exist anymore. Thus, here in 5:17, we see Jesus teaching his disciples that he did not come to destroy the Law but to obey and to affirm its validity and existence. The sense of Jesus affirming the validity and continuity of the Law is stressed by the comparison of the verse with *"Think not that I have come to abolish the law,"* Μὴ νομίσητε ὅτι ἦλθον καταλῦσαι τὸν νόμον in v. 17 and of v. 18: *"For truly, I say to you, till heaven and earth pass away, not an iota, not a dot, will pass from the law until all is accomplished"* ἀμὴν γὰρ λέγω ὑμῖν· ἕως ἂν παρέλθῃ ὁ οὐρανὸς καὶ ἡ γῆ, ἰῶτα ἓν ἢ μία κεραία οὐ μὴ παρέλθῃ ἀπὸ τοῦ νόμου, ἕως ἂν πάντα γένηται. Loader says, "The emphasis here is on Law in particular and upholding it and giving instruction so that it is rightly fulfilled."[61] Loader continues, "How does God's authority in Jesus relate to God's authority in the Law and the Prophets. Matthew seems bent on saying: no conflict."[62]

The above discussion identifies that by taking the comparison in 5:17 seriously the interpretation of 5:17 could come to mean that Jesus did not come to abolish the Law but to fulfill—to do—the Law, as the Law will not pass away until the heaven and earth pass away (5:18). This interpretation takes the comparison in 5:17 seriously into consideration. In addition, it takes the immediate context of the comparison and its function in the narrative into consideration.

6.2.2 Law Abiding Ideal Disciple (5:18–20)

Matt 5:18 starts with Matthew's statement 'verily I say unto you' which emphasizes the truthfulness of the following statement made that the Law will not be destroyed before the passing away of the world.[63] In addition, it follows with *"until heaven and earth pass away, not the smallest letter or stroke shall pass away from the Law, until all is accomplished,"* ἕως ἂν παρέλθῃ ὁ οὐρανὸς καὶ ἡ γῆ, ἰῶτα ἓν ἢ μία κεραία οὐ μὴ παρέλθῃ ἀπὸ τοῦ νόμου,

60. Ibid., 81.
61. Loader, *Jesus' Attitude towards the Law*, 167.
62. Ibid.,168.
63. It occurs 31 times in Matthew while 13 times in Mark and only six times in Luke.

ἕως ἂν πάντα γένηται. Here too, the phrase "all is accomplished," ἕως ἂν πάντα γένηται is compared with "until heaven and earth passed away," ἕως ἂν παρέλθῃ ὁ οὐρανὸς καὶ ἡ γῆ. Most scholars understand this passage to mean that "the Law will remain valid in all its parts 'until all things come to pass.'

The verb γίνομαι, 'come to pass' is frequently used by Matthew in the middle voice to express the coming to pass of some event; indeed, it is used that way in some of the introductions to formula quotations (Matt 1:12; 21:4; 26:54-56).[64] The significance of this interpretation is that Jesus meant that the Law will remain valid until all things come to pass. However, when all things came to pass the Law will be demolished. Manson thinks that the Law will be abolished in the end of days, when the heaven and earth would pass away because, "man may no longer require the kind of revelation of God's will that was necessary for him in this world."[65] However, though this interpretation could be correct, the stress of this passage lies on the eternal aspect of the Law than 'fulfillment of all things.' Meier assumes, "we may not be able to be sure whether, in the earliest Jewish-Christian form of the saying, 'till heaven and earth pass away' may have been simply a rhetorical way of expressing 'never.' But in Matthew's own eyes, the phrase in 5:18b probably refers to a future apocalyptic which *will* occur"[66] [Italics his]. I strongly disagree with this.

In 5:18, we find a parallelism where 18b and 18d begins with ἕως meaning until. Jesus in v.18 says *"an iota or a stroke will not pass away* until heaven and earth pass away," ἕως ἂν παρέλθῃ ὁ οὐρανὸς καὶ ἡ γῆ ("and until all is accomplished," ἕως ἂν πάντα γένηται. The comparison here is that "an iota or a stroke will not pass away" which is kept against "until heaven and earth passed away" and "until all are accomplished."

The comparative parallelism, "until heaven and earth passed away" and "until all are accomplished" could be synonymous or different. There are two ways we can understand this: 1. either both clauses meant the same event, or 2. they both meant different events. If both represent the same event it would mean that the Law would pass away only when heaven and earth pass away. If these two clauses represent different time frames then the Law would pass away when the heaven and earth pass away: end times and/ or when everything will be accomplished. Likewise, πάντα γένηται could mean two things: 1. all will be accomplished in the end times; 2. all things are accomplished in Christ.

64. Meier, *The Vision of Matthew*, 230.
65. Manson, *The Sayings of Jesus*, 154.
66. Meier, *The Vision of Matthew*, 232-233.

> **Mat 5:18**
>
> 18a. For truly I say to you,
> 18b. *until heaven and earth pass away,*
> 18c. **not the smallest letter or stroke shall pass from the Law**
> 18d. *until all is accomplished.*

If we take the first position we should affirm that both 18b and 18d are synonymous but if we take the second position we should conclude that the Law had to pass away after the death-resurrection of Christ. Many Evangelical scholars hold the second position.[67] However, why would we take the second position when the first position of 18d reitterates what is mentioned in 18b? If so, there is a double affirmation by Jesus in 5:18 (b and d) that the Law will not pass away until the end of days and thus all believers must obey the Law.[68] One more reason why both 18b and 18d form a synonymous parallelism is that both clauses have a verb in aorist subjunctive third person singular, which suggests both are kept in parallel (παρέλθῃ and γένηται). It is, thus, absurd why one must take πάντα γένηται to mean 'all are accomplished in Christ' while the same verse, in 18b, gives a clearer meaning that all will be accomplished only in the end of days. Thus, Law will only pass away in the end of days. This interpretation suggests the eternal aspect of the Law which is attested quite frequently in Jewish literature. Manson rightly comments, "There was no point on which devout Palestinian Jews were more sensitive than on any attempt to tamper with the Law, which was for them something given directly by God Himself, and therefore perfect and irreformable."[69]

If the Law is not set aside by Jesus Christ and if it is continued until the end of days the ideal disciple must obey the Law as it was, not set aside. It is little different from Menninger's views. Menninger understands Jesus fulfilling the Law as a 'continuity' of the Law while setting aside of the Law as its 'discontinuity.'[70] However, he does not explain how a particular thing could logically continue while it is already discontinued? When the Law is set aside it is discontinued. He should have at least said that by the fulfilling of the Law Jesus completes the Law and thus discontinued the Law.

67. Menninger, *Israel and the Church*, 109.
68. Hagner, *Matthew 1–13*, 108.
69. Manson, *The Sayings of Jesus*, 153.
70. Menninger, *Israel and the Church*, 104.

However, he holds that the Law is continuing while it is discontinued by the Lord Himself, which is quite logically absurd. In addition, he himself says elsewhere that "either Jesus retains the Law or sets it aside, we cannot have both."[71] Thus, I concur with the interpretation that in Jesus the Law is fulfilled in the sense that it is discontinued as absurd and distorts the interpretation of Matthew. In addition, I stress that Jesus did not come to abolish the Law but to obey and 'establish' the Law. Thus, in 5:17, Jesus shared his relationship to the Law. In 5:18, he stressed the continuing validity of the Law. Now, in 5:19 & 20, he must state the relationship of the Law to the disciple.

6.2.3 The Law and the Ideal Disciple (5:19-20)

Matt 5:19 clearly shows Jesus' perception of the relationship of the disciples to the Law. He says, *"Whoever then annuls one of the least of these commandments, and so teaches others, shall be called least in the kingdom of heaven; but whoever keeps and teaches them, he shall be called great in the kingdom of heaven,"* ὃς ἐὰν οὖν λύσῃ μίαν τῶν ἐντολῶν τούτων τῶν ἐλαχίστων καὶ διδάξῃ οὕτως τοὺς ἀνθρώπους, ἐλάχιστος κληθήσεται ἐν τῇ βασιλείᾳ τῶν οὐρανῶν· ὃς δ' ἂν ποιήσῃ καὶ διδάξῃ, οὗτος μέγας κληθήσεται ἐν τῇ βασιλείᾳ τῶν οὐρανῶν. Here also, Jesus uses comparison. *"The one who annuls the Law is the least in the Kingdom of Heaven,"* ὃς ἐὰν οὖν λύσῃ μίαν τῶν ἐντολῶν τούτων τῶν ἐλαχίστων ... ἐλάχιστος κληθήσεται ἐν τῇ βασιλείᾳ τῶν οὐρανῶν but *"the one who keeps and teaches them is called great in the Kingdom of Heaven,"* ὃς δ' ἂν ποιήσῃ καὶ διδάξῃ, οὗτος μέγας κληθήσεται ἐν τῇ βασιλείᾳ τῶν οὐρανῶν. Jesus could have just described the disciple in simple terms saying, the one who keeps the Law will be called great in the kingdom of heaven. However, he uses comparison. This comparison brings a powerful contrast and directs the disciple to obey the Law inorder to be greater rather than to disobey the Law and be the least in the kingdom of heaven.

I don't think it is appropriate to take this verse to mean that though you break the commandment you are in the kingdom of God but you will be least in the kingdom of heaven. Because, in v. 20, Jesus says that unless one's righteousness exceeds that of the Pharisees (by keeping the Law) he/she cannot enter the kingdom of heaven. Thus, even the entrance to the kingdom of heaven is warranted by better obedience of the Law. Thus, if someone breaks (λύσῃ) the commandment and teaches others the same he/she is considered least in the kingdom of heaven, which could be equivalent to saying he/she is not eligible to enter the kingdom of heaven, in the light of 5:20.

---

71. Ibid., 118.

6.2.3.1 The Ideal Disciple Compared with Paul?

Manson pointed out that it was Paul who was thought of in 5:19.[72] Paul's so-called anti-nomian views in Romans and Galatians made few scholars think that Matthew was in opposition with Paul in terms of the obedience of the Law. As Paul was stressing his Gentile believers to shun away from certain aspects of the Law, people say, Matthew wrote this verse, keeping Paul in mind to say that if Paul continues to 'teach' others not to obey the Law he will be called least in the kingdom of heaven. Could Paul be compared with the ideal disciple in this passage?

Obviously Paul shares many negative comments about the Law, like: *"For Christ is the end of the law for righteousness to everyone who believes" (Rom 10:4).* "Christ redeemed us from the curse of the Law" (Gal 3:13). However, Paul also shared several positive comments of the Law:

> Do we then nullify the Law through faith? May it never be! On the contrary, we establish the Law. (Rom 3:31)

> What shall we say then? Is the Law sin? May it never be! (Rom 7:7)

> So then, the Law is holy, and the commandment is holy and righteous and good. (Rom 7:12)

> I agree with the Law, confessing that it is good. (Rom 7:16)

This is the dilemma in Pauline studies. Thus, though Paul stated things against the Law in several places he also stressed the positive character of the Law. Thus, we cannot ignore that Paul was pro-nomian in certain aspects. We see that Paul submitted himself to the synagogue disciplines, because he mentions in 2 Corinthians 11:24 that he received thirty-nine lashes five times; shaving of the head (Acts 21:24), and that he visited the Temple and also worshipped regularly at the Synagogue. These details show his continuing commitment to the Law. Thus, Paul could not have been against the Law. However, it is obvious that he was against the idea of the Law being imposed by the Jews over the Gentile converts inorder for them to be considered as the fully-saved people. Thus, Paul stated strongly that Law does not bring righteousness but faith does. So, for Paul, Law is secondary in the requirement for salvation while faith is more important in the aspect of salvation. However, Matthew seems to write in a totally different context. Matthew's Jesus was talking to his disciples at the time when they were already believers. The Law and obedience to it is not mentioned here as an entry requirement for salvation but as something which would be

---

72. Manson, *The Sayings of Jesus*, 154.

considered as the rules for the staying inside the saved community. In this perspective, Paul would have shared the same idea as that of Matthew. Thus, Matthew and Paul were not contradictory but shared the same intention, I suppose. Thus, Paul is not compared with the ideal disciple in this passage.

6.2.3.2 The Ideal Disciple Compared with Pharisees and Scribes

The key teaching in v.19 is that *"whoever keeps and teaches them, he shall be called great in the kingdom of heaven,"* ὃς δ᾽ ἂν ποιήσῃ καὶ διδάξῃ, οὗτος μέγας κληθήσεται ἐν τῇ βασιλείᾳ τῶν οὐρανῶν. Thus, Jesus directly commends the one who keeps the Law. In other words, Jesus teaches his disciples to keep the Law. Matt 5:17 stressed that the Law was not destroyed by the Lord but was confirmed as he himself keeps the Law. In addition, in 5:18, the Messiah stressed the eternal continuity of the Law and thus, he commands the ideal disciple to keep the Law in 5:19. In 5:20, Jesus exhorts or even commands his disciple to keep the Law so that he/she may enter the kingdom of God.

Matt 5:20 contains a classic comparison. It starts with *"For I say to you,"* Λέγω γὰρ ὑμῖν and continue to say, *"that unless your righteousness surpasses that of the scribes and Pharisees, you shall not enter the kingdom of heaven,"* ἐὰν μὴ περισσεύσῃ ὑμῶν ἡ δικαιοσύνη πλεῖον τῶν γραμματέων καὶ Φαρισαίων, οὐ μὴ εἰσέλθητε εἰς τὴν βασιλείαν τῶν οὐρανῶν. The comparison implies that the Pharisees have some kind of righteousness. However, the righteousness of the ideal disciple of Jesus 'must exceed the righteousness of the Pharisees.' How could this be possible? What is this righteousness? What are the implications of this comparison?

One serious question that arises when trying to understand this verse is how could one qauntify righteousness in order to possess sufficient righteousness to surpass the righteousness of the scribes and the Pharisees. It was believed before Sanders' *Paul and Palestinian Judaism* that Jewish contemporaries of Jesus obeyed the Law in order to achieve salvation.[73] Scholars thought that the Jews of Jesus' time amassed merits by obedience to the Law. However, in that tedious work, Sanders pointed out that the Jews did not obey the Law for their salvation but they considered themselves as already saved people, by God's choosing of Abraham, and the covenant with him, and by the salvation from Egypt. If so, how do we understand the word 'surpassing righteousness'?

In the immediate context of 5:17-48, Matthew tells his readers, *"beware of practicing your righteousness before men to be noticed by them; otherwise*

---

73. Sanders, *Paul and Palestinian Judaism*.

you have no reward with your Father who is in heaven" Προσέχετε δὲ τὴν δικαιοσύνην ὑμῶν μὴ ποιεῖν ἔμπροσθεν τῶν ἀνθρώπων πρὸς τὸ θεαθῆναι αὐτοῖς· εἰ δὲ μή γε, μισθὸν οὐκ ἔχετε παρὰ τῷ πατρὶ ὑμῶν τῷ ἐν τοῖς οὐρανοῖς (6:1). In 5:17–48, Matthew expounded the Law and 5:20 shows that the ideal disciples' righteousness should surpass that of the Pharisees, and in 6.1 Matthew shows that his disciples should not perform righteousness in front of others. So, what is practicing righteousness? I think, for Matthew, in this context of 5:1—7:29, practicing righteousness is to obey the Law as expounded by his/her master teacher, Jesus the Messiah.

For Meier, Justice or righteousness in Matthew means "God's saving activity or gift of salvation in the end time."[74] I don't think this is what is meant here in Matthew, while this interpretation could be Pauline. It is not appropriate to interpolate Pauline idea of righteousness here. Though both use the same word, Paul does not give much of the 'doing' aspect to the righteousness but for Matthew obeying the Law is righteousness. For Paul, righteousness is given by God in the work of Christ through the faith of the believer in Jesus Christ. However, for Matthew, one must obey the Law and that is righteousness. Thus, Jesus' teaching in 5:20 *"that unless your righteousness surpasses that of the scribes and Pharisees, you shall not enter the kingdom of heaven,"* ἐὰν μὴ περισσεύσῃ ὑμῶν ἡ δικαιοσύνη πλεῖον τῶν γραμματέων καὶ Φαρισαίων, οὐ μὴ εἰσέλθητε εἰς τὴν βασιλείαν τῶν οὐρανῶν basically means unless the ideal disciple of Jesus keep the Law far better than the Pharisees and scribes they cannot enter the kingdom of God. Thus, through 5:17–20, Jesus characterizes the ideal disciple as the one who keeps the Law. The ideal disciple is not like the Pharisees and scribes but is the one who better obeys the Law, the way in which his master expounded in 5:21–48.[75] Thus, the ideal disciple is not characterized as an antinomian but a Law-abiding disciple of Christ. Thus, comparisons in 5:20 help in this interpretation.

6.2.3.3 Karma vs. Dharma

Does practicing righteousness mean achieving merits (like karma) by obedience? It is not *karma*—an Indian term which signifies the effect that one gets by his/her actions. One usually receives karma, in the Indian sense, if he/she does any action—good or bad. Applying this to the Jewish observance of the Law many suggested that Jewish people thought of receiving good karma through obedience. However, as noticed from Sanders' writings

---

74. Meier, *The Vision of Matthew*, 225.
75. Hagner, *Matthew 1–13*, 109.

karma would not mean anything if it doesn't lead one towards salvation because Jews did not consider themselves as obeying the Law for salvation. If so, we can attribute another Indian term for the Jewish observance of the Torah in order to understand their attitude of obedience to the Torah, and that is *dharma*.

The term dharma means duty, the duty of every man. If a man was born in a barber family he inherits his father's duty, i.e., to do the hairdressing of the community. If he neglects it, it affects the whole community such that the whole community would lack a barber and thus everyone would roam around unshaven and with long hair. Thus, one's important goal in life in Indian thought is to perform his/her duty, dharma. I think this explains the attitude expected of the ideal disciple in the Sermon on the Mount. It is also true in the Jewish worldview. As they were born a Jew they are to keep the dharma, the duty of the community, to observe the Torah. Thus, the Jew did not think of amassing karma but obeying their dharma. The only difference between the two is that the term karma includes the salvific effect of the duty performed while dharma stresses the duty itself. In this sense Jesus was not describing his ideal disciple as amassing merits by working the Law but exhorts him/her to perform the duty, that is, obeying the Law.

For Watchman Nee, 'to exceed the righteousness of the Pharisees and the scribes,' just means that the disciple should obey the commands of the Lord, primarily (5:21–48).[76] The reason he gives is that the Law of Old Testament was incomplete and those who obeyed those laws did not have complete righteousness. For this reason, Jesus came, gave new commands, and raised the standards of the Mount Sinai in the Sermon on the Mount. He says, "The teaching of the Lord Jesus on the Mount is higher than that which was given to Moses on Mount Sinai. The righteousness that is derived from keeping the teaching on the Mount is higher than that which is derived from keeping the Law which the scribes and Pharisees try to keep."[77] Thus, for Nee, when the disciple obeys the commands of Jesus then he naturally exceeds the righteousness of Pharisees and scribes. Nee did not just stop with this but raises this regulation of Jesus as literally binding to all believers. I agree with Nee saying that Jesus wanted the disciple to obey the Law as interpreted by him but I disagree with his statement that Jesus gave a new Law apart from the Law of Moses and thus the disciple should obey only Jesus' commandments and not the Mosaic ones. The narrative doesn't seem to point towards this interpretation when we take the whole context into consideration. From 5:21 onwards, Jesus begins to quote Old Testament

76. Nee, *Interpreting Matthew*, 84.
77. Ibid., 84.

teachings (Law) in order to give his teachings on it. Many thought that Jesus gives antitheses to the Old Testament commandments. However, Jesus did not give antitheses but he gave his interpretation of the Law with his Messianic authority just as several rabbis of his time did, which were thought of as authoritative teachings for their respective communities. Thus, how could one surpass righteousness of the Scribes and the Pharisees in the obedience of the Law? How could one 'rightly obey' the commandments? This is what is explained in detail in 5:21–48.

The portion following 5:20 shows how the ideal disciple could surpass the righteousness of the Pharisees and Scribes.[78] The intention of Matt 5:17–20 is that when the audience hear Jesus revoking major social and religious institutions of the Law (divorce, oaths, legal retaliation), they should not think that Jesus came to destroy the Old Testament revelation. Thus, the comparison in 5:20 acts as a transition: as a summary to 5:17–19 and also as an introduction to 5:21–48, the so-called antitheses.[79] Through the comparison in 5:20 Jesus depicted the ideal disciple as the one who obeys the Law expounded by the Messiah in 5:21–48, by which he/she would surpass the righteousness of the Scribes and Pharisees. This depiction of the ideal disciple comes to fore by the comparison in 5:20, which says that unless your righteousness surpasses *that* of the scribes and Pharisees, you will not enter the kingdom of heaven. It is now time to turn to the other comparisons Jesus uses in 5:21–48 which are called antitheses and their function in the characterization of the ideal disciple.

6.3 Jesus, the Law and the Antitheses (5:21–48)

6.3.1 Are the Antitheses Anti-theses?

Six times in 5:21–48 Jesus talks about 'it was said,' 21, 27, 31, 33, 38, and 43. In these instances, five times (excluding 5:15) they are accompanied with the phrase 'You have heard.' Glasscock assumes that in 5:21–48 Jesus basically attacks the oral traditions of the Jews. He supports this idea from the use of 'heard' in the phrases, "you have heard that it was said . . . but I say" (5:31).[80] It need not be so. Manson points out that 'You have heard' could mean that Jesus is referring to the synagogue reading of the Scriptures.[81] Meier says, "'it was said' is the reverent 'divine passive,' which has God as

---

78. Also Gundry, *Matthew*, 82.
79. Menninger, *Israel and the Church*, 113 also Hare, *Matthew*, 49.
80. Glasscock, *Matthew*, 116.
81. Manson, *The Sayings of Jesus*, 155.

the understood agent."[82] Thus, God's words heard in the synagogue is what is probably meant in this passage. Thus, in 5:21-48, Jesus uses God's words expressed in the Law in order to give his teachings.

Jesus says *"You have heard that it was said . . . but I say,"* Ἠκούσατε ὅτι ἐρρέθη . . . ἐγὼ δὲ λέγω ὑμῖν (which appears in 5:22, 28, 32, 34, 39, 44). Here are the comparisons in which Jesus compares what the disciples have heard with what he is going to teach. These comparisons bring varied interpretation as seen above. Many scholars consider 'But I say to you' as meaning that Jesus said something contrary to the Law because he uses 'but I say to you' as a means of contrast. Meier shows a prevalent reading of this passage: "Jesus as Fulfiller of the Law gives six examples of his eschatological fulfillment in the six antithesis (5:21-48). In six instances of Pentateuchal Law, Jesus contrasts what God said to the wilderness-generation of Israel at Sinai with what Jesus himself says to his disciples now."[83] Margaret Davies opposes this interpretation and say:

> The introductory formula, used at the beginning of each example, 'you have heard that it was said to people of old . . . and/but I say to you . . . has often been construed by Christians as antithetical, and the Greek δέ has been translated 'but.' Jesus' teaching in this section, however, is not the antithesis of the older teaching. It does not teach that his followers should murder whenever they feel like it, nor commit adultery, nor divorce at their convenience, nor abrogate oaths, nor retaliate excessively, nor hate other people. The formula is therefore best translated 'and I say to you', since the new teaching is an elaboration of the older teaching.[84]

According to Davies, then, these antitheses are not really antitheses, meaning contrasts but comparisons which are intended to highlight a characteristic trait. Many suggested that "Jesus opposed the old maxim" in the six so-called antitheses.[85] However, how can he oppose the Law when he himself stated quite emphatically that he did not come to destroy but to fulfill? Thus, it should not be interpreted as Jesus teaching against the Old Maxims but it should be understood as something which shows the continuity. Thus, δέ should be translated as a continuance rather than something

---

82. Meier, *The Vision of Matthew*, 63.
83. Ibid., 63
84. Davies, *Matthew*, 52.
85. Daube, *The New Testament and Rabbinic Judaism*, 254.

in opposition. J. Andrew Overman rightly points out, "There is a common and older copulative sense to δέ, which suggests more coordination or continuity."[86]

Gundry emphatically proclaims, "The term 'antitheses' designates the material incorrectly. . . . Jesus contradicts neither the Law nor current rabbinic interpretations of it."[87] Though I am not as sure as Gundry that Jesus did not oppose his current rabbinic interpretations (as it is hard to rely on the rabbinic material in existence at present as representing the teachings of Jesus' time) I am sure that Jesus' teaching in 5:21-48 is not delivered against the Law (Torah). Loader suggests, "Matthew's apparent familiarity with disputes reflected in early rabbinic tradition and his focus predominantly on Pharisees seem to indicate that his community must still be in some relationship with such circles."[88] Thus, I consider the passage in concern 5:17-48 is also about clarifying Jesus' interpretation of the Law over and against the Pharisaic and scribal interpretations.[89] To make these clarifications, Jesus uses comparisons in 5:21-48 which are called as antitheses.[90] By using these comparisons Jesus describes how the ideal disciple must live.

The ideal disciple, thus, must live unlike the Pharisees and scribes (5:20).[91] The ideal disciple has heard that he/she 'should not commit murder,' οὐ φονεύσεις but Jesus says to him in the comparison in 5:21-22 that he/she should not even get angry, ὁ ὀργιζόμενος τῷ ἀδελφῷ αὐτοῦ ἔνοχος ἔσται τῇ κρίσει. Likewise in 5:27-28, Jesus compares the Old Testament teaching with his teaching to show that the ideal disciple must not look at a woman lustfully, πᾶς ὁ βλέπων γυναῖκα πρὸς τὸ ἐπιθυμῆσαι αὐτὴν ἤδη ἐμοίχευσεν αὐτὴν ἐν τῇ καρδίᾳ αὐτοῦ while the Old Testament taught only that 'one should not commit adultery,' οὐ μοιχεύσεις (5:27). Likewise, the other so-called antitheses (5:31-32: Divorce; 5:33-34: vows; 5:38-39: Do not resist; and 5:43-44: Love your enemies) are kept in comparison with Jesus' teachings so as to highlight the characteristic traits expected of the ideal disciple from his/her master, the Messiah, Jesus Christ. In the following subtitles these comparisons will be looked at closely to identify the characteristic features highlighted by Jesus through the use of these comparisons.

---

86. Overman, *Church and Community in Crisis*, 81.
87. Gundry, *Matthew*, 83.
88. Loader, *Jesus' Attitude towards the Law*, 151.
89. Also Menninger, *Israel and the Church*, 113.
90. Hagner, *Matthew 1-13*, 109.
91. Ibid., 109.

6.3.2 Jesus' Interpretation vs. Pharisaic and Scribal Interpretation

It is striking to see that in the Gospel of Matthew the Law concerning divorce and concerning oaths are kept as antithesis to the teachings of the Pharisees. Is this a coincidence that the majority of the positions of the Pharisees, which were negated in other places of the Gospel, are also placed in ch. 5, which follows the statement that the righteousness of the ideal disciple should exceed that of the Pharisees? I don't think so. It is possible that these six antithesis mentioned in ch. 5 are kept purposefully against some of the Pharisaic teachings.[92] Jesus expounds the Law against the interpretation of the Pharisees. This is justified by the mention of some characteristic features in Matt 6, in which Jesus did not want his followers to behave like the Pharisees. In Matt 6, Pharisees were called hypocrites who gave alms to the poor for publicity (6:2–4), prayed on the street for publicity (6:5–13), and fasted for publicity (16–18). These are the things Jesus did not want his followers to do. In addition, these teachings in Matt 6 are also continuous, kept in the same section, which starts from 5:17. Therefore, the key verse to understand these passages is v. 20: *"For I tell you that unless your righteousness surpasses that of the Pharisees and the teachers of the law, you will certainly not enter the kingdom of heaven,"* Λέγω γὰρ ὑμῖν ὅτι ἐὰν μὴ περισσεύσῃ ὑμῶν ἡ δικαιοσύνη πλεῖον τῶν γραμματέων καὶ Φαρισαίων, οὐ μὴ εἰσέλθητε εἰς τὴν βασιλείαν τῶν οὐρανῶν. Thus, it is probable that Jesus' interpretation of the Torah in Matt 5 is kept as antithesis to the teachings of the Pharisees.

The comparisons are not just made against the Pharisees but it also includes the scribes with the Pharisees. Glasscock says, "scribes were the religious scholars of the time. Their primary function was to copy and preserve the Scriptures. The scribes were also expositors of the Law, often called Lawyers, and normally members of the party of Pharisees."[93] One should note that in Matthew the Pharisees are Jesus' dialogue partners in most instances where Jesus negates some of their teachings throughout the Gospel. The major teachings of the Pharisees, which Matthew explicitly disagrees includes: washing of the hands before eating (9:10–13 and 15:1–2), fasting (9:14–15), Sabbath (12:1–14), their traditions (15:1–6), divorce (19:3–9), loving God and neighbor (22:34–40), oaths (23:15–22), and other regulations mentioned in Matt 23. In these passages the readers get to know the position of Matthew's Jesus over and against the teachings of the Pharisees.

---

92. Ibid., 109.
93. Glasscock, *Matthew*, 119.

Among these teachings, the teachings about divorce, loving the neighbor and about the oaths are found in the Matt 5 respectively, (5:31–32), (5:43–44), and (5:33–37). Thus, as the Pharisees and scribes are the dialogue partners of Jesus, Jesus compares his teachings with the teachings of the Pharisees in these comparisons. Thus, the function of the comparisons are to highlight the teachings of Jesus which characterizes how the ideal disciple ought to live (one without anger, without lust, with truth in his/her words, one who resists evil, the one who loves his/her enemies) which were kept against the teachings of the Pharisees and Scribes.[94]

In the Christian view, when Jesus is seen as the one fighting against the Pharisaic interpretation of the Torah, it was seen by many as Jesus, the Christian leader fighting against Jewish way of living. The comparisons are usually interpreted as contrasts and antithetical. This is an absurd interpretation in light of the many debates that went on between the various Jewish groups of the first Century CE (ex. Qumran writings accusing the leaders of the Temple in the *Temple Scroll*). Jacob Neusner is right in pointing out that the Jesus Movement was not a non-Jewish sect from the beginning, it was a Christian Jewish movement where Jews interpreted the scriptures (Old Testament) in light of their Messiah's advent and teaching.[95] Thus, Jesus' words against the Pharisees were not against Judaism per se but one Jewish group's interpretation of the Torah against another Jewish group's interpretation of the Torah. Hummel puts it rightly, "Matthew's church has its own Christian halakah, alongside the Pharisaic; its own rules for community and devotion, alongside the Jewish ones; its own tradition of the Law beside that of the rabbis; its own church discipline, while it is still itself subject to Pharisaic jurisdiction; its own teaching authority, which it sets beside the seat of Moses, on which the 'scribes and Pharisees' sit."[96]

Loader, thus, suggests that Matthew using comparisons in the antitheses to expound the Torah in 5:17–48 on two fronts. "One front is against lax Christianity who believe the Law has been abolished or modified (7:15–23; 24:10–11). With this in mind he has Jesus strike out against any suggestion that Torah has lost validity. The other front is against rabbinic casuistry. In response, Matthew emphasizes that Jesus maintains the validity of the Law and has Jesus expound the centrality of love in interpreting Torah."[97] Thus, Jesus stressed the idea that the ideal disciple must obey the Law while he

---

94. Hagner, *Matthew 1–13*, 109.

95. Chilton and Neusner, *Judaism in the New Testament*, 6.

96. R. Hummel, *Die Auseinandersetzung zwischen Kirche* cited in Loader, *Jesus' Attitude towards the Law*, 138.

97. Loader, *Jesus' Attitude towards the Law*, 137.

also clarified it against the interpretations of the Pharisaic and the scribal interpretations. It is time then to browse through the comparisons, the so-called antitheses and see how these comparisons function in Jesus' characterization of the ideal disciple.

6.3.3 Murder vs. Anger

In 5:21 and 22 Jesus says, *"You have heard that it was said to the men of old, 'You shall not kill; and whoever kills shall be liable to judgment.' But I say to you that every one who is angry with his brother shall be liable to judgment . . . "*Ἠκούσατε ὅτι ἐρρέθη τοῖς ἀρχαίοις· οὐ φονεύσεις· ὃς δ' ἂν φονεύσῃ, ἔνοχος ἔσται τῇ κρίσει. ἐγὼ δὲ λέγω ὑμῖν ὅτι πᾶς ὁ ὀργιζόμενος τῷ ἀδελφῷ αὐτοῦ ἔνοχος ἔσται τῇ κρίσει. Jesus quotes Old Testament from Exod 20:13 and Deut 5:17, the sixth commandment of the Decalogue and compares it with his own teaching.

This comparison highlights one important difference between the teaching of the Law and the teaching of Jesus. While the Law is concerned with overt action, Jesus' teaching sheds lights on the root of the problem so that the disciple is better able to obey the Law. Manson says, "The point of the antithesis [comparison] lies in the contrast between the outward act, of which an earthly court can take cognizance, and the inward disposition."[98] Thus, the comparison is about the outward action and the inward disposition. Anger is the root cause of commiting murder. One could kill without anger but one cannot murder without anger.[99] Thus, Jesus shows that anger is the root of the problem of murder and thus, the ideal disciple must keep watch over anger so that they will not disobey the Law, "thou shall not murder," οὐ φονεύσεις.[100]

Some see this comparison as antithetical where Jesus gave new ideals which were different from the Law. Jesus' intentions here, it seems, is not to give new laws but to show the root of the problem to the ideal disciple, which is anger, so that he/she could obey the Law better. Comparisons do not always function as antithetical. Comparisons need not always play as antagonist to a protagonist. Comparisons could simply function as a foil to highlight a few characteristic features intended to be highlighted rather

---

98. Manson, *The Sayings of Jesus*, 155.

99. Interestingly, ὁ ὀργιζόμενος is kept in present tense. Wallace calls this as Present Retained in Indirect Discourse. Technically, the participle should be in aorist tense. However, the present tense is retained in the indirect speech. Wallace, *Greek Grammar*, 537–538.

100. Hagner, *Matthew 1–13*, 1012.

than just one archetypal function as antithesis. Thus, this comparison in 5:21–22 functions as a foil to bring out how the ideal disciple should behave, as one who should not get angry. Thus, understanding the right function of the comparison is important for the interpretation of the Sermon on the Mount.

Jesus says, *"and whoever shall say to his brother, 'Raca,' shall be guilty before the supreme court; and whoever shall say, 'You fool,' shall be guilty enough to go into the fiery hell,"* ὃς δ' ἂν εἴπῃ τῷ ἀδελφῷ αὐτοῦ· ῥακά, ἔνοχος ἔσται τῷ συνεδρίῳ· ὃς δ' ἂν εἴπῃ· μωρέ, ἔνοχος ἔσται εἰς τὴν γέενναν τοῦ πυρός (Matt 5:22). ῥακα is not a Greek word. It is better to take it as a transliteration of the Aramaic word רֵקָא which means 'empty' or empty headed or 'stupid' or 'blockhead,' etc.[101] If μωρέ is taken as a Greek word then it would mean 'fool.' However, Manson suggests that it could have been derived from the Hebrew word מוֹרֶה which would mean more than mere stupid: 'stubborn,' 'rebellious,' and so 'obstinately wicked.'[102] Either way, one thing is clear, μωρέ is a harsher word than ῥακα. Many suggest that the council here means the Sanhedrin, the highest court of the Jewish legal system.[103] If we consider it so, we could postulate that Sanhedrin had a rule which prohibited anyone to call his neighbor ῥακα, for which the violators were punished by the council. Nevertheless, if we consider it as divine judgment of the eschatological time it would be synonymous with the next phrase 'danger of the hell of fire,' τὴν γέενναν τοῦ πυρός. Thus, this could also be synonymous and the word council could also mean the final divine judgment.

This interpretation is consistent with other passages where anger is seen as the root cause of murder. *"Anyone who hates his brother is a murderer, and you know that no murderer has eternal life abiding in him,"* πᾶς ὁ μισῶν τὸν ἀδελφὸν αὐτοῦ ἀνθρωποκτόνος ἐστίν, καὶ οἴδατε ὅτι πᾶς ἀνθρωποκτόνος οὐκ ἔχει ζωὴν αἰώνιον ἐν αὐτῷ μένουσαν (1 John 3:15). *"Be angry but do not sin; do not let the sun go down on your anger,"* ὀργίζεσθε καὶ μὴ ἁμαρτάνετε· ὁ ἥλιος μὴ ἐπιδυέτω ἐπὶ τῷ παροργισμῷ ὑμῶν (Eph 4:26). Several other verses talk about peace and not anger, *"live in peace,"* εἰρηνεύετε (1 Thess 5:13); *"pursue peace with all men,"* Εἰρήνην διώκετε μετὰ πάντων (Heb 12:14); *"and pursue the things which make for peace,"* Ἄρα οὖν τὰ τῆς εἰρήνης διώκωμεν (Rom 14:19); *"Peace-maker,"* εἰρηνοποιοί (Matt 5:9).

In addition, the Law certainly condemned anger displayed towards a brother. Lev 19:17–18 reads, *"You shall not hate your brother in your heart,*

---

101. Manson, *The Sayings of Jesus*, 156.
102. Ibid., 156.
103. Ibid., 156.

but you shall reason with your neighbor, lest you bear sin because of him. You shall not take vengeance or bear any grudge against the sons of your own people, but you shall love your neighbor as yourself . . . " Rabbi Eliezer mentioned that anger would lead to murder. A saying attributed to R. Eliezer (c. 90 CE) runs like this: 'He who hates his neighbor, lo he belongs to the shedders of blood.'[104] Thus, Hare mentions, "It is not in the least suggested that these commandments are outdated [by the Lord]. In each case it is a matter of probing deeper behind the commandment to the will of God. Its explicit reference is to the extreme case, but the underlying purpose of God condemns the anger that gives birth to physical violence and murder."[105] Likewise, here, with the periphrastic participle construction Jesus commands his disciple to make friends with others quickly, ἴσθι εὐνοῶν τῷ ἀντιδίκῳ σου ταχύ (5:25) in order to avoid imprisonment.[106] The subjunctive verb in the indefinite temporal clause, ἂν ἀποδῷς, indicates that the disciple would never be able to come out of the imprisonment until the last penny, τὸν ἔσχατον κοδράντην, is paid (5:26).[107]

Therefore, the ideal disciple is exhorted and characterized as the one who should reconcile to the brother with whom he is angry before he sacrifices in the Temple (5:23–26). This passage shows that the setting is still inside Judaism where Temple sacrifice was still the center of the Christian worship. The disciple, assuming he is from Galilee, must make friends with his neighbor quickly because it will be hard for him to leave the sacrifice in the crowded Temple altar and go for reconciliation before the sacrifice. Hare points out that it is impossible to leave the offerings on the altar. In his imagination he ridicules the situation that one must leave a live pair of pigeons or a live goat on the altar to be reconciled to his neighbor.[108] Even Jewish writings point out the importance of reconciliation with the neighbors before God. "For transgressions that are between man and God the Day of Atonement effects atonement, but for transgressions that are between a man and his fellow the Day of Atonement effects only if he has appeased his fellow" (*Yoma* 8:9).

Thus, Jesus did not give a new law in the comparison in 5:21–22. It is obvious that similar teachings were in other Judaisms also. Jesus as the Messiah of the new Judaism, Christianity, must teach these things to his disciples so that they could keep the Law effectively. The comparison, then, is intended

---

104. Ibid., 155.
105. Hare, *Matthew*, 51.
106. Wallace, *Greek Grammar*, 647.
107. Ibid., 479.
108. Hare, *Matthew*, 52.

to characterize the disciple as the one who is loving and forgiving of his/her fellow disciple so that he/she would not go to the extreme of killing others.

6.3.4 Adultery vs. Lust

In the next comparison in 5:27-28 Jesus says, *"You have heard that it was said, 'You shall not commit adultery.' But I say to you that every one who looks at a woman lustfully has already committed adultery with her in his heart,"* Ἠκούσατε ὅτι ἐρρέθη· οὐ μοιχεύσεις. ἐγὼ δὲ λέγω ὑμῖν ὅτι πᾶς ὁ βλέπων γυναῖκα πρὸς τὸ ἐπιθυμῆσαι αὐτὴν ἤδη ἐμοίχευσεν αὐτὴν ἐν τῇ καρδίᾳ αὐτοῦ. Here again the Law is compared with Jesus' teaching to characterize how the disciple should live. However, Jesus does not negate the Law here but made it more stringent. Jesus quotes Exod 20:14 and Deut 5:18 which says *"Thou shall not commit adultery,"* לֹא תִּנְאָף. οὐ μοιχεύσεις, where the cohortative indicative is used here to identify the command of the Old Testament Law.[109] In addition, Wallace identifies that οὐ μοιχεύσεις is imperatival future, thus, identifying that the Old Testament Law is kept in comparison here for the teaching of Jesus Christ.[110]

For Jesus, committing the act of adultery is not the only sin, but even lust which leads one to adultery is also a sin. In this comparison, Jesus rightly gives his disciples the teaching which avoids the root of the problem so that they would not commit the crime itself. There are several other Jewish writings which mentioned against lust (Job 31:1; Sir 23:4-6; 26:9-1; *T. Iss* 7:2; *Pss. Sol.* 4:4-5). *Kalla* § I says, "He who looks at a woman with desire is as one who has criminal intercourse with her."[111] Thus, Jesus did not give a new Law but he resembles other Jewish teachers in teaching his ideal disciple that lust is the root cause of adultery and so, in order to effectively keep the Law the disciples should shun away from lust. Thus, the comparison in 5:27-28, which says, *"You have heard that it was said, . . . But I say to you,"* Ἠκούσατε ὅτι ἐρρέθη· οὐ μοιχεύσεις. ἐγὼ δὲ λέγω ὑμῖν is aimed at characterizing the ideal disciple as the one who should not only avoid committing adultery but also the one who should not even lust after another woman, else he may eventually be led to adultery. Jesus internalizes the Law.[112] This characterization is aimed at helping the disciple not to break the Law (Exod 20:14; Deut 5:18), which prohibits adultery. Thus, this comparison is also

---

109. Wallace, *Greek Grammar*, 452.

110. Ibid., 569. In addition, Wallace points out that future indicative with οὐ shows prohibitive commands in Wallace, *Greek Grammar*, 723.

111. Manson, *The Sayings of Jesus*, 157.

112. Hagner, *Matthew 1-13*, 121.

not an antithetical comparison but a foil to bring forth the teaching of Jesus which in turn helps the disciple to keep the very Law it compares with.

6.3.5 Divorce vs. No Divorce

The third 'antithesis' is little different from others, perhaps that is the reason why the normal form used for all the other five is not followed in this so-called antithesis. The regular phrase, "you have heard" is missing in this antithesis which leaves it to Ἐρρέθη ... ἐγὼ δὲ λέγω ὑμῖν (Matt 5:31–32). Jesus says, "It was also said, *'Whoever divorces his wife, let him give her a certificate of divorce.'* But I say to you *that every one who divorces his wife, except on the ground of unchastity, makes her an adulteress; and whoever marries a divorced woman commits adultery*" (Matt 5:31–32). Though the conventional formula, *"you have heard"* is missing, *"It was also said,"* and *"But I say to you,"* Ἐρρέθη ... ἐγὼ δὲ λέγω ὑμῖν highlights the comparison in these verses. Wallace points out that Ἐρρέθη ... ἐγὼ δὲ λέγω indicates comparison. He says, "The nominative personal pronoun is most commonly used for emphasis. The emphasis may involve some sort of *contrast*. In such instances, two subjects are normally in view, though one might be only implied. This contrast is either of kind (antithetical) or degree (comparison)."[113] Though this could be contrast it could also be considered as comparison here in the context of the Sermon on the Mount.

While divorce was allowed by the Law Jesus does not allow divorce except in the case of adultery in this comparison. Is Jesus then giving a new law? Is he then characterizing the ideal disciple as an antinomian? This comparison, in 5:31–32, shows that Jesus' teaching, in one sense, is against the Law but in another sense, it is interpreted in a more stringent manner. Jesus is in one way not contradicting the Law but he is using a stringent interpretation of the very Law, given in Deut 24:1. Deuteronomy 24:1 gives the condition for divorce in the Law:

> כִּי־יִקַּח אִישׁ אִשָּׁה וּבְעָלָהּ וְהָיָה אִם־לֹא תִמְצָא־חֵן בְּעֵינָיו כִּי־מָצָא בָהּ
> עֶרְוַת דָּבָר וְכָתַב לָהּ סֵפֶר כְּרִיתֻת וְנָתַן בְּיָדָהּ וְשִׁלְּחָהּ מִבֵּיתוֹ: וְיָצְאָה מִבֵּיתוֹ
> וְהָלְכָה וְהָיְתָה לְאִישׁ־אַחֵר׃

> *"When a man takes a wife and marries her, and it happens that she finds no favor in his eyes* because he has found some indecency in her, *and he writes her a certificate of divorce and puts it in her hand and sends her out from his house."*

---

113. Wallace, *Greek Grammar*, 321.

The phrase כִּי־מָצָא בָהּ עֶרְוַת דָּבָר, *'because He has found some indecency in her'* caused several interpretations. The contemporaries of Jesus, Hillel and Shammai differed greatly on the ground of divorce and in the interpretation of this phrase. While they interpreted the same phrase from Deut 24:1, עֶרְוַת דָּבָר, they had two different interpretations. While the school of Hillel suggested the Hebrew phrase meant 'shamefulness (or nakedness) of a matter,' School of Shammai suggested it is 'matter of shamefulness (or nakedness)' (*m. Git.* 9:10).[114] According to Hillel's interpretation, it could be any event which could bring shame for the wife. An example would be overcooked bread. However, according to Shammaites' interpretation, it should the matter of nakedness, i.e., adultery and nothing else is eligible as the grounds for divorce. Thus, Jesus here seems to agree with the school of Shammai.[115] Glasscock rightly comments, "It appears that Deut 24 was written to protect women from being casually discarded by their husbands, but this had been twisted by some rabbis to give men the freedom to do just that (cf. Hillel's view)."[116] Thus, Jesus' comparison in 5:31–32 was not antithetical but functions as a foil again and reinstate what was originally meant in the Law.

Glasscock notes that "The instruction in Deut 24 was intended to restrict the casual discarding of one's wife."[117] I think Shammaites' interpretation was the closest one to the teaching of Deut 24, of which Jesus sides with. By the time of Jesus it is possible that divorce had become a major social problem. Men could easily divorce their wives for any reason if the condition could be anything that is shameful (according to Hillel's view). In addition, there are many evidences that Hillel's views were more prevalently practiced than Shammaites'. If a man sees a beautiful woman on the street and if he wants to take her as a wife all he needs to do is go home and wait for his wife to make a small mistake like burning the food, which would have been common in those days as cooking was done on wood fire. Thus, Jesus seeing the problem that women were frequently being divorced for no valid reason and seeing the social implications which created more divorced old women as men could look for young, beautiful wives, had to bring back the original intention of divorce, i.e., adultery as the only grounds for divorce. Because, only when one commits adultery she breaks the bonds of the marriage. Glasscock puts it this way, "To prostitute the privilege of intimacy with someone other than one's own partner is to break the bond of

---

114. Gundry, *Matthew*, 90–91.
115. Manson, *The Sayings of Jesus*, 158.
116. Glasscock, *Matthew*, 129.
117. Ibid., 126–7.

oneness."[118] Gundry points out "Matthew reasons that an act of immorality by the wife has already made her an adulteress; hence, the husband who divorces her does not bear responsibility of making her an adulteress by pushing her into an illicit marriage to another man."[119] Thus, Jesus did not negate the Old Testament Law but interpreted it with his Messianic authority so that it could be adhered to properly.[120] Sanders says, "Moses did not command divorce, he permitted it; and to prohibit what he permitted is by no means the same as to permit what he prohibited."[121] Thus, the comparison in 5:31–32 highlights the ideal disciple as the one who does not divorce his wife, except for unchastity.

6.3.6 Vows and Oaths

Matt 5:33–37 is concerned with vows and oaths. Jesus says, *"Again, you have heard that the ancients were told, 'you shall not make false vows, but shall fulfill your vows to the Lord.' "But I say to you, make no oath at all . . . But let your statement be, 'Yes, yes' or 'No, no'; and anything beyond these is of evil,"* Πάλιν ἠκούσατε ὅτι ἐρρέθη τοῖς ἀρχαίοις· οὐκ ἐπιορκήσεις, ἀποδώσεις δὲ τῷ κυρίῳ τοὺς ὅρκους σου. ἐγὼ δὲ λέγω ὑμῖν μὴ ὀμόσαι ὅλως . . . ἔστω δὲ ὁ λόγος ὑμῶν ναὶ ναί, οὒ οὔ· τὸ δὲ περισσὸν τούτων ἐκ τοῦ πονηροῦ ἐστιν. This comparison identifies that, in the Old Testament Law, vows were allowed but according to the teachings of Jesus the ideal disciple should not make a vow but his/her 'yes' should be 'yes' and 'no' should be 'no'. In the Old Testament Law, vows were allowed but perjury of the vows was prohibited. Prohibition of perjury is in Lev 19:12 and Deut 5:11.[122] Manson says, "The Law does not forbid oaths; but it does forbid perjury, which is regarded as a profanation of the name of God."[123]

Oath taking was common among the Jews.[124] Jephthah is a good example for taking oaths (Judg 11:29–39). The Essenes had an aversion to oaths in general, but they took an oath on admission into the sect (see *CD* 15:5; 1*QS* 5:7–11; Josephus, *J.W.* 2.8.6–7). In the time of Jesus, vows were common in the government. All citizens were required to take oath of allegiance to the ruler (Josephus, *J.W.* 2.135–39; *A.J.* 15:371).

118. Ibid., 129.
119. Gundry, *Matthew*, 91.
120. Hagner, *Matthew 1–13*, 125.
121. Sanders, *Jesus and Judaism*, 256–7.
122. Also Numbers 30:2; Deut 23:21, 23.
123. Manson, *The Sayings of Jesus*, 158.
124. Glasscock, *Matthew*, 131.

Jesus used four common objects as examples for oath taking: heaven, earth, Jerusalem, and one's own head. Glasscock points out, "An oath was a binding agreement, and to swear by something or someone called that thing or person into account. Since man is not the ultimate master of the things around him, he has no authority to call any of them to account."[125] Sanders points out, "Oaths were important for society because they guaranteed a word or action by appealing to God and calling down his curse if it was broken."[126] However, oaths are not required if everyone's words are true where the 'yes' is 'yes' and the 'no' is 'no.'[127] Thus, Jesus does not go against the Old Testament but stresses the needlessness of the permission of oaths if everyone speaks only the truth.

To make a vow brings in the possibility of breaking the vow. If everyone lives by their words, saying if their 'yes' is 'yes' and 'no' is 'no,' then there is no need for the vows and oaths. This does not mean that Jesus was going against the Old Testament Law. Through this comparison he is just providing a way to help a person not to break an oath or a vow. Thus, this comparison also is not targeted at keeping the teaching of Jesus as antithetical to that of the Old Testament but to help the ideal disciple to live without breaking oaths or vows. Thus, the characterization of the ideal disciple is shown here as the one who does not make a vow or an oath but as the one who speaks the truth. Thus, comparisons also aid the characterization of the ideal disciple to show that he/she is not antinomian but pro-nomian.

6.3.7 Eye for an Eye vs. Do not Resist

In Mat 5:38–39, Jesus says, "*You have heard that it was said, 'Eye for eye, and tooth for tooth.' But I tell you, Do not resist an evil person. If someone strikes you on the right cheek, turn to him the other also,*" Ἠκούσατε ὅτι ἐρρέθη· ὀφθαλμὸν ἀντὶ ὀφθαλμοῦ καὶ ὀδόντα ἀντὶ ὀδόντος. ἐγὼ δὲ λέγω ὑμῖν μὴ ἀντιστῆναι τῷ πονηρῷ· ἀλλ' ὅστις σε ῥαπίζει εἰς τὴν δεξιὰν σιαγόνα σου, στρέψον αὐτῷ καὶ τὴν ἄλλην. Here, the comparison is with what the disciple has heard, 'Eye for an Eye'—a teaching on retribution with Jesus' teaching against retribution which says, "Do not resist an evil person." Here, there seems to be an antithetical teaching present. In 5:38–42, Jesus teaches against retribution. Jewish Law teaches retribution such that the one who committed a crime should be avenged according to his crime. Exod 21:23–25 says: "23 *But if there is any further injury, then you shall appoint as a penalty life*

---

125. Ibid.,131.
126. Sanders, *Jewish Law from Jesus to the Mishnah*, 51.
127. So also Matt 23:16–22; Jas 5:12.

for life, 24 *eye for eye, tooth for tooth, hand for hand, foot for foot,* 25 *burn for burn, wound for wound, bruise for bruise."*[128] Lev 24:19–20 says: *"*19 *And if a man injures his neighbor, just as he has done, so it shall be done to him:* 20 *fracture for fracture, eye for eye, tooth for tooth; just as he has injured a man, so it shall be inflicted on him."* These laws were important for an emerging country as it was in the context of Exodus, and Deuteronomy. However, when the country is in foreign power, which has its own laws in dealing with these crimes, these criminal punishments are not required anymore. It is possible that these laws were used by anti-Roman sympathizers of Jesus' time to retaliate against Romans. Thus, Jesus wants to tell his disciples that they should not retaliate but show the right cheek when smitten on the left cheek; let them have the coat when they sue to take the shirt; and to walk an extra mile. These words were borrowed by Mahatma Gandhi and used in the freedom struggle against the British where the power of this statement was proved. Though retribution was allowed in the Law it was not intended to stop the crime. However, the Sermon on the Mount was not just punishing the ones who committed the crime but intended to stop the ones from committing the crime. Thus, in the Christian community, if all do not retaliate but love even the enemies (5:44) then there is no need for the retribution laws.

By the time of Jesus Jews did not follow the laws of retribution literally. Both Mishna and Mekhilta avoid any form of literal interpretation of 'Eye for an eye' but the penalty was to pay for the damages.[129] Thus, Jesus did not state anything new to the common Jewish practices of his time. In addition, he did not give a new Law but interpreted it according to the needs of his time. Moreover, it seems obvious that Jesus is interpreting Lev 19:18: *"You shall not take vengeance, nor bear any grudge against the sons of your people, but you shall love your neighbor as yourself; I am the Lord."* The first part of this passage talks about not taking vengeance among the Jews, which is the essence of Jesus' teaching in 5:38–42; while the second part of Lev 19:18 is about 'Loving the neighbors.' This is exactly what is taught in 5:42–48. Thus, Jesus did not give a new Law but interpreted the Law to the Christian community. Thus, though this comparison seems to have been kept antithetical to the Old Testament Law it was not kept antithetical to the prevalent practices of the people of Jesus' time and the Old Testament teaching in Lev 19:18. This comparison then uses Lev 19:18 to interpret the Law in Lev 24:19–20.

---

128. Also in Deut 19:21.
129. Daube, *The New Testament and Rabbinic Judaism,* 255.

Using one scripture to interpret another scripture was a common way of interpretation in those days.[130] Thus, in one way this comparison of Jesus does not show antithesis either, however, it helps the ideal disciple to live better by living in harmony and love, with his/her fellow citizens. The characterization of the ideal disciple here is that he/she should not follow the practice of retribution but he/she should show love and consideration to others.

6.3.8 Love your Neighbors vs. Love your Enemies

In 5:43-44, Jesus says, "*You have heard that it was said, 'you shall love your neighbor, and hate your enemy.' But I say to you, love your enemies, and pray for those who persecute you,*" Ἠκούσατε ὅτι ἐρρέθη· ἀγαπήσεις τὸν πλησίον σου καὶ μισήσεις τὸν ἐχθρόν σου. ἐγὼ δὲ λέγω ὑμῖν· ἀγαπᾶτε τοὺς ἐχθροὺς ὑμῶν καὶ προσεύχεσθε ὑπὲρ τῶν διωκόντων ὑμᾶς. This comparison in 5:43-44 is unique where Jesus compares "You have heard *that it was said*, 'you shall love your neighbor, *and hate your enemy*'" with his teaching "But I say to you, love your enemies." The ideal disciple should love his/her enemies and pray for the ones who persecute him/her so that—ὅπως γένησθε υἱοὶ τοῦ πατρὸς ὑμῶν τοῦ ἐν οὐρανοῖς . . . you may be sons of your Father who is in heaven (5:45). There is another reason why the ideal disciple should love the enemies. It is mentioned in 5:45 and 48. The ideal disciple should love the enemies because he/she should be perfect just like the Father is perfect, ἔσεσθε οὖν ὑμεῖς τέλειοι ὡς ὁ πατὴρ ὑμῶν ὁ οὐράνιος τέλειός ἐστιν (5:48). In addition, as the Father "*. . . causes His sun to rise on the evil and the good, and sends rain on the righteous and the unrighteous,*" ὅτι τὸν ἥλιον αὐτοῦ ἀνατέλλει ἐπὶ πονηροὺς καὶ ἀγαθοὺς καὶ βρέχει ἐπὶ δικαίους καὶ ἀδίκους (5:45), so the ideal disciple should also be like the Father and be perfect by loving the enemies, ἀγαπᾶτε τοὺς ἐχθροὺς ὑμῶν.

In addition, there are two comparisons here, very similar to the ones being found in Matt 6 and 7. As 5:46 and 47 are transition verses the similar comparisons found in Matt 6-7 are also found in the 5:46 and 47. Jesus

---

130. This method is called כיוצא בו במקום אחר "as is found in another place" [Neusner, *Rabbinic Literature: An Essential Giude*, 20]. Difficult passages are interpreted by comparison with clear passages containing similar principles. If Messiah is to sit at God's right hand then it may be inferred that when the Son of Man comes with the clouds (Dan 7:13-14), he will be seated at the right hand of God and will judge his enemies [Craig A. Evans, "Jewish Exegesis," *Dictionary for the Theological Interpretation of the Bible* (ed. Kevin J. Vanhoozer, London: SPCK, 2005), 381. Ps 110:1 was explained by Rabbi Aqiba *b.khag.* 14*a*; *b. Sanh.* 38*b* in relation with Daniel 7:9]. This is evidently what Jesus implied in his reply to Caiaphas (Mk 14:62).

says, if you love only those who love you what benefit do you have, ἐὰν γὰρ ἀγαπήσητε τοὺς ἀγαπῶντας ὑμᾶς, τίνα μισθὸν ἔχετε; (5:46). There is no specific benefit in this because even the Tax-collectors love in this way, οὐχὶ καὶ οἱ τελῶναι τὸ αὐτὸ ποιοῦσιν; (5:46). The ideal disciple here is compared with the tax collectors. Comparative characterization is found here. While the tax collectors love those who love them they should be rewarded also. Why should the ideal disciple specifically be rewarded with the kingdom of heaven while they have the same love as that of the tax-collectors? This could be considered as one of the most ironic comparisons in the Sermon on the Mount. While the other comparisons compare the disciple with other religious people such as Pharisees and scribes, here Jesus uses strong comparison by bringing the tax-collectors as the foil. J. Vernon McGee says, "The *tax collector* was at the bottom of the religious ladder; the *Pharisee* was at the top. *Tax collectors* were grouped right down there with the sinners; the *Pharisees* were considered to be the most acceptable ones to God."[131] Thus, if the ideal disciple was compared with the Pharisees it would be better for him/her than being compared with the tax-collector. If the ideal disciple only loves the ones who love him/her he/she is no better than the tax-collectors. Thus, the ideal disciple is characterized as the one who is better than the tax-collectors by their love for even their enemies.

Again in 5:47, Jesus compares the ideal disciple with the gentiles. He says, καὶ ἐὰν ἀσπάσησθε τοὺς ἀδελφοὺς ὑμῶν μόνον, τί περισσὸν ποιεῖτε; οὐχὶ καὶ οἱ ἐθνικοὶ τὸ αὐτὸ ποιοῦσιν, *"And if you greet your brothers only, what do you do more than others? Do not even the Gentiles do the same?"* (5:47). The ideal disciple again is compared with the gentiles in 5:47. The same principles found in the comparison with the tax-collectors are at work here too. The ideal disciple should be better than the gentiles. While the gentiles greet only their brothers the ideal disciple should greet and love even the enemies, ἀγαπᾶτε τοὺς ἐχθροὺς ὑμῶν.

No exact parallels of the teaching to love the enemies are found in the Jewish literature. It was usually believed by the Jews that God would vindicate Israel and would punish its persecutors (2 Macc 4:38; 7:36; Judith 11:10). The Essenes of Qumran exhorted followers to share love among people of their community and hate those who were not of their community (1QS 1:1:4, 10; 2:4–9; 1QM 4:1–2; 15:6; 1QH 5:4).[132] However, Jesus, when he died on the Cross, showed his love for his enemies by praying for their forgiveness. This is exactly what Jesus expected from his disciples. Every

---

131. McGee, *J. Vernon McGee on Prayer*, 17.

132. Even Gandhi could not apply this verse and love the British. Though Gandhi did not retaliate against the British he did not love them either.

Jewish community had their particular differences from the other Jewish sects in the interpretation of the Scriptures. This is one of the unique doctrines of the Christian Judaism. Through this command then Jesus commands his ideal disciple to love even enemies. This comparison shows the expected quality of the ideal disciple as he is the one who should love even his enemies much like his own master. The comparison shows the similarity to Jesus' own life and expects the disciple to model his/her life after the life of his/her master.

6.4 Jesus vs. Teachers of Judaisms of His Time

Though we argued our case that the comparisons in the Sermon on the Mount should not be considered as antitheses but as foils to foster the characterization of the ideal disciple, the case still needs to be strengthened by comparing what Jesus does in the Sermon on the Mount with the other teachings prevalent in Judaism of his time. This will be the concentration of this section. One of the major reasons why the comparisons are misunderstood by other interpreters is that many interpret Matt 5 out of the context of its time. Matthew's Gospel must be read alongside other Jewish writings of its time so that these comparisons can be understood better. Matthew's Gospel is the 'most Judaizing' of all the Gospels. Thus, one must understand the Judaism of the late antiquity, its sects and their leaders' teachings and their authority in order to understand the comparisons in the Sermon on the Mount better.

Neusner, an expert in Judaism, says that there were several sects of Judaism in the time of Jesus. All of them held the view that the Torah was authoritative and binding for their communities. Neusner says, "If we examine the communities of the faithful of Judaism, whether now or in antiquity, we are struck by the diversity of those communities and their faiths, all of them calling themselves 'Israel' and their faiths 'the Torah.'"[133] While Pharisees, and Essenes adhered to the whole Tanakh, the Sadducees only accepted the Torah (Pentateuch) as authoritative (Josephus, *B.J.* 13. 297–98). However, all Jewish sects accepted the Old Testament scriptures, interpreted them according to their own situations, and used the Scriptures to prove their beliefs. Neusner points out one interesting observation, i.e., the Judaism of the first century BCE and CE is so diverse that it is hard to say that one doctrine of a particular sect is said to be believed by other Jewish sects as well.

---

133. Chilton and Neusner, *Judaism in the New Testament*, 20.

> Most knowledgeable people now reject the conception of a single Judaism, everywhere paramount. A requirement of theology, the dogma of a single, valid Judaism contradicts the facts of history at every point in the history of Judaism, which finds its dynamic in the on-going struggle among *Judaisms* to gain the position of the sole, authentic re-presentation of the Torah. Further, along with the notion of a single official Judaism, we give up the notion of a unitary, internally harmonious Judaism, a lowest common denominator among a variety of diverse statements and systems. And logic further insists that we let go of the notion of an incremental, cumulative, 'traditional' Judaism. At the same time, and for the same reason, we dismiss as vacuous and hopelessly general the notion of a single Judaism characteristic of a given age, e.g. the first century BC and AD, and we reject as groundless the conception that all documents of said age tell us about one and the same religious community, therefore, a single Israel and its Torah. It follows that the sources of a given period of time do not tell us about a single Judaism, characteristic of that time. They tell us about their writers' premises, the Judaic thinking that underpins the Judaic system they have put forth-and that alone.[134] (Italics mine)

In the fifth line of the above quote, it should be noted that Neusner uses Judaism*s*, meaning there were several Judaisms in the first century BCE and CE. Thus, he named one of his books, *Judaism in the New Testament: Practices and Beliefs*, where the plurals, practice*s* and belief*s* should be noted because it shows that there were several practices and beliefs diversely present in that said period of time.[135] In this book, Neusner and Bruce Chilton tried to interpret the New Testament in the presupposition that New Testament books were Jewish writings. If so, New Testament documents show one kind of Judaism, Christian Judaism, and Mishnah and Talmud show Rabbinic Judaism, and Qumran writings show the Judaism of the Essenes of Qumran. Though all these different writings are of Judaism they speak about their particular beliefs of their particular sect. He further comments, "Once we recognize the diverse character of various bodies of Judaic writings, we take up a single body of what appear on the surface to be closely congruent documents and read them.... For we insist that each piece of writing or set of cognate writings tells us about the Judaism to which it wishes to attest."[136] Thus, each sect used the Torah to prove the doctrines of

134. Ibid., 6.
135. Ibid..
136. Ibid., 7.

the particular Jewish sect. In addition, each community had authoritative leaders who had special interpretative authority to interpret the Scripture, ex. Hillel and Shammai. It is time to look at some of the interpretations of some sects and see how it could help interpret the comparisons in the Sermon on the Mount.

6.4.1 Teacher of Righteousness and the Law

In the Qumran community there was an authoritative interpreter of the Scriptures called Teacher of Righteousness. The Dead Sea Scrolls know the Teacher as 'the Interpreter of the Law' in documents such as *The Community Rule, The Damascus Document, The Commentary on Habakkuk*, and *Midrash on the Last Days*. Authors of the scrolls know the Teacher as Teacher, Teacher of the Community, Teacher of Righteousness,[137] Interpreter, and Interpreter of the Law[138]. The fact that the Teacher has the authority to interpret the Law reflects his role in the community because the Law is pivotal to the Community. In the *Thanksgiving Hymns*, for instance, the Teacher refers to himself as having the waters of the covenant confirmed in his heart for those who seek it, for God has 'hidden Thy Law [within (him)].'[139] In this passage, the Teacher of Righteousness not only knows the Law, but his knowledge of the Law is given to him by God. As in Numbers 12:6–8 when Moses receives the Law directly from the mouth of God, the Teacher also receives the Law from the mouth of God (1*QpHab* II 2–3). The community respects the Teacher's legal understanding and uses his interpretations for redemption. *CD* 28–30 says: "But all those who hold fast to these precepts and coming in accordance with the Law, who heed the voice of the Teacher and confess before God, saying, 'Truly we have sinned . . . by walking counter to the precepts of the covenant' . . . ; they shall rejoice and their hearts shall be strong" (*CD* 28–30). The Teacher of Righteousness had special interpretative skills which gave him the authority to comment on the prophetic books and give its fuller futuristic meaning for his eschatological community. "The Teacher of Righteousness is one 'to whom God made known all the mysteries of the words of His servants the Prophets" (1*QpHab*

---

137. *CD* I, 11; *CD* VIII, 20:15, 20, 28, 33. 1Q14 I, 6. 1*QpHab* I, 12; II, 3; IV,10; VII,5, VIII,20; IX, 10; XI,6. 4Q171 III, 15; IV,8,26. 4Q173 I,5.

138. 1*QS* VIII,13. *CD* VI 8; VI, 18. 4QD a/e I, 20. 4Q174 I,12.

139. 1*QH* VIII, 8–10; 12. See also 1*QH* VI 10–12: 'to magnify the Law and the truth and to enlighten the members of your council in the midst of the sons of men' and 1*QH* VII 18–21: 'For in your righteousness you have appointed me for your Covenant, and I have clung to your truth and [gone forward in your ways].'

VII, 16). It seems that the community was fascinated with the prophetic books as they were expecting the apocalyptic end which was imminent for them.

The Teacher of Righteousness had special interpretive skills or revelation through which he could reveal the mysteries written by the prophets, which even the prophets were not aware of. 1*QpHab* 7:4–5 explains this characteristic feature of the Teacher of Righteousness: "And God told Habakkuk to write down that which would happen to the final generation, but He did not make known to him when time would come to an end. And as for that which He said, *That he who reads may read it speedily* (Hab 2:2): interpreted, this concerns the Teacher of Righteousness, to whom God made known all the mysteries of the words of His servants the Prophets" (Italics: Scripture). In another instance, the author of a *pesher* shows the interpretative skill of the Teacher while commenting on the prophetic book, Habakkuk.

> *[Behold the nations and see, marvel and be astonished; for I accomplish a deed in your days, but you will not believe it when] told.* They, the men of violence and the breakers of the Covenant, will not believe when they hear all that [is to happen to] the final generation from the Priest [in whose heart] God set [understanding] that he might interpret all the words of His servants the Prophets, through whom He foretold all that would happen to his people and [His land]. (1*QpHab II*, 5–10) (Italics: Scripture)

In this passage, the Teacher is portrayed as a priest who has the divine power to interpret the Scriptures, namely the Prophetic Books. If we read the quote carefully we will see that the Teacher had special revelation which added even more details to the Scriptures. These interpretations of the Teacher were considered authoritative to the community and essential for every member of the community. Most of the community rules and regulations were formed by the interpretations of the teacher. It is interesting that the Teacher is different from other exegetes because he does not merely apply scripture to his situation, but rather claims that scripture is written with him in mind. Thus, the Teacher had equal authority to the prophets: "Who have listened to the voice of the Teacher of Righteousness and have not despised the precepts of righteousness when they heard them; they shall rejoice and their hearts shall be strong, and they shall prevail over all the sons of the earth. God will forgive them and they shall see His salvation because they took refuge in His holy name. (*CD XIII*, 30–5)

In the Dead Sea Scrolls, the sectarians commented on the Old Testament prophetic books and the book of Psalms.[140] The *pesharim* are basically commentaries on the Old Testament books.[141] These *pesharim* were usually categorized into two categories: *continuous*, which interpret a single book section by section, and *thematic*, which consist of certain citations grouped around a thematic idea. Likewise, in Math 5, Jesus was basically commenting on the Old Testament documents in thematic fashion to give the exhortation on how the ideal disciple should live.

In the Gospels, though it is not explicitly stated that Jesus had such an authority to interpret the Scripture, Jesus in Matthew is portrayed as the one who had similar authority to interpret the Old Testament Scripture and thematically commenting on it to give the rules of his newly formed Christian-Jewish sect by characterizing the ideal disciple with exhortations and teachings. Jesus is characterized as *the* Teacher who interprets the Law in the right manner, which would serve as the rules for the Matthean community. Thus, Jesus is shown in the Sermon on the Mount as the one using the comparisons to characterize the ideal disciple.

6.4.2 Rabbi Hillel and the Law

Another important figure in the history of the rabbis in Israel is Hillel. Neusner says, "When we take up the question of the Pharisees, we focus attention on Hillel in particular because he was the greatest figure of that group."[142] Neusner dates historical Hillel to have lived by 50 BCE to 10 CE, which makes Hillel as a 'near-contemporary' to Jesus.[143] There are quite a number of similarities between Hillel and Jesus. Hillel gives an inverted golden rule of Jesus saying, "What is hateful to yourself do not do to your neighbor. That is the entire Torah. All the rest is commentary" (*Talmud Shabbat* 31a). Neusner notes that Hillel was not just an interpreter of the Law but also a legislator of the Law.[144] The legislator is the one who

---

140. 1*QpHab*; 1*QpMic*; 1*QpZeph*; 1*QpPs*; 3*QpIsa*; 4*QIsa a-e*; 4*QpHos a, b*; 4*QpMic*; 4*QpNah*; 4*QpZeph*; 4*QpPs ab*.

141. It should be noted that the term *pesher* should not only restricted to the commentaries on the prophetic books because in the DSS *pesharim* of the Psalms are also included. As the Qumran community were more inclined on unraveling the mysteries of the prophetic books they used this style of writing commentaries for the prophetic books and psalms. It nevertheless negates the possibility of similar composition of commentaries among the other Jewish sects on other books of the Tanakh.

142. Neusner, *Judaism in the beginning of Christianity*, 63.

143. Ibid., 64.

144. Ibid., 64.

could make the Law. One must understand that in the intertestamental period Jews thought that God's direct words were not common among them. Therefore, no one after Malachi spoke anymore as though they received the word directly from the Lord saying, 'Thus says the Lord'. Thus, they considered Old Testament to constitute the religious, moral and social Law which taught them how one should live within the community. This view emphasized the importance of the Torah and so the Jewish teachers were not willing to write something and say, "thus says the Lord."[145] Hence, the religious leaders of the Judaism of the later intertestamental time handled the scripture carefully. In this period of time, Hillel is mentioned as a legislator who gave new law to the people which basically went against one of the Old Testament commandment. Deut 15:1–3 states that:

> 1. *At the end of seven years you shall grant a remission of debts.*
>
> 2. And this is the manner of remission: every creditor shall release what he has loaned to his neighbor; he shall not exact it of his neighbor and his brother, because the Lord's remission has been proclaimed.
>
> 3. From a foreigner you may exact it, *but your hand shall release whatever of yours is with your brother.*

According to the Torah the lender must remit all the loans of the debtor on the dawn of the seventh year in the septennial cycle. Practically, it was said, it did not serve the purpose of the Law however it had adverse effect on the teaching of the Law. The Law teaches that when someone borrows money from a lender, the loan must be cancelled at the dawn of the seventh year. If this continually happens the lender will have nothing to give. No business, ancient or modern, could withstand periodic debt cancellation without seriously undermining the financial security of the lenders. It does not only cause damage to the lender but also to the poor because very few would come forward to lend money as they know it would be cancelled on the seventh year. Thus, the principle of the Torah, which is to help the poor, is affected by the Torah itself. For this reason, Rabbinic literatures say, 'Hillel legislated the *prozbul*,' a law concerning the lending and the cancellation of the loan. The *prozbul* is nothing but a system where the lender deposits a certificate, called the *prozbul* to the court, in which the court takes over the debts and preserved them from being annulled in the Seventh Year. Thus, the debts would remain even after the seventh year because the loan is not from the lender's hand but from the court.

---

145. Some used another medium where they shared what they wanted to say through Pseudepigrapha.

A. Whatever of yours that is with your brother your hand should release (Deut 15:3)-but not he who gives his mortgages to the court.

B. On this basis, they said

C. Hillel ordained the prozbul.

D. On the account of the order of the world.

E. That he saw the people, that they held back from lending to one another and transgressed what is written in the Torah

F. He arose and ordained the prozbul.

G. And this is the formula of the prozbul: 'I give to you, so-and-so and so-and-so, the judges in such-and-such place, every debt which I have, that I may collect it whenever I like,' and the judges seal below or the witnesses (*Sifre Deut* 113).[146]

Thus, Hillel legislated a law, *prozbul*, which is basically against the Law but justified by the Law by saying that the Law just mentions 'that which is in the hands of you' (Deut 15:3) but does not say anything against 'that which is in the hands of the court'. Thus, Hillel said one could leave his property with the court that the loan will not be cancelled on the seventh year. Though this interpretation is against the Law the Hillelites justified it by saying it was for the benefit of the people (on the account of the order of the world). Thus, one must notice that Hillel had authority to interpret the Scriptures even to the point of going against the Law so that the order of the world could be maintained.[147] This is an authority Jewish leaders of the sects possessed, which is quite peculiar to them.

If a Jewish leader had an authority to overwrite the Scripture because of the order of the world how much more the Messiah himself should have. It does not mean that the Jewish leader or the Messiah nullifies the Law but they expound the Law for the betterment of their community. Hillel was not considered as the one who abrogated the Law though he basically legislated a law which was against the Torah. Likewise, Jesus in the comparisons of Matt 5:21–48 mentions several so called antithesis which sound like antithesis but if one look closely in the view of the Jewish leaders' authority to interpret the Law these are not to be considered as antitheses but explicatory of the Law.

---

146. Neusner, *From Politics to Piety*, 14.

147. Jesus was against this way of interpreting the Scripture of the Pharisees that in Matt 15 he points out that the Korban law of giving gifts to the temple nullified the Torah which said honor your father and mother.

There is also one other phenomenon one must consider before concluding on the subject of comparisons of the Sermon on the Mount in 5:21–48. As Jesus had the authority even to contradict the Law like Hillel and the Teacher of Righteousness, Jesus uses comparisons to complement the Law instead of contradicting. This point is stressed in this section through the examples from the Teacher of Righteousness and Hillel. In the next section, one other method used by the Rabbis called 'Building fence around the Torah' will be seen so that we are able to better understand the function of the comparisons in the Sermon on the Mount. To this now we turn.

6.4.3 Building Fence Around the Torah

The Qumran community criticizes an unidentified group referred to only as "builders of the wall" (*CD* 4.19–20). Probably this criticism was directed against the Pharisees, who created extra-biblical laws in order to protect the Law (see *m. Abot* 1.1: "And make a fence around the Law") (see also *CD* 8.12–13, 18; 19.31). "Moses received the Torah from Sinai, and handed it down to Joshua, and Joshua to the elders, and the elders to the prophets, and the prophets delivered it to the men of the Great Synagogue. They said three things, 'Be deliberate in judgment; raise up many disciples; and make a fence about the Torah'" (*Abot* 1.1). The word, Torah basically means the "written Law," the first five books of the Old Testament. However, the Pharisees believed that God also gave "oral law"[148] on Mt. Sinai, which Moses transmitted to Joshua and Joshua to the elders (*Abot* 1.1). The elders, then, transmitted it to the prophets and the prophets to the Great Synagogue, the elders of the Pharisees. The men of the Great Synagogue said three things and the third one is "make fence about the Torah." Thus, Abot shows that making fence around the Torah is a teaching of the Pharisees that went back to the time of Moses himself who received it from God. Though this is a justification of the Pharisees' teaching one must notice that this 'fencing around the Torah' is such an important aspect of the Pharisees that they date it back to Moses receiving it from God.

'Fencing around the Torah' thus refers to the regulations that were formulated by the Jewish elders formulated to ensure that they don't break the Law of the Old Testament. In *Abot* 3:17, Rabi Akiba (40–135 CE) also teaches the same principle of fencing around the Torah: "R. Akiba said, ' . . . The Massorah is a rampart around the Torah; tithes are a safeguard to riches; good resolves are a fence to abstinence; a hedge around wisdom is

---

148. The "oral law" (תּוֹרָה שֶׁבְּעַל־פֶּה) is nothing but that which develops, illuminates, and comments upon the "written law" (תּוֹרָה שֶׁבִּכְתָב).

silence'" (*Abot* 3.17). It is important to note that Rabbi Akiba was mentioned as the one teaching about the fencing around the Torah because after the destruction of the Temple in 70 C. E. Rabi Akiba was the major figure of the Jewish elders for the transmission of the oral Torah. Thus, R. Akiba ben Joseph teaching the 'Fencing around the Torah' is important. Here, in *Abot* 3.17, R. Akiba points out that the oral Torah (Massorah) is the fence around the Torah. Most of the Mishnaic teachings are the oral Torah. The oral Torah elaborates how one should obey the Torah effectively. The rabbis expounded on the Torah on how one must obey a certain Law in a particular situation. For example, on the regulations of how one must keep the Sabbath, *Mishnah Shabbat* gives 39 prohibitions so that that one does not break the law:

> The chief categories of acts of labor [prohibited on the Sabbath] are forty less one:
>
> 1. one who sows,
> 2. ploughs,
> 3. reaps,
> 4. binds sheaves,
> 5. threshes,
> 6. winnows,
> 7. selects [fit from unfit produce or crops],
> 8. grinds,
> 9. sifts,
> 10. kneads,
> 11. bakes,
> 12. one who shears wool,
> 13. washes it,
> 14. beats it,
> 15. dyes it,
> 16. spins,
> 17. weaves,
> 18. makes two loops,
> 19. weaves two threads,
> 20. separates two threads,
> 21. ties,
> 22. unties,
> 23. sews two stitches,
> 24. tears in order to sew two stitches,
> 25. one who traps a deer,
> 26. slaughters it,
> 27. flays it,

28. salts it,
29. cures its hide,
30. scrapes it,
31. and cuts it up,
32. one who writes two letters,
33. erases two letters in order to write two letters
34. one who builds,
35. tears down,
36. one who put out a fire,
37. kindles a fire
38. one who hits with a hammer
39. one who transports an object from one domain to another:

These are the forty categories of labor less one. (*m. Šabb.* 7:2)

Old Testament teaches that the people of God should keep the Sabbath by resting (Deut 5:12) and by not doing any work. It is clearly emphasized in Exod 31:13–14: "13 *You yourself are to speak to the Israelites: You will keep my Sabbaths, for this is a sign between me and you throughout your generations, given in order that you may know that I, the Lord, sanctify you. 14 You will keep the Sabbath, because it is holy for you; everyone who profanes it will be put to death; whoever does any work on it will be cut off from among the people*" (NAU). Old Testament does not give much detail on what works are which are prohibited, except a few, like 'not to kindle the fire on Sabbath,' etc., in Exod 35:3. Thus, the rabbis, the leaders of the Jewish sects, had to expound the Torah on how one should observe the Torah. The Pharisees were important in this respect. They purportedly created this 'building wall around the Torah' so that their followers would not break the Torah. These are not just regulations but building the fence. In order to find the Jewish elders' technique of interpreting the Torah and also their regulations to prohibit the breaking of the Torah we must look into the building of the fence in Mishnah Shabbat.

One who builds—how much does he build so as to be liable (to punishment for violating the prohibition)?

One who builds in any measure at all.

One who hews stone, hits with a hammer or adze, or bores—in any measure at all is liable.

This is the governing principle: Whoever on the Sabbath performs a forbidden act of labor and [the result of] his act of labor endures is liable.

12:2

One who plough in any measure whatsoever, is liable.

One who weeds, one who cuts off dead leaves, and one who prunes, in any measure whatsoever, is liable.

One who gathers branches of wood: if to improve the field—in any measure at all; if for a fire—a measure of wood sufficient to cook a small egg—is liable.

One who gathers herbs, if it is to improve the field—in any measure at all; if it is for cattle to eat—in the measure of a lamb's mouthful, is liable.

12:3

One who writes two letters, whether with the right hand or with the left, whether the same letter or two different letters, whether with different pigments, in any alphabet—is liable.

12:4

One who writes two letters at one time, inadvertently, is liable.

If one wrote with ink, caustic, red dye, gum, or copperas, or with anything that leaves a mark, on two walls forming a corner, or on two leaves of a tablet, which are read with one another—is liable.

One who writes on his flesh is liable. One who scratches a mark on his flesh—Rabbi Eliezer declares him liable to a sin offering [he must bring a sacrifice in the Temple to atone for his sin], while Rabbi Joshua declares him exempt.

12:5

If one wrote with fluids, fruit juice, dirt from the street, writer's sand, or with anything that does not leave a lasting mark, he is exempt (from punishment).

If one wrote with the back of his hand, with his foot, mouth, or elbow; if he wrote one letter alongside a letter already written; if he wrote a letter on top of a letter [already written]; . . . if he wrote one on the ground and one on the beam; if he wrote two letters on the two walls of the house, on the two sides of a leaf of paper, so that they cannot be read with one another, he is exempt.

(*m. Šabb.* 12:1)

Here, it is clear that several practical suggestions were given on how one must refrain from building, plowing, and writing in order that he/she would not break the Torah of Sabbath observance. The Old Testament does not teach these details. However, these minute details of practical life were mentioned by the Jewish rabbis so that the Law would not be broken.

Though the Pharisaic group is the one considered as doing this fencing around the Torah we see similar regulations in the Qumran writings also. One example could also be given concerning the obedience of the Sabbath.

> As to the Sabbath to keep it according to its law, ... no man shall do work on the sixth day from the time in which the globe of the sun is removed from the gate in its fullness, for it is He who said, "Keep the Sabbath day to sanctify it." And on the day of the Sabbath no man shall utter a word of folly. And surely none shall demand any debt of his neighbor. None shall judge on matters of property, and gain. None shall speak on matters of work and labor to be done on the following morning.... No man shall walk in the field to do the work of his affairs on the day of the Sabbath. None shall walk outside his city more than a thousand cubits.... No man shall eat on the day of the Sabbath but of that which is prepared or perishing in the field. None shall eat or drink but from that which was in the camp. But if he was on the way and went down to wash he may drink where he stands, ... but he shall not draw into any vessel. No man shall send the son of the stranger to do his affairs on the day of the Sabbath.... No man shall put on garments that are filthy or were brought by a gentile unless they were washed in water or rubbed off with frankincense.... No man shall mingle of his own will on the Sabbath.... No man shall walk after the animal to feed it outside of his city more than two thousand cubits.... None shall lift his hand to beat it with his fist.... If it be stubborn he shall not remove it out of his house.... No man shall carry anything from the house to the outside or from the outside into the house and if he be in the gate he shall not carry out anything of it or bring in anything into it. None shall open the cover of a vessel that is pasted on the Sabbath.... No man shall carry on him spices to go out and come in on the Sabbath.
> ... None shall move in the house on the day of the Sabbath rock or earth. No nurse shall bear the suckling child to go out and to come in on the Sabbath.... No man shall provoke his manservant or his maidservant or his hireling on the day of the Sabbath.... No man shall deliver an animal on the day of the Sabbath.... And if it falls into a pit or ditch, he shall not raise

it on the Sabbath.... No man shall rest in a place near to the gentiles on the day of the Sabbath.... No man shall profane the Sabbath for the sake of wealth and gain.

... And if any person falls into a gathering of water or into a place of ... he shall not bring him up by a ladder or a cord or instrument.... No man shall bring anything on the altar on the Sabbath, save the burnt-offering of the Sabbath, for so it is written, "Save your Sabbaths." [CD 14]

Thus, even Qumran community, which calls the Pharisees as the builders of walls, use the same interpretive techniques by 'building fence around the Torah' so that they will not break the Law. Sanders mentions, "It is a general principle that greater stringency than the Law requires is not illegal. The *ḥeberim* and the Essenes, to name two obvious groups, took on themselves stringent requirements not in Mosaic Law, and they doubtless did so on religious grounds."[149] He continues to say, "It is not against the Law to be stricter than the Law requires. Only those who think that it is can readily harmonize the antitheses with the view that Jesus opposed aspects of the Law."[150] Thus, Jesus used a similar Jewish interpretative technique, building fence around the Torah, so that his ideal disciple would not break the Law. Thus, as the ideal disciple is exhorted to shun away from anger so that he would not commit murder, he is exhorted to shun away from lust so that he would not commit adultery. Divorce should be avoided on behalf of the world order that not many women would suffer just because their husbands divorce them for no valid reasons. Oaths are not needed when 'yes' is 'yes' and 'no' is 'no'. There is no need to retaliate against others because the disciples are to love even the enemies. Thus, Jesus basically built fence around the Torah so that the intention of the Scripture would be fulfilled by the obedience of the interpretations of the Messiah by the ideal disciple. Thus, the ideal disciple is characterized as the one who obeys the Law by following the fence laid around the Torah by his/her master and Messiah, Jesus Christ, by not being angry, by not lusting after other women, by not divorcing, by being truthful and by loving one another, even the enemies. Thus, this characterization of the ideal disciple is not of an antinomian disciple but the one who follows the Law by the fence laid by his master.

---

149. Sanders, *Jesus and Judaism*, 256.
150. Ibid., 260.

6.5 Conclusion

In this chapter, Jesus' use of the comparisons in 5:17–48, in the Sermon on the Mount was dealt with. Through the many comparisons Jesus characterizes the ideal disciple as the one who keeps the Law, as he also does. In 5:17–18, Jesus showed that he is not an antinomian. Further, from 5:19–48, Jesus' exhortation to the disciples and consequentially by his characterization of the ideal disciple he has shown that the ideal disciple is also not an antinomian but the one who follows the Law expounded by his/her master, Jesus Christ. These comparisons helped in this characterization as a polemic against the Pharisaic and scribal teachings and the obedience of the Law, and against the assumptions of the Jesus' teachings on the Law. Thus, in this chapter it was argued that the comparisons in the so-called antithesis are not antithetical comparisons rather they function as foils to bring out the characterization of the ideal disciple, i.e., the one who keeps the Law far better than the Pharisees and scribes. Thus, comparisons aid greatly in the characterization of the ideal disciple in Matt 5:17–48.

Chapter 7

Comparative Characterization in Matthew 6:1—7:29

7.1 Introduction

UNTIL MATT 5:48, JESUS expounded the Law and exhorted the disciple to obey the Law in the way he expounded the Law. By doing this, he also characterized the ideal disciple as the one who obeys the Law as explicated by the master, Jesus Christ so that his/her righteousness would exceed that of the Pharisees and scribes (5:20). Morris says, "The previous section (5:17–48) has made it very clear that Jesus was not opposed to keeping the Law; rather, he was firmly committed to it and in a much more wholehearted way than his Pharisaic opponents."[1] Morris points out that the whole of Matt 5:21–48 should be understood as Jesus teaching the Law against the teachings of the scribes and the Pharisees.[2] This was done with the many comparisons—so called antitheses, in chapter 5. These kinds of comparisons continue well into chapters 6 and 7. Jesus uses comparisons in comparing the ideal disciple with Pharisees and even with gentiles to characterize the ideal disciple in these chapters. These comparisons will be the concentration of this study in this chapter. Here again, Jesus' use of comparisons will be identified and studied to recognize their function as a foil and their purpose to elucidate the characteristic features of the ideal disciple.

The focus of this chapter is to identify the characterization of the ideal disciple in chapters 6 and 7 of the Sermon on the Mount and to look at the functions of the comparisons in chapters 6 and 7.

---

1. Morris, *The Gospel According to Matthew*, 135.
2. Also Gundry, *Matthew*, 101.

7.2 Beware of Practicing Righteousness (6:1–34)

Even in ch. 6, Christ continues his teachings that true righteousness must exceed that of the scribes and Pharisees (5:20).[3] The continuity is obvious by the comparisons he uses in 6.2, 5–16, with the hypocrites to teach how the ideal disciple should live. Hans Dieter Betz identifies that Jesus' teachings in the Sermon on the Mount are kept in comparison with the teachings of the scribes and Pharisees. He says:

> The definition of the Sermon on the Mount is that, now the way to attain righteousness is not just like that of the scholars, to be read from the paper. For this reason, righteousness can therefore only be spoken in the comparison and contrast. It is enough to note that they are quantitatively and qualitatively different from the scribes and the Pharisees and it must be superior than theirs.
>
> The question is but now, why the Sermon on the Mount is just kept as an antitype to the teaching of the scribes and the Pharisees. The expression the scribes and Pharisees shows an already existing stereotyping in advance, which was probably there since Jesus' time and even since John the Baptist's, reflecting an existing dispute. Historically, Jesus seems to be its Torah Interpreter, especially in the confrontation with the scribes and Pharisees. The words of the Sermon on the Mount can look back on these conflicts, but even in the reliance on them, as it is clear from the antitheses. The δικαιοσύνη required by God after the Sermon on the Mount can therefore not simply be provided through external observation of rules, as we saw in the scribes and Pharisees practiced.[4]

---

3. Glasscock, *Matthew*, 141.

4. The original text in German is as the following: *Die Definition der Bergpredigt zeichnet sich nun dadurch aus, daß der ihr gelehrte Weg zur Gerechtigkeit nicht einfach vom Papier abgelesen werden kann. Von dieser Gerechtigkeit kann deshalb auch nur im Vergleich und im Kontrast gesprochen warden. Es genügt festzustellen, daß sie sich quantitativ und qualitativ von der Schriftgelehrten und Pharisäer unterscheiden und ihr überlegen sein muß. Die Frage ist nun aber, warum die Bergpredigt gerade in der Lehre der Schriftgelehrten und Pharisäer ihren Antityp sieht. Der Ausdruck Schriftgelehrten und Pharisäer setzt dabei ja schon eine gewisse Stereotypisierung voraus, die wohl die seit Jesu und sogar seit Johannes dem Täufer bestehende Auseinandersetzung widerspiegel. Historisch gesehen hat Jesus offenbar seine Toraauffassung vor allem in der Auseinandersetzung mit den Schriftgelehrten und Pharisäern entwickelt. Die Bergpredigt blickt auf diese Auseinandersetzungen zurück, nimmt aber selbst im Rückgriff an ihnen teil, wie sich aus den Antithesen ergibt. Die von Gott geforderte* δικαιοσύνη *kann nach der Bergpredigt demnach nicht einfach durch äußerliche Beobachtung von Vorschriften erbracht werden, wie man dies bei den Schriftgelehrten und Pharisäern praktiziert sah* (Betz, Studien zur Bergpredigt, 47).

Here, Betz clearly points out that *Gerechtigkeit* could only be spoken "in comparison and contrast" with the scribes and the Pharisees because of the existing disputes with them from the time of John the Baptist. Thus, the comparison is used. Further, Betz states that Jesus developed his understanding of the Torah (Toraaufassung) in discussion and debate with scribes and Pharisees. Though it is not the concentration of this study to go into the historical aspects of the conflict between Jesus and the Pharisees and scribes it is important to note that Betz keeps Jesus' teachings, including the antitheses, in contrast and in comparison to the teachings of the scribes and the Pharisees.

These comparisons, thus, characterize the ideal disciple. In Matt 6:1, Jesus warns the disciple by saying, *"Beware of practicing your righteousness before men to be noticed by them,"* Προσέχετε δὲ τὴν δικαιοσύνην ὑμῶν μὴ ποιεῖν ἔμπροσθεν τῶν ἀνθρώπων πρὸς τὸ θεαθῆναι αὐτοῖς. The word "beware" προσέχετε—indicates warning and prohibition. The disciple should be careful about practicing righteousness before men (ἔμπροσθεν τῶν ἀνθρώπων). Further more, they should never practice righteousness before men. The consequences for practicing righteousness before men would mean he/she will have no reward from the Father who is in heaven (6:1). The mention of οὐρανοις indicates that the rewards will not be in heaven or towards heaven. It is already mentioned in 5:20 that *"unless your righteousness exceeds that of the Pharisees you will not enter into the kingdom of heaven,"* ἐὰν μὴ περισσεύσῃ ὑμῶν ἡ δικαιοσύνη πλεῖον τῶν γραμματέων καὶ Φαρισαίων, οὐ μὴ εἰσέλθητε εἰς τὴν βασιλείαν τῶν οὐρανῶν. Thus, the disciple practicing righteousness like the Pharisees before men (6:2), will not have any reward from the Father in heaven. Thus, he may not enter into the kingdom of heaven. This is how serious a folly it is to practice righteousness before men. In what way could one practice righteousness before men? Three examples are given: prayer, almsgiving and fasting. All these three areas are identified as common practices often preached and exhorted by the religious leaders of that time, as practicing righteousness.[5] Tob 12:8 says, "Prayer is good when accompanied by fasting, almsgiving, and righteousness." Thus, practice of righteousness is identified with prayer, fasting and almsgiving. Gundry calls these the three main pillars of Jewish piety.[6] Thus, Jesus, a product of his time, used these three elements to identify the abuse of these elements of religious piety in chapter 6. Jesus deals with these elements of religious piety in the following passages:

5. Glasscock, *Matthew*, 142.
6. Gundry, *Matthew*, 101.

Almsgiving:
    6:1-4: Don't give to the poor before men like the hypocrites

Prayer:
    6:5-6: Don't pray before people like the hypocrites
    6:7-15: Don't pray with meaningless words like the gentiles

Fasting:
    6:16-18: Don't fast before men like the hypocrites

In addition to these, Jesus also includes few other elements of practical living. In 6:19-21, Jesus encourages the ideal disciple to store wealth in heaven rather storing wealth on the earth. This could be a transition passage because, in 6:1-18 Jesus shares that religious piety practiced before men will produce only μισθός, "reward" or "wealth" in the earth and not in heaven. Thus, 6:19-21 could be a summary of 6:1-18, which says don't store your reward on the earth but store it in heaven. The Father in heaven gives rewards in heaven. Thus, the ideal disciple must seek the rewards in heaven and store the rewards in heaven by giving alms secretly, ποιῇς ἐλεημοσύνην (6:1-4); by praying privately, προσεύχομαι (6:5-15); and by fasting properly, νηστεύω (6:16-18). Thus, 6:19-21 functions as a summary for 6:1-18. In addition, the concept of do not store up in earth is brought back in 6:24-34 in which Jesus teaches the disciple not to serve money. Thus, 6:19-21 functions as a transition passage in this chapter. In 6:22-23, a seemingly unrelated teaching about the eyes is mentioned. After this, in 6:24-34, Jesus teaches the disciple not to serve money but only God by not worrying about the essentials of life but to trust God. Thus ends Matthew chapter 6. While the teachings of Jesus in Matt 7 are dealt with in 7.3 of this chapter, and the teachings of Jesus in Matt 6 are further dealt with in 7.2 of this chapter. To this now we proceed.

7.2.1 Not Giving Alms before Men like the Hypocrites (6:1-4)

Though Matt 6:1 functions as an introduction to the whole chapter, even to chapter 7, it is, however, immediately connected to 6:2-4. The disciple must be careful on how he/she would do righteousness before men. As mentioned above, δικαιοσύνη in Matthew functions quite differently from Pauline usage. Boice identifies the trouble in translating δικαιοσύνη by giving few alternatives and say: "We might say piety, but *piety* usually refers to what we call a pious attitude. *Devotion* is a possibility, but we usually limit devotions to such matters as Bible reading and prayer. *Religion* might work if what we mean is 'Do not make public displays of your religion in order to attract other people's attention.'"[7] Thus, Boice points out that NIV's translation which says "acts of righteousness" could be the better translation.[8] Then, this would mean, in Matt 6:1, Jesus says, *"Beware of practicing your acts of righteousness before men to be noticed by them."* It is interesting that Jesus mentions "before men," ἔμπροσθεν τῶν ἀνθρώπων, and also adds "to be noticed by them," πρὸς τὸ θεαθῆναι αὐτοῖς. This shows the stress Jesus wants to place on the performance of the acts of righteousness "before men" and "to be noticed by them." τὸ θεαθῆναι, the infinitive to be noticed by them, αὐτοῖς, is an adverbial use of the infinitive indicating purpose.[9] Thus, the better translation would be "Beware of practicing your righteousness before men *for the purpose of* being noticed by men." The disciple does the "acts of righteousness" for the purpose of being noticed by them. Jesus then characterizes the ideal disciple as the one who does not do the "acts of righteousness" "before men" "to be noticed by them." If he/she does then he/she "will have no reward from the Father in heaven," μισθὸν οὐκ ἔχετε παρὰ τῷ πατρὶ ὑμῶν τῷ ἐν τοῖς οὐρανοῖς (Matt 6:1).

This doing of the "acts of righteousness" "before men" and "for the purpose of being praised by them," τὴν δικαιοσύνην ὑμῶν . . . ποιεῖν ἔμπροσθεν τῶν ἀνθρώπων πρὸς τὸ θεαθῆναι αὐτοῖς, is related to Matt 6:2–4. In 6:2, Jesus says, "so when you give to poor, do not sound a trumpet before you . . . " It is quite interesting that Jesus uses οὖν here in the beginning of 6:2. οὖν connects 6:1 to 6:2. The things mentioned in 6:1 give rise to the things mentioned in 6:2. How should the disciple not do the acts of righteousness (τὴν δικαιοσύνην ὑμῶν . . . ποιεῖν) before men and to be noticed by them? It is when the ideal disciple gives alms properly to the poor, Ὅταν οὖν ποιῇς ἐλεημοσύνην (6:2–4).

Giving to the poor is encouraged and even commanded in the Old Testament. Deut 15:11 says, *"There will always be poor people in the land. Therefore I command you to be openhanded toward you brothers and toward the poor and needy in your land."* Further, there are many verses in the Old Testament which share similar ideas:

> Deut 15:4: However, there should be no poor among you, for in the land the Lord your God is giving you to possess as your inheritance, he will richly bless you,

---

7. Boice, *The Gospel of Matthew*, 96.
8. Ibid., 96.
9. Wallace, *Greek Grammar*, 592.

Deut 15:6: For the Lord your God will bless you as he has promised, and you will lend to many nations but will borrow from none. You will rule over many nations but none will rule over you.

⁷ If there is a poor man among your brothers in any of the towns of the land that the Lord your God is giving you, do not be hardhearted or tightfisted toward your poor brother.

⁸ Rather be openhanded and freely lend him whatever he needs.

⁹ Be careful not to harbor this wicked thought: "The seventh year, the year for canceling debts, is near," so that you do not show ill will toward your needy brother and give him nothing. He may then appeal to the Lord against you, and you will be found guilty of sin.

¹⁰ Give generously to him and do so without a grudging heart; then because of this the Lord your God will bless you in all your work and in everything you put your hand to.

¹¹ There will always be poor people in the land. Therefore I command you to be openhanded toward your brothers and toward the poor and needy in your land.

Pro 14:31: He who oppresses the poor shows contempt for their Maker, but whoever is kind to the needy honors God.

Pro 19:17: He who is kind to the poor lends to the Lord, and he will reward him for what he has done.

Pro 22:9: A generous man will himself be blessed, for he shares his food with the poor.

Isaiah 3:14: The Lord enters into judgment against the elders and leaders of his people: "It is you who have ruined my vineyard; the plunder from the poor is in your houses.

¹⁵ What do you mean by crushing my people and grinding the faces of the poor?" declares the Lord, the Lord Almighty.

Thus, giving to the poor was essential for Jewish piety. However, these acts of righteousness were used by many for their personal benefits. For Jesus says, *"So when you give to the poor do not sound a trumpet before you, as the hypocrites do in the synagogues and in the streets, so that they may be honored by men. Truly I say to you, they have their reward in full"* (6:2). The comparison here is quite evident. The hypocrites here play as the foil to bring out the characteristic features expected of the disciple.

When the hypocrites give to the poor they sound a trumpet before them, μὴ σαλπίσῃς ἔμπροσθέν σου (Matt 6:2). This happens in two places: in the synagogues and also in the streets, συναγωγαῖς καὶ ἐν ταῖς ῥύμαις

(Matt 6:2). It should be noticed that both, συναγωγαῖς and ῥύμαις are public places. Morris says, "The synagogue was a public place, and a generous gift made there would certainly be noticed. So it was with the streets. Jesus selects two very public places where hypocritical gifts may be given and he warns his followers against following the practice. People who engage in that kind of giving are interested in being praised by men; It is the praise and not the helping of the needy in which they are primarily interested."[10] Thus, Jesus chooses two strategic places to identify how attention-craving the so-called "acts of righteousness" of the hypocrites are.

It is not clear if the hypocrites really used trumpets before giving the gifts, μὴ σαλπίσῃς ἔμπροσθέν σου. Glasscock identifies that blowing the trumpet was important in the Old Testament to gather people together in the time of Moses.[11] However, no literature mentions that Jews blew trumpet before giving alms. This could have been a figurative speech. Glasscock says, "It is possible that Jesus was being sarcastic and used the ceremony of trumpet blowing as illustrating how ridiculous that Pharisees had become even in minor charities."[12] Through this comparison, then Jesus points out the negative aspects of practicing righteousness of the hypocrites.

An important question to ask at this juncture is who these hypocrites are. The word, ὑποκριταί was used for actors on stage plays who acted out a certain character.[13] Thus, Gundry says ὑποκριταί "here refers to acting in pretense of concern for the needy when the real concern is for the admiration from other men."[14] Thus, the hypocrites were those people who were not genuinely concerned for the poor but their real concern was to establish a reputation for piety.

Who are these hypocrites? Pharisees are frequently called as ὑποκριταί in the Gospels, and especially in Matthew (Matt 6:2,5,16; 7:5; 15:7; 22:18;23:13, 14, 15, 23, 25, 27, 29; 24:51; also in Mark 7:6; Luke 6:42; 12:56; and 13:15). In addition, in the context of the Sermon on the Mount where the comparison is explicitly kept against the Pharisees in 5:20 it is understandable that Pharisees are intended here by the use of ὑποκριταί in 6:2 (also in 6:5 & 16). Thus, Pharisees are kept as foils for the ideal disciple who "blow trumpet," σαλπίσῃς, not literally though but metaphorically (like blowing your horns in colloquial terms), while giving alms to the poor.[15]

10. Morris, *The Gospel According to Matthew*, 137.
11. Glasscock, *Matthew*, 142.
12. Ibid., 142.
13. Gundry, *Matthew*, 102.
14. Ibid., 102.
15. Blomberg, *Matthew*, 116.

The last clause in 6:2 shows that by giving alms to the poor "before men," ἔμπροσθεν τῶν ἀνθρώπων, in public places Pharisees *"have their reward in full,"* ἀπέχουσιν τὸν μισθὸν αὐτῶν. By giving alms in public the Pharisees will not get the reward from the Father in heaven (6:2). However, they receive their reward in full from men as they seek to be "honored by men," δοξασθῶσιν ὑπὸ τῶν ἀνθρώπων (6:2). The verb form ἀπέχουσιν is in the present tense but it contains a notion of the perfect, an action happened in the past of whose effect is still being felt in the present time. They are not receiving the reward at the present. They have received the reward when they gave alms before people. However, it is kept in the present because these kinds of actions happen frequently even in the time of the narration. Thus, it should be considered as perfective present, to meaning "they have received their reward."[16] By this, Jesus identifies that the action's reward had been given and still is continuous as they continue to give alms before people. Glasscock says that "the choice seems to be between whose reward a person desires—the recognition of men or the recognition of God."[17] This is not just about pleasing men but it is about not pleasing God and much more than that, i.e., displeasing God. Pharisaic concentration on the acts of righteousness to be honored by men shows dishonoring of God Himself. Blomberg says, the Pharisees' "motive for giving or soliciting reflects hypocrisy, pretending to honor God when in fact one is distracting attention from him."[18] It is as if the Pharisees want to be glorified rather than glorifying the Father (against 6:16).[19]

In Matt 5:16, Jesus taught that the disciple should do good works before men by saying, *"Let your light shine before men in such a way that they may see your good works, and glorify your Father who is in heaven."* However, in 6:1–18, Jesus says do not do "acts of righteousness before men," τὴν δικαιοσύνην ὑμῶν μὴ ποιεῖν ἔμπροσθεν τῶν ἀνθρώπων. In one place (5:16), the ideal disciple should do good works before men but in another place he/she should not do the good works before men. Is Jesus then contradicting himself? No! He is not! If the good works are done to glorify God alone then it could be practiced before men (5:16). However, "if the motive for doing righteousness is to gain recognition for themselves, it is going to cost them God's reward."[20] Blomberg says, "The positive alternative Jesus commands is that we should give in such a way that there is no temptation for others

16. Wallace, *Greek Grammar*, 533.
17. Glasscock, *Matthew*, 142.
18. Blomberg, *Matthew*, 117.
19. Garland, *Reading Matthew*, 78.
20. Glasscock, *Matthew*, 142.

to glorify the giver than God."[21] Thus, 5:16 does not contradict 6:2 rather contributes to each other. If one does good works to please God it can be done before people but if the good works were done to gain attention to oneself then it must done in private. Thus, it is the motive of the disciple who gives alms that is in consideration here in 6:2 rather than the action of giving alms themselves.

In Matt 6:3–5, Jesus says, *"But when you give to poor, do not let your left hand know what your right hand is doing, so that your giving will be in secret, and your Father who sees what is done in secret will reward you."* Here there is a comparison. While the Pharisees give in public, in the synagogues and in street corners, the ideal disciple is exhorted to give in secret. In addition, Jesus clearly says trumpeting about giving alms to others will not fetch any reward but giving alms in secret will fetch the attention of the Father for he says, *"You Father who sees what is done in secret will reward you,"* ὁ πατήρ σου ὁ βλέπων ἐν τῷ κρυπτῷ ἀποδώσει σοι.

Jesus words: 'Let not your left hand know what your right hand is doing,' μὴ γνώτω ἡ ἀριστερά σου τί ποιεῖ ἡ δεξιά σου (6:3), need not be understood literally. It is hard for the left hand to be kept in secret from what the right hand is doing. It also does not mean that the ideal disciple should not keep track of the money donated or even be financially accountable to others in such donations.[22] What it means is that the motive for giving should not be for "the desire for praise from others."[23] μὴ γνώτω comes with μή in subjunctive mood. Thus, it indicates strong prohibition.[24] The ideal disciple should not let the right hand know what the left hand gives. This means there is a strong prohibition of ostentation while alms giving. Garland says, "If the goal of religiosity is to earn the admiration of others, one can easily succeed; but it cancels out any hope of a reward from the Father. If one seeks credit from others, one cannot expect extra credit from God. The voucher already has been cashed in."[25] Thus, the disciple should give alms only in secret.

Secrecy of giving alms is common in rabbinic teachings. For rabbis say:

> There were two chambers in the Temple, one the chamber of secrets, into which the devout used to put their gifts in secret

21. Blomberg, *Matthew*, 117.
22. Ibid., 117.
23. Ibid., 117.
24. Wallace, *Greek Grammar*, 487.
25. Garland, *Reading Matthew*, 78.

and the poor of good family received support from in secret (*m. Shekalim* 5:6)

Just as there was a chamber of secret donations for the poor in Jerusalem temple, so there was such a chamber in each and every town. (*t. Shekalim* 2:16)

R. Yannai once saw a man give money to a poor man publicly; he said: "It would have been better to give him nothing than to have given it to him and put him to shame" (*Koheleth Rabbah* 12:14)

The one who gives in secret is greatest than Moses (*b. Baba Batra* 9b)

There are three things whose virtuousness the Holy One proclaims every day: the bachelor who lives in a big city and does not sin; the poor who turns over a find to its owner; and a rich man who gives the tenth of his fruits in secret. (*b. Pesah* 113a, b)

Thus, the reward for giving alms in secret was a common teaching in rabbinic times. In addition, this could have been a prevalent teaching in Jesus' time as well. Thus, Jesus teaches his ideal disciple to be a better person in practicing Jewish piety by giving alms in secret unlike the Pharisees who would not get the reward from the Father. Matt 6:4 clearly indicates that it is the Father who rewards the disciple unlike the Pharisees, who get their earthly reward from men.[26] This comparison is heightened by the use of the participle with an article in 6:4. Jesus says, ὁ πατήρ σου ὁ βλέπων ἐν τῷ κρυπτῷ ἀποδώσει σοι. In addition to ὁ πατήρ, Jesus adds ὁ βλέπων to show that it is the Father who rewards the disciple. The presence of βλέπων with ὁ which indicates the adjectival proper function of βλέπων shows the stress Jesus keeps in comparison to the rewards received by Pharisees from τῶν ἀνθρώπων.[27] Thus, even the participle here highlights the comparison.

The comparison of the disciple with the Pharisees, thus, functions quite beautifully in the characterization of the ideal disciple. The ideal disciple should not give alms before men to get the admiration and appreciation from men. However, the ideal disciple must do it in secrecy so that God will be glorified. This depiction would not have taken this effect if Jesus did not use the Pharisees as the foil in this narrative. The function of the foil brought forth a powerful portrayal of who the Pharisees are and how the disciple should not be like them and how the disciple should really do the

---

26. Hagner, *Matthew 1–13*, 142.
27. Wallace, *Greek Grammar*, 617.

"acts of righteousness," δικαιοσύνην ... ποιεῖν (6:1).[28] This is the power of comparisons in the characterization of the ideal disciple in the Sermon on the Mount.

7.2.2 Not Praying before People like the Hypocrites (6:5-6)

In Matt 6:5, Jesus gives another teaching very similar to 6:2-4. This is also one of the "acts of righteousness," δικαιοσύνην ... ποιεῖν (6:1), prevalent in Jewish practice of piety, which is prayer. He says in 6:5, *"when you pray (ὅταν προσεύχησθε) you are not to be like the hypocrites (οὐκ ἔσεσθε ὡς οἱ ὑποκριταί); for they love to stand and pray in the synagogues and on the street corners so that they may be seen by men (ὅτι φιλοῦσιν ἐν ταῖς συναγωγαῖς καὶ ... προσεύχεσθαι). Truly I say to you, they have their reward in full."* Prayers were essential part of Jewish piety.[29] *m. Berakoth* 1:4 says: "In the morning two Benedictions are said before [the shema] and one after; and in the evening two Benedictions are said before and two after." Sirach 39:5 says, "The ideal scribe is the one who rises early to seek the Lord and petition the Most High." Thus, prayer had an important role in Jewish religiosity.

The characterization of the ideal disciple is driven by the exhortation of Jesus where he says *"when you pray you are not be like the hypocrites,"* ὅταν προσεύχησθε, οὐκ ἔσεσθε ὡς οἱ ὑποκριταί (6:5a). ὅταν here is similar to 6:2 and thus brings similar syntactical pattern in this verse also. ὅταν with subjunctive forms subjunctive in indefinite temporal clause, indicating "a future contingency from the perspective of the time of the main verb."[30] Thus, the temporal idea is stressed. "Whenever" the ideal disciple prays he/she should not be like the hypocrites. Here again, the hypocrites, οἱ ὑποκριταί, should mean the Pharisees. How the disciple should not be like the Pharisees is exemplified in this passage.

The Pharisees, here, are characterized as the ones who pray in the public places, in the synagogues and in street corners, to be seen by men, ὅπως φανῶσιν τοῖς ἀνθρώποις (6:5). The accusations are very similar accusation to the ones laid in 6:2. It might be acceptable that the Pharisees pray in the synagogues as the synagogues were considered places of worship for the Jews. However, it is interesting that the Pharisees would also pray in the street corners, ἐν ταῖς γωνίαις τῶν πλατειῶν (6:5). Why would they pray in the streets? Morris suggests that "The junction of two streets would be very public place and to pray there, in a place not especially given over to

28. Hagner, *Matthew 1-13*, 141.
29. Ibid., 145.
30. Wallace, *Greek Grammar*, 479.

religious exercises and with many people to observe what was going on, was to court notice and to win approbation of people who liked to observe religious activities in progress,"[31] He further adds, "There were prayers that were offered at prescribed times (cf. Ps 55:17; Dan 6:10; Acts 3:1), and it was not beyond the ingenuity that they were in public place at the time of prayer and thus 'compelled' to pray where they would be seen."[32] Either way, it is interesting that Jesus uses the word φιλέω, love in 6:5 to show that the Pharisees loved to stand and pray in the public places. Wallace shows that φιλοῦσιν is potential indicative, which shows desire as it is coupled with προσεύχεσθαι to show how the Pharisees love to show off their praying to others but not to the Father.[33] The stress of the use of this potential indicative is to show the desire of the Pharisees for ostentation. It is not just that they had to do the prayer at a particular time but it is their love of showing piety in front of others that is accused by Jesus here. Thus, their intense love to showcase the piety is condemned by Christ while the sincerity of the ideal disciple is exhorted and rewarded.

Glasscock says, "They love to be seen praying and therefore speak to be heard by men and not by God."[34] Boice points out that "In order to be his disciple, . . . those who are his must practice their religion from the heart and not for the notice, approbation, and reward of men."[35] Thus, the ideal disciple must shun away from praying in public. This does not mean that the disciple should shun away from public prayers such as communal prayers. Rather, praying in public to get the attention of others should be prohibited.

If one prays in a public place "so that he/she may be seen by men," he/she will not get the reward from heaven. Jesus says, *"But you, when you pray, go into your inner room, close your door and pray to your Father who is in secret, and your Father who sees what is done in secret will reward you"* σὺ δὲ ὅταν προσεύχῃ, εἴσελθε εἰς τὸ ταμεῖόν σου καὶ κλείσας τὴν θύραν σου πρόσευξαι τῷ πατρί σου τῷ ἐν τῷ κρυπτῷ· καὶ ὁ πατήρ σου ὁ βλέπων ἐν τῷ κρυπτῷ ἀποδώσει σοι (6:6). Jesus, thus, characterizes the ideal disciple in v.6 as the one who goes into the inner room closes the door and prays to the Father in secret so that he/she will be rewarded by the Father. Thus, the ideal disciple should be exactly opposite to the Pharisees who 'love' to pray in public such as in the synagogues and in the street corners.

---

31. Morris, *The Gospel According to Matthew*, 140.
32. Ibid., 140.
33. Wallace, *Greek Grammar*, 451.
34. Glasscock, *Matthew*, 144.
35. Boice, *Matthew*, 98.

Inner room with doors locked, εἴσελθε εἰς τὸ ταμεῖόν σου καὶ κλείσας τὴν θύραν σου πρόσευξαι (6:6), is kept in comparison and contrast with synagogues and street corners ἐν ταῖς συναγωγαῖς καὶ ἐν ταῖς γωνίαις τῶν πλατειῶν (6:5). When the Pharisees pray in the synagogue and in the street corners seeking attention from other men, the ideal disciple should pray in the closed inner room, seeking only the attention of the Father.[36] The characterization of the ideal disciple comes with colors with the use of these comparisons with the hypocrites. Thus, 6:5–6 uses comparisons to characterize the ideal as the one who only wants to please the Father by his/her religious piety of prayer rather than practicing it in public, unlike the Pharisees.

7.2.3 Not Praying with Meaningless Words like the Gentiles (6:7–15)

Though 6:7–15, as a whole, talks about prayer, the first part 6:7–8 has the comparison and exhortation on how to pray the prayer, while vv.9–15 gives the model prayer, "The Lord's Prayer." Jesus, in 6:7 says, *"And when you are praying, do not use meaningless repetition as the Gentiles do, for they suppose that they will be heard for their many words,"* Προσευχόμενοι δὲ μὴ βατταλογήσητε ὥσπερ οἱ ἐθνικοί, δοκοῦσιν γὰρ ὅτι ἐν τῇ πολυλογίᾳ αὐτῶν εἰσακουσθήσονται. It is interesting that, here, Jesus is characterizing the ideal disciple by comparing him/her with the gentiles, οἱ ἐθνικοί. Usually comparisons in the Sermon on the Mount are done with Pharisees and scribes. However, here, (and later in 6:32) Jesus uses the gentiles as foil to bring out the characteristic features expected of the ideal disciple. The ideal disciple should not be like the gentiles because the gentiles use "meaningless repetitions," βατταλογήσητε. The verb, βατταλογήσητε is translated as "vain repetition" in KJV. By the use of temporal verbal participle, Προσευχόμενοι Jesus indicates that when the ideal disciple prays he/she should not be like the gentiles. This shows that Jesus was not just against the repetition of prayers, such as the Lord's Prayer but the ones with vain repetitions.[37]

These vain repetitions could be identified as Gentiles using various names to please their gods and goddesses. It was customary in the pagan religions that the one who prays would bring forth the various names of the gods or goddesses concerned so that in some ways he/she would appease the god or the goddess and trick the god or goddess into favoring him/her. This similar phenomenon was seen in the gentile worship in Jesus' times.

---

36. Hagner, *Matthew 1–13*, 156.
37. Morris, *The Gospel According to Matthew*, 141.

Garland says, "One had to invoke the gods with meticulous care so as not to offend them; but since the gods had completely different functions and domains of power under different names, one had to be sure to utter the right name to get the response one wanted."[38] Lucius in Apulieius' *Metamorphoses* prays:

> *O blessed Queen of Heaven, whether thou be the Dame Ceres [Demeter]* which art the original and motherly source of all fruitful things in earth, who after the finding of thy daughter Proserpina [Persephone], through thy great joy which thou diddest presently conceive, madest barrain and unfruitful ground to be plowed and sown, and now thou inhabitest in the land of Eleusie [Eleusis]; or *whether thou be the celestial Venus* . . . [or] *horrible Proserpina* . . . thou hast the power to stop and put away the invasion of the hags and ghosts which appeared unto men, and to keep them down in the closures [womb] of the earth; thou which nourishes all the fruits of the world by thy vigor and force; *with whatsoever name is or fashion it is lawful to call upon thee*, I pray thee, to end my great travaile . . . (Apuleius, *Metam.* [*The Golden Ass*] 11.2) [Italics for Emphasis]

After Lucius went to sleep he sees the vision of Demeter, who then proclaims who she is by the many names attributed to her:

> . . . My name, my divinity is adored throughout the world, in diverse manners, in variable customs, and by many names. For the Phrygians that are the first of all men call me the *Mother of the gods of Pessinus*; the Athenians, which are sprung from their own soil, *Cecropian Minerva*; the Cyprians, which are girt about by the sea, *Paphian Venus*; the Cretans, which bear arrows, *Dictynian Diana*; the Sicilians, which speak three tongues, *infernal Prosperpine*; the Elusinians, their ancient goddess *Ceres*; some *Juno*, others *Bellona*, others *Hecate*, others *Ramnusie* . . . ; and the Egyptians, which are excellent in all kind of ancient doctrine, and by their proper ceremonies accustomed to worship me, do call me by my true name, *Queen Isis*. (Apuleius, *Metam.*11.2)

It is interesting to see that the goddess appeared before Lucius as he used correct names for the goddess. In addition, the author of the *Metamorphoses* gives more attributes with names of the goddess so that these names would be used in prayers by the readers. Another example could be seen in Catullus' *Poem 34*:

---

38. Garland, *Reading Matthew*, 79.

> *Diana*, we are in your care, we chaste girls and boys. Come, chaste boys and girls, let us sing in praise of *Diana*.
>
> O *daughter of Leto*, mighty *offspring of mightiest Jupiter*, you who were born beside the Delian olive tree, *queen of the mountains and the green forests and the trackless glens and the murmuring streams*.
>
> *You are called Juno Lucina* by women in the agony of childbirth. *You are called powerful Trivia. You are called Luna*, with your borrowed light.
>
> *You, goddess*, measuring out the year's progress by your monthly phases, do fill the farmer's humble storerooms with fine produce.
>
> *Hallowed be thy name, whatever name it is that you prefer*. And, as in years past you have been accustomed to do, so now, too, protect and preserve the race of Romulus with your kindly favor. (Catullus, *Poems* 34)

It is interesting to see that the Poet Catullus invokes the different names of the goddess Diana to strike at the right place from various angles. The goddess Diana is the daughter of Leto, as she is the queen of the mountain and the green forests. She is called Juno Lucina for the women who give birth. She is Trivia for those who seek power. She is Luna who is the moon god who fills the storerooms of the farmer. In addition, the poet is cautious that he might have missed some names or pronounced wrong names which might not be appropriated for suitable circumstances. Thus, he says, may your name be glorified, whatever the name you prefer. Identifying and pronouncing the right name of the god or the goddess seems to be the key in pagan prayers. Thus, Jesus says the disciple should not pray with "the many words" like the gentiles.

Garland puts it nicely: "Jesus teaches that one does not need to reel off a litany of divine aliases to conjure up a reluctant God in prayer; one need simply invoke God as Father and may then pray in spirit of confidence that the Father will respond."[39] Therefore, the disciple need not trick God by using 'vain' repetitive words because the *"Father knows what the disciple needs before he/she asks Him,"* οἶδεν ὁ πατὴρ ὑμῶν ὧν χρείαν ἔχετε πρὸ τοῦ ὑμᾶς αἰτῆσαι αὐτόν (6:8). God, the Father is a merciful God who desires to help His children and thus, He need not be tricked. Thus, the ideal disciple is characterized as the one who does not trick God the Father but the one who asks with trust in prayer.

---

39. Ibid., 79.

When the heavenly Father feeds the birds of the air, τὰ πετεινὰ τοῦ οὐρανοῦ (6:26) and clothes the grass of the field, τὸν χόρτον τοῦ ἀγροῦ (6:30), how much more that He would feed the disciple and clothe him/her, οὐ πολλῷ μᾶλλον ὑμᾶς (6:26 &30). Thus, the disciple need not trick God but should smiply "trust [Him] as one would direct requests to a loving Father."[40] Thus, the disciple should not be like the gentiles when they pray (6:8). The ideal disciple should not use meaningless words but rather pray to God about what he/she needs with the prayer the Lord himself teaches in 6:9–15. Thus, the characterization of the ideal disciple in 6:7 & 8 and its beauty is brought up by the use of comparisons with the gentiles.

7.2.3.1 Lord's Prayer

In Matt 6:9–13, Jesus teaches the disciple how to pray. He gives an example of the prayer which the disciple should use when he prays. This prayer is famously called the Lord's Prayer. However, it has been suggested that it should be called the 'disciple's prayer' rather than Lord's Prayer because Jesus should never have been able to pray this prayer, as it also includes "forgive our sins," καὶ ἄφες ἡμῖν τὰ ὀφειλήματα ἡμῶν (Mat 6:12).[41]

Jesus, in 6:9, says, *"Pray, then in this way,"* οὕτως οὖν προσεύχεσθε ὑμεῖς. Jesus does not say 'pray this prayer' but 'pray in this manner.' Thus, Boice calls this prayer as "model prayer."[42] He continues, "It is not a prayer to be memorized and repeated mechanically, though it is not wrong to repeat these words thoughtfully in a liturgical service."[43] Thus, this model prayer is the format in which the disciple should pray. It is even acceptable to recite this prayer, but meaningfully. Boice reminds that the English slang, "pitter-patter" comes from the Latin words of the beginning of the Lord's Prayer (*Pater Noster*) to mean blabbering.[44] Thus, the Lord's Prayer is not intended to be prayed blindly by the disciple but as a format which should be meant seriously while praying, unlike the gentiles.

In the Lord's Prayer (6:9–13), Jesus gives six petitions the disciple must follow.[45] The first three are concerned with honoring God, God's kingdom, and God's will while the other three are about the concerns of the human

---

40. Ibid., 79.
41. Boice, *The Gospel of Matthew*, 90.
42. Ibid., 98.
43. Ibid., 98.
44. Ibid., 98.
45. Ibid., 98.

beings and their neighbors.⁴⁶ Boice identifies how similar this structure is to the Ten Commandments where the first four commandments were laws about the relationship with God while the other six were about one's relationship with his/her neighbor.⁴⁷

7.2.3.1.1 First Petition: Hallowed be Thy Name

In the first petition, Jesus exhorts his disciple to honor the name of God. However, the word he used to say this is quite unique and demands attention. The ideal disciple should pray *"Our Father in heaven, Hallowed be your Name."* God is addressed here as the Father. Though many identify that the idea of God as the Father is not frequently mentioned in the pagan religions or in Judaism, Talbert shows examples where people call their god as father from pagan religions and from the Old Testament sources.⁴⁸ Thus, it seems common to identify God as the Father. In addition, it should be noted that God is identified frequently in the Sermon on the Mount as the Father. Therefore, the first petition is about honoring God.

In 6:9, the word Father is modified with a personal pronoun. Gundry points out that the use of the first person plural pronoun rather than a singular pronoun indicates that this prayer should be said as communal prayer rather than an individual prayer.⁴⁹ Either way, the point to be noticed is the personal connection that the prayer makes with the identification of God as the Father of the disciple. In the beatitudes it was mentioned that the ideal disciple will be called as the "sons of God," ὅτι αὐτοὶ υἱοὶ θεοῦ κληθήσονται. However, here the disciple already calls God as "our Father," Πάτερ ἡμῶν.

This personal connection to the Father is elevated to another level by the description of who this Father is, "the one who is in heaven," ὁ ἐν τοῖς οὐρανοῖς (Mat 6:9). Thus, Boice says, "The God to whom we pray is personal and caring. But he is also the holy and sovereign God, who is in heaven."⁵⁰ In other words, the characterization of the ideal disciple in 6:9 takes a new height that the ideal disciple is the child of the holy and sovereign God, who is in heaven, Πάτερ . . . ὁ ἐν τοῖς οὐρανοῖς (Mat 6:9). Thus, this disciple should, in his first petition, glorify his/her Father saying, "Hallowed be your name!" ἁγιασθήτω τὸ ὄνομά σου (Mat 6:9).

---

46. Ibid., 98.
47. Ibid., 98.
48. Talbert, *Reading the Sermon on the Mount*, 110–112.
49. Gundry, *Matthew*, 102.
50. Boice, *The Gospel of Matthew*, 99.

7.2.3.1.2 Second and Third Petition: Thy Kingdom Come, Thy Will be Done

The second petition is about God's kingdom to come, ἐλθέτω ἡ βασιλεία σου, (6:10a). The third petition is about God's will be done, γενηθήτω τὸ θέλημά σου (6:10b). In one way, both petitions are to be considered simultaneous actions. God's will must be done in God's kingdom and God's will must be done to enter into God's kingdom. If God's will should be understood as Jesus' teaching in the Sermon on the Mount then it is understandable that in the third petition, the disciple is advised to obey the teachings in the Sermon on the Mount. The ideal disciple is thus, characterized as the one eagerly waits for God's kingdom and for God's will to be done, even by obeying the Sermon on the Mount.

7.2.3.1.3 Fourth Petition: Give us the Daily Bread

In 6:11, Jesus moves from God's concerns to human concerns. The ideal disciple should pray, "Give us this day our daily bread," τὸν ἄρτον ἡμῶν τὸν ἐπιούσιον δὸς ἡμῖν σήμερον (6:11). Blomberg says that the rare adjective ἐπιούσιος, though traditionally translated as 'daily' could also mean "tomorrow."[51] Thus, this prayer indicates that the disciple must be totally dependent on God alone for his/her survival. It should be obvious that this bread, τὸν ἄρτον, is not just bread alone but all that is essential for one's life.[52] Some early church fathers considered this bread as the Holy Communion which is unlikely to have been mentioned here.[53] Thus, the ideal disciple is characterized as the person who depends on God for his survival. It is also possible that the comparison in 6:32 with the gentiles is alluded to in this verse.

In 6:24–34, Jesus teaches that the ideal disciple should not be like the gentiles who seek all the things of the world and are concerned with the worries of this world such as what to eat, τί φάγητε (6:26), and what to wear, τί ἐνδύσησθε (6:30), etc. As the ideal disciple is exhorted to pray for the daily food in 6:11, it is possible that the ideal disciple, even here, is characterized against the gentiles (comparative characterization), who do not have trust in God but worry about their essentials of life for their next day.

---

51. Blomberg, *Matthew*, 119.
52. Boice, *The Gospel of Matthew*, 99.
53. Morris, *The Gospel According to Matthew*, 146.

7.2.3.1.4 Fifth Petition: Forgive Us our Debts

In 6:12, Jesus teaches the ideal disciple to pray for God's forgiveness. He says, *"And forgive us our debts, as we also have forgiven our debtors,"* καὶ ἄφες ἡμῖν τὰ ὀφειλήματα ἡμῶν, ὡς καὶ ἡμεῖς ἀφήκαμεν τοῖς ὀφειλέταις ἡμῶν (Mat 6:12). This petition for forgiveness of sins is quite interesting. In 6:11, the disciple should pray for his/her daily bread and it will be granted to him/her without any condition, τὸν ἄρτον ἡμῶν τὸν ἐπιούσιον δὸς ἡμῖν σήμερον.[54] However, in 6:12, the disciple should pray for forgiveness of his/her sins, καὶ ἄφες ἡμῖν τὰ ὀφειλήματα ἡμῶν. However, the granting of this forgiveness of sins depends on the condition that the disciple should also forgive his/her debtors, ὡς καὶ ἡμεῖς ἀφήκαμεν τοῖς ὀφειλέταις ἡμῶν (Mat 6:12). Morris says, "the prayer recognizes that we have no right to seek forgiveness for our own sins if we are withholding forgiveness from other, and perhaps even that we cannot really seek it."[55] Thus, the ideal disciple is characterized in this verse as the one who prays for the forgiveness of his/her sins from God. By the same time, he/she is also characterized as the one who forgives others of their sins. It seems like this idea of forgiving others is such an important aspect of the characterization of the ideal disciple in the Sermon on the Mount that this idea is brought back, even after the Lord's Prayer in 6:14–15.

7.2.3.1.5 Sixth Petition: Lead us not into Temptations

In 6:13, Jesus says, *"And do not lead us into temptation, but deliver us from evil,"* καὶ μὴ εἰσενέγκῃς ἡμᾶς εἰς πειρασμόν, ἀλλὰ ῥῦσαι ἡμᾶς ἀπὸ τοῦ πονηροῦ. What does πειρασμός mean here? Morris says, "The word has the basic meaning 'test,' and when used of Satan's testing of people with a view to their failing the test it comes to mean 'temptation.' It has usually been understood in this way in this prayer."[56] Hence, the ideal disciple should pray that God the Father should keep him/her away from any temptation, πειρασμός. In addition, how should the word, πονηρός be translated, as evil one or as evil? If it should be understood as the substantial adjective then it should mean that the disciple prays that God would deliver him/her from the evil one, Satan. In addition, the word evil, πονηρός could also indicate the collective aspect of evil. By translating this word as 'evil' in a collective sense it would also incorporate the evil one. Thus, it is better to interpret it

---

54. Hagner, *Matthew 1–13*, 173.
55. Morris, *The Gospel According to Matthew*, 147.
56. Ibid., 148.

as evil which is all inclusive evil that God should deliver the disciple from, τοῦ πονηροῦ, including the evil one.[57]

In the second part of 6:13 and in the last part of the Lord's Prayer there is a textual problem, the doxology: *"For Yours is the kingdom and the power and the glory forever, Amen,"* ὅτι σοῦ ἐστιν ἡ βασιλεία καὶ ἡ δύναμις καὶ ἡ δόξα εἰς τοὺς αἰῶνας· ἀμήν. Morris suggests that the absence of the doxology in some early manuscripts should be seen as unintentional, as "its absence ... may be because it was simply assumed."[58] Either way, through this inclusion in 6:13, the disciple is characterized as the one who gives all glory, and power and the kingdom to God alone. The disciple is thus characterized as the one who glorifies God, just like the first petition's characterization.

7.2.3.1.6 Forgive others to be Forgiven

Though the section on the Lord's Prayer is completed in 6:13, 6:14–15 continues what was discussed in 6:12—forgive others to be forgiven of sins. 6:14 & 15 reiterates the idea repeatedly: *"For if you forgive others for their transgressions, your heavenly Father will also forgive you. But if you do not forgive others, then your Father will not forgive your transgressions,"* Ἐὰν γὰρ ἀφῆτε τοῖς ἀνθρώποις τὰ παραπτώματα αὐτῶν, ἀφήσει καὶ ὑμῖν ὁ πατὴρ ὑμῶν ὁ οὐράνιος· ἐὰν δὲ μὴ ἀφῆτε τοῖς ἀνθρώποις τὰ παραπτώματα αὐτῶν, οὐδὲ ὁ πατὴρ ὑμῶν ἀφήσει τὰ παραπτώματα ὑμῶν. There is nothing new mentioned here in 6:14–15. All that is said in 6:14–15 is already mentioned in 6:12. In addition, there is not much difference in message from 6:14 to 6:15. Both share the same thought while the message kept in negation in 6:15, ἐὰν δὲ μὴ ἀφῆτε τοῖς ἀνθρώποις τὰ παραπτώματα αὐτῶν, οὐδὲ ὁ πατὴρ ὑμῶν ἀφήσει τὰ παραπτώματα ὑμῶν. Morris puts it this way, "But is the adversative conjunction that introduces the other side of the coin. The change that puts offenses in the second clause in this verse instead of in the first clause as in verse 14 is largely stylistic, but it perhaps emphasizes the activity of forgiving rather than the nature of the offenses. Forgiveness is important for the followers if Jesus, whereas the nature of the offenses committed against them is not. Jesus is saying that to fail to forgive others is to demonstrate that one has not felt the saving touch of God."[59] Thus, the ideal disciple is characterized as the one who forgives those who sinned against him. In addition, he is also portrayed as the one who is forgiven of the Father from his/her sins.

57. Ibid., 148–149.
58. Ibid., 149.
59. Ibid., 149.

Though there is no apparent comparison present in the Lord's prayer (6:9–15), Boice says that the whole of Lord's prayer itself is kept in contrast and thus, can be compared with the ostentatious prayers of the Pharisees (6:1–4) and the repetitive prayers of the gentiles (6:5–6).[60] Thus, the characterization of the ideal disciple in 6:9–15 deals with comparative characterization.

7.2.4 Not Fasting before Men like the Pharisees (6:16–18)

In Matt 6:16–18, Jesus brings fasting, another important aspect of Jewish piety as the third illustration of the principle enunciated in 6:1. The phrase "whenever you fast," Ὅταν δὲ νηστεύητε is similar to "when you give," Ὅταν... ποιῇς ἐλεημοσύνην (6:2) and "when you pray," ὅταν προσεύχησθε (6:5), which is used here. Whenever the disciple fasts he/she should not put on a gloomy face like the hypocrites (6:16–18). The Pharisees are used again in this section to play as foil to bring out the characteristic features expected of the ideal disciple.

It is shown that the Pharisees' main reason to "put on a gloomy face," μὴ γίνεσθε ὡς... σκυθρωποί and "to neglect their appearance," ἀφανίζουσιν γὰρ τὰ πρόσωπα αὐτῶν is "so that they will be noticed by men when they are fasting," ὅπως φανῶσιν τοῖς ἀνθρώποις νηστεύοντες (Mat 6:16). As the hypocrites crave for attention from men, even through the acts of religious piety such as fasting they will not get heavenly reward as they get their rewards in full from men (6:16). Jesus further says, σὺ δέ "but You" (Mat 6:17) to the disciple to identify that the disciple is kept in comparison to the Pharisees. Gundry shows an important point, for he says, "In the style characteristic of Matthew's composition, v.16 and vv.17–18 run along parallel lines. They both begin with references to fasting introduced by δέ (to be translated 'and' in v.16, 'but' in v.17). From there on, the parallels are antithetic: hypocrites verses disciples, sullenness verses putting oil on the head, disfiguring faces verses washing the face, display in fasting verses hiding one's fasting, and full receipt of reward in the present versus future repayment by the Father."[61] Thus, the ideal disciple is kept in comparison once again in this section to highlight the expected norm of the disciple, as the one who fasts sincerely from the heart and not just to be seen by men.

Fasting was an important act of piety in Jewish practices. Tob 12:8 identifies the importance of fasting. In the Old Testament fasting was commanded to be practiced only on the Day of Atonement (Lev 16:29–31).

60. Boice, *The Gospel of Matthew*, 98.
61. Gundry, *Matthew*, 110.

However, after the Babylonian exile many fasts were regulated to commemorate the past disasters to the nation.[62] Thus, by post-exilic Judaism fasting became a common practice in Judaism (Zech 8:19; Neh 9:1; Ps 35:13; Neh 1:4 and Dan 9:3). Extensive fasting of the Jews was so popular that even Emperor Augustus boasted that he fasts even more than a Jew (Tacitus, *Ann.* 5.4). If so, fasting was a common practice in Jewish religiosity. Even Matthew points out that Jesus fasted for forty days (4:2-11). Thus, Jesus was not against the practice of fasting but his point of concern was the reason for and the manner in which the fasting should be observed. Jesus, then, was characterizing the ideal disciple as the one who fasts only for the Lord, and not to gain attention from men.

In the above sections, from 6:1-18, through the three sub-sections there is one theme which runs through. This theme found in all three sub-sections of 6:1-18 (1. Giving in 6:1-4; 2. Praying in 6:5-15; and 3. Fasting in 6:16-18) emphasizes the comparison which separates "seeking human reward" from "desiring to please God."[63] Thus, comparisons abound in the Sermon on the Mount. In addition, these comparisons contribute to the characterization of the ideal disciple.

7.2.5 Not Storing on Earth but in Heaven (6:19-23)

In this passage, Jesus teaches about storing up treasures in heaven in 6:19-21 and he teaches about the eye being the lamp of the body in 6:22-23. Interestingly, similar comparisons used in 6:2-4; 5-6; and 6:16-18 are found in 6:19 and 20 also. The comparison is quite beautifully made as follows: v. 19 says "do not store up treasures for yourselves," Μὴ θησαυρίζετε ὑμῖν θησαυροὺς, while v.20 says, "store up treasures for yourselves" θησαυρίζετε δὲ ὑμῖν θησαυροὺς. While v.19 says, "on earth," ἐπὶ τῆς γῆς, v. 20 says "on heaven," ἐν οὐρανῷ. While v. 19 says "where moth and rust destroy," ὅπου σὴς καὶ βρῶσις ἀφανίζει v.20 says "where neither moth nor rust destroy," ὅπου οὔτε σὴς οὔτε βρῶσις ἀφανίζει. While v. 19 says "where thieves break in and steal," ὅπου κλέπται διορύσσουσιν καὶ κλέπτουσιν v. 20 says "where thieves do not break in or steal," ὅπου κλέπται οὐ διορύσσουσιν οὐδὲ κλέπτουσιν. Thus, the comparisons are kept side by side to give a complex characterization to highlight the expected characteristic trait of the ideal disciple, which is, the one who does not store up treasures on earth but in heaven.

The reason why the disciple should not store up treasure on earth, Μὴ θησαυρίζετε ὑμῖν θησαυροὺς ἐπὶ τῆς γῆς, is that on earth the treasure is

---

62. Boice, *The Gospel of Matthew*, 101.
63. Blomberg, *Matthew*, 122.

not safe. On earth, the treasure may be destroyed by moth, rust or even by thieves. However, treasures stored in heaven will be secure and would last eternally. How should one store treasures in heaven? Jesus does not explain this clearly.

In Jewish literature there are few mentions on how to store up treasures in heaven. In Tob 4:8–9, by giving of one's possession, it says, "so you will be laying up good treasures for yourself." *Sirach* 29:10–12 which mentions about helping a poor man says, "Lay up your treasure according to the commandments of the Most High." *m. Peah* 1:1 says, "These are things whose fruits a man enjoys in this world while the capital is laid up for him in the world to come: honoring father and mother, deeds of loving kindness, making peace between a man and his fellow; and the study of the Law is equal to them all." *t. Peah* 4:18:D says, "My ancestors stored up treasures for his world, but I, through giving charity, have stored up treasures for the heavenly world above." In light of these sayings it is possible that storing up treasures in heaven could mean giving alms to the poor. In addition, there is one other reason why we must consider that 'store up treasure' is about generosity.

Immediately after 6:21, out of nowhere Jesus keeps the teaching about eye being "the lamp of the body," Ὁ λύχνος τοῦ σώματός ἐστιν ὁ ὀφθαλμός in 6:22–23. Further, Jesus says οὖν ᾖ ὁ ὀφθαλμός σου ἁπλοῦς. NAU translates this as "if your eye is clear." However, it should be noticed that ἁπλοῦς means simple, single or sincere.[64] It should also be noted that ἁπλοῦς and its cognates often connotes generosity (Pro 11:24–26 LXX; 1 Chr 29:17 LXX; *T. Iss* 3:4; Rom 12:8; 2 Cor 8:2; 9:11, 13; Jas 1:5). In addition, evil eye often means stinginess and greed (Matt 20:15, Deut 15:9 LXX; 28:54–46 LXX; Prov 23:6; 28:22 LXX; Tob 4:7; Sir 14:10; *m. 'Abot* 5:16). Through this, Jesus says in 6:22–23: *"The eye is the lamp of the body; so then if your eye is single, your whole body will be full of light. But if your eye is evil your whole body will be full of darkness. If then the light that is in you is darkness how great is the darkness,"* Ὁ λύχνος τοῦ σώματός ἐστιν ὁ ὀφθαλμός. ἐὰν οὖν ᾖ ὁ ὀφθαλμός σου ἁπλοῦς, ὅλον τὸ σῶμά σου φωτεινὸν ἔσται. ἐὰν δὲ ὁ ὀφθαλμός σου πονηρὸς ᾖ, ὅλον τὸ σῶμά σου σκοτεινὸν ἔσται. εἰ οὖν τὸ φῶς τὸ ἐν σοὶ σκότος ἐστίν, τὸ σκότος πόσον. Through this parable Jesus teaches that if the eye is single, ἁπλοῦς, meaning generous, then the whole body will be full of light, ὅλον τὸ σῶμά σου φωτεινὸν ἔσται. If the disciple is generous he will acquire light, and store up treasure in heaven. However, if the eye is evil (stingy) then the whole body will be full of darkness. Thus, if the disciple is stingy then he will only store treasures on earth but without light because there are no treasures stored in heaven. Here again, in 6:22–23,

---

64. Schneider, ἁπλοῦς, *EDNT*, 1:124.

with comparisons of "single eye," ᾗ ὁ ὀφθαλμός σου ἁπλοῦς, and "evil eye," ὁ ὀφθαλμός σου πονηρὸς ᾗ, and "body with light," ὅλον τὸ σῶμά σου φωτεινὸν ἔσται, and "body with darkness," ὅλον τὸ σῶμά σου σκοτεινὸν ἔσται in 6:22 and 23 respectively, Jesus characterized the ideal disciple as the one who should be generous, and not stingy. Thus, it should be assumed that the teaching on storing up treasures in 6:19–20 should mean giving alms to the poor on earth.

Comparisons, contrasts and irony play a big role in this passage. As storing up treasure on earth is contrasted with storing up treasure in heaven, being generous is contrasted with being stingy. The irony is this: by being generous on this earth the disciple would store up treasures in heaven. By being stingy on earth one would store up treasures on earth, which would eventually be destroyed by moth and rust, or stolen by thieves or would pass away when heaven and earth pass away.[65] Garland says, "Since the earth is temporal and heaven is eternal, it is only prudent to store treasures in heaven. The way to store wealth in heaven that will escape the ravages of earth is to give it away on earth."[66] Gundry says, "Now the parable teaches generosity as opposed to greediness and goes against antinomians whose evil lack of love makes them niggardly."[67] The comparisons in this section beautifies the characterization of the ideal disciple as the one who is generous and stores up treasures in heaven and not as the one who is stingy on earth and looses light and only holds on to the temporary treasures.

Moreover, v. 21 gives one more reason why the ideal disciple must practice giving generously. If he/she is concentrating on acquiring wealth alone in this world his/her heart would be attached to this world and eventually he/she would loose the kingdom-mindedness. John Stott calls this "materialism which tethers our hearts to the earth."[68] This does not mean that the disciple should not work and should not earn money. "It is worldly-mindedness to which he is objecting, the concentration on prosperity in this world to the neglect of all else."[69] Morris further states that, "the place we choose for our treasures tells something about ourselves."[70] Thus, the ideal disciple is characterized as the one whose heart is set on the kingdom of heaven where he/she would store up treasures by giving alms to the poor and the needy. Thus,

65. Boice, *The Gospel of Matthew*, 104.
66. Garland, *Reading Matthew*, 82.
67. Gundry, *Mathhew*, 113.
68. Stott, *A Deeper Look at the Sermon on the Mount*, 131.
69. Morris, *The Gospel According to Matthew*, 152.
70. Ibid., 153.

comparative characterization aids in the characterization of the ideal disciple, which depicts the ideal disciple as a generous person in this section, 6:19–23.

7.2.6 Not Serving Money like Gentiles but God (6:24–34)

Talbert identifies that Matt 6:24 is similar to 6:21 and 6:22–23, where the comparisons of the two treasures (6:21) and the two eyes (6:22–23) are kept similar to the two masters of 6:24.[71] Though the comparisons are similar it is probable that 6:24 is connected more with 6:25–34 than to 6:21–23. The idea mentioned in 6:21–23 is also similar to 6:24. Jesus characterizes the ideal disciple as the one who is a giver and not a greedy person in 6:21–23. Similarly, in 6:24, Jesus characterized the ideal disciple as the one who serves God alone, and not Mammon, money. Though the ideas in both passages are similar, 6:24 is quite different and connects well with the idea stressed in 6:25–34.

In 6:25–34, Jesus teaches the disciple not to worry about the essentials of life such as food, drink, and clothings. In 6:24, moreover, Jesus teaches about serving God and not money. One would go after money only because of the worries about the future. The worry about the future would in turn force the person to be obsessed with money.[72] Thus, Jesus exhorts against this obsessive acquisition of money, and serving money with removing the worry about the essentials of life in 6:24–34. In addition, in 6:24, Jesus stressed that the disciple should not serve money but God and in 6:33 he also exhorted the disciple to seek first the kingdom of God so that all the material needs of this world would be added unto the disciple. This shows how 6:24 is closely related with 6:25–34. Thus, 6:24 is studied along with 6:25–34.

In 6:24, Jesus brings forth another comparison, the two masters. These two masters are identified as God and wealth. Thus, Jesus says, *"No one can serve two masters; for either he will hate the one and love the other, or he will be devoted to one and despise the other. You cannot serve God and wealth,"* Οὐδεὶς δύναται δυσὶ κυρίοις δουλεύειν· ἢ γὰρ τὸν ἕνα μισήσει καὶ τὸν ἕτερον ἀγαπήσει, ἢ ἑνὸς ἀνθέξεται καὶ τοῦ ἑτέρου καταφρονήσει. οὐ δύνασθε θεῷ δουλεύειν καὶ μαμωνᾷ (Mat 6:24). Thus, in 6:24, Jesus exhorts the ideal disciple to shun away from serving wealth. The comparison is quite interesting. This completeness of the comparison extends up to 6:32. The gentiles are identified as the ones who go after the material things of the

---

71. Talbert, *Reading the Sermon on the Mount*, 124.
72. Boice, *The Gospel of Matthew*, 106.

world. For he says: "For the gentiles eagerly seek all these things," πάντα γὰρ ταῦτα τὰ ἔθνη ἐπιζητοῦσιν (6:32).

Earlier, gentiles were used in the comparison in the teaching against long prayers. Here, the gentiles are placed as foil to show that they run after the material things of the world. In pagan religions, god is used as a vehicle to improve good life. Pagan gods are sought after for prosperity and good health. However, Jewish religion is based more on the covenant with Yahweh.[73] In the Old Testament religion, it is the covenant which produces the blessings (Deut 11:26 & 27), and thus, God comes first and then the blessings of this world. This idea is stressed again in 6:33, where Jesus said, *"Seek first His kingdom and His righteousness, and all these things will be added to you,"* ζητεῖτε δὲ πρῶτον τὴν βασιλείαν τοῦ θεοῦ καὶ τὴν δικαιοσύνην αὐτοῦ, καὶ ταῦτα πάντα προστεθήσεται ὑμῖν. Thus, the ideal disciple should not seek God just for the material and physical blessings of this world like the pagans, but for who God is and for His kingdom's sake and for His righteousness' sake. When the disciple seeks God for who He is, then all the material needs will be added to him/her, ταῦτα πάντα προστεθήσεται ὑμῖν (6:33). Through this comparison then the ideal disciple is characterized as a person who loves God (6:24), and who seeks God alone (6:33), and His kingdom and His righteousness (6:33), and not money (6:24) like the gentiles who are obsessed with serving money (6:32).

Matt 6:24 brings this imagery of slavery in its use of comparison, Οὐδεὶς δύναται δυσὶ κυρίοις δουλεύειν. In the ancient world slaves had shared ownership (Acts 16:16). However, as per 6:24, it seems like common knowledge that the slave in shared ownership would never be able to love both masters equally. He/she would love one almost better than the other. Thus, to love one and to hate one would mean not serving both equally. Thus, Jesus points out that it would be impossible for the ideal disciple to serve both money and God and thus, he/she should choose to serve God alone. However, choosing to serve God alone does not mean that he/she should not get his/her hands on the money. Matt 6:33 shows that when the disciple's priority is seeking God alone all these things, the essential needs of life, will be added unto him/her because the Father knows what the disciple needs (6:32b). In addition, if the Father would feed the mere birds of the air, and would clothe the flowers of the wild, and the grass of the field, would He not take care of the disciples much more, οὐχ ὑμεῖς μᾶλλον διαφέρετε αὐτῶν (6:26). Thus, the disciple should not worry about the essentials of life but seek God and serve God alone.

---

73. Dumbrell, *Covenant and Creation*, 15.

This section (6:24–34) seems to concentrate more on worrying than just about teachings on money. In 6:15, Jesus says, *"Do not be worried about your life, as to what you will eat or what you will drink; nor for your body as to what you will put on. Is not life more than food, and body more than clothing."* Διὰ τοῦτο λέγω ὑμῖν· μὴ μεριμνᾶτε τῇ ψυχῇ ὑμῶν τί φάγητε ἢ τί πίητε, μηδὲ τῷ σώματι ὑμῶν τί ἐνδύσησθε. οὐχὶ ἡ ψυχὴ πλεῖόν ἐστιν τῆς τροφῆς καὶ τὸ σῶμα τοῦ ἐνδύματος. Thus, Jesus characterizes the ideal disciple as the one who is worry-free. The disciple should not worry about what he/she will eat, or drink or wear. Interestingly, two comparisons are kept in this verse. "Is not life more [important] than food," οὐχὶ ἡ ψυχὴ πλεῖόν ἐστιν τῆς τροφῆς and is not "body more [important] than clothing," καὶ τὸ σῶμα τοῦ ἐνδύματος (6:25). Here, through these two comparisons, Jesus points out some essential things to the disciples. While the world [the gentiles] runs after these things (6:32) and is concerned more about food it forgets the importance of this life itself, ἡ ψυχή. In addition, it is also possible that the eternal life is implied here. If so, while the gentiles search after food, they forget the importance of eternal life. Consequently, while the gentiles run after the cloths, ἔνδυμα they forget the importance of God-given body itself. Unlike the gentiles, the disciple must realize the importance of this life, eternal life, and the God-given body and appreciate God who gave these things than just worrying about food, drink and clothes.

The reasoning for not worrying about food, drinks, and clothes are not clear in 6:25 but will be explained further in 6:26–31. Food, drinks and clothes are essentials to live in this world. However, by looking at the importance of God-given life (this life and the future life), and the God-given body (6:25) the disciple should identify that all these things are not just achieved by the disciple alone but were given freely by God and thus should put trust in God alone, who knows what the disciple needs and would give, as He takes care of the birds of the air, wild lilies and the grass of the field (6:26–31).

Why one should not worry is explained in 6:26–31. The disciple is asked to look at the birds of the air in 6:26. The birds do not sow, nor reap, nor gather grains into barns but the heavenly Father feeds them, ὁ πατὴρ ὑμῶν ὁ οὐράνιος τρέφει αὐτά (6:26). Likewise, the heavenly Father would also feed the disciple. In addition, in 6:28, Jesus says that the disciple should not worry about what he/she would wear. The disciple is asked to observe the lilies of the wild. "They do not toil nor do they spin," οὐ κοπιῶσιν οὐδὲ νήθουσιν (6:28). However, its beauty is much higher than the clothes of the great king Solomon himself, "in all his glory," ἐν πάσῃ τῇ δόξῃ αὐτοῦ (6:29). This again is similar to Jesus' teaching in 6:30. There is a comparison here. The clothes of the lilies of the wild are much better than the clothes of the great king Solomon himself. If God could do this, then how much more that he would clothe the ideal disciple. Comparisons are used to bring out the provisions awaiting the ideal disciple. Here, Jesus points out that God clothed the grass of the field and thus would also clothe the disciple. Through the comparisons Jesus characterizes the ideal disciple as the one who should not worry about the clothes but the one who seeks first the kingdom of God.

In addition, interestingly, in 6:26, Jesus says, *"Are you not worth more than they"* (the birds of the air), οὐχ ὑμεῖς μᾶλλον διαφέρετε αὐτῶν. In addition, in 6:30, when he mentioned about the grass, he says that if God could clothe the grass *"which is alive today and tomorrow is thrown into the furnace, will He not much more clothe you?"* σήμερον ὄντα καὶ αὔριον εἰς κλίβανον βαλλόμενον. These two statements indicate comparisons. The ideal disciple is compared with the birds of the air and the grass of the field. Though this comparison is missing in 6:29, in the analogy of wild flowers, one must assume that the comparison mentioned in 6:30, *"will he not much more clothe you,"* οὐ πολλῷ μᾶλλον ὑμᾶς should be applied even in 6:29 because of the similarity of the content, clothing. Thus, the disciple is compared with all three analogies, the birds of the air, τὰ πετεινὰ τοῦ οὐρανοῦ (6:26), the flowers of the wild, τὰ κρίνα τοῦ ἀγροῦ (6:28), and the grass of the field, οὐ πολλῷ μᾶλλον ὑμᾶς (6:30). Through these comparisons a sarcastic reality is shared. If God could take care of these birds, flowers, and grass how much more that He would care for the disciple.

The sarcasm and comparison are stressed again on another level in 6:30, by his mention that if God could take care of the grass of the field which is alive today and will be thrown in the furnace tomorrow how much more that he will clothe the disciple. Glasscock says, "The comparison accentuates the priority of kingdom matters and God's standards over material commodities including even one's own life."[74] This comparison is again stressed by the use of "you little of faith" in 6:30. Thus, the disciple should take note of how God takes care of the birds of the air, flowers of the wild, and the grass of the field, and should put faith in God that He who gave the body and life would take care of the disciple. This is the characterization of the ideal disciple. Added to this, 6:27, 31 and 34 stress the idea that in the light of these comparisons mentioned in 6:24–34 the ideal disciple should not worry about the food, drinks and clothes. To this now we turn.

---

74. Glasscock, *Matthew*, 157.

7.2.6.1 Not Worrying

In 6:27, Jesus tells his disciples that by worrying one cannot add "a single cubit" to the years of life. The word cubit, πῆχυς was originally used for the forearm.[75] The length of the forearm is then used as a measure, approximately eighteen inches.[76] However, it should be noticed that cubit is a length measure but "years of life" is chronological measure. NIV thus translates ἡλικία—(meaning age) as height. Thus, for NIV, one cannot add one cubit to the height. Johannes Schneider says that ἡλικία means 'age' in Septuagint and 'size' in Sir. 26:17.[77] However, it seems "years" should be the better translation because many would be more concerned about increasing years of life than their height.[78] Schneider points out that ἡλικία should be translated as 'span of life' as it goes well with the context.[79] Whatever it may be, the message is clear, as the disciple cannot add anything to one's own life he/she must realize the sovereignty of God who gave him/her the life, eternal life and the body (6:24) and should put trust in God that He knows what the disciple needs (6:32), and thus should trust in God that He will provide all that is needed much more than the way He provides for the birds, lilies and the grass (6:26, 28–30). Therefore, the comparisons of the birds, lilies and grass play important roles in the characterization of the disciple.

In 6:31, Jesus reiterates, *"Do not worry then, saying what will we eat? Or what will we drink? Or what will we wear for clothing"?* μὴ οὖν μεριμνήσητε λέγοντες· τί φάγωμεν; ἤ· τί πίωμεν; ἤ· τί περιβαλώμεθα. In 6:34, Jesus again says, *"So do not worry about tomorrow, for tomorrow will care for itself. Each day has enough trouble of its own,"* μὴ οὖν μεριμνήσητε εἰς τὴν αὔριον, ἡ γὰρ αὔριον μεριμνήσει ἑαυτῆς· ἀρκετὸν τῇ ἡμέρᾳ ἡ κακία αὐτῆς. Thus, through the repetition it is clear that Jesus is characterizing the ideal disciple as the one who does not worry about what he/she should eat, drink, or wear, but as the one who trusts in God and seeks first His kingdom and His righteousness, unlike the gentiles who are obsessed with acquiring wealth and serve Mammon. Thus, comparative characterization again brings out the beauty of the several levels of comparisons found in 6:24–34. The ideal disciple should then be worry-free about the essentials of life but should trust in God and should seek God and His kingdom first so that all the essentials of life will be added to him/her.

---

75. Morris, *The Gospel According to Matthew*, 158.
76. Glasscock, *Matthew*, 156.
77. Schneider, "ἡλικία," *TDNT* 2:943–945.
78. Morris, *The Gospel According to Matthew*, 158.
79. Schneider, "ἡλικία," 944.

Therefore, in summary, comparative characterization indicates how the ideal disciple is characterized with the use of the many comparisons. In 6:1-4, Jesus characterized the ideal disciple as the one who gives alms to the poor in secret and not ostentatiously like the hypocrites. In 6:5-6, he characterized the ideal disciple as the one who does not pray ostentatiously like the hypocrites. In 6:7-15, Jesus characterized the ideal disciple as the one who prays with the model prayer taught by Jesus and as the one who does not pray with meaningless repetitive words like the gentiles. In 6:16-18, Jesus characterized the ideal disciple as the one who does not fast ostentatiously like the hypocrites. In 6:19-23, Jesus characterized the ideal disciple as the one who stores treasures in heaven by being generous to others (6:22), and not by being stingy (6:23). In 6:24-34, Jesus characterized the ideal disciple as the one who does not serve money like the gentiles, but as the one who serves God alone, by not worrying about the essentials of life such as food, drink, and clothing. Thus, comparative characterization helped in the characterization of the ideal disciple in chapter 6 of the Sermon on the Mount. With this, the study of chapter 6 ends. In the next section, chapter 7 of Matthew will be studied to identify the function of the comparison in the characterization of the ideal disciple.

7.3 Comparisons and Their Function in Matthew 7 (7:1-29)

Matthew chapter 7 is again a continuation of Jesus' characterization of how the ideal disciple should live in the Sermon on the Mount. Few commentators suggest that there is no connection between chapter 7 and the rest of the Sermon on the Mount.[80] However, Gundry rightly points out that the comparison of surpassing the righteousness of the scribes and Pharisees mentioned in 5:20 still runs through chapter 7 of Matthew.[81] Thus, the judgmental spirit of the Pharisees should not be found in the disciples (7:1-6); Trusting God and asking to receive from Him is inculcated in 7:6-12; Teachings on entering the narrow gates is mentioned in 7:13-14; and warnings about false teachers are stressed in 7:15-27, including the teachings on the house built on the rocks which means being true to Jesus' teaching which are mentioned in 7:24-25. Thus, Matt 7 is a continuation of Jesus' teaching on how the disciple must live. Even here, Jesus uses comparisons to elucidate the characterization of the ideal disciple. The following portion

80. Glasscock, *Matthew,* 161.
81. Gundry, *Matthew,* 121.

of this chapter in this book will deal with Jesus' characterization of the ideal disciple in Matt 7, and the use of comparisons and their functions in Matt 7.

7.3.1 Not Judging Others like the Hypocrites (7:1–6)

In Matt 7:1–5, Jesus deals with the problem of judging others. In 7:1–2, Jesus says, "*Do not judge so that you will not be judged. For in the way you judged and by your standard of measure, it will be measured to you,*" Μὴ κρίνετε, ἵνα μὴ κριθῆτε· ἐν ᾧ γὰρ κρίματι κρίνετε κριθήσεσθε, καὶ ἐν ᾧ μέτρῳ μετρεῖτε μετρηθήσεται ὑμῖν. There is a subtle comparison here. The teaching on not judging is compared with its consequence by which you will be judged, Μὴ κρίνετε—ἵνα μὴ κριθῆτε. Both are kept side by side. The ideal disciple should not judge others so that he/she will not be judged likewise (6:1). The judgment once pronounced on others consequently brings forth judgment on oneself with the same measure he/she judged others (6:2). The positive aspect of not judging others is that there will not be a measure by which judgment could be pronounced against oneself. If the disciple judges someone, he/she has already created a measure by which the judgment will be pronounced on himself/herself. On the contrary, if the disciple had not pronounced judgment then there is no measure and that there is a possibility of acquittal from the judgment itself. Gundry suggests that this judgment should be considered as the final judgment.[82]

In 7:3–5, Jesus brings his favorite foil to elucidate how the disciple should live, once again. The ideal disciple should not be like the hypocrites, ὑποκριτοι, the Pharisees who have a log in their own eyes judge or criticize another, who only has a speck (6:3–5). Pharisees are commonly characterized in the Gospels as the ones who criticize Jesus and others. They are usually portrayed as fault finders (Matt 9:11, 34; 12:2, 14, 24, 38; 15:1–2, 16:1; 22:34–36; Mark 2:16, 24; 7:1–5; 8:11; 10:2; 12:13–15; Lk 5:21, 30; 6:2, 7; 7:36–39; 11:37–38, 53; 14:1–3; 15:2; 16:14; 19:39; John 8:3–5; 9:13–15). Unlike the Pharisees, the disciple should first work on "taking the log out," ἔκβαλε πρῶτον ἐκ τοῦ ὀφθαλμοῦ σοῦ τὴν δοκόν, of his/her own eye (7:5). Glasscock rightly points out that Jesus "selected one of the most typical of Pharisaic faults and used it to introduce the closing lessons of his discourse."[83] Thus, Jesus uses comparisons of the hypocrites to characterize the ideal disciple as the one who does not judge others.

The imperative on not to judge others does not mean that the disciple should not "make any sound judgments or evaluate moral and ethical

---

82. Gundry, *Matthew*, 120.
83. Glasscock, *Matthew*, 162.

situation."⁸⁴ This would contradict the teachings of Jesus in the Sermon on the Mount. Rather, the command on not to judge is primarily targeted against having a judgmental spirit rather than sound judgment. Glasscock puts it this way, "The censorious critic is a fault-finder who is negative and destructive towards other people and enjoys actively seeking out their failings. He puts the worst possible construction on their motives, pours cold water on their schemes and is ungenerous toward their mistakes."⁸⁵ Gundry points out, "Jesus does not teach the wrongness of taking a speck out of a brother's eye, i.e., rebuking a fellow disciple for a sin. Rather, Jesus teaches the wrongness of doing so with the larger sin of self-righteousness on one's own part. Self-righteousness makes the rebuke a hypocritical 'act' of showiness instead of a genuine attempt to ensure the wellbeing of the sinning brother."⁸⁶ Thus, Jesus was not against judging people per se but against self-righteous judging and the showiness. Jesus already taught extensively about the showiness in the ostentatious practices of the acts of righteousness in 6:1–18. Here again, he characterizes the ideal disciple as the one who avoids showiness in judging others. As found throughout the Sermon on the Mount, the interior character of the disciple is targeted even in this pericope than the action of judging itself. This teaching is like the teachings of Jesus in 6:1–18, where the interior qualities of piety were the concerns of Jesus rather than the actions of almsgiving, prayer, and fasting.⁸⁷ Thus, the ideal disciple is characterized as the one who does not judge others for self-righteous reasons, unlike the hypocrites, the Pharisees.

7.3.1.1 Swine and Dogs

Interestingly, Matt 7:6, which is an ambiguous passage to interpret, is placed right after 7:1–5. Jesus says, *"Do not give what is holy to dogs, and throw your pearls before swine,"* Μὴ δῶτε τὸ ἅγιον τοῖς κυσὶν μηδὲ βάλητε τοὺς μαργαρίτας ὑμῶν ἔμπροσθεν τῶν χοίρων. This comparison of the disciple with the dogs and swine is ambiguous as this verse does not seem to be connected either with 7:1–5 or with 7:7–11 at the first look. In one sense, if this passage is connected with 7:1–5, then the analogy of the dog and the swine would relate to the Pharisees. However, what is the holy thing that the disciple

---

84. Ibid., 162.
85. Ibid., 162.
86. Gundry, *Matthew*, 122.
87. Talbert, *Reading the Sermon on the Mount*, 108 says, "The aim of Matthew 6:1–18 is not the privatization of piety but the purification of motive in one's relation to God. Piety may be public, but when it is, it should be for God's sake."

should not throw at them? What are these pearls? Could these be the valuable judgments mentioned in 7:1–5? Gundry says that "The prohibition of giving dogs what is sacred and of throwing pearls to pigs warns against easy conditions of entrance into the church."[88] This could be a possible interpretation.

If the judgments of 7:1–5 could be considered as the teachings of Jesus then the obedience to the teachings of Jesus would entrust the entrance of the outsider, including a Pharisee. However, if the recipient of these teachings is as hard as the Pharisee who is more judgmental of every one and more critical of every teaching it is better that the teachings of Jesus, which would be the judgments of Christ should not even be thrown at them. Thus, holy things could be interpreted as the teachings of Jesus and the judgments of Christ and thus, they should not be thrown freely at the outsiders such as Pharisees. Thus, 7:6 adds one more level of prohibition to 7:1–5, which says do not judge saying do not give your judgment to the outsiders as they would not know how to value these teachings like pigs and dogs who would not know how to value the holy things. Comparisons and analogies still continue to play an important role in the characterization of the ideal disciple. Thus, according to 7:6, the ideal disciple should not have the judgmental spirit of the Pharisees and in addition, he/she should not throw judgments to the outsiders who would not know how to value the teachings of Christ.

7.3.2 Asking like a Child to Receive (7:7–12)

In 7:7, Jesus says, *"Ask, and it will be given to you; seek, and you will find; knock and it will be opened to you,"* Αἰτεῖτε καὶ δοθήσεται ὑμῖν, ζητεῖτε καὶ εὑρήσετε, κρούετε καὶ ἀνοιγήσεται ὑμῖν. Jesus just preached on prayer in 6:7–15. The disciples were exhorted earlier on not to pray ostentatiously and not to pray with meaningless words. However, Jesus asks the disciples to pray. He also taught in detail on how to pray in the Lord's Prayer (6:9–13). Again in 6:25–34, Jesus mentioned that the disciple should not be anxious about what to eat, what to drink and what to wear as God the Father knows the needs of the disciple and would give all these things automatically (6:32–33). However, this condition of the Father does not mean that the disciple should not pray and ask. Jesus may not share the idea mentioned in Jas 4:2: *"You do not have because you do not ask God,"* οὐκ ἔχετε διὰ τὸ μὴ αἰτεῖσθαι ὑμᾶς. According to James, the disciple does not have because he/she did not ask God. However, according to Matthew in the Sermon on the Mount, when one seeks God, automatically all things will be added to him/her, ζητεῖτε δὲ πρῶτον τὴν βασιλείαν τοῦ θεοῦ καὶ τὴν δικαιοσύνην

---

88. Gundry, *Matthew*, 122.

αὐτοῦ, καὶ ταῦτα πάντα προστεθήσεται ὑμῖν (6:33). The disciple need not ask because the Father knows the needs of the disciple (6:32). If so, why should the disciple ask in 7:7?

The idea is simple. The disciple should ask God with the trust that God would give exactly the same thing that he/she asked. This is the important teaching of this passage. The human father would not give a stone if the child asked for bread (ἄρτος—λίθος 7:9), and as the human father would not give a snake if the child asked for a fish (ἰχθύς—ὄφις 7:10), likewise, the heavenly Father will also give the things exactly as asked by the disciple. Comparisons of stone to bread and snake to fish are used. Through this teaching Jesus' words targets against the mistrust on the part of the disciple of God. Thus, why should the disciple ask God in prayer? It is to show his/her trust and dependence on God the Father. The Father knows the needs of the disciple, οἶδεν γὰρ ὁ πατὴρ ὑμῶν ὁ οὐράνιος ὅτι χρῄζετε τούτων ἁπάντων (6:32). However, the disciple must ask the Father so that he/she will show the dependence on and trust in the Father. Thus, the ideal disciple is characterized as the one who has trust in God the Father for all his/her needs.

Moreover, in as much as this passage characterizes the ideal disciple with the exhortations, it also describes who the Father is. This is evident in 7:9–11. In 7:9, Jesus asks, will a Father give a stone when his son asks for a bread loaf? In addition, in 7:10, again he asks, will a man give a snake if his child asks for a fish? It is obvious that even a human father would not trick his child by giving a small stone resembling a bread loaf instead of bread or a snake instead of fish.[89] Thus, Jesus points out *"If you, then, being evil, know how to give good gifts to your children how much more will your Father who is in heaven give what is good to those who ask Him,"* εἰ οὖν ὑμεῖς πονηροὶ ὄντες οἴδατε δόματα ἀγαθὰ διδόναι τοῖς τέκνοις ὑμῶν, πόσῳ μᾶλλον ὁ πατὴρ ὑμῶν ὁ ἐν τοῖς οὐρανοῖς δώσει ἀγαθὰ τοῖς αἰτοῦσιν αὐτόν (7:11). The phrase "how much more," οὐ πολλῷ μᾶλλον ὑμᾶς in 6:30 brings out the comparison aspect to the fore. If human beings, who are fallible and evil, know how to love and care for their children how much more would God, the loving Father of all creations show love and care by giving what the disciple asks?

God the Father is not like the pagan gods who are sometimes even hostile to the human beings. Boice says, "If God were like the pagans imagined him to be capricious, selfish, even vengeful—the one who prays would be on guard and would even try to bribe God or win him over. But if God is gracious, as Jesus taught, then we need not be afraid to ask him for whatever

---

89. Blomberg, *Matthew*, 130.

we need at any time."⁹⁰ Thus, God, the Father is characterized here as the loving God with his comparisons with the human fathers. This is the beauty of this section, 7:6–11. It characterizes both the disciple and the Father. God the Father is characterized as the one who loves His children and gives whatever the children ask, like or much more than the human fathers. The disciple is, thus, characterized as the one who shows his/her dependency on God by asking, seeking, and knocking for all the needs.

7.3.2.1 Golden Rule: Treating Others Better

In 7:12, Jesus gives one of his well-known teachings saying, *"In everything, therefore, treat people the same way you want them to treat you, for this is the Law and the Prophets,"* Πάντα οὖν ὅσα ἐὰν θέλητε ἵνα ποιῶσιν ὑμῖν οἱ ἄνθρωποι, οὕτως καὶ ὑμεῖς ποιεῖτε αὐτοῖς· οὗτος γάρ ἐστιν ὁ νόμος καὶ οἱ προφῆται. This verse seems to be common among Jewish circles and a negative form of this teaching is found in Tob 4:15 and *b. Shabbath* 31a. Tob 4:15 says, "What you hate, do not do to anyone." *b. Shabbath* 31a says, "What is hateful to you, do not do to your neighbor; that is the whole Torah, while the rest is the commentary thereof." Rabbi Hillel's saying, in *b. Shabbath* 31a, seems closer to Jesus's saying though the teaching in Jesus is in the positive while Hillel's is in the negative.

Blomberg identifies that it is easier to keep Hillel's negative teaching while it is harder to keep Jesus' positive teaching.⁹¹ Do not do to others what you do not want them to do to you, would mean that the disciple should not do to others what he/she doesn't want the others to do to him/her. For example, if the disciple doesn't want others to disrespect him/her he/she should not disrespect others. However, according to the teachings of Jesus, if the disciple wants to be treated with respect by others, he should actively engage in respecting others. The latter is harder than the former. Gundry says, "The positive form of the Golden Rule demands on acts of love, not mere avoidance of harming others, as in the negative form."⁹² That is the reason why this rule of Jesus is called Golden Rule and the teaching of Hillel and Tobit are considered as Silver Rule.⁹³

In addition, the similarity with Hillel's saying shows that Jesus, along with Hillel assumes that the important teaching of the Old Testament is to love others. In Matt 22:37–40, Jesus says:

90. Boice, *The Gospel of Matthew*, 108.
91. Blomberg, *Matthew*, 131.
92. Gundry, *Matthew*, 109.
93. Blomberg, *Matthew*, 131.

> ³⁷ And He said to him, 'You shall love the Lord your God with all your heart, and with all your soul, and with all your mind.
>
> ³⁸ This is the great and foremost commandment.
>
> ³⁹ The second is like it, 'You shall love your neighbor as yourself.
>
> ⁴⁰ On these two commandments depend the whole Law and the Prophets.

According to Jesus and Rabbi Hillel, then, the Old Testament teachings are summarized in loving God and loving the neighbors. However, in 7:12, it is summarized furthermore. To love the neighbors is the important teaching of Jesus Christ, for he says, loving others *"is the Law and the Prophets,"* οὗτος γάρ ἐστιν ὁ νόμος καὶ οἱ προφῆται (7:12). Loving God is not included here. In addition, the mention of "the Law and Prophets," ὁ νόμος καὶ οἱ προφῆται echoes Jesus' use of the same phrase in 5:17. Boice suggests, "This is Jesus' summary, and not only of the Law and the Prophets. It is also a summary of the entire body of the sermon, for the phrase 'the Law and the Prophets' is the *inclusio* that both introduces the main section of the sermon (at Matt 5:17) and now concludes it."[94] Thus, according to Boice, 7:12 begins the conclusion of the Sermon on the Mount. Therefore, the content in between should be considered as the teachings on how to be the ideal disciple over against the righteousness of the Pharisees and the scribes.

Interestingly, in the light of 7:12's and 5:17's use of ὁ νόμος καὶ οἱ προφῆται, Blomberg says, "Thus, . . . in the first antithesis (5:21–26) even if we succeed in not murdering and in not hating or verbally abusing others, we still have not completely obeyed until we earnestly seek others' well-being. With its reference to the 'Law and the Prophets,' 7:12 ties back in with 5:17 and provides a frame to bracket the body of the sermon."[95] Thus, according to Blomberg, obeying the Law, according to the interpretation of Jesus in 5:17–48, is not enough to enter into the kingdom of heaven. To enter into the kingdom of heaven the ideal disciple should love others as mentioned in 7:12.

Gundry also mentions, "The reference to the Law and the Prophets indicates that the extended definition of surpassing righteousness, which began with Jesus coming to fulfill the Law and the Prophets (5:17), has drawn to a close."[96] This is an interesting observation of Gundry. Accordingly,, the whole Sermon on the Mount should be understood as Jesus teaching his disciples on how to surpass the righteousness of the Pharisees

---

94. Boice, *The Gospel of Matthew,* 109.
95. Bloomberg, *Matthew,* 131.
96. Gundry, *Matthew,* 125.

and scribes. Thus, 7:12 characterizes the disciple not only as the person who does not do what he/she does not want others to do him/her but also as the one who does to others what he expects others to do to him/her. Thus, 7:12 shows the disciple as the one who is generous and helping and loving his/her neighbors.

How does this passage connect to the rest of the sermon? It is interesting that οὖν in 7:12 connects as resulted expectation of the teachings in 7:6–11. In light of the gracious and giving God of 7:6–11, the ideal disciple must show love and care to his/her neighbors. Thus, Blomberg says, "In view of God's generosity to us, treating others in a manner we would like ourselves to be treated is the least we can do."[97] A closer look at this verse suggests that there is a comparison here. How the disciple must treat others is compared with how he wants to be treated. Thus, through this comparison Jesus shows the characterization of the ideal disciple. Therefore, the ideal disciple is the one who treats others in the way he/she wants others to treat him/her in light of the graciousness and the generosity of the Father mentioned in 7:6–11.

7.3.3 Final Comparisons and Entering the Narrow Gates (7:12–27)

In this section, 7:13–27, comparisons are widely used showing their importance in the Sermon on the Mount. Gundry says, "The Sermon on the Mount concludes with a series of exhortation set in the framework of a contrast between two ways of righteousness and lawlessness."[98] Comparisons between narrow gate and wide gate are placed in 7:13–14. Comparisons of sheep and wolves are kept in 7:15. Comparisons of grape and fig fruits with thorns and thistles are mentioned in 7:16. Comparisons of good tree and good fruit with bad tree and bad fruit are found in 7:17–20. Comparisons of those who call Jesus their Lord and those who are really his disciple are identified in 7:21–23. Comparison of the one who builds on the rock and the one who builds on the sand is cited in 7:24–27. Thus, this last section of the Sermon on the Mount is crowded with many comparisons. Gundry says,

> The narrow gate and constricted road contrast with the wide gate and broad road (vv.13–14). Hearing and doing Jesus' words contrast hearing and not doing them and define the narrow way as hearing and doing, the broad way as hearing and not doing

97. Blomberg, *Matthew*, 130–131.
98. Gundry, *Matthew*, 126.

(vv.24–27). In between lies a warning not to heed the siren call to lawlessness of those false prophets whose use of the title 'Lord' for Jesus contrasts with their disobedience to his teaching concerning the heavenly Father's will (vv.15–23). And the contrast between entrance into life and consignment to destruction at the last judgment overarches the whole.[99]

Thus, comparisons and contrasts color this section in 7:13–27 and aid in the characterization of the ideal disciple.

It is interesting that in all these comparisons and contrasts two categories emerge. Blomberg says, "In each case (each comparison) the first category refers to those who hear, and are saved; the second, to those who only hear and so are destroyed. In each case eternal life and judgment are at stake."[100] Thus, all comparisons in this section are targeted to show how the ideal disciple should take the narrow gate of suffering, and how to be a good tree and good fruit, and build the house on the rock by hearing the word of God, the Sermon on the Mount, and by obeying the word of God. Thus, in this section, the Sermon on the Mount does not add more "new commandments but encourages obedience to those already given."[101] This is the unique contribution of the characterization of the ideal disciple in this section, 7:13–27. To this now we turn.

7.3.3.1 Entering the Narrow Gate

In 7:13–14, Jesus uses a beautiful comparison of narrow gate and wide gate. This comparison brings many comparisons in its detail.

Table 1: Wide Gate vs. Narrow Gate (7:13–14)

Wide Gate (7:13)	Narrow Gate (7:14)
Gate is wide	Gate is small
Way is broad	Way is narrow
Leads to destruction	Leads to life
Many enter into it	Only few who find it

The narrow gate is kept in contrast with the wide gate. The wide gate is wide, and its way is broad, it leads to destruction, and many enter into it (7:13). In

---

99. Ibid., 126.
100. Blomberg, *Matthew*, 131.
101. Ibid., 131.

contrast, the narrow gate is small, its way is narrow and it leads to life and only few find it. The interesting part in this analogy is the use of comparisons and contrasts in many levels. All details mentioned about the wide gate are kept in contrast with all the details kept about the narrow gate. Thus, this comparison is deliberate and the contrast is conspicuous. Thus, comparative characterization is beautifully employed in 7:13–14.

Garland points out that this imagery of wide gate and narrow gate, in this comparison, comes from the city. He says, "If one is entering a city, a broad, constructed road leads to the king's palace or somewhere very useful and can be safely traversed. If one is exiting a city, precipitous path would lead through robber's territory."[102] Thus, the imagery from the roads of the city is used to teach the importance of entering the path of righteousness.

In 7:13–14, Jesus does not clarify what the road is and how the narrow gate is narrow, etc. However, one thing is clear that the narrow gate leads to life while the wide gate leads to destruction. In addition, not many take the narrow gate. When these two comparisons are put together, this comparison shows that many would not take this path of righteousness and thus would end up in destruction. However, few will find this narrow path of righteousness and they will find life. Thus, the ideal disciple is characterized as the one, who though among the few, would enter into life through the narrow gate.

In addition, Gundry points out that the narrow road could indicate persecution and suffering.[103] Garland says, "The broad way offers more pleasant excursion and avoids danger. The passage for the followers of Christ, if they choose the right gate, will be a tight squeeze and lined with suffering."[104] Thus, it is possible that this narrow gate indicates a path of persecution. Gundry says that this narrowness in the passage through the narrow gate indicates "the strictures of the surpassing righteousness just taught by Jesus as a requirement for entering the kingdom."[105] Thus, it is obvious that 7:13–14 continue the teachings of Jesus from 5:17–20 in which the disciples are exhorted to surpass the righteousness by passing through the narrow gate of suffering to life.

One more question needs to be answered. How should the disciple pass through the narrow gate? As mentioned above, the overarching theme in this section is the message in 7:24, i.e., hearing the words of Jesus and

---

102. Garland, *Reading Matthew*, 88.
103. Gundry, *Matthew*, 126.
104. Garland, *Reading Matthew*, 88.
105. Gundry, *Matthew*, 127.

acting on the words of Jesus.[106] Thus, to enter the narrow gate of suffering the ideal disciple of Jesus must obey the words of Jesus Christ. Thus, the ideal disciple of Jesus is characterized as the person who is among the few who would enter into the narrow gate of persecution but find life.

7.3.3.2 Beware of False Prophets (7:15–23)

In 7:15–23, Jesus gives four analogies: False prophets in 7:15a and 7:21–23; Sheep and wolves in 7:15; Grapes, figs and thorns in 7:16; and Good tree with good fruits and bad tree with bad fruits in 7:17–20. In all these analogies comparisons are found extensively. Thus, comparative characterization could be used in this section to identify the characterization of the ideal disciple in 7:15–23.

7.3.3.2.1 SHEEP VS. WOLVES

In 7:15, Jesus warns in his own style, "Beware of false prophets." This phrase seems much connected with 7:21–23 of which 7:15–19 are essentially a part. In 7:15, Jesus teaches the disciple to be aware of the false prophets. In 7:16–19, he gives clues by which the disciple could know the difference between the false prophets and his true disciples. In addition, in 7:21–23, Jesus explains the characteristics of the false prophets and how the ideal disciple must be different from them.

In 7:15, Jesus identifies that these false prophets are the wolves in sheep's clothing. Inside they are "ravenous wolves," λύκοι ἅρπαγες but outside they look like sheep, προβάτων (7:15). Morris suggests that these false prophets could be the ones who would hinder the disciple and make the narrow gate narrower by creating problems for them.[107] On the contrary, 7:13–25 does not warn in any way that the disciple should not listen to the false teachings of the false prophets or stay away from these false prophets. Thus, it should be assumed that these false prophets are not to be equaled with the false teachers like the ones found in Galatians.

The main characteristic features of the false prophets in 7:15–27 is that they do not obey the words of the Lord (7:36). Their actions were not the same as their words (7:23). They are like the hypocrites, they say one thing but they are different from what they profess (7:15, sheep but wolves). Thus, the portrayal of the false prophets in 7:15–23 is a warning to the disciple

---

106. Boice, *The Gospel of Matthew*, 109.
107. Morris, *The Gospel According to Matthew*, 176.

that he/she should know about these false prophets and that the disciple should not be like them (7:24–27).

In 7:15, then, Jesus uses comparison of sheep and the wolves. The sheep is a peaceful animal but the wolves are identified as ἅρπαγες, "ravenous" wolves (7:15). This could mean that these wolves are the false prophets. Like the wolves these false prophets may try to devour the sheep, whom they are impersonating. If the sheep is considered as the disciple then, these false prophets' main objective is to destroy the sheep. From other point of view, there is a possibility that these wolves need not try to devour the sheep but they are just identified as the ones in contrast to the sheep. It is possible that Jesus characterizes these wolves as the people who are anti to the teachings of Jesus but they appear as if they are disciples. This idea goes well with the other analogies mentioned in this section.

Grapes and figs coming out of thorns is another analogy (7:16). These false prophets are like thorns in reality not useful to many but they act like grapes and figs. Thus, these false prophets are the classic impersonators just like the hypocrites who act like the disciples but in truth they are not. This interpretation goes well with the whole theme of chapters 6 and 7 of the Matthew, where the ideal disciple is compared with the hypocrites who constantly behave differently from what they profess about themselves. Thus, in 7:15, the disciple is compared against the false teachers who do not follow the teachings of Christ (7:24), who practice lawlessness (7:23), and those who may bring suffering on the disciples (7:15, as they are wolves). Thus, the ideal disciple is compared with them and characterized as the one who obeys the words of Jesus (7:24) and follows the Law (7:23) and is not hypocritical like those who impersonate sheep when they truly are wolves.

7.3.3.2.2 Grapes vs. Thorns and Figs vs. Thistles

In 7:16, Jesus gives two comparisons. First, *"Grapes cannot be gathered from thorn bushes,"* μήτι συλλέγουσιν ἀπὸ ἀκανθῶν σταφυλὰς, and the next "Figs cannot be gathered from thistles," ἢ ἀπὸ τριβόλων σῦκα. Grapes and thorn bushes are not to be found together. They are antithetical. While grapes are sweet, healthy, and useful fruits the thorn bushes are generally not useful plants. How could a grape be found on a thorny plant. Grapes should only be found in grapevines. In addition, figs could only be found in a fig tree and not in thistles.

Jesus uses these illustrations to answer this question: How could the disciple identify the false prophets?[108] It is by looking at their fruits. Grapes

---

108. Ibid., 177.

cannot come from thorns likewise figs cannot come from thistles. In the same ways, good characters cannot come from false prophets. Thus, the ideal disciple should know if someone among his/her community consistently producing bad fruits, bad character then he/she should know that they are false prophets. In addition, the ideal disciple is also in one way characterized by the overall context of 7:15–27 that he/she should not be like the false prophets who produce bad character but he should follow the words of Jesus and produce good fruits like grapes and figs. Thus, the contrasting ideas of grapes and figs with thorns and thistles give a beautiful comparative characterization.

7.3.3.2.3 Good Tree vs. Bad Tree and Good Fruit vs. Bad Fruit

The same thought is stressed in 7:16 is continued through 7:17–20. First, in 7:17–18, a comparison is given with the components such as good tree, good fruit, bad tree and bad fruit. The common knowledge is that a good tree will produce good fruit and bad tree would produce bad fruit (7:17). In contrast, good tree cannot produce a bad fruit and so also a bad tree cannot produce a good fruit. These contrasting ideas are kept together to form good comparisons here. As a good tree could only produce good fruits, a true disciple would only produce good character.[109] As a bad tree could only produce bad fruit a false prophet would only produce bad character. Thus, the disciple can identify who the false prophet is by identifying his/her characters (7:20).[110] Therefore, if the ideal disciple should not be like a false prophet he/she should not produce bad fruits, bad character but should produce only good fruits, good character, by obeying the words of Jesus Christ (7:24). Thus, through the use of comparisons and exhortations Jesus characterizes the ideal disciple as the one who would have good characters, by following his teachings.

7.3.3.2.4 False Prophets vs. True Disciple

In 7:21, Jesus says, *"Not everyone who says to me, 'Lord,' 'Lord' will enter the kingdom of heaven, but he who does the will of My Father who is in heaven will enter,"* Οὐ πᾶς ὁ λέγων μοι· κύριε κύριε, εἰσελεύσεται εἰς τὴν βασιλείαν τῶν οὐρανῶν, ἀλλ' ὁ ποιῶν τὸ θέλημα τοῦ πατρός μου τοῦ ἐν τοῖς οὐρανοῖς.

---

109. Glasscock, *Matthew*, 172.
110. Gundry, *Matthew*, 130.

Here, Jesus clearly compares the false prophets mentioned in 7:15a with the ones who will do the will of the Father.[111] In addition, it is clearly mentioned that the false prophets will not enter into the kingdom of heaven but the true disciple, the one who does Father's will, will enter the kingdom of heaven ἀλλ' ὁ ποιῶν τὸ θέλημα τοῦ πατρός μου τοῦ ἐν τοῖς οὐρανοῖς. There seems to be a parallelism in 7:21 to 5:20. In 5:20, Jesus mentioned that unless the disciple's righteousness surpasses the righteousness of the Pharisees and scribes he/she will not enter into the kingdom of heaven. Thus, in 5:20, the entry requirement to kingdom of heaven is to surpass the righteousness of the Pharisees and scribes. However, here in 7:21, the entry requirement to the kingdom of heaven is to do the will of the Father.[112] Thus, it is possible to assume that to surpass the righteousness of the Pharisees and scribes is to do the will of the Father. Thus, the disciple is exhorted and characterized as the one who should do the will of the Father.

Entry to the kingdom of heaven is not granted by calling the right name of the Lord.[113] For those who just call Jesus as 'Lord, Lord' and the ones who did prophecy in his name, and the ones who cast out demons and perform miracles in his name would not get a clean chit to enter into the kingdom of heaven. Just by the performances of ministry the disciple cannot get the entrance into the kingdom of heaven.[114] He/she will be thrown out and will be called as lawless, οἱ ἐργαζόμενοι τὴν ἀνομίαν (7:23).

Jesus calls them as lawless people, τὴν ἀνομίαν. The will of the Father must be the Law. The ones who do not keep the will of the Father must be considered as lawless people, τὴν ἀνομίαν.[115] In addition, Gundry identifies that, "For Matthew, then, the will of the heavenly Father appears in the things Jesus say."[116] Thus, if the will of the Father is the Law and if the will of the Father is Jesus' teachings (7:24), then it must be assumed that Jesus' teachings are also law. Thus, by following the teachings of Jesus one would not become lawless like the false prophets in 7:23. Jesus does expound the Law in 5:17–48. Thus, the ideal disciple is characterized as the one who should not be like the false prophets who only do ministry but do not follow the words of Jesus Christ. The ideal disciple is therefore the one who does the will of the Father expounded by Jesus in the Sermon on the Mount, and the one who enters into the kingdom of heaven. Thus, here again, in

---

111. Ibid., 130.
112. Morris, *The Gospel According to Matthew*, 178–179.
113. Ibid., 179.
114. Glasscock, *Matthew*, 175.
115. Morris, *The Gospel According to Matthew*, 180.
116. Gundry, *Matthew*, 131.

7:21–22, Jesus compares the ideal disciple with the false prophets to characterize the ideal disciple.

7.3.3.2.5 House Built on Rock vs. House Built on Sand (7:24–27)

In the last section of the Sermon on the Mount, 7:24–27, Jesus gives another comparison which is about a man building a house on the rock and another man building a house on sand. In 7:24, Jesus says, *"Therefore everyone who hears these words of Mine and acts on them, may be compared to a wise man who built his house on the rock,"* Πᾶς οὖν ὅστις ἀκούει μου τοὺς λόγους τούτους καὶ ποιεῖ αὐτούς, ὁμοιωθήσεται ἀνδρὶ φρονίμῳ, ὅστις ᾠκοδόμησεν αὐτοῦ τὴν οἰκίαν ἐπὶ τὴν πέτραν. This man is compared with another man in 7:26: *"Everyone who hears these words of Mine and does not act on them, will be like a foolish man who built his house on the sand,"* καὶ πᾶς ὁ ἀκούων μου τοὺς λόγους τούτους καὶ μὴ ποιῶν αὐτοὺς ὁμοιωθήσεται ἀνδρὶ μωρῷ, ὅστις ᾠκοδόμησεν αὐτοῦ τὴν οἰκίαν ἐπὶ τὴν ἄμμον. The comparisons could be explicated in table 2.

Table 2: House Built on Rock vs. House Built on Sand (7:24–27)

Man Build House on Rock (7:24–25)	Man Built House on Sand (7:26–27)
-Hears these words of Mine	-Hears these words of Mine
-Acts on them	-Does not act on them
-Wise man	-Foolish man
-Built house on Rock	-Built house on Sand
-Rain fell	-Rain fell
-Flood came	-Flood came
-Winds blew	-Winds blew
-Slammed against the house	-Slammed against the house
-It did not fall	-It fell
-It had been founded on the rock	-Great was its fall

The table once again points out the beauty and the details of the comparisons in 7:24–27. Most elements of the comparison are contrasted with other elements of the comparison. The comparisons show the main difference among them. The wise man is considered wise because he hears the words of Jesus and acts on them, ὅστις ἀκούει μου τοὺς λόγους τούτους καὶ ποιεῖ αὐτούς (Matt 7:24). That is, he obeys the teachings of Jesus. Jesus here says, "words of Mine," μου τοὺς λόγους, which obviously should mean the teachings of Jesus in Matthew including the Sermon on the Mount.[117] Thus, obeying the teachings of Jesus means building the house on the rock, which will not be destroyed even when rain falls, flood comes, winds blow, and slams against the house and thus, the house will not fall.

Gundry points out that this fall should be considered as final judgment.[118] Matt 7:21 could be given as proof for this interpretation. By obeying the will of the Father the disciple could enter into the kingdom of heaven (7:21). As mentioned above, if Jesus' words exemplify the will of the Father, then, obeying Jesus' words would open the kingdom of heaven. And thus, it is similar to building the house on the rock that even when the rain falls, the final judgment, the house will not be able to be destroyed.

Similar teachings about building one's house on rock and sand are found in Jewish literatures and also in Greco-Roman literatures. Rabbi Elisha ben Abuyah says: "One in whom there are good works, who has studied much Torah, to what may he be likened? To a person who builds first with stones and afterward with bricks: even when much water comes and collects by their side, it does not dislodge them. But one in whom there are no good works, though he studied Torah, to what may he be likened? To a person who builds first with bricks and afterward with stones: even when a little water gathers, it overthrows them immediately" ('Avot R. Nat. 24). In the Greco-Roman world, Seneca in *Epistulae Morales* says: "Suppose that two buildings have been erected, unlike as to their foundations, but equal in height and grandeur. One is built on faultless ground, and the process of erection goes right ahead. In the other case, the foundations have exhausted the building materials, for they have sunk into soft and shifting ground and much labor has been wasted in reaching the solid rock" (Seneca, *Ep.* 52). Jesus uses similar imagery to characterize the ideal disciple as the one who obeys the words of Jesus by using the analogy of building a strong foundation.

However, the compared contrasted comparisons in 7:26–27 give a totally opposite view. The foolish one hears the words of Jesus, the will of the Father (7:21), but does not act on those words of Jesus, and thus it is considered as the house built on the sand. Talbert identifies that the Palestinian house had no strong foundation.[119] Thus, the strength of the house was on the soil. Thus, if the house is built on sand when the rain falls, floods come,

---

117. Morris, *The Gospel According to Matthew*, 181.
118. Gundry, *Matthew*, 133.
119. Talbert, *Reading the Sermon on the Mount*, 142.

winds blow, and slam against the house, the house would fall, and that too it would be a great fall (7:27). Likewise, the disciple who does not keep the teachings of Jesus would fall a great fall at the final judgment.[120] Thus, this portion of the Sermon on the Mount characterizes the ideal disciple as the one who hears the teachings of Jesus and acts on it by obeying them so that he/she would not fall in the final judgment unlike the false prophets who hear and do not act on Jesus' teachings but falls a great fall in the final judgment. Thus, these comparisons bring forth a beautiful comparative characterization which elucidates the characterization of the ideal disciple as the one who obeys the teachings of Jesus, in 7:13–27.

7.4 Conclusion

Doing righteousness is a theme that runs from 5:17 to 7:27.[121] Jesus' warning not to do righteousness 'before men' in 6:1 introduces what Jesus is intending to deal with in the characterization of the ideal disciple in chapter 6. Three acts of righteousness are of major concern in this chapter for Jesus: almsgiving (6:2–4), prayer (6:5–15), and fasting (6:16–18). Technically, it is not just about almsgiving or prayer or fasting but how to give alms, and how to pray and how to fast is the concentration here. Thus, he mentions 'whenever you give alms' (6:2), 'whenever you pray' (6:5), 'whenever you fast' (6:16). Therefore, the ideal disciple is characterized as the one who gives alms properly, who prays properly, and who fasts properly. How to give alms properly, or to pray properly, or to fast properly? To answer these Jesus used three comparisons which explained the proper way of giving alms, and the proper way of praying, and the proper way of fasting. The ideal disciple should not be like the Pharisees, the hypocrites who perform the religious duties in front of others to be glorified. In addition, the ideal disciple should not be like the gentiles who use repetitive meaningless words in their prayer. The disciple should then perform these 'acts of righteousness' (6:1) with sincerity and truth. Thus, comparisons played vital roles in the characterization of the ideal disciple.

In 6:19–23, Jesus showed that the ideal disciple must be the one who stores wealth in heaven by giving generously and the one who does not hold back. In 6:24–34, Jesus characterized the ideal disciple as the one who does not worry about the essentials of life like food, drinks, and clothing but trusts God unlike the gentiles who runs after them with worry. Comparisons

---

120. Gundry, *Matthew*, 133.
121. Chamblin, *Matthew*, 386.

of the ideal disciple with Pharisees and gentiles were kept frequently in Matthew chapter 6.

This idea ran through chapter 7 of the Sermon on the Mount. In 7:1–5, the ideal disciple was characterized as the one who would not judge others, unlike the Pharisees who always criticize others. In 7:6–12, the disciple was characterized as the one who would present his/her needs by asking, seeking and knowing God to show his/her trust and dependency on God. In 7:13–27, Jesus showed that the disciple needs to pass through the narrow gate by not being like the false prophets, who do not obey the words of the Lord. Thus, the ideal disciple, in 7:13–27, is characterized using the many comparisons such as sheep and wolves (7:15), grapes and figs with thorns and thistles (7:16), the good tree with good fruits and bad tree with bad fruits (7:17–20), false prophets with true disciple (7:21–23), and the house built on the rock and house built on sand (7:24–27). Through these, the ideal disciple is characterized as the one who follows the teachings of Jesus in the Sermon on the Mount with sincerity of practicing piety and generous giving. Therefore, comparative characterization helps in recreating the character of the ideal disciple, by analyzing the use of comparisons in the Sermon on the Mount to see its function in depicting the character of the ideal disciple in the Sermon on the Mount.

Chapter 8

Comparative Characterization of the Ideal Disciple in the Sermon on the Mount and Its Implications

8.1 Introduction

JOHN CALVIN IDENTIFIED THE importance of the Sermon on Mount as "a brief summary of the doctrine of Christ . . . collected out of his many and various discourses."[1] This brief summary of the doctrine of Christ has been studied in this study. In the first seven chapters, the study was introduced and the course of this study was charted in the first chapter. In the second chapter, the literary review was given by identifying the key views of the key interpreters of the Sermon on the Mount. In chapters 3 and 4, the methodology was described. Literary criticism, narrative criticism and the importance of the use of comparisons and the methodology, comparative characterization were described. In chapter 5, characterization of the ideal disciple was exemplified by interpreting Matt 5:1–16. There, it was argued that the Sermon on the Mount characterizes the ideal disciple by its imperatival portrayal of how the ideal disciple should be. In chapter 6, Matt 5:17–48 was studied with the so-called antitheses to the continual identification of the function of the comparisons in the characterization of the ideal disciple. Further, in chapter 7, Matt 6 and 7 were studied to identify the many comparisons present in them and also to identify their teleological purpose of characterizing the ideal disciple against the hypocrites and the Gentiles. Thus, in this chapter, the concluding remarks of the study will be mentioned.

---

1. Calvin, *Commentary on a Harmony of the Gospel*, 258–259.

8.2 Significance of Comparative Characterization in the Sermon on the Mount

One of the important stresses of this study is the importance of the use of the methodology, comparative characterization in the interpretation of the Sermon on the Mount. Comparisons abound in all kinds of literature, be it ancient, modern or post-modern. Humanity and human communications frequently use comparisons. In addition, comparison is an anthropological and social phenomenon in the area of communication and perception. As long as literature and communication exist so will comparisons. As surely as comparisons are present comparative characterization will be used. Thus, the use of comparative characterization is stressed in this study.

In addition, in this study it was identified that the Sermon on the Mount's important function is to characterize the ideal disciple. By narrating how a disciple must live, in 5:1—7:29, Jesus characterized the ideal disciple in the Sermon on the Mount. Though this portion of the text is crowded with second person imperatival narrations, the narrative characterizes the ideal disciple. This could also be called as *imperatival characterization*. Jesus characterizes the ideal disciple by giving imperatives such as, "do not sound a trumpet before you" (Mat 6:2), "when you pray, go into your inner room" (Mat 6:6), etc. Through these imperatives, a comprehensive portrayal of the disciple of Jesus was narrated and thus, characterized. Thus, comparisons are used to aid the characterization and they add beauty to the communication. Thus, comparative characterization in this study is used to identify the characterization of the ideal disciple portrayed by Jesus with the many imperatives and descriptions.

As mentioned earlier in this study, the Sermon on the Mount abounds with comparisons. Why are so many the comparisons present in the Sermon on the Mount? What is the function of these comparisons in the Sermon on the Mount? These were the concerns of this study. Through the interpretation of the three chapters, Matt 5, 6, & 7, it was identified that the comparisons in the Sermon on the Mount had a major function in the characterization of the ideal disciple. The conclusions of which will be summarized in the three following subtitles.

8.2.1 Comparative Characterization in the Beatitudes (5:1–16)

Sermon on the Mount uses the beatitudes with comparisons, contrasts, and irony, which are quite unique when it is compared with a similar beatitude of Menander. Menander in fragment 114k says, "Blessed is the man who has both mind and money for he employs the latter for what he should" (Menander 114K). Here, Menander describes the blessed person as the one who has mind and money because he will spend his money wisely. Interestingly, this beatitude has been just a description of the blessedness of the person who has money and mind. This beatitude is quite different from the beatitudes of the Sermon on the Mount. Here, there is no comparison or contrast, unlike the Sermon on the Mount. In the Sermon on the Mount, the beatitudes use comparisons and contrasts which depict who the disciple is at present and who he is or who he will be in the kingdom of heaven. For example, in the first beatitude, though the disciple is 'poor in the spirit' in the present condition he/she is blessed because he/she possesses the kingdom of heaven. This contrast is brought out by the comparison in this beatitude. Thus, the complex characterization of the ideal disciple comes to the fore in the beatitudes of the Sermon on the Mount, unlike the beatitude of Menander.

In the beatitudes, Jesus depicts a complex portrayal of who this ideal disciple is. This complex portrayal of who the ideal disciple is depicted as who he/she is at the present and who the ideal disciple will be in the kingdom perspective. The following are the characterizations of the ideal disciple in Matt 5:1–16.

5:3	The ideal disciple is "poor in spirit" but he is the one who possesses the kingdom of Heaven
5:4	The ideal disciple is mourning at present but he/she is the one who is truly comforted.
5:5	The ideal disciple is meek but he/she will inherit the earth.
5:6	The ideal disciple will receive the righteousness which he/she hungers and thirsts for.
5:7	The ideal disciple shows mercy and also receives mercy from the Father.
5:8	The ideal disciple is pure at heart by cleansing the heart from all malice, and thus will see God.
5:9	The ideal disciple is the child of God as he/she makes peace.
5:10–12	The ideal disciple undergoes persecution with joy as he/she possesses the kingdom of heaven.
5:13–16	The ideal disciple should be like the salt and light by being true to his/her nature, in the way he/she is portrayed in the Sermon on the Mount, if not he/she is of no use.

Therefore, in these characterizations of the ideal disciple, the ideal disciple is portrayed as the person who is "poor in the spirit," but also as the one who possesses "the kingdom of heaven"; as the "one who mourns" but also as the one who is "comforted"; "the meek," but also as the one who "inherits the earth"; "the one who is hungry and thirsty for righteousness," but also as the one who is "satisfied"; "the merciful," and also the one who "receives mercy"; "the pure in heart," but also as the one who "sees God"; "peace makers" but also as the one who is "son(s) of God"; "persecuted for the sake of righteousness" but also as the one who possesses the "kingdom of heaven" (5:3-10). In addition, in 5:13-16, Jesus portrayed the ideal disciple as salt and light, the one who should continue to be a disciple by his/her obedience to the teachings of Christ. The followers of Christ should take these characterizations into consideration and should align their lives with the portrayal depicted by Jesus.

8.2.2 Comparative Characterization in the Antitheses (5:17-48)

Chamblin says that the so-called antitheses are kept as "representatives" of good works mentioned in 5:16.[2] Thus, by not getting angry at his/her brother (5:21-26); and not lusting after other man's wife (5:27-30); and by not divorcing one's wife for no valid reason (5:31-32); and by being truthful all the time (5:33-37); and by not choosing retribution for the crimes committed against one (5:38-42); and by loving even enemies (5:43-48), the ideal disciple is characterized as the one who keeps the Law better than the Pharisees and scribes. The following are the depictions of the ideal disciple in 5:17-48:

5:17-20   As Jesus is not against the Law the ideal disciple must also obey the Law in a better way and should surpass the righteousness of the Pharisees and the scribes to enter into the kingdom of heaven.

5:21-26   The ideal disciple should avoid getting angry because it might make him/her to break the Law, which says, 'thou shall not kill.'

5:27-30   The ideal disciple should not look at a woman lustfully because it might make him to break the Law, 'thou shall not commit adultery.'

5:31-32   The ideal disciple should not divorce his wife except on the grounds of adultery because it goes against the Law mentioned in Deut 24:1.

5:33-37   The ideal disciple should just be truthful all the time because making a vow might cause him/her to break the vow also.

---

2. Chamblin, *Matthew*, 339.

5:38–42 The ideal disciple should not do retribution for the crime committed against him/her but he/she should go an extra mile to live in harmony with the neighbors.

5:43–48 The ideal disciple should not stop at only loving the neighbors but he/she should also love the enemies.

Therefore, the ideal disciple is depicted in this section as the one who internalizes the Law and takes it to the heart. The ideal disciple is not just the one who obeys the Law outwardly but the one who internalizes the Law into the heart and obeys God by obeying the Torah in the way Jesus interpreted them. Thus, the ideal disciple is not an antinomian but the one who adheres to the Law, in the way Jesus expounded it. Hagner points out that "Jesus' words stress that the Law is to be preserved not as punctiliously interpreted and observed by the Pharisees but as definitively interpreted by Jesus the Messiah. That is to follow the authoritative teaching of Jesus is to be faithful to the whole meaning of the law."[3] Therefore, the ideal disciple is characterized as the one who should keep the Law in the way Jesus expounded so that his/her righteousness would surpass the righteousness of the Pharisees and scribes (5:20), and would pave way for the disciple to enter into the kingdom of heaven. Hence, the follower of Christ should not be an antinomian but the one who obeys the Law as expounded by Christ in the Sermon on the Mount.

8.2.3 Comparative Characterization in Matt 6–7

Jesus characterized the ideal disciple in Matt 6–7 along similar lines with his previous teachings in 5:13–16 and in 5:20. In 5:13–16, Jesus mentioned that the disciple must be a true disciple like salt and light. In addition, in 5:20, Jesus mentioned that the disciple must surpass the righteousness of the Pharisees and scribes. Clubbing both these ideas, Jesus gives elaborate teachings on how the ideal disciple should be a true disciple in the practice of piety and spiritual activities over and against the hypocrites and the gentiles.

6:1–4 The ideal disciple should not perform the "acts of righteousness," especially, almsgiving in front of people to get honor from them as it would nullify the reward from the Father in heaven.

6:5–6 The ideal disciple should not perform the spiritual activities like the hypocrites, especially ostentatious prayer to get honor from people as it would nullify the rewards from the Father in heaven.

3. Hagner, *Matthew 1–13*, 106.

6:7-15   The ideal disciple should not pray with meaningless words like the gentiles but should pray as were taught by Jesus in the Lord's prayer, which emphasizes glorifying the Father (6:10,13), shows dependency on God (6:11, 13a), seeks forgiveness (6:12), and which emphasizes the importance of forgiving others (6:12; 14-15).

6:16-18   The ideal disciple should not perform spiritual activities like the hypocrites, especially fasting, only to be seen by people and to get honor from them as it would nullify the reward from the Father in heaven.

6:19-23   The ideal disciple should not store up treasures on earth but in heaven, where it would be eternally safe, by being generous to others (6:22), and not by being stingy (6:23).

6:24-34   The ideal disciple should not serve money like the gentiles, but serve God alone, by not worrying about the essentials of life such as food, drink, and clothing, as God would feed the disciple much more than the way He provides for the birds of the air (6:26), and lilies of the wild (6:28), and the grass of the field (6:30).

7:1-5   The ideal disciple should not judge others, like the hypocrites, but correct himself/herself first, before edifying others.

7:6-11   As the ideal disciple should not worry about the essentials of life (6:24-34), he/she should show dependence in God by asking, seeking and knocking—by trusting in Him that He will give exactly what is asked, much more than the human fathers, who know how to give good gifts to their children.

7:12-27   The ideal disciple should enter the narrow gate which leads to the kingdom of heaven, and should know who the wolves are by their fruits (their character, 7:16-20), and should not be like them, who build the house on sand by not obeying the words of the Lord (7:21-22; 26-27), but should be wise by obeying the teachings of the Lord (6:23-25).

Continuing on the idea of internalization of the Law, found in 5:17-48, Jesus here also brings the idea of internalization of the spiritual activities and their purposes in Mat 6-7. Jesus' main thrust of Matt 6 is doing the "acts of righteousness" only for the glory of God and not to get honor from people. The ideal disciple should not be like the hypocrites, the Pharisees who are obsessed with receiving honor from people through their spiritual activities such as, almsgiving (6:1-4), prayer (6:5-6), and fasting (6:16-18). In addition, the ideal disciple should not be like the gentiles who pray with meaningless words (6:7-15), and who are mainly concerned with the essentials of this world (7:12-27). The ideal disciple should trust in God that He will give all he/she needs and would give all that he/she asks (7:1-11). Thus, the ideal disciple should not store up treasures in earth but in heaven by giving to others (6:24-34). Thus, the ideal disciple is characterized by Jesus as the one who truly practices the spiritual activities and also as the one who trusts and lives for God alone and not for the wealth of this world. This characterization is achieved by the many comparisons Jesus used in the Sermon on the Mount. Thus, the follower of Christ should not practice spirituality ostentatiously but with sincerity to glorify the Lord. The ideal disciple should not be anxious about life and serve money alone. He/she should also obey the Lord by being wise in building the house on the rock. He/she should be good examples by following the teachings of Jesus in the Sermon on the Mount.

To summarize, five important themes arise in the characterization of the ideal disciple in the Sermon on the Mount. First, in the beatitudes, the disciple should know who he/she is in the kingdom of heaven. For example, the ideal disciple may be poor in spirit at present but he/she possesses the kingdom of heaven. Thus, the ideal disciple should know who he/she is in the kingdom of heaven. Second, in Matt 5:17-48, Jesus characterizes the disciple as the one who internalizes the Torah, the teachings of the Old Testament and obeys the Law better than the Pharisees and scribes, to enter into the kingdom of heaven. This internalization is brought out by not getting angry at others inorder to obey the command about not killing, and by not lusting after others inorder to obey the command on not committing adultery, etc. Third, in Matt 6, the main theme emerges as doing the "acts of righteousness," spiritual activities, such as prayer, fasting and almsgiving sincerely for the Lord and not to get honor from others. Fourth, in Matt 7, the main theme emerges as trusting in God for all the essentials of life, and to seek, ask and knock for the daily needs with trust in God that He would give exactly what was asked. Last but not the least, fifth, a theme that runs through the Sermon on the Mount, which is to be a true disciple by obeying all that Jesus commanded. The ideal disciple is not just the one who calls Jesus as Lord but the one who obeys him completely which is similar to building the house on the rock. Thus, Jesus characterized the ideal disciple in this manner in these three chapters, Matt 5–7.

The main objective in this study was to show how comparisons function in the characterization of the ideal disciple in the Sermon on the Mount. As it was shown above in the literary review most writers who wrote on the Sermon on the Mount concentrated on the applicability of the Sermon on the Mount. However, in this study, the focus is on how the ideal disciple is characterized using the comparisons which are found so frequently in the Sermon on the Mount. This idea is stressed throughout this study and the characterization of the ideal disciple is brought forth by using comparative characterization. Thus, it is time to conclude that comparative characterization is a good method to use in the interpretation of the Sermon on the

Mount to identify the characterization of the ideal disciple and to know how the ideal disciple of Christ should live.

8.3 Conclusion

To reiterate, the Sermon on the Mount should be considered as a document which characterizes the ideal disciple through its prohibitions, commands, descriptions, and characterizations.[4] Thus, Jesus characterizes the ideal disciple in the Sermon on the Mount using comparisons which can be found throughout the Sermon on the Mount. In addition, the important contribution of this study is the identification that these comparisons function in the characterization of the ideal disciple. While commenting on 6:1–18, Senior points out that "the three traditional expressions of Jewish piety [are] almsgiving, prayer, and fasting (6:1–18). In each case negative examples are used as a foil to illustrate authentic piety, either on the part of the 'hypocrites' whose actions are done merely for show and do not reflect their interior spirit, or 'gentiles' who are ignorant of authentic piety (6:7, 32)."[5] Senior clearly identifies that the hypocrites and the gentiles are kept as foils to bring out the characterization of the disciple. Thus, he pinpoints the comparative characterization in the Sermon on the Mount. Thus, Senior ascertains that in the Sermon on the Mount the hypocrites—the Pharisees, and the Gentiles are kept as foils to characterize how the disciple should live. This characterization is identified as the comparative characterization. Through these comparisons it is also noticed that the characterization of the ideal disciple has taken a round shape. From the Beatitudes, and in the uses of analogies such as salt and light, and in the teachings of the Law in 5:17–48, where the righteousness of the disciple is exhorted to exceed that of the Pharisees and scribes, and in the teachings of religious piety such as giving, praying, and fasting in Matt 6, and in the teachings on not to judge, to ask and be aware of the false prophets in Matt 7, the ideal disciple is characterized in a rounded form. Through these characterizations, the ideal disciple is taught how to live in this world. As many of the characterization of the disciple are similar to the portrayal of Jesus himself, the Sermon on

---

4. For example, when Jesus describes the one who is angry with his brother is guilty, he uses the participle with an article, ὁ ὀργιζόμενος which should be treated as generic article, meaning it is a description of anyone who is a disciple who is angry is guilty before the court (Wallace, *Greek Grammar*, 230). Jesus also uses indefinite plurals in the Sermon on the Mount like in Matt 7:16 which generalize the characterization of the ones Jesus is portraying in the Sermon on the Mount (Wallace, *Greek Grammar*, 402–403).

5. Senior, *The Gospel of Matthew*, 106.

the Mount seems to exhort the ideal disciple to imitate Jesus. The disciple must imitate Jesus in the way he keeps the law (5:17–48), in the way he prays (6:5–6), etc. Thus, the characterization of the ideal disciple in the Sermon on the Mount teaches the disciple how to be a disciple. For this purpose comparisons and comparative characterization is used in this study to study the Sermon on the Mount. It is only apt to end this study with the words of John Stott:

> There is no single paragraph of the Sermon on the Mount where this contrast between Christian and non-Christian standards is not drawn. It is the underlying and uniting theme of the sermon; everything else is variation of it. Sometimes it is the Gentiles or pagan nations with which Jesus contrasts his followers. At other times he contrasts them with Jews.[6]

Thus, comparative characterization is a great tool to the study of the Sermon on the Mount.

---

6. Stott, *The Sermon on the Mount*, 6.

Bibliography

Abbott, Margery Post. *Historical Dictionary of the Friends (Quakers)*. 2nd Edition. Plymouth: Scarecrow, 2012.
Abrams, M. H., and Geoffrey Galt Harpham. *A Glossary of Literary Terms*. 9th Edition. Boston: Wadsworth Cengage Learning, 2009.
Allen, Charles Livingstone. *The Sermon on the Mount*. Westwood: Revell, 1966.
Allen, J. P. *The Sermon on the Mount the Kingdom of God in its Nature and Characteristics*. Nashville: Broadman, 1959.
Allison, Dale C. *The Sermon on the Mount Inspiring the Moral Imagination: Companions to the New Testament*. New York: Crossroad, 1999.
Allstrom, Elizabeth C., and Mel Silverman. *Truly, I say to You*. New York: Abingdon, 1966.
Alt, Franz. *Frieden ist möglich: Die Politik der Bergpredigt*. München: Piper, 1983.
———. *Peace is Possible: The Politics of the Sermon on the Mount*. New York: Schocken, 1985.
Alter, Robert. *The Art of Biblical Narrative*. New York: Basic Books, 1981.
———. *The David Story: A Translation with Commentary of 1 and 2 Samuel*. New York: W.W. Norton 1999.
———. *World of Biblical Literature*. New York: Basic Books, 1981.
Andrews, C. F. *The Sermon on the Mount*. London: G. Allen & Unwin, 1942.
Arbel, Vita Daphna. *Beholders of Divine Secrets: Mysticism and Myth in the Hekhalot and Merkavah Literature*. Albany: State University of New York, 2003.
Arnold, Eberhard. *Salt and Light: Talks and Writings on the Sermon on the Mount*. Rifton: Plough, 1967.
Arnold, Eberhard, and Jürgen Moltmann. *Salt and Light: Living the Sermon on the Mount*. Farmington: Plough, 1998.
Asmussen, Hans. *Die Bergpredigt Eine Auslegung von Matth. Kap. 5-7*. Göttingen: Vandenhoeck & Ruprecht, 1939.
Atkins, Gaius Glenn. *From the Hillside*. Boston: Pilgrim, 1948.
Augustine. *The Sermon on the Mount Expounded and The Harmony of the Evangelists*. Translated by William Findlay. Edinburgh: T&T Clark, 1986.
———. *Commentary on the Lord's Sermon on the Mount with Seventeen Related Sermons*. Fathers of the Church. New York: Fathers of the Church Inc., 1951.

Augustine, and Denis Joseph Kavanagh. *Commentary on the Lord's Sermon on the Mount with Seventeen Related Sermons.* New York: Father's of the Church Inc., 1951.
Augustine, and Francine Cardman. *The Preaching of Augustine.* Philadelphia: Fortress, 1973.
Augustine, and John James Jepson. *The Lord's Sermon on the Mount.* Westminster: Newman, 1948.
Augustine, and Richard Chenevix Trench. *Exposition of the Sermon on the Mount.* London: John W. Parker, 1851.
Aune, David E. *The New Testament in Its Literary Environment.* Philadelphia: Westminster, 1987.
Aveling, Edward Bibbins. *The Sermon on the Mount.* London: Freethought, 1881.
Balmforth, Ramsden. *Spiritual Agnosticism and the Sermon on the Mount in Relation to Problems of Social Reconstruction.* London: C.W. Daniel, 1921.
Barclay, Robert. "An Apology for the True Christian Divinity," in *Truth Triumphant.* Edited by Benjamin C. Stanton. New York: Medico-Chirurgical Review, 1831.
Barclay, William. *The Old Law and the New Law.* Philadelphia: Westminster, 1972.
Bar-Efrat, Shimon. *Narrative Art in the Bible.* Journal for the study of Old Testament Supplement Series 70. London: T&T Clark, 2004.
Bauman, Clarence. *The Sermon on the Mount the Modern Quest for its Meaning.* Macon: Mercer University Press, 1985.
Beardslee, William A. *Literary Criticism of the New Testament.* Philadelphia: Fortress, 1969.
Bennema, Cornelis. "A Theory of Character in the Fourth Gospel with reference to Ancient and Modern Literature." *Biblical Interpretation* 17 (2009): 375-421.
Bercot, David W. *Will the Real Heretics Please Stand up: A New Look at Today's Evangelical Church in the Light of Early Christianity.* Tyler: Scroll, 1989.
Bergen, Robert D. *First, Second Samuel.* The New American Commentary. Nashville: Broadman, 1996.
Berlin, Adele. *Poetics and Interpretation of Biblical Narrative.* Winona Lake: Eisenbrauns, 1994.
Betz, Hans Dieter. *Studien zur Bergpredigt.* Tübingen: J. C. B. Mohr, 1985.
Betz, Hans Dieter, and Adela Yarbro Collins. *The Sermon on the Mount: A Commentary on the Sermon on the Mount, Including the Sermon on the Plain (Matthew 5:3—7:27 and Luke 6:20-49).* Edited by Adela Yarbro Collins. Hermeneia: A Critical and Historical Commentary on the Bible. Minneapolis: Fortress, 1995.
Betz, Hans Dieter, and Laurence L. Welborn. *Essays on the Sermon on the Mount.* Translated by Laurence L. Welborn. Philadelphia: Fortress, 1985.
Beyer, Hermann Wolfgang. *Der Christ und die Bergpredigt nach Luthers Deutung.* München: Kaiser, 1933.
Beyschlag, Karlmann. *Die Bergpredigt und Franz von Assisi.* Beiträge zur Förderung christlicher Theologie 2. Reihe, Gütersloh: Bertelsmann, 1955.
Blair, Edward Payson. *Leader's Guide to the Study of the Sermon on the Mount: The Quadrennial Emphasis Bible Study, 1968-1972.* Nashville: Abingdon, 1968.
Bligh, John. *The Sermon on the Mount: A Discussion on Matthew 5-7.* Slough: St Paul, 1975.
Blomberg, Craig L. *Matthew.* The New American Commentary. Nashville: Broadman, 1992.

Blumhardt, Johann Christoph. *Die Bergpredigt Jesu: Übersichtliche Auslegung*. Stuttgart-Hohenheim: Hänssler, 1969.
Boardman, George Dana. *Studies in the Mountain Instruction*. New York: D. Appleton, 1880.
Bock, Darrell L., and Buist M. Fanning. *Interpreting the New Testament Text*. Wheaton: Crossway, 2006.
Boice, James Montgomery. *The Gospel of Matthew: The King and the Kingdom: Matthew 1–17*. Vol. 1 of *The Gospel of Matthew*. Grand Rapids: Baker, 2001.
Boice, James Montgomery. *The Sermon on the Mount: An Exposition*. Grand Rapids: Zondervan, 1972.
Bone, Harry, B. M. Cherrington, and Henry P. Van Dusen. *Ten Studies in the Sermon on the Mount*. New York: Council of Christian Associations Distributed by Association Press, 1926.
Bonhoeffer, Dietrich. *The Cost of Discipleship*. New York: Macmillan, 1959.
———. *The Extraordinariness of the Christian Life a Bible study on the Sermon on the Mount*. New York: National Student Christian Federation, 1964.
Borgman, Paul. *David, Saul, and God: Rediscovering an Ancient Story*. Oxford: Oxford University Press, 2008.
Boring, M. Eugene. *Matthew and Mark*. New International Bible Commentary of the New Testament. Nashville: Abingdon, 1995.
Bossuet, Jacques Bénigne. *The Sermon on the Mount*. New York: Longmans, Green, 1900.
Bowman, Robert C. *Sermon on the Mount*. Covenant Bible Study Series. Elgin: Brethren Press, 1988.
Brewster, Harold Sydney. *The Simple Gospel*. New York: Macmillan, 1922.
Briscoe, D. Stuart. *Now for Something Totally Different a Study of the Sermon on the Mount*. Waco: Word, 1978.
Broadhead, Edwin Keith. *Demand and Grace the Sermon on the Mount*. Macon: Smyth & Helwys, 1999.
Brooks, Oscar Stephen. *The Sermon on the Mount Authentic Human Values*. Lanham: University Press of America, 1985.
Brouwer, Anneus Marinus. *De Bergrede*. Zeist: Ruys, 1930.
Brouwer, Wayne. *Being a Believer in an Unbelieving World Contemporary Reflections on the Sermon on the Mount*. Peabody: Hendrickson, 1999.
Brown, Charles Reynolds. *The Religion of a Layman*. New York: Macmillan, 1920.
Browne, John R. *The Great Sermon*. Boston: Stratford, 1935.
Brunner, Frederick Dale. *The Christbook: Matthew 1–12*. Vol. 1 of *The Christbook*. Grand Rapids: Eerdmans, 2004.
Buck, Gertrude, and Elisabeth Woodbridge Morris. *A Course in Narrative Writing*. New York: Henry Holt & Company, 1906.
Burnett, F.W. "Characterization and Reader Construction of Characters in the Gospels." *Semeia 63* (1993).
Burns, Jim. *The Word on the Sermon on the Mount*. Youth Builders Group Bible Studies. Ventura: Gospel Light, 1996.
Burroway, Janet. *Writing Fiction: A Guide to Narrative Craft*. Boston: Little Brown, 1982.
Buttrick, David. *Speaking Jesus: Homiletic Theology and the Sermon on the Mount*. Louisville: Westminster John Knox, 2002.

Calvin, John. *Commentary on a Harmony of the Evangelists, Matthew, Mark and Luke.* Vol.1 of *Commentary on a Harmony of the Evangelists.* Translated by William Pringle. Grand Rapids: Eerdmans, 1949.

———. *Commentary on a Harmony of the Gospel.* Grand Rapids: Eerdmans, 1956.

———. *The Institutes of the Christian Religion.* Translated by Henry Beveridge. Edinburgh: Calvin Translation Society, 1846.

Carlsen, G. Robert. *Encounters.* 4 volumes. New York: McGraw-Hill, 1985.

Carpenter, William Boyd. *The Great Charter of Christ Being Studies in the Sermon on the Mount.* New York: T. Whittaker, 1896.

Carson, D. A. *The Sermon on the Mount an Evangelical Exposition of Matthew 5–7.* Grand Rapids: Baker, 1978.

Carter, Warren. *What are they Saying about Matthew's Sermon on the Mount?* New York: Paulist, 1994.

Chalkley, Thomas. *Some Observations on Christ's Sermon on the Mount.* London: W&S Graves, 1815.

Chambers, Oswald. *Studies in the Sermon on the Mount.* London: Marshall, 1932.

Chamblin, J. Knox. *Matthew.* Vol. 1 of *Matthew.* A Mentor Commentary. Ross-shire: Mentor Imprint, 2010.

Chappell, Clovis Gillham. *The Sermon on the Mount.* Nashville: Cokesbury, 1930.

Chatman, S. *Story and Discourse: Narrative Structure in Fiction and Film.* London: Cornell University Press, 1978.

Chilton, Bruce, and Jacob Neusner. *Judaism in the New Testament: Practices and Belief.* New York: Routledge, 1995.

Chrysostom, John, and Jaroslav Jan Pelikan. *The Preaching of Chrysostom.* Edited by Jaroslav Jan Pelikan. Philadelphia: Fortress, 1967.

Cohon, Beryl David. *Jacob's well: Some Jewish Sources and Parallels to the Sermon on the Mount.* New York: Bookman Associates, 1956.

Coleman, Lyman. *Sermon on the Mount.* Littleton: Serendipity House, 1991.

Coleridge, Henry James. *The Sermon on the Mount.* Quarterly Series. London: Burns and Oates, 1882.

Connick, Charles Milo. *Build on the Rock: You and the Sermon on the Mount.* Westwood: Revell, 1960.

Conrad. *Die Bergpredigt: Ihre Behandlung und Auslegung in der Schule.* Brandenburg: Gedruckt bei J.J. Wiesike, 1860.

Cooper, Dale. *Sermon on the Mount a Study Guide.* Revelation Series for Adults. Grand Rapids: Education Department of Christian Reformed Church, 1981.

Cox, Billy J. *Forty Days on the Mountain.* New York: Vantage, 1976.

Crain, Jeanie C. *Reading the Bible as Literature.* Cambridge: Polity Press, 2010.

Croft, Steven, Stephen Cottrell, Paula Gooder, and Robert Atwell. *Pilgrim: The Beatitudes: Follow Stage, Book 4.* London: Church House, 2014.

Crowe, Charles M. *Sermons from the Mount.* Nashville: Abingdon, 1954.

Culpepper, Alan. *Anatomy of the Fourth Gospel: A Study in Literary Design.* Philadelphia: Fortress, 1983.

Daily, Starr. *The Magnificent Love: A Gospel of Divine Love Based on the Sermon on the Mount.* Westwood: Revell, 1964.

Daube, David. *The New Testament and Rabbinic Judaism.* Salem: Ayer Company, 1984.

Davenport, Gene L. *Into the Darkness Discipleship in the Sermon on the Mount.* Nashville: Abingdon, 1988.

Davies, Margaret. *Matthew. A New Biblical Commentary*. Sheffield: JSOT, 1993.
Davies, W. D. *The Sermon on the Mount*. Cambridge: Cambridge University Press, 1966.
———. *The Setting of the Sermon on the Mount*. Cambridge: Cambridge University Press, 1964.
Denck, Hans. "Concerning True Love." *Early Anabaptist Spirituality: Selected Writings*. Edited by Daniel Liechty. Mahwah, NJ: Paulist, 1994.
Derrett, J. Duncan M. *The Ascetic Discourse: An Explanation of the Sermon on the Mount*. Eilsbrunn: Ko'amar, 1989.
———. *The Sermon on the Mount: A Manual for Living*. Northampton: Pilkington, 1994.
Dibelius, Martin. *The Sermon on the Mount*. New York: Scribner's, 1940.
Dietzfelbinger, Christian. *Die Antithesen der Bergpredigt*. München: Kaiser, 1975.
Dimitroff, Stojan. *Der Sinn der Forderungen Jesu in der Bergpredigt*. Sofia: Druck S.M. Staikoff, 1938.
Dockery, David S., and David E. Garland. *Seeking the Kingdom the Sermon on the Mount Made Practical for Today*. Wheaton: H. Shaw, 1992.
Dodd, C. H. *Apostolic Preaching and Its Developments*. Chicago: Willett, Clark & Co., 1937.
———. *Gospel and Law*. New York: Columbia University Press, 1951.
———. *History & the Gospel*. New York: Scribner's, 1938.
———. *The Founder of Christianity*. New York: MacMillan Company, 1970.
Dods, Marcus, James Denney, and James Moffatt. *The Literal Interpretation of the Sermon on the Mount*. London: Hodder & Stoughton, 1904.
Doke, Joseph J. *M.K. Gandhi: An Indian Patriot in South Africa*. Madras: G.A. Nateson & Ca, 1919.
Dorinani, Daniel M. *The Sermon on the Mount: The Character of a Disciple*. New Jersey: P&R Publishing, 2006.
Drewitz, Ingeborg, and Wolfgang Erk. *Der Verbotene Friede: Reflexionen zur Bergpredigt aus zwei Deutschen Staaten*. Stuttgart: Radius, 1982.
Driver, John. *Kingdom Citizens*. Scottdale: Herald, 1980.
Dumbrell, W. J. *Covenant and Creation: A Theology of the OT Covenants*. Grand Rapids: Baker, 1984.
Dupont, Jacques. *Les Béatitudes*. Etudes Bibliques. Bruges: Abbaye de Saint-André, 1958.
Dykes, J. Oswald. *The Beatitudes of the Kingdom*. London: James Nisbet, 1873.
———. *The Laws of the Kingdom*. New York: R. Carter, 1873.
———. *The Manifesto of the King an Exposition of the Sermon on the Mount*. London: James Nisbet, 1881.
———. *The Relations of the Kingdom to the World*. New York: R. Carter, 1874.
Eddleman, H. Leo. *Teachings of Jesus in Matthew 5–7*. Nashville: Convention, 1955.
Ervast, Pekka. *The Esoteric School of Jesus*. Nevada: Blue Dolphin, 1999.
Eyton, John. *The Lord Jesus Christ's Sermon on the Mount with a Course of Questions and Answers, Explaining that Valuable Portions of Scripture*. Baltimore: J. Kingston, 1969.
Faulkner, William. *A Rose for Emily*. Logan: Perfection Learning Corporation, 2007.
Ferguson, Sinclair B. *Kingdom Life in a Fallen World Living out the Sermon on the Mount. The Christian Character Library*. Colorado Springs: NavPress, 1986.

———. *The Sermon on the Mount Kingdom Life in a Fallen World*. Edinburgh Carlisle: Banner of Truth Trust, 1987.
Findlay, James Alexander. *The Realism of Jesus: A Paraphrase and Exposition of the Sermon on the Mount*. London: Hodder and Stoughton, 1900.
Fisher, Fred L. *The Sermon on the Mount*. Nashville: Broadman, 1976.
Fitzgerald, Ernest A. *There's No Other Way*. Nashville: Abingdon, 1970.
Forbes, Christopher. "Paul and Rhetorical Comparison." *Paul in the Greco-Roman World*. Edited by J. Paul Samply. New York: Trinity, 2003.
Forbes, John. *The Symmetrical Structure of Scripture*. Edinburgh: T&T Clark, 1854.
Foulkes, Richard Tolan. *Ethics in the Dead Sea Manual of Discipline and in the Sermon on the Mount*. Princeton: Princeton University Press, 1960.
Fox, Emmet. *The Sermon on the Mount the Key to Success in Life and The Lord's Prayer: An Interpretation*. San Francisco: Harper & Row, 1989.
———. *The Sermon on the Mount: A General Introduction to Scientific Christianity in the Form of a Spiritual Key to Matthew V, VI, and VII*. New York: Church of the Hearing Christ, 1934.
Friedlander, Gerald. *The Jewish Sources of the Sermon on the Mount*. New York: George Routledge Bloch, 1911.
Frost, Bede. *Founded Upon a Rock: An Introduction to the Sermon on the Mount*. New York: The Macmillan, 1935.
Gandhi, M.K. "Letter to Tolstoy." *Modern Review*. October, 1916.
———. *An Autobiography*. Boston: Beacon, 1957.
Gandhi, Mahatma. "Christianity and Hinduism." *Mahatma Gandhi*. 8th edition. Edited by Sarvepalli Radhakrishnan. New Delhi: Jaico, 2007.
———. "The Place of Jesus." *Mahatma Gandhi*. 8th edition. Edited by Sarvepalli Radhakrishnan. New Delhi: Jaico, 2007.
Garland, David E. *Reading Matthew: A Literary and Theological Commentary on the First Gospel*. New York: Crossroad, 1993.
Genung, George F. *The Magna Charta of the Kingdom of God: Plain Studies of our Lord's Sermon on the Mount*. Philadelphia: American Baptist Publication Society, 1985.
Glasscock, Ed. *Matthew*. Moody Gospel Commentary. Chicago: Moody, 1997.
Goguel, Maurice. *La vie de Jesus-Christ*. Paris: Payot, 1932.
Gore, Charles. *The Social Doctrine of the Sermon on the Mount*. London: Percival, 1892.
Govett, Robert. *The Sermon on the Mount Expounded*. London: James Nisbet, 1861.
Gray, William David. *The Sermon on the Mount*. Louisville: Pentecostal Publishing Company, 1925.
Green, Bryan. *Being and Believing*. New York: Scribner's, 1956.
Greidanus, Sydney. *The Modern Preacher and the Ancient Text: Interpreting and Preaching Biblical Literature*. Grand Rapids: Eerdmans, 1988.
Griffith-Jones, Ebenezer. *The Sermon on the Mount a Practical Exposition*. Manchester: J. Robinson, 1903.
Guelich, Robert A. *The Sermon on the Mount a Foundation for Understanding*. Waco: Word, 1982.
Gundry, Robert H. *Matthew: A Commentary on His literary and Theological Art*. Grand Rapids: Eerdmans, 1982.
Gunn, David M. "Narrative Criticism." *To Each Its Own Meaning: An Introduction to Biblical Criticisms and Their Application*. Edited by Steven L. McKenzie and Stephen R. Haynes. Louisville: Westminster John Knox, 1999.

Habel, Norman C. *Literary Criticism of the Bible*. Philadelphia, Fortress, 1971.
Hagner, Donald A. *Matthew 1–13*. Word Biblical Commentary 33A. Dallas: Word, 1997.
Hamilton, Edward Lawrence. *The Laws & Principles of the Kingdom of Heaven as Contained in the Sermon on the Mount*. London: Marshall, 1927.
Hare, Douglas R. A. *Mathew*. Interpretation. Louisville: John Knox, 1993.
Hargrove, Hubbard Hoyt. *At the Master's Feet: A Series of Expository Sermons from the Sermon on the Mount*. Nashville: Broadman, 1944.
Harmon, William, and C. Hugh Holman, *A Handbook to Literature*. 8th Edition. Upper Saddle River: Prentice Hall, 1999.
Harnack, Adolf von. *What is Christianity?* Translated by Thomas B. Saunders. New York: Harper & Row, 1957.
Harrington, Daniel. *The Gospel of Matthew*. Sacra Pagina Series 1. Collegeville: Liturgical, 1991.
Harrison, George W. M. "The Semiotics of Plutarch's Συγκρίσεις: The Hellenistic Lives of Demetrius-Antony and Agesiaus-Pompey," in *Revue belge de philologie et d'histoire*. 73, (1995).
Harrison, Martin. *The Language of Theatre*. London: Routledge, 1998.
Hayes, Doremus Almy. *The Heights of Christian Living a Study of the Sermon on the Mount*. New York: Abingdon, 1929.
Heim, Karl. *Die Bergpredigt Jesu*. Tübingen: Furche-Verlag, 1949.
Hendrickx, Herman. *The Sermon on the Mount: Studies in the Synoptic Gospels*. London: Geoffrey Chapman, 1984.
Hendriksen, William. *Exposition of the Gospel According to Matthew*. New Testament Commentary, Grand Rapids: Baker, 1973.
———. *The Sermon on the Mount*. Grand Rapids: Eerdmans, 1934.
Henson, William Eugene. *The Inaugural Message of the King: A Brief Exposition of the Sermon on the Mount*. New York: Vantage, 1954.
Hicks, B. R. *The Sermon on the Mount: Step by Step to Spiritual Maturity*. Jeffersonville: Christ Gospel, 1981.
Hill, Daniel Harvey. *A Consideration of the Sermon on the Mount*. Philadelphia: WS&A Martien, 1858.
Hill, David. *The Gospel of Matthew*. New Century Bible Commentary. Grand Rapids: Eerdmans, 1972.
Hogan, Martin. *The Sermon on the Mount in St. Ephrem's Commentary on the Diatessaron*. New York: Peter Lang, 1999.
Holmes, John Haynes. "Homage." *Mahatma Gandhi*. 8th edition. Edited by Sarvepalli Radhakrishnan. New Delhi: Jaico, 2007.
Hughes, R. Kent. *Sermon on the Mount: The Message of the Kingdom*. Wheaton: Crossway, 2001.
Hugo, Victor. *Les Misérables*. Bruxelles: A. Lacroix, Verboeckhoven & Cie 1862.
Hummel, R. *Die Auseinandersetzung zwischen Kirche und Judentum im Matthäusevangelium*. Beiträge zur Evangelischen Theologie 33. Munich: Kaiser, 1966.
Hunter, Archibald Macbride. *Design for Life an Exposition of the Sermon on the Mount: Its Making, Its Exegesis and Its Meaning*. London: SCM, 1953.
Isaac, Jules. *Jesus and Israel*. Translated by Sally Gran. New York: Holt, Rinehart & Winston, 1971.

Jameson, John Gordon. *The Gospel of the Kingdom in the Sermon on the Mount*. London: W. Hodge, 1951.
Jeremias, Joachim, and Norman Perrin. *The Sermon on the Mount*. London: Athlone, 1961.
Jeremias, Joachim. *Die Bergpredigt*. Calwer Hefte zur Förderung biblischen Glaubens und Christlichen Lebens. Stuttgart: Calwer, 1960.
Johnson, Luke Timothy. "The Sermon on the Mount." *The Oxford Companion to Christian Thought*. Edited by Adrian Hastings. Oxford: Oxford University Press, 2000.
Jones, E. Stanley. "Gandhi-Portrayal of a Friend." *Mahatma Gandhi*. 8th edition. Edited by Sarvepalli Radhakrishnan. New Delhi: Jaico, 2007.
———. *The Christ of the Mount a Working Philosophy of Life*. New York: Abingdon, 1931.
Joosse, Nanne Pieter George. *The Sermon on the Mount in the Arabic Diatessaron*. Amsterdam: Centrale Huisdrukkerij VU, 1997.
Jordan, Clarence. *Sermon on the Mount*. Philadelphia: Judson, 1952.
Juárez Muñoz, J. Fernando. *El Sermón de la Montaña*. Guatemala: Talleres Gutenberg, 1944.
Kaiser Jr., Walter C. "Narrative," in *Cracking Old Testament Codes: A Guide to Interpreting the Literary Genres of the Old Testament*. Edited by D. Brent Sandy and Ronald L. Giese. Jr. Nashville: Broadman & Holman, 1995.
Kant, Immanuel. *The Critique of Practical Reason*. Translated by Thomas Kingsmill Abbott. Radford: Wilder, 2008.
Keener, Craig S. *A Commentary on the Gospel of Matthew*. Grand Rapids: Eerdmans, 1999.
Keith, Pierre. "Les Citation d'Osée 6:6 dans les Oracles Sybillius," in *Car c'est l'amour qui me plait, non le Sacrifice: Recherches sur Osée 6:6 et son interprétation Juive et Chrétienne*. Edited by Eberhard Bons. Leiden: E. J. Brill, 2004.
Kepler, Thomas S. *Jesus' Design for Living*. Nashville: Abingdon, 1955.
Kissinger, Warren S. *The Sermon on the Mount: A History of Interpretation and Bibliography*. Metuchen: Scarecrow, 1975.
Kittel, G., G. Friedrich. *Theological Dictionary of New Testament*, Translated by G. W. Bromiley. 10 volumes. Grand Rapids: Eerdmans, 1964–1976.
Kodjak, Andreij. *A Structural Analysis of the Sermon on the Mount*. Berlin: Mouton de Gruyter, 1986.
Lacy, Donald Charles. *Called To Be*. Lima, Ohio: CSS, 1978.
Ligon, Ernest Mayfield. *The Psychology of Christian Personality*. New York: Macmillan, 1935.
Ligon, Greg. *Bonhoeffer's Cost of Discipleship*. Nashville: Broadman & Holman, 1998.
Lindsay, A. D. *The Moral Teaching of Jesus: An Examination of the Sermon on the Mount*. New York: Harper & Brothers, 1937.
Link, Charles E. *Jesus' Epilogue to the Sermon on the Mount: A Study of the Lord's Prayer*. Lima: CSS, 1995.
Lloyd-Jones, David Martyn. *Studies in the Sermon on the Mount*. Grand Rapids: Eerdmans, 1959.
Loader, William R. G. *Jesus' Attitude Towards the Law: A Study of the Gospels*. Tubingen: J.C.B. Mohr, 1997.

Loken, Israel P. *The Old Testament Historical Books: An Introduction.* Momence: Xulon Press, 2008.

Loosley, Ernest. *The Challenge from the Mount.* London: Epworth, 1964.

Loy, M. *The Sermon on the Mount: A Practical Study of Chapters V-VII of St. Matthew's Gospel.* Columbus: Lutheran Book Concern, 1909.

Luther, Martin. *Commentary on the Sermon on the Mount.* Translated by Charles A. Hay. Philadelphia: Lutheran Publication Society, 1892.

Luther, Martin, and Charles Augustus Hay. *Commentary on the Sermon on the Mount.* Philadelphia: Lutheran, 1892.

Luther, Martin, and Martin E. Marty. *The Place of Trust: Martin Luther on the Sermon on the Mount.* Edited by Martin E. Marty. San Francisco: Harper & Row, 1983.

Lüthi, Walter, and Robert. Brunner. *The Sermon on the Mount.* Edinburgh: Oliver and Boyd, 1963.

Lyttelton, E. *Studies in the Sermon on the Mount.* London: Longmans, Green, 1905.

Mann, Gerald. *Why does Jesus Make me Nervous? Taking the Sermon on the Mount Seriously.* Waco: Word, 1980.

Manson, T. W. *The Sayings of Jesus.* London: SCM, 1949.

Marriott, Horace. *The Sermon on the Mount.* New York: Macmillan, 1925.

Massey, Isabel Ann. "Interpreting the Sermon on the Mount in the Light of Jewish Tradition as Evidenced in the Palestinian Targums of the Pentateuch: Selected Themes." *Studies in the Bible and Early Christianity.* Lewiston: E. Mellen, 1991.

McAfee, Cleland Boyd. "Studies in the Sermon on the Mount." *ATLA Monograph Preservation Program.* New York: Fleming H. Revell, 1910.

———. *Studies in the Sermon on the Mount.* New York: Fleming H. Revell, 1989.

McArthur, Harvey K. *Understanding the Sermon on the Mount.* New York: Harper, 1960.

McEachern, Alton H. *From the Mountain.* Nashville: Broadman, 1983.

McGee, J. Vernon. *J. Vernon McGee on Prayer.* Nashville: Thomas Nelson, 2002.

McKeown, James. *Genesis.* Two Horizons Old Testament Commentary. Grand Rapids: Eerdmans, 2008.

Meier, John P. *The Vision of Matthew: Christ, Church, and Morality in the First Gospel.* New York: Paulist, 1979.

Meistad, Tore. *Martin Luther and John Wesley on the Sermon on the Mount. Pietist and Wesleyan Studies.* Lanham: Scarecrow, 1999.

———. *To be a Christian in the World: Martin Luther's and John Wesley's Interpretation of the Sermon on the Mount.* Trondheim: University of Trondheim, 1989.

Menninger, Richard E. *Israel and the Church in the Gospel of Matthew.* New York: Peter Lang, 1994.

Mercer, Jerry. *Jesus Christ Sermon on the Mount.* Nashville: Graded, 1985.

Meyer, F. B. *The Directory of the Devout Life: Meditations on the Sermon on the Mount.* New York: Fleming H. Revell, 1904.

Miller, John W. *The Christian Way: A Guide to the Christian Life Based on the Sermon on the Mount.* Scottdale: Herald, 1969.

Moltmann, Jürgen., and Werner H. Schmidt. *Nachfolge und Bergpredigt.* München: Kaiser, 1982.

Morris, Leon. *The Gospel According to Matthew.* Grand Rapids: Eerdmans, 1992.

Mortley, R. J. *Rhetores Graeci.* Translated by L. Spengel. Vol. 2 of *Rhetores Graeci.* Frankfurt: Minerva, 1966.

Mouton, Richard G. *The Modern Reader's Bible.* New York, Macmillan, 1895.

Murthy, B. Srinivasa. *Mahatma Gandhi and Leo Tolstoy Letters.* Long Beach: Long Beach, 1987.
Myres, William V. *Design for Happiness.* Nashville: Broadman, 1961.
N.A, "Rural Poverty in Asia." [cited April 5th, 2014] Online: http://www.ruralpovertyportal.org/in/ region /home/tags/asia.
N.A. "Antagonist." n.p. *Encyclopædia Britannica: Ultimate Reference Suite on CD-ROM,* 2009.
N.A. "Foil." n.p. *Encyclopædia Britannica: Ultimate Reference Suite on CD-ROM,* 2009.
Nee, Watchman. *Interpreting Matthew.* New York: Christian Fellowship, 1989.
Neumann, Frederick. *The New Heart: An Introduction to the Sermon on the Mount.* Princeton: Princeton University Press, 1991.
Neusner, Jacob. *Judaism in the beginning of Christianity.* London: SPCK, 1984.
Newson, Carol Ann. *The Self as Symbolic Space: Constructing Identity and Community at Qumran.* Studies on the Texts of the Desert of Judah 52. Leiden: E. J. Brill, 2004.
Ohrn, Arnold T. *The Gospel and the Sermon on the Mount.* New York: Revell, 1948.
Ortiz, Juan C. *Disciple: A Handbook for New Believers.* Lake Mary: Charisma House, 1995.
Overman, J. Andrew. *Church and Community in Crisis: The Gospel According to Matthew.* Valley Forge: TPI, 1996.
Palmer, Earl F. *The Enormous Exception Meeting Christ in the Sermon on the Mount.* Waco: Word, 1986.
Parker, Hankins F. *Earth's Greatest Sermon: A Practical Application of the Sermon on the Mount.* New York: American, 1966.
Parker, Joseph. *Peacemaking: A Sermon for the Times.* London: Judd & Glass, 1800.
Pathrapankal, Joseph. *The Christian Programme: A Theological and Pastoral Study of the Sermon on the Mount.* Bangalore: Dharmaram, 1999.
Patte, Daniel. *Discipleship according to the Sermon on the Mount: Four Legitimate Readings, Four Plausible Views of Discipleship, and Their Relative Values.* Valley Forge: Trinity Press, 1996.
———. *The Challenge of Discipleship a Critical Study of the Sermon on the Mount as Scripture.* Harrisburg: Trinity, 1999.
Paul, John. *Blessed Are the Pure of Heart: Catechesis on the Sermon on the Mount and Writings of St. Paul.* Boston: St. Paul Editions, 1983.
Pelikan, Jaroslav Jan. *Divine Rhetoric: The Sermon on the Mount as Message and as Model in Augustine, Chrysostom, and Luther.* Crestwood: St. Vladimir's Seminary, 2001.
Pennington, Chester A. *The Word among Us.* Philadelphia: United Church, 1973.
Pentecost, J. Dwight. *Design for Living the Sermon on the Mount.* Chicago: Moody, 1975.
———. *The Sermon on the Mount: Contemporary Insights for a Christian Lifestyle.* Portland: Multnomah, 1980.
Peterson, Norman R. *Literary Criticism for New Testament Critics.* Philadelphia: Fortress, 1978.
Pink, Arthur Walkington. *An Exposition of the Sermon on the Mount.* Swengel: Bible Truth Depot, 1950.
Plotzke, Urban Werner. *God's Own Magna Charta.* Westminster: Newman, 1963.
Plummer, George Winslow. *The Applied Psychology of the Sermon on the Mount.* New York: Seminary of Biblical Research, 1927.

Pontifex, John, and John Newton. "Persecuted and Forgotten? A Report on Christians oppressed for their faith 2011-2013." [Cited on 3-2-2014] Online: http://catholicebooks.wordpress.com/2014/01/07/online-text-persecuted-and-forgotten-a-report-on-christians-oppressed-for-their-faith-2011-2013/.

Powell, Mark Allen. *What is Narrative Criticism? A New Approach to the Bible*. London: SPCK, 1993.

Powys, Llewelyn. "The Triumph of the Spirit, Radhakrishnan." *Mahatma Gandhi*. 8th edition. Edited by Sarvepalli Radhakrishnan. New Delhi: Jaico, 2007.

Prabhavananda. *The Sermon on the Mount according to Vedanta*. London: G. Allen & Unwin, 1964.

Radhakrishnan, Sarvepalli. *Mahatma Gandhi*. New Delhi: Jaico, 2007.

Ragaz, Leonhard. *Die Bergpredigt Jesu*. Bern: H. Lang, 1945.

Renan, Ernest. *Vie de Jesus*, 4th ed. Paris: Michel-Levy, 1863.

Resseguie, James L. *Narrative Criticism of the New Testament: An Introduction*. Grand Rapids: Baker, 2005.

Richards, Hubert J. *The Beatitudes for Children*. Collegeville: Liturgical Press McCrimmons, 1988.

Ridderbos, Herman N. *De Strekking der Bergrede naar Mattheus*. Kampen: Kok, 1936.

Rimmon-Kenan, Shlomith. *Narrative Fiction: Contemporary Poetics*. 2d edition. New York: Routledge, 2002.

Ritschl, Albrecht. *The Christian Doctrine of Justification & Reconciliation*. 2d edition. Translated by H. R. Machintosh and A. B. Macaulay. Edinburgh: T&T Clark, 1902.

Robinson, Arthur William. *Studies in the Teaching of the Sermon on the Mount*. London: Student Christian Movement, 1922.

Robinson, Haddon W. *The Christian Salt & Light Company: A Contemporary Study of the Sermon on the Mount*. Grand Rapids: Discovery House, 1988.

Royster, Dmitri. *The Kingdom of God the Sermon on the Mount*. Crestwood: St. Vladimir's Seminary, 1992.

Ryken, Leland. *How to Read the Bible as Literature*. Grand Rapids: Academie, 1984.

———. *The Literature of the Bible*. Grand Rapids: Zondervan, 1974.

———. *The New Testament in Literary Criticism*. New York: Frederick Ungar, 1984.

Rynne, Terrence J. *Gandhi & Jesus: The Saving Power of Non-Violence*. Maryknoll: Orbis, 2008.

Sanders, E. P. *Jewish Law from Jesus to the Mishnah*. London: SCM, 1990.

———. *Paul and Palestinian Judaism: A Comparison of Patterns of Religion*. London: SCM, 1977.

———. *Jesus and Judaism*. Philadelphia: Fortress, 1985.

Savage, H. E. *The Gospel of the Kingdom*. London: Longmans, Green, 1910.

Scaer, David P. *The Sermon on the Mount the Church's First Statement of the Gospel*. St. Louis: Concordia, 2000.

Schabert, Arnold. *Die Bergpredigt*. München: Claudius, 1966.

Scher, Andrew R. *The Master-Speech: The Sermon in the Mount: A Nonsectarian Interpretation of Matthew 5-7*. New York: Exposition, 1954.

Schlatter, Adolf von. *Die Gabe des Christus: Eine Auslegung der Bergpredigt. Theologie und Dienst*. Giessen: Brunnen, 1982.

Schonfield, Hugh Joseph. *The Speech that Moved the World*. London: Search, 1932.

Schweitzer, Albert. *Out of My Life and Thought: An Autobiography*. Maryland: JHU Press, 1933.

———. *The Mystery of the Kingdom of God*. Translated by Walter Lowrie. New York: Dodd, Mead and Co., 1914.

———. *The Mysticism of Paul the Apostle*. Translated by William Montgomery. New York: Seabury, 1968.

Schweizer, Eduard. *Die Bergpredigt*. Göttingen: Vandenhoeck & Ruprecht, 1984.

Scott, Melville. *The Christian Covenant*. London: G. Allen, 1912.

Senior, Donald. *The Gospel of Matthew: Interpreting Biblical Texts*. Nashville: Abingdon, 1997.

Shaw, Bernard. "Religion and War." *The Religious Speeches of Bernard Shaw*. Edited by Warren S. Smith. New York: McGraw-Hill, 1965.

Shearer, John Bunyan. *The Sermon on the Mount: A Study*. Richmond: Presbyterian Committee of Publication, 1906.

Sheean, Vincent. "Last Days." *Mahatma Gandhi*. 8th edition. Edited by Sarvepalli Radhakrishnan. New Delhi: Jaico, 2007.

Shepherd, J. Barrie. *Prayers from the Mount*. Philadelphia: Westminster, 1986.

Shinn, Everett. *The Sermon on the Mount*. Philadelphia: J. C. Winston Company, 1946.

Shinn, Roger Lincoln. *The Sermon on the Mount*. Philadelphia: United Church, 1962.

Sitaramayya, Pattabhi. "The Wisdom of Gandhiji." *Mahatma Gandhi*. 8th ed. Edited by Sarvepalli Radhakrishnan. New Delhi: Jaico, 2007.

Smith, T. C. *The Sermon on the Mount: A Study Guide*. Greenville: Smyth & Helwys, 1992.

Stafford, Geoffrey Wardle. *The Sermon on the Mount: The Charter of Christianity*. New York: Abingdon, 1927.

Stapfer, Edmond. *Jesus-Christ pendant son ministere*, vol. II of *Jesus-Christ sa personae, son autorite, son oeuvre*. Paris: Fischbacher, 1897.

Stassen, Glen Harold, and David P. Gushee. *Kingdom Ethics: Following Jesus in Contemporary Context*. Downers Grove: InterVarsity, 2002.

Staudinger, Josef. *Die Bergpredigt*. Wien: Herder, 1957.

Stewart, Don H. *Matthew 5–7: Design for Discipleship*. Nashville: Convention, 1992.

Stoll, Brigitta. *Zur Auslegungs-und Wirkungsgeschichte der Bergpredigt in Kommentaren, Predigten und hagiographischer Literatur von der Merowingerzeit bis um 1200*. Tübingen: J. C. B. Mohr, 1988.

Stott, John R. W. *Sermon on the Mount: 12 Studies for Individuals or Groups: A Lifeguide Bible Study*. London: Scripture InterVarsity, 2000.

———. *Christian Counter Culture: The Message of the Sermon on the Mount*. Bible Speaks Today. London: InterVarsity, 1978.

———. *A Deeper Look at the Sermon on the Mount: Living out the way of Jesus*. Downers Grove: InterVarsity, 2013.

———. *The Sermon on the Mount*. Downers Grove: InterVarsity, 2000.

Strack, H. and Billerbeck, P. *Kommentar zum Neuen Testament aus Talmud und Midrash, I: Matthäus. I*. München: Beck,1966.

Strang, Lewis Clinton. *The Master and the Modern Spirit*. New York: Roland, 1925.

Strecker, Georg, and O.C. Dean. *The Sermon on the Mount: An Exegetical Commentary*. Translated by O.C. Dean. Nashville: Abingdon, 1988.

Suber, Howard. *The Power of Film*. Studio City: Michael Wiese Production, 2006.

Swindoll, Charles R. *Simple Faith*. Dallas: Word, 1991.

Talbert, Charles H. *Matthew: Paideia Commentaries on the New Testament*. Grand Rapids: Baker, 2010.

———. *Reading the Sermon on the Mount: Character Formation and Decision Making in Matthew 5–7*. Columbia: University of South Carolina, 2004.

Thompson, Ernest Trice. *The Sermon on the Mount and its Meaning for Today*. Richmond: John Knox, 1946.

Thornton, Henry. *Family Commentary upon the Sermon on the Mount*. New York: Swords, Stanford, 1841.

Tillich, Paul. *A History of Christian Thought*. Edited by Carl E. Braaten. New York: Harper & Row, 1968.

Tolstoy, Leo. "My Confession." *My Confession, My Religion and, The Gospel in Brief*. New York: Thomas Y. Crowell, 1899.

———. *The Kingdom of God is Within You*. Editore: Wildside Press LLC, 2006.

———. *What I Believe*. Translated by C. Popoff. London: Eliot Stock, 1885.

Tov, Emmanuel. "The Scribes of the Texts Found in the Judean Desert." *The Quest for Context & Meaning: Studies in Biblical Intertextuality in Honor of James A. Sanders*. Edited by Craig A. Evans and Shemaryahu Talmon. Leiden: E. J. Brill, 1997.

Treasure, Geoff. *Living Right Side Up*. Wheaton: Victor, 1977.

Turco, Lewis. *The Book of Literary Terms: The Genres of Fiction, Drama, Non-Fiction, Literary Criticism and Scholarship*. Hanover: University Press of New England, 1999.

Uspensky, Boris. *Poetics of Composition: The Structure of the Artistic Text and Typology of a Compositional Form*. Los Angeles: University of California Press, 1973.

Vanhoozer, Kevin J., *Dictionary for the Theological Interpretation of the Bible*. London: SPCK, 2005.

Vaughan, C. J. *Characteristics of Christ's Teaching Drawn from the Sermon on the Mount*. New York: Wilbur B. Ketcham, 1859.

Vincent, Father Albert. *Le Judaisme [Judaism]*. Paris: Bloud et Gay, 1932.

Wallace, Daniel B. *Greek Grammar Beyond the Basics: An Exegetical Syntax of the New Testament*. Grand Rapids: Zondervan, 1996.

Ward, Keith. *The Rule of Love: Reflections on the Sermon of the Mount*. London: Daybreak, 1989.

Warden, Michael D. *Why be Normal? A Creative Study of the Sermon on the Mount*. Cincinnati: Standard, 1998.

Waylen, Hector. *Mountain Pathways: A Study in the Ethics of the Sermon on the Mount*. London: Sherratt & Hughes, 1909.

Weber, Gerard P., and Robert L. Miller. *Breaking Open the Gospel of Matthew the Sermon on the Mount*. Cincinnati: St. Anthony Messenger, 1998.

Weiss, Johannes. *Jesus' Proclamation of the Kingdom of God*. Translated by Richard Hyde Hiers and David Larrimore Holland. Chico: Scholars Press, 1985.

Welch, John W. *The Sermon at the Temple and the Sermon on the Mount: A Latter-Day Saint Approach*. Salt Lake City: Deseret, 1990.

Wenzel, Renate Egger. *Ben Sira's God: Proceedings of the International Ben Sira Conference*. Berlin: Walter de Gruyter, 2002.

Wesley, John, and Kenneth C. Kinghorn. *John Wesley on the Sermon on the Mount: The Standard Sermons in Modern English*. Vol. 1 of *John Wesley on the Sermon on the Mount*. Nashville: Abingdon, 2002.

Wesley, John. and Weakley Jr, Clare G. *Happiness Unlimited: Commentary on the Sermon on the Mount*. Plainfield: Logos, 1979.

Westerholm, Stephen. "The Law in the Sermon on the Mount: Matt. 5:17–18." *Criswell Theological Review* 6, 1992.

White, Ellen Gould Harmon. *Thoughts from the Mount of Blessing*. Mountain View: Pacific, 1900.

Wierzbicka, Anna. *What did Jesus Mean? Explaining the Sermon on the Mount and the Parables in Simple and Universal Human Concepts*. Oxford: Oxford University Press, 2001.

Williams, Joel. *Other Followers of Jesus: Minor Characters as Major Figures in Mark's Gospel*. Shefield: Sheffield Academic, 1994.

Wilson, Frank Theodore. *Unconditional Spiritual Surrender Studies from the Sermon on the Mount*. Philadelphia: Board of Christian Education of the Presbyterian Church in the USA, 1946.

Windisch, Hans. *The Meaning of the Sermon on the Mount a Contribution to the Historical Understanding of the Gospels and to the Problem of their True Exegesis*. Philadelphia: Westminster, 1951.

Woellner, Fredric Philip. *The Highlands of the Mind: A Psychological Analysis of the Sermon on the Mount*. Pasadena: Sunday Morning, 1930.

Wood, James Douglas. *The Sermon on the Mount and its Application*. London: Geoffrey Bles, 1963.

Worth, Roland H. *The Sermon on the Mount: Its Old Testament Roots*. New York: Paulist, 1997.

Wright III, Benjamin G. "Jubilees, Sirach, and Sapiential Tradition." *Enoch and the Mosaic Torah: The Evidence of Jubilees*. Edited by Gabrielle Boccaccini and Giovanni Ibba. Grand Rapids: Eerdmans, 2009.

Wright, Thomas Henry. *The Sermon on the Mount for Today*. Edinburgh: T&T Clark, 1927.

Wright, William Burnet. *Master and Men; or, The Sermon on the Mountain Practiced on the Plain*. Boston: Houghton, Mifflin, 1898.

Yri, Norvald. "Seek God's Righteousness: Righteousness in the Gospel of Matthew." *Right with God: Justification in the Bible and the World*. Edited by D. A. Carson. Grand Rapids: Baker, 1992.

www.ingramcontent.com/pod-product-compliance
Lightning Source LLC
Chambersburg PA
CBHW071242230426
43668CB00011B/1555